The Yoknapatawpha Chronicle
of Gavin Stevens

The
Yoknapatawpha
Chronicle
of Gavin Stevens

JOHN KENNY CRANE

Selinsgrove: Susquehanna University Press
London and Toronto: Associated University Presses

Associated University Presses
440 Forsgate Drive
Cranbury, NJ 08512

Associated University Presses
25 Sicilian Avenue
London WC1A 2QH, England

Associated University Presses
2133 Royal Windsor Drive
Unit 1
Mississauga, Ontario
Canada L5J 1K5

The paper used in this publication meets the requirements
of the American National Standard for Permanence of Paper
for Printed Library Materials Z39.48-1984.

Library of Congress Cataloging-in-Publication Data

Crane, John Kenny, 1942–
 The Yoknapatawpha chronicle of Gavin Stevens.

 Includes index.
 1. Faulkner, William, 1897–1962—Criticism and
interpretation—Handbooks, manuals, etc.
2. Yoknapatawpha County (Imaginary place)—Chronology
—Handbooks, manuals, etc. I. Title.
PS3511.A86Z774 1988 813'.52 87-42809
ISBN 0-941664-90-2 (alk. paper)

Printed in the United States of America

This book is for
PHILIP YOUNG

Contents

Author's Preface

In writing this book my intention was not to retell Faulkner for the layman, for that cannot be done and still have Faulkner be who Faulkner is. Rather it was to straighten out, insofar as possible, the labyrinthine history of Yoknapatawpha County, history which most of his books seem to presume that we know by instinct even if we are encountering a Faulkner novel or story for the first time. More than this, however, something beyond reading all his novels and all his stories is required to satisfy this presumption, for only then does a reader with a flawless memory have all the "facts" he or she needs to go back and better understand the complex interrelationship of human beings and events for a second and perhaps third reading of *all* the novels and *all* the stories. I once heard *Absalom, Absalom!* described as a book that still has 378 pages to go after the reader has reached page 378—it must be read again in the light of what one has struggled to learn up until then. In a sense all of Faulkner's writing is this way—how much more meaningful is a second reading of, say, *The Unvanquished* after *Sartoris* has been digested as well. Or vice versa. Likewise, I suppose *The Town* or *The Mansion* make good sense in themselves; but how much more sense they make with *The Hamlet* to precede them. And how much more ominous *The Hamlet* is if the contents of its two sequels are also known.

The problem, though, is perhaps intensified by fragments of information that float into and out of various Faulkner books with little, if any, elaboration on their context, magnitude, import, or drama. For instance, Colonel John Sartoris, a man whose name is the most important the county has ever known, is fully portrayed in only one book—*The Unvanquished*. Yet references to him or the things he did (or supposedly did)—from his organization of the Mississippi Second in the Civil War to his degeneration into a common horse thief by the end of it, to his murder of the two Burdens the next decade, to his own death at the hands of Redmond that same year—these appear piecemeal in ten novels and five short stories. Likewise, Faulkner makes frequent references to the county's early Indians—Ikkemotubbe, Issetibbeha, and Moketubbe—but how often is he clear about their relationships to one another, about each man's character, or about the many details that (if the reader only knew them from the three short stories in which they appear) would so illuminate his reasons for bringing them up in some six novels that do not even concern them? Or consider the MacCallums, who stand for a certain brand of natural goodness and honor if one knows their history, but who pale considerably if the reader encounters them as individual entities in a given book or, more likely, recollects them only vaguely from another. They are rarely at center stage, yet their presence in the wings is almost always significant. But the resulting nuances of association are often missed by all but inveterate readers of the Yoknapatawpha saga.

And surely this problem is more severe when one considers the predicament of those readers who continually encounter the important name of Uncle Ike McCaslin who, they probably *do* know, was in on the hunt for the big bear named Old Ben but who, they might *not* know, is the descendant of a whole string of McCaslins who represent both the wrong and shame of the South and the brand of honor on which the South, even to this day, believes it rests. It is this sort of problem, which has for decades separated Faulkner from many intelligent readers and confused his vision for those who doggedly pursue him, that this volume tries to confront.

It is my hope that this book is interesting enough on its own and possesses enough continuity (something that chronicles often lack) to be read from front to back and, thus, construct the stage for the magnificent dramatic presentations that Faulkner's novels contain. This book, however, is also referenced in three ways to make it a work for solving the sorts of difficulties I outlined above. First, at the end of the volume every character the chronicle mentions is indexed according to all the pages on which he or she is mentioned. Thus, the reader can gain a quick outline of the full range of the financial activities of Flem Snopes, for instance. Or the reader can realize, where he or she might otherwise not, that the house Flem relieves Manfred DeSpain of in 1927 is the same one his father, Ab Snopes, tracked horse manure into in 1894. Or the reader can grasp the fact that "Dry September" has a deceptive title in that it refers less to the climate or the mood than to the fact that the story's two main characters—Jackson McLendon and Minnie Cooper—are each entering their forties and have had twelve-year droughts since their last meaningful achievements: McLendon's decoration for valor in World War I and the ever-more-plain Miss Cooper's affair with a man she thought would marry her, both of which occurred in 1917. Or, as I said earlier, he or she can understand more of Ike McCaslin by grasping the heritage handed to him (or withheld from him) by his father and his uncles (Buck and Buddy McCaslin), his notorious grandfather (Old Carothers McCaslin), or his well-intentioned but weak-willed maternal uncle (Hubert

[10]

Beauchamp). Also at the end of this book are genealogies of Faulkner's fictional families, I believe the fullest yet offered, so that one can realize the relationships of disparate characters. Uncle Ike McCaslin, for example, is Lucas Beauchamp's cousin but is really nobody's uncle. Ab Snopes, perhaps surprisingly, turns out to be Percy Grimm's uncle. Carothers McCaslin is at one and the same moment Tomey's Turl's father and grandfather. Charles Bon is Henry Sutpen's half brother and, therefore, also Judith's. And so on.

The second system of referencing concerns the dates in the square brackets in the text. The most meaningful thing I can say about these is that they are references to "other significant dates" that connect with the incident being related in the present year. For instance, in the year 1869, Aunt Jenny Sartoris DuPre relates, to a Scottish railroad engineer, the story of her brother Bayard I and Jeb Stuart raiding Pope's kitchen tent during the Civil War. The date [1862] in the text refers the reader to that year to read of the event in its proper context and fuller detail. Or, in the text for 1894, the first reference to the triple-named character Buck Thorpe, Jackson and Longstreet Fentry, and Ripsnorter occurs. The date [1897] in the text refers the reader to the year in which the boy is taken from Fentry back to the Thorpe family. At that point, in the 1897 text entry, the dates [1903] and [1917] refer to the date on which Fentry returns to Yoknapatawpha County after six years of self-imposed exile and to the year in which Buck Thorpe meets his demise, both of which are referred to in the sentences adjoining those bracketed dates. In every instance in which I have provided such a bracketed notation, the inference the reader should make is that a more complete understanding of the meaning of this incident in the county's history can be had by consulting those years in the text.

The third system of referencing is the notations in decorative brackets or "braces." Whether it be a capital letter or a short story title enclosed in quotation marks, the implication always is that the information given in the text has been primarily extracted from the novel coded by the capital letter or from the story whose title is provided. Thus, in the text for 1881, the information about the Ab Snopes–Pat Stamper horse deal comes from *The Hamlet* and is marked {H}. The reader should consult the key that follows this Preface for the list of symbols I have used. Likewise, in 1894, Sarty's desertion of the Snopes family is taken from "Barn Burning," as the information in curved braces indicates. And, in 1873, the murder of the two Burdens by John Sartoris comes both from *Light in August* {L} and *The Unvanquished* {U}, both of which describe the event in question.

I have placed the text, however, in the mouth of (or perhaps more properly in the pen of) Gavin Stevens instead of my own for a number of reasons. First, I felt the story should be told by a character who participated in much of it, not by a Northerner who has it third-hand at best. Second, Stevens as a narrator can be permitted to moralize for Faulkner himself, something a

[11]

literary critic is not supposed to do. Third, Stevens is a man who would undertake a project such as this. He enters into long, involved, esoteric, open-ended projects, such as a chronicle is by definition—witness his translation of the Old Testament out of the Hebrew into classical Greek. He is interested in the county as such, the history of places, the intermixing of families, the glory of the past and the ignominy of the present, the reasons why it all happened as it did. And he is prone to reflect upon the helplessness of man at the hands of fate, the fact that all men are equally helpless, and the reality that all human beings would be better off understanding that their individual destinies are inextricably tied with those of others and, therefore, ought to get on with the business of helping one another out. For all these reasons, and probably for others as well that I cannot articulate even for myself, I have chosen to let Gavin tell Faulkner's story of Yoknapatawpha for him. Throughout I have tried to imitate, not so much Faulkner's style, as the style in which Faulkner allows Stevens to speak—the mixture of Harvard lawyer and Heidelberg Ph.D. with the backwoodsy downhomeyness of a Mississippi boy at once proud and ashamed of the heritage his forbears have handed him. Perhaps I have in mind the way Stevens speaks to Chick Mallison during their car rides in *Intruder in the Dust;* that seemed to me to be in the manner in which he would address the reader of a chronicle such as this.

Some may find gratuitous, however, my use of Chick Mallison and Melissa Meek as editors of this chronicle. I did this simply because a chronicle needs an editor, especially because chroniclers usually die before they can polish or tie anything up. Unlike fiction, history does not structure itself according to neatly organized complications, reversals, climaxes, and denouements. So Chick was chosen because, for him, every word his Uncle Gavin spoke was gospel, worthy of preservation and dissemination. And Melissa Meek was chosen because her humane interest in people, as she demonstrates in her futile attempt to save Caddy Compson in the "Appendix" to *The Sound and the Fury,* would drive her toward accuracy of detail—the things Gavin would not have known about the people named in such a chronicle as this the spinster librarian could have tracked down. In short, the Mallison–Meek combination is the reason why this chronicle can contain no loose ends as it would have for Stevens—the loose ends they would have either tied up or cut off. Gavin himself would have left such things hanging loose, for he knew too well that fate would have seen to their knotting up eventually.

As I said at the outset, this book is intended to alleviate, not increase, the confusion that so many readers at all levels complain about. Thus, I have put aside my instincts toward absolute scholarly accuracy and made the adjustments that anyone familiar with Faulkner's work knows have to be made to bring about a book such as this. I speak of the conflicts of date, detail, or genealogy that sometimes occur. Some are easily solved. For instance, there are two versions of the story in which John Sartoris accidentally captured a Yankee regiment: one in *The Unvanquished* in which he does it after meeting Bayard and Ringo along the road, the other in *Sartoris* in which it occurs as the grand finale of the horse race between Colonel Sartoris and a man named Zeb Fothergill. I have let both of these stand, for it can be argued that they occurred in different years. Likewise, Boon Hogganbeck one day fired a gun wildly on the Jefferson Square, wounding a girl and breaking a window. This event, though, is used twice: once it is set in the 1880s and Boon is bailed out by General Compson; the second time it is set in 1904 and Boon is rescued by Maury Priest. In Faulkner's mind these were probably the same event, and only the two plot lines of *Go Down, Moses* and *The Reivers* have altered the details. Again, I have given these two events independent identities, Boon being who Boon was.

Others were impossible to reconcile, however, without altering what Faulkner said. These are very few in terms of percentages. I feel, though, that I should admit to the following at the outset, lest I be accused of un-acknowledged tampering with a greater writer's work:

1) The Indian genealogies and dates are not consistent. For example, in "Red Leaves" Ikkemotubbe is Issetibbeha's father, while in "A Justice" and "A Courtship" Ikkemotubbe is himself Issetibbeha's nephew. Other facts in the genealogy are likewise troublesome. I have chosen to solve this by following what the bulk of evidence in Faulkner seems to suggest was the case—that Ikkemotubbe was Issetibbeha's junior and killed him to assume the chieftainship of the tribe. Consequently, in retelling "Red Leaves" under 1803, I have altered some details to bring about conformity. I must admit, however, that, as a novelist myself, I am not comfortable in doing so.

2) Readers of Faulkner know that Chick Mallison has two birth dates: 1914 in *The Town* and *The Mansion,* and 1924 in *Intruder in the Dust* and most of the stories in *Knight's Gambit.* This cannot be properly rectified, but I have chosen the later date because Chick is a crucial character in only one of those books—*Intruder in the Dust;* this has forced me to alter his role in the Snopes fight of the two trilogy books, however—again something I am uncomfortable about.

3) For a long time Faulkner called V. K. Ratliff by the name of V. K. Suratt, especially in *Sartoris* and *As I Lay Dying.* He is always called Ratliff in this chronicle.

4) I have had to assume that certain Yoknapatawphans knew each other, though Faulkner never says they did. Certainly, for example, twenty-one-year-old Gavin Stevens and nineteen-year-old Quentin Compson would have known each other at Harvard when Quentin committed suicide in his own freshman and Gavin's junior year.

5) Some of the dates of birth and marriage given at the opening of each year's entry in the chronicle are estimates, though I do not list them as such

since Lawyer Stevens would have had access to such information. In each case, however, I have tried to pick a logical year, and in many cases, the *only* year in which, just from a physiological standpoint, it could have happened. Will Varner, for example, married his second wife in 1944, a dozen years after the death of his first one. Hence, I have assumed the first Mrs. Varner died in 1932. At this point Varner himself would have to be a minimum of ninety-two, especially since his seventeenth child, Eula, was born in 1889. Getting Will married at nineteen and giving Mrs. Varner no barren year would still force us to place Will's birth date in 1852, Jody's (the ninth child) in 1880, and make Will about fifty-two when he first encountered Flem Snopes in 1904. But Will Varner is always described as a man who will never die because he is simply too important to do so; so ninety-two still seems middle-aged in his particular case. I have also let Ike McCaslin die in 1947, only because Faulkner tells us several times that he "lived to be eighty" and we know his birth date to be 1867. I have also let Gavin Stevens die in 1947, simply because Faulkner gives us no facts about Yoknapatawpha County after 1946 and, perhaps, because it seemed fitting that he be allowed to die in the same year as Ike, Stevens's complement in so many ways.

6) In the same respect, a few Faulknerian incidents, especially the contents of some of the short stories, are only approximately datable. Again I have chosen the most logical date when the precise date cannot be determined— really an infrequent dilemma in Faulkner's work.

7) Faulkner has written five novels and some two dozen short stories which do not involve the county or its people. After an earlier attempt to blend them in, I decided to omit them entirely as disunifying and not even "vintage" Faulkner anyway.

8) I am aware that some of the years here do not correspond with dates given in *The Portable Faulkner,* Malcolm Cowley's landmark work which rescued America's greatest modern writer from obscurity. However, Cowley wrote in 1946, and much of what Faulkner thereafter created would prevent certain of Cowley's dates from retaining credibility. "Red Leaves" just could not have happened after 1833, nor could "Spotted Horses" have happened so early as 1900. Thus, I have deviated from Cowley where Faulkner's facts compelled me to but have retained most of Cowley's other dates, some of which are indisputable.

9) Sam Fathers, we know, died just after Old Ben did in 1883; yet, in "A Justice," Faulkner has him telling a story to the Compson children at the turn of the century. This is clearly an oversight on Faulkner's part.

The expert Faulknerian will notice other variations I was forced to make and perhaps some I wasn't, shouldn't have, and probably am unaware of. For the latter I apologize; for the former I beg forgiveness, but I had no reasonable alternative unless I were to make this book a different one entirely, aimed from the outset at a different audience.

If this book serves either to open Faulkner's work to those who have heretofore shied away from it or to alleviate confusion for those who love it but experience the difficulties we all do, it will have been worth writing. For me it was both a labor of love and an open admission that Faulkner led me to Styron (hence my book *The Root of All Evil* in 1985) and that he taught me how to write a novel of my own (*The Legacy of Ladysmith* in 1986), however terrible and intimidating it is to write anything in his shadow.

John Kenny Crane

Key to Abbreviations

The following are abbreviations used to indicate the source(s) of each of the incidents recounted in the chronicle. Short stories are listed throughout by their titles, but novels are referred to by the following letters:

{A} *Absalom, Absalom!* (1936)
{B} *A Fable* (1954)
{D} *As I Lay Dying* (1930)
{F} *The Sound and the Fury* (1929)
{G} *Go Down, Moses* (1942)
{H} *The Hamlet* (1940)
{I} *Intruder in the Dust* (1948)
{K} *Knight's Gambit* (1949)
{L} *Light in August* (1932)
{M} *The Mansion* (1959)
{N} *Requiem for a Nun* (1951)
{O} *Flags in the Dust* (1973)
{R} *The Reivers* (1962)
{S} *Sartoris* (1929)
{T} *The Town* (1957)
{U} *The Unvanquished* (1938)
{W} *The Wild Palms* (1939)
{Y} *Sanctuary* (1931)
{Z} *Big Woods* (1955)

The Yoknapatawpha Chronicle
of Gavin Stevens

A YOKNAPATAWPHA CHRONICLE

Compiled by
Gavin Stevens, County Attorney
Yoknapatawpha County, Mississippi

Edited by
Charles J. Mallison, Jr.,
Nephew of Gavin Stevens and Executor of His Estate

and by
Melissa Meek, Librarian (Retired)
City of Jefferson, Mississippi

Preface

When my Uncle Gavin died in 1947, this chronicle was found among papers he had periodically scattered about his desk in the months (and probably years) before the heart attack that took his life. For a quarter of a century after that it lay in the Records Office of the Yoknapatawpha County Courthouse, referred to only occasionally by someone or other who had some vague or malicious interest in our county's past. It took me this long to realize, I suppose, that what he had written had significance for more than just the few who even knew it existed. The private struggles of human beings are rarely recorded and then only by men or women whose "objectivity" is their most treasured asset.

Uncle Gavin's words are anything but objective. He loved the South, both its long-lost ideal and its ever-present reality; and, consequently, he distrusted (though did not hate) the North. He believed in formal education but believed it only a refinement of the natural wisdom any human being possesses if he or she would take the time to know their own heart. He felt that the white race would have to be in charge for some time to come; but he labored constantly to shorten that time and help our Negro citizens wait out the years it would take until their heritage could be blended with that of the race which had once, wrongly, owned them. He would have preferred that our agrarian economy be allowed to operate apart from the industrialization and mechanization which so enthralled and later enveloped the rest of the country; but he knew that it couldn't and worked to prove to the rest of us that the fact that we could no longer be McCaslins or Sartorises did not have to make us Snopeses either. All these personal beliefs are starkly evident in this chronicle.

But what is even more evident is Uncle Gavin's belief that every person's life is all he or she has, that it is, therefore, worthy of record, and that each would have done better than he or she did if only they had been shown how to. Furthermore, in accord with those legendary words Judith Sutpen spoke to General Compson's wife and which that lady passed on to the rest of us, he believed that the words and actions and individual fates of all humans were tightly intertwined with those of every other one—that what one did affected the lives of many others without one's even intending it to, and for this reason each of us had a sacred obligation to be careful about what it was he or she *was* doing. As this chronicle demonstrates, some were more careful than others; and Gavin Stevens respected them for it.

Uncle Gavin was an impossible yet somehow understandable combination of a hard-core determinist and an inveterate believer that most of us must accept responsibility for what we do nonetheless. I do not speak of historical determinism only, for surely every Southerner does (or ought to) believe in that—had it not been for Federal interference in our affairs and a ruinous war that therefore had to be fought, we would be different—and better—than we are. Rather I speak of what philosophers call logical determinism, of which Aristotle was an opponent but of which Diodorus Cronus (an obscure philosopher Uncle Gavin read avidly) was a convincing advocate. As these pages consistently show, he held a belief that everything that happens is preplotted to happen at some moment long before those who seem to "make" it happen ever think of doing so. As he writes without reservation, Popeye Vitelli was destined to come here long before his diseased father ever went to bed with his hapless mother; and 1929 was the year it was bound to happen. And Joe Christmas, who was murdered in a local minister's house when I was six years old, was doomed to that end from the minute his father's circus train bogged down on a muddy road in Arkansas. Yet, as Uncle Gavin remarks in his narration of the Bundren funeral cortege in 1930, each of us has to believe that this is not so, even though each of us suspects it is; and it is how we act in the face of it, no matter what we believe, that really counts. Men like Ike McCaslin, V. K. Ratliff, Hawkshaw Stribling and women like Eunice Habersham, Jenny DuPre, and more others than I can count—these people taught us *how* to act and *how* to accept the fact that what we were acting amidst was not, and never could be, of our own choosing. And Uncle Gavin taught us all this probably more than anyone else I can think of.

I must confess that much of the information in Uncle Gavin's pages makes no sense to me. He records events that I have no idea how he even knew about; I am not even sure why he considered them important enough to write down. Some of the people whose names he records as having been born, married, or laid to rest each year I could identify only with the help of painstaking research; others I cannot identify at all. Some Uncle Gavin did not even have names for. Yet I cannot excise any such people or events from his pages—they lived and they happened and therefore they meant something and still do. If they didn't, they wouldn't have lived or happened in the first place. The tragedy, though, is twofold: if Gavin had never heard of some of them, no one would have remembered them; and many of those whom he never heard of are now forgotten. Yet each of us *has* a meaning; and each of us does, no matter how shallowly, leave his or her "scratch on the blank face of oblivion," even if other people never know, or want to know, who it was that made it.

On April 16, 1861, Cecilia Farmer, daughter of the town jailer, carved her name and that date into the jailhouse window with a diamond ring as she watched young townsmen ride out to war. In his account of the events of 1934, Uncle Gavin takes note of my interest in that scratching and the fact that I was curious about what it meant. I now think I know what it means; it means that Cecilia Farmer existed, tried her best at whatever fate gave her to try at, and demanded to be remembered for having so tried.

This chronicle is but one of the scratches left by Gavin Stevens. The people he helped, the innocent he saved from accusation, the public spirit he engendered in Yoknapatawpha County, the example he set—these are his others. With these pages, though, he carved the names and dates for other men who, though they had not the wherewithal to do it for themselves, needed nonetheless to be remembered for having done the best they could at something they never asked to have to do.

Charles J. Mallison, Jr.
May 1986
Jefferson, Mississippi

A Yoknapatawpha Chronicle

1540

In 1532 Francisco Pizarro had landed at Tumbes in Peru and ascended the Andes to Cajamarca. Here he encountered the Inca chieftain Atahualpa and, having lured him close by open profession of friendship, seized him and had him put to death. Among those in Pizarro's contingent upon whom such easy acquisition of wealth, land, and slaves was to have the greatest effect was Hernando de Soto. In a game of chance that was to pay dividends different from those he sought, de Soto invested his share of the Peruvian take in an expedition which landed in Florida in 1539. During the next four years, in a quest for gold which proved entirely in vain, he and his men prowled what is today the south central United States, being in all probability the first white men to cross the Mississippi and—equally probably—de Soto the first white man buried in it. They are purported to have gone as far west as Oklahoma. Though he was to die a defeated man in 1542, de Soto had accidentally managed to open a vast territory to white explorers and settlers who followed. If such be the correct term, it was in 1540 that de Soto "opened" what is today the state of Mississippi, a land of rich woodland inhabited by Indians—Chickasaws and Choctaws primarily but other tribes as well—to the whites, the half-whites, the Negroes, and the various alternative mixtures of human blood which would at first slowly (but ultimately totally) conquer and, some say, rape the virginal land they traversed at will {Z}.

1699

Born: Quentin MacLachan Compson (d. 1783)

[27]

1700–1710

The Indian word *yoknapatawpha,* from which this county derives its name, began to be associated, in the mind of the white settler, with the north central section of what is today the state of Mississippi. Translated literally it means "water runs slow through flat land" and has reference probably to the Tallahatchie and Yoknapatawpha rivers which form the northern and southern borders of the county.

Also during this decade, true to the theory that unrelated events in distant places shape the future as much if not more than related events in the present place, Quentin MacLachan Compson, to be the first of four Quentin Compsons, son of a printer in Glasgow, Scotland, was orphaned and taken to his mother's people in the Perth Highlands and there raised {F}.

At roughly this same time, Quentin—as were so many loyal Scotsmen— was orphaned as well by the evaporation of Scottish independence and the formation of Great Britain, this in 1707, with the union of England and Scotland.

1743

Born: Three Basket, Chickasaw brave

1746

Having fought and lost in the Scottish uprising against King George I, Quentin Compson I emigrated from Culloden Moor to Carolina with little save the claymore he wore in the day and slept under at night {F}.

1747

It was in this year, approximately, that the Yoknapatawpha Chickasaws first began holding Negro slaves. Legends have it that the Indians maimed them immediately upon acquisition to impede their propensity to flee.

1751

Born: Issetibbeha (d. 1803), Chickasaw chief

[28]

1763

Born: Black slave of Issetibbeha (d. 1803)

In this year the Treaty of Paris, actually a series of different treaties, was signed by England, France, and Spain, effectively ending the Seven Years War in Europe. France lost Canada and its possessions east of the Mississippi River, including, of course, the land which is today the State of Mississippi, to England; and it ceded as well the land known as West Louisiana to its ally Spain in compensation for Spain's loss of Florida to England.

1770

Issetibbeha, upon the death of the Chickasaw chieftain who was apparently his father but whose name no one has discovered, became first among his tribe, the chief, "The Man" {"Red Leaves"}.

1772

Born: Lucius Quintus Carothers McCaslin (d. 1837)

1773

Born: David Hogganbeck

Born: Moketubbe, son of Issetibbeha and his first wife

1774

Born: Ikkemotubbe (d. 1817), son of Mohataha

1775

In this year apparently, Issetibbeha, now twenty-four, sold forty Negroes to a trader from the Mississippi River port today known as Memphis. Ever since the Chickasaws began holding slaves in the previous decade, they had to confront the problem of Malthusian multiplication, even though Malthus had yet to say anything about such things in print {"Red Leaves"}. Unable to feed or clothe so much unnecessary help, the Indians had at first thought, without much relish, of eating them. Later the decision was made to barter them to the white man who, for some reason the tribe could not fully comprehend, wanted as many of them as he could get. However, the Indians still faced the problem of what to do with so much money once they acquired it, a difficulty they never fully grasped nor solved. Issetibbeha, however, invested the money from this particular sale in a sabbatical to Paris, which was currently ruled by Louis XVI and Marie Antoinette. The trip itself must not have cost him enough, however, for he soon lent about three hundred dollars to his new friend, the Chevalier Soeur Blonde de Vitry. As a result Issetibbeha seems to have gotten himself squired through the best French circles, something at first inconsistent with our conception of this savage but not so strange when one recalls that the Indians of Yoknapatawpha had been getting used to the white man's habits—luxury, laziness, and grossness—ever since shifting their workload to the back of the ever geometrically multiplying Negroes.

In this year, of course, at Lexington and Concord in the North, the colonists fired the first shots of the American Revolution.

1776

After twelve months in Paris, Issetibbeha returned in this year of American independence to Yoknapatawpha County, or at least to what would be later called that. He carried with him a gilt bed, girandoles, a purple dress for his sister, and a pair of red slippers which were at once and everlastingly coveted by his three-year-old son, Moketubbe {"Red Leaves"}. If the racial integrity of the Chickasaws had been on the decline before this, the decadent example Issetibbeha was henceforth to set would initiate a process of degeneration and corruption which would not be reversed for the next sixty years until the Indians were driven by the white man's "Man," Andrew Jackson, to Oklahoma [1832].

1777

Born: Sister of Herman Basket, the last acknowledged and undisputed beauty of the Chickasaw tribe in Yoknapatawpha

The black slave who was, three years from now, to become Issetibbeha's personal valet [1780] and, twenty-six years from now to be forced into a

[30]

common grave with him [1803], was captured off Kamerun by a white trader and shipped to slave-hungry America {"Red Leaves"}. He lived for ninety days between decks in the dreadful heat and humidity of the tropical latitudes, crammed together with other black men with whom he held in common only race and future. His sole contact with the world beyond his confines seems to have been the overheard voice of the ship's drunken captain, intoning above him in slobbering phrases pietistic verses from the Bible he must sincerely have thought he was living by.

In the North, the American Revolution, in progress now for two years, reached its first turning point on October 17th as the American forces under Horatio Gates defeated the British under Burgoyne at Saratoga. In Burgoyne's army there was an ensign named Ratcliffe, and it was his descendants who were eventually to settle in Yoknapatawpha County {T}, change their name via simple phonetical mutational laziness to "Ratliff," and engender a male offspring who would become the most verbose and the proudest resident of the county [1874]. Since it was to be this man, V. K. Ratliff, who would introduce to it the sewing machine, the vacuum cleaner, the radio, and the television, the defeat of Burgoyne at Saratoga stands as a landmark date in the onset of dubious modernism in Yoknapatawpha County.

1778

Born: Jason Lycurgus Compson, the first of four so named

Charles Stuart Compson, son of Quentin I and father of Jason Lycurgus, fought for the British in Georgia, the state in which Tory and patriot sentiment was probably most equally divided. In one battle he was left for dead in a swamp by his own men and by the Americans who pursued them through it {F}. He still carried his father's claymore [1746] when he later set out for the North on his homemade wooden leg in search of him, his son, and his Carolina home, not knowing that they would already be gone, to escape this very same war, by the time he got there.

1779

Born: Thucydus (d. 1854), black slave, who was to become the husband of Eunice, who was herself to become the black mistress of Lucius Quintus Carothers McCaslin

Early this year Quentin Compson I fled with his grandson (Jason I) from Carolina to Kentucky to escape the implications—political and military—of the Revolutionary War. Having lost to one British king in Scotland, he resolved, it seems, not to repeat his mistake in so apparently hopeless a cause as this one {F}. He still carried the tartan he brought from his homeland in 1746. He is thought to have wound up finally in Daniel Boone's settlement.

1780

The black slave, now 17, who was taken in the Kamerun three years before [1777], was officially installed this year as Issetibbeha's personal body servant {"Red Leaves"}.

1781

In this year Great Britain ceded West Florida, including Mississippi, back to Spain, an act which was to provoke the West Florida Controversy in the latter half of this decade and the first half of the next.

In the North, the Yorktown campaign effectively concluded British military operations in America when Cornwallis surrendered to Washington and Rochambeau on October 19th. Though it would be two more years until America would be recognized as an independent nation [1783], by yet another Treaty of Paris, the Revolution was over. As our fledgling country prepared to unite, however, many (and Charles Stuart Compson—still without home or family—was among them) continued to have designs on disrupting this cause against which they had almost died fighting {F}.

1783

Died: Quentin MacLachan Compson (b. 1699)

Charles Stuart Compson, the traitor Compson in a family which would someday produce a Governor and a General (not to mention several more traitors), finally caught up after four years of trying [1778] with his father and son in Harrodsburg, Kentucky, just in time to bury the former {F}. Charles remained in the community, however, and tried his hand at being a schoolteacher, a trade no one with the name Compson would ever be happy at and one which Charles himself would eventually reject in favor of ones as flamboyant as his name would someday demand.

In this year the American Revolution officially ended when John Adams, Benjamin Franklin, and John Jay settled territorial problems with the British in the latest Treaty of Paris.

1788

In this year the Constitution of the United States was officially ratified by the necessary nine states, thereby instituting the government which was to begin to function within the next twelve months.

In Yoknapatawpha County in this landmark year, Andrew Jackson, solicitor for North Carolina and Tennessee, burned sticks in treaty with Issetibbeha and gave the chief a coat in token of good will {"A Courtship"}. None of the Indians, and maybe not even Jackson himself, could know that it would be this man, four decades later [1832], who would banish them all and all like them to Oklahoma where there was little of apparent value in the white man's terms and even the oil would be overlooked by the Indians until the white man had realized that it was worth enough to drill for.

The Presidency of George Washington, 1789–1797

1789

Things were apparently quiet among the Chickasaws in these years. They were largely overlooked by the government which was beginning its work in the North; and they had not yet begun to gamble and trade their land [1813] and self-respect away to Compsons, McCaslins, and Sutpens, as they would before long [1816] [1833]. Issetibbeha continued his long tenure as "The Man" in the Yoknapatawpha district. His son—the fat, squat, repulsive Moketubbe—had attained the age of sixteen; and, in this same year, he gave up the activity which legend has it {"Red Leaves"} had occupied him for the previous thirteen [1776]: the futile attempt to don the red shoes which his father had brought back from Paris, apparently realizing that they were too small for him even at three and by some incontrovertible law of fate would continue to remain so until his dying day. Some say that he would later try them one more time [1803], while in pursuit of his father's slave during his short tenure as "The Man," but that the pain drove him to distraction. These shoes were, in Moketubbe's mind, some talisman of power, some scepter of reign; so perhaps it turned out for the best that he never had power long enough for these to compel to retaliatory tyranny.

1790

At about this time Charles Stuart Compson gave up teaching school in Harrodsburg, Kentucky, and entered upon a career of outright gambling.

[33]

Though, as has been indicated earlier, this is a profession more suited to a Compson {F}, it would some years hence [1801] result in a move by his enemies to run him out of the country and, others said, out of the world if they could have caught him.

About this year as well, the Huguenot named Louis Grenier, a Paris-educated architect who also practiced a little law on the side, crossed the mountains from Virginia and Carolina to Mississippi {R}. True to his French heritage he had fought against the British in the American Revolution; and one version of the facts has it that it was he who gave Jefferson, the seat of Yoknapatawpha County, its name. He was to have direct descendants in the county, though his name would be phonetically butchered, into the 1930s, the ill-fated Lonnie Grinnup being the last to possess it (or at least any name which derived from it) [1938].

Lastly, a United States Agency was established to deal with Indian matters in the Mississippi Territory, and the Negro Slave population of the state was estimated at 650,000.

1791

Born: Son of Dr. Habersham

1793

Died: Judge Lemuel Stevens

In this year, near Savannah, Georgia, Eli Whitney invented the cotton gin.

1795

Born: A son to Issetibbeha (d. 1803)

Born: Quentin Compson II, later "Governor Compson"

1796

Married: Herman Basket's Sister and Log-in-the-Creek

This was a critical year in the history of prewhite Yoknapatawpha County. David Hogganbeck, twenty-three, had been piloting Captain Studenmare's steamboat into the Tallahatchie River for several years {"A Courtship"}. The Indians had come to anticipate him, the boat, and the wares it brought to help absorb their unwanted money; they knew all this would arrive when the river, swollen by spring rains, attained the level of a line David had drawn for them on the landing, a line which silently announced that the boat now had enough depth of water to "walk in." While in the settlement each year, David would play the fiddle and attempt (and generally succeed at) doing every-thing twice as much and twice as well as the Indians could. He would run, dance, and eat twice as long as any brave who offered him a challenge, for (legend has it) he was twice their size. It was in this year, however, that he first became romantically interested in Herman Basket's beautiful sister; but it was also in this year that the manly Ikkemotubbe, a nephew of Issetibbeha's who was a year younger than David, became inclined toward this same maiden gem.

Yet, by the time that summer that the water had begun to recede below the all-important mark on the landing, neither had surfaced as the "intended" of Herman Basket's Sister. When David, as a consequence, refused to pilot the boat out until it was settled, Captain Studenmare promptly fired him, though Studenmare himself apparently had no skill to pilot the boat toward the safer waters of the Mississippi. Instead Studenmare borrowed Issetibbeha's wagon and, with the boat Negroes riding with him, set out for Natchez. David reminded him as he departed that he would be along in the steamboat's dinghy in the spring to pick up his pay at a Natchez saloon.

To settle the matter of Herman Basket's Sister, Hogganbeck and Ik-kemotubbe engaged in a number of rituals to determine the better man—but none could identify a clear winner. Finally, at whose suggestion no one is now sure, the two suitors agreed to race each other to the "Cave," a well-known testing spot for Indian courage, 130 miles away. The first man to arrive, fire a gunshot inside, and emerge (no mean trick since the roof of the cave was known to be quite delicate) was to be declared the victor, the better man, the man who would become the husband of Herman Basket's Sister. In a chase which lasted many days, David and Ikkemotubbe passed each other and even lent each other brotherly assistance on many occasions; but it was the smaller, more mobile Ikkemotubbe who eventually entered the Cave first, fired the shot, and had the roof fall in on him before he could get out. Hot on his heels, though, was David who got inside just in time to prop a portion of the ceiling on his back so Ikkemotubbe could escape and return with help. Since other tribesmen had been following immediately behind, however, David—after having endured much suffering and internal bleeding—was freed many days before he expected to be. The question of the winner, thus, was still unsettled. But it was also moot. Herman Basket's Sister, unim-pressed by the gauntlets David and Ikkemotubbe had run to curry her favor, had married the lazy, drunk, harmonica-playing Log-in-the-Creek, clearly

[35]

preferring a domestic husband to whatever David or Ikkemotubbe were prepared to be.

But in the history of Yoknapatawpha County, the real significance of this event is yet to be mentioned. Unable to remain and endure their mutual loss, Ikkemotubbe and David Hogganbeck journeyed to New Orleans on Captain Studenmare's steamboat, which David had managed to extricate despite the shallow water {"A Justice"}. Ikkemotubbe would not return for seven years [1803], spending that time with his old friend the Chevalier Soeur Blonde de Vitry, who taught him to be a leader and eventually "Du Homme," the "Man," the Chief of the Chickasaws {"Red Leaves"}. Unfortunately, however, Ikkemotubbe was not in the line of succession for this position, being as he was the son of Issetibbeha's sister, Mohataha. Between Ikkemotubbe and the kingship stood four men who had prior claim: Issetibbeha himself; his first son, Moketubbe; his infant son born in 1795; and the chief's brother, Sometimes Wake-up. Yet in 1803 Ikkemotubbe would become "The Man" nonetheless.

THE PRESIDENCY OF JOHN ADAMS, 1797–1801

1797

With the firing of David Hogganbeck by Captain Studenmare, the steamboat which now came up the river about four times a year was piloted by David Callicoat. Callicoat continued in this capacity until the steamboat eventually ran aground and "died" on a trip in 1799 {"A Justice"}. Despite the fact that Ikkemotubbe was in New Orleans during these years, he apparently knew him or at least knew of his piloting skills. At one point he even adopted his name before he selected "Doom" instead.

1798

With Ikkemotubbe in New Orleans and the white man yet to arrive, this year was apparently uneventful in Yoknapatawpha. Issetibbeha gave the coveted red slippers to Moketubbe on his twenty-fifth birthday, though Moketubbe had long since given up trying to don them {"A Justice"}.

Mississippi this year ended Spain's rule by beginning to fly the flag of the United States, though it would be two more decades [1817] before it was to become the new republic's twentieth state.

1799

Born: Theophilus "Uncle Buck" McCaslin (d. 1869)

Born: Amodeus "Uncle Buddy" McCaslin (d. 1869)

Sometime during this year Captain Studenmare's steamboat, presumably piloted by David Callicoat, ran aground on a sandbar in the Tallahatchie River and there, as the Indians said, died {"A Justice"}. Ikkemotubbe, however, would resurrect it in four more years [1803].

This year was most important, however, because it marked the arrival of the first white settlers in Yoknapatawpha County. During a period when Issetibbeha was absent from the district, attending a state function with another chief named Wolf's Friend (who sat, as Mohataha later would, under a crimson umbrella during the heat of the day), Dr. Habersham, his eight-year-old motherless son, Louis Grenier, and Alec Holston arrived from Virginia and Carolina by way of the Cumberland Gap. Holston's role is somewhat obscure, though he seems to have been a kind of factotum of Habersham's, perhaps a groom and bodyguard for the doctor and a sort of tutor for the boy. They established, at the site of what is today the town of Jefferson, a Chickasaw Agency and trading post {N}. Grenier soon obtained a land patent and began to import slaves.

1800

The settlement which Habersham established at the present location of Jefferson came to be known by his name and stayed that way for several decades [1831]. He and Issetibbeha apparently got along famously, and Habersham this year was appointed the first Indian agent in the district {N}. Another white man named Wyott built a store and ferryboat landing at the Tallahatchie River crossing in the northern portion of the County. This ferry was to serve as the most convenient means of fording the river until an iron bridge replaced it some one hundred years later {R}. And Alec Holston established the Holston House, the first tavern in the district. Because he had dragged a fifteen-pound lock from his Carolina home, he became (even though the lock had nothing to secure) the symbol and the protector of individual rights in the district {N}. Curiously, the lock was equated by the white residents with freedom; and Holston was looked to by all, Indians included, for advice and approval.

1801

Died: David Callicoat, in New Orleans

Undoubtedly because relations between Issetibbeha's Chickasaws and the settling whites had been so superb, the United States government was able to conclude a treaty with the Chickasaw nation in order that the Natchez Trace could become a wagon road for white settlers moving south.

Elsewhere, Charles Stuart Compson, becoming more of a brigand every year, was participating in a plan with James Wilkinson to split off the whole Mississippi Valley from the United States and merge it with Spain {F}. Unlike the other conspirators, however, Compson could not keep quiet about his beliefs and activities and so became the only one of them forced to leave the country. He was ultimately chased out of Kentucky and the United States, some of his pursuers being the very men he was supposed to be coconspiring with.

1802

Married: Ikkemotubbe and a quadroon Haitian girl, in New Orleans

When Ikkemotubbe married a Haitian girl in New Orleans, the girl's brother pursued him about the city, either to prevent the marriage or at least terminate it before it had a chance to produce offspring {"Red Leaves"}. Though the matter is murky to this day, one version of the facts has it that the legendary Sam Fathers was the first child of this union, though it was to be Sam himself, as an old man speaking to impressionable young boys, who would most insist upon this version of his genealogy.

1803

Born: Sam Fathers (d. 1883), formerly "Had-Two-Fathers"

Married: Slave of Ikkemotubbe and his quadroon wife

Died: Issetibbeha (b. 1751)

Died: Youngest son of Issetibbeha (b. 1795)

Died: Three white slave traders

Died: Black slave of Issetibbeha (b. 1763)

Unquestionably this was a momentous year in the history of Yok-napatawpha County. The fact that this was the year of the Louisiana Purchase and thus Mississippi no longer represented the southwestern frontier of the United States was dwarfed by local events.

The number of slaves being held by the Chickasaws had quintupled over the past several decades, and once again they had to be sold off to the white man. As a result many cattle-dealing slave traders loitered about the county waiting to make trades with the Indians for what the latter considered incredibly low stakes {"Red Leaves"}.

When Ikkemotubbe disembarked after his seven-year absence in New Orleans [1796], he brought with him six to eight *more* blacks, in addition to his quadroon wife, the Chevalier Soeur Blonde de Vitry, a gold-laced hat and cloak, a small gold snuff box filled with strong-smelling white powder which looked like salt, and a wicker wine hamper containing four puppies {"A Justice"} {"A Courtship"}. Before beginning the three-day journey from the Tallahatchie landing to Issetibbeha's plantation {G}, Ikkemotubbe apparently noticed Studenmare's stranded steamboat in the river where it had run aground four years earlier [1799]. He coveted it instantly and decided to have the steamboat moved inland to the plantation. But first he had to be about the business of becoming "The Man," despite the fact that four Indian males technically stood in his way.

In what became known in Yoknapatawpha Indian lore as the "bullet of bread," Ikkemotubbe used some of the strange white powder to poison (secretly) his uncle, "The Man" Issetibbeha; (openly) one of the puppies; and (secretly again) Issetibbeha's eight-year-old son, the next in line after the slovenly Moketubbe to be The Man {"A Justice"}. Sometime thereafter he poisoned another puppy in Moketubbe's presence; and, after only a very short time as The Man, Moketubbe abdicated in favor of Issetibbeha's brother, Sometimes Wake-up. Perhaps it took another dead dog to persuade Sometimes Wake-up to abdicate as well, but it can be assumed that the word was pretty widespread by now about what the bullet of bread could do to the unsuspecting communicant. Sometimes Wake-up, then, never served as The Man, and Ikkemotubbe assumed power, probably in the spring of this year. He became known to Indians and whites alike as "Du Homme," or, more easily, "Doom." Though blame cannot be laid entirely on his shoulders, perhaps the Chevalier Soeur Blonde de Vitry can stand as an effective symbol for the doom civilized behavior brought to the native instincts of the Indians and eventually to the human race as a whole.

During the few weeks that Moketubbe served as The Man—between the

[39]

death of his father and the death of the second puppy—he was required by tribal custom to see to the burial of Issetibbeha's personal slave, horse, and dog in the same grave with their master {"Red Leaves"}. The horse and dog, not understanding the tribal law, were, of course, easy marks. The slave, who had served the chief for twenty-three years, knew better, however, and took to the hills to escape his personal doom. Many braves, old and young, were sent in pursuit, among them Three Basket and Louis Berry, the two who ultimately ran the exhausted Negro to ground. But during the chase the slave was secretly aided by other slaves and openly admired by the Indians for his abilities to escape and endure. Finally, after being so badly bitten by a snake that he considered chopping off his own arm with a hatchet, he was caught—naked and mud-caked—sitting on a log and singing to himself. He was brought to Moketubbe and allowed to finish a final meal before being put to death and laid to rest with the chief he had served.

This was, insofar as can be determined, Moketubbe's sole achievement in his tenure as The Man. Perhaps Ikkemotubbe even waited till this was completed because it was clearly not the duty he, as new Chief and Doom, would care to open with. Moketubbe apparently had little interest in the Manship anyway, especially after wearing the painful red slippers, his symbol of power, all through the prolonged slave chase. His lust for power was no doubt waning, however, when the second puppy died before him from the bullet of bread.

Ikkemotubbe's first action as The Man was to have the stranded steamboat moved to the plantation, a distance of twelve hard miles {"A Justice"}. Assembling some of the plantation slaves and the several he had brought back from New Orleans, he led his party to the Tallahatchie and commenced to extricate the boat, which the steamboat-fascinated Doom was planning to make his home. He managed to secure rights to the boat, which he found already inhabited on the sandbar by three white slave traders, by trading them the six or eight unwanted New Orleans blacks. However, Crawfishford, a brave, coveted one of the lighter-skinned women and, with the aid of Herman Basket, killed the three white men who now owned her and dumped them in the river. From that point forward Crawfishford lost all interest in the boat-moving, and he daily feigned sickness to stay behind with her at the plantation. Responding to the woman's husband's complaint about Crawfishford's activities, Ikkemotubbe—during the six or seven months it took him to roll the boat on logs to the plantation—had to devise means for keeping Crawfishford away from this quadroon woman. He also had to devise a means to determine to which man she really belonged. After a series of cockfights and other trials, all of which provided little resolution, the woman in question gave birth to a very light-skinned child. The baby was, of course, the man the county later knew as Sam Fathers; but it was at least evidence to Ikkemotubbe that the child belonged to Crawfishford and not to

[40]

the woman's husband. So, once the steamboat project was completed, Doom ordered Crawfishford, with the assistance of his too close ally Herman Basket to build a huge fence around the woman's house, a fence only the black husband would be able to scale. The child, named "Had-Two-Fathers" by Doom himself, was awarded to Crawfishford to bring up.

It must be pointed out again, though, that this version of Sam's parentage does not jibe with Sam's own version nor with that offered by many old-timers in the County. Some say that Ikkemotubbe, much like Thomas Sutpen after him [1831], learned of his own wife's black blood too late {G}. Thus he was confronted with the problem of unloading an unwanted, wrong-shaded heir to his Manship and Doomship. To solve this, the alternate version has it, he pronounced a marriage between his wife and a black slave. This would make Sam Fathers the son of Doom he liked to claim to be (and very well might have been).

1804

Born: Mother of Rosa Coldfield (d. 1845)

Born: The black child of the slave cuckolded by Crawfishford

Doom had by this year attained full control of the disintegrating Chickasaw nation in northern Mississippi, and Napoleon became Emperor of France. Doom was living in his steamboat on the plantation.

In this year, also, President Thomas Jefferson gave the city plan for Jackson, Mississippi, to Territorial Governor Clayborne {N}.

1807

Born: Thomas Sutpen (d. 1869)

Born: Wash Jones (d. 1869)

Not in Yoknapatawpha yet but acquiring slaves at a fast rate, Lucius Quintus Carothers McCaslin bought Eunice, the black girl with whom he would enter into an illegitimate, morganatic relationship in about two years {G} [1809].

1808

Died: Wife of Lucius Quintus Carothers McCaslin

[41]

1809

Married: Thucydus and Eunice, two McCaslin slaves

1810

Born: Tomasina, illegitimate, half-black daughter of Lucius Quintus Carothers McCaslin and his slave Eunice (d. 1833)

Born: Aunt of Rosa Coldfield

At approximately this time, the white community eventually to be known
as Jefferson [1831] made its decision to attach the symbolic Holston lock to
the town mailbag {N}, the only thing it seemed to have which was worth
locking up or, at least, the only thing which ever got far enough beyond the
settlement's grasp to get stolen by someone who did not give a damn for this
community or probably any other either. However, despite real dangers
along the route, the mail carrier named Pettigrew refused to lug fifteen
pounds of useless metal back and forth to Nashville. Thus, for reasons hard to
explain but perhaps somewhat easier to understand, the lock was affixed to
the bag only during the times it lay securely in the back room of Ratcliffe's
trading post.

1811

Jason Lycurgus Compson came up the Natchez trace this year with a pair
of pistols and a fast mare {F}, long since out of association with his on-the-
lam father who was probably long since out of the country by now [1801].
He arrived at the Chickasaw agency at Okatoba, also known as "Old Jefferson."

1812

Born: Calvin Burden I (d. 1873)

America's nationalist feelings were strengthened this year and for the
ensuing two because of the ongoing war with Great Britain over neutrality

of the seas. In Yoknapatawpha, the white community continued to solidify itself; its leaders were beginning to muster themselves into a new, non-Indian aristocracy of land and slaveholders, even though they were still short on both. Also, Jason Lycurgus Compson became the first agent's clerk and then partner in the Chickasaw agency {F}.

1813

Ikkemotubbe did something this year which might support the contention that it was *he*, not Crawfishford, who sired Sam Fathers [1803]: he sold Sam, his mother, and her husband to Lucius Quintus Carothers McCaslin [1807], a new white settler in the district, whose activities in slave-buying and slave-mating have already been mentioned [1810]. By this year, McCaslin had made his way over the mountains from Carolina {G} to Yoknapatawpha with his Negroes and foxhounds {R}. He acquired some land from the Indians and built a two-roomed, mud-chinked half-domicile/half-fort upon it.

Yet if McCaslin felt he must properly fortify himself against the Indians (or was it his own race he distrusted?), other whites continued to feel safe, indeed brotherly, in their intercourse with the Chickasaws. To the east, however, was the Creek War; but even this was, before long, brought under control by Andrew Jackson.

1815

Jason Lycurgus Compson became half-owner, with Ratcliffe, of a store. He stocked it with money won by his mare in races against the inferior mounts of Ikkemotubbe's braves, races he always limited to a quarter-mile or three furlongs, which was as long as her speed could hold out {F}.

1816

Married: Son of Dr. Habersham and Issetibbeha's granddaughter

The horse-loving Ikkemotubbe, impressed by the victories won by Jason Compson's mare against the best steeds his braves could bring forward, traded a square mile of land to Compson in return for the horse {N}. This land would someday occupy the center of Jefferson and be known as the Compson Mile [1840]. It would later be sold by the family [1908] to send a son to Harvard {F}; and the people they sold it to would eventually turn it into a golf course and, later still, a housing project [1945]. But the first fragment of it would go, not many years hence [1834], when the town bought it to build a courthouse on.

While Doom was involved in horse and land trading, some Chickasaw braves, with or without his knowledge, killed several Negro slaves by whipping and burning them, apparently for some minor offenses or, maybe, just for fun.

THE PRESIDENCY OF JAMES MONROE, 1817–1825

1817

Born: Jason Compson II (d. 1900), later "General Compson"

Died: Ikkemotubbe (b. 1774)

After having many flags flying above it, Mississippi was admitted to the Union this year as the nation's twentieth state.

In the Yoknapatawpha district, this year was marked by the death of Ikkemotubbe, "Doom," though the causes are unknown to this day. What is known is that it took three days to catch his slave for common burial {"Red Leaves"}, just as it took three days to run down Issetibbeha's some years earlier [1803]. The Chickasaws were clearly testing the propensity of the blacks to endure; and, if they were not winning, the Negroes were putting up a hard fight.

1818

Born: Ellen Coldfield (d. 1863)

1819

In another state this year, it is thought in the western part of Virginia, Thomas Sutpen, a man whose life was so greatly to affect Yoknapatawpha County {A}, was submitting to his single year of formal schooling. According to his account of it many years later, the only information he heard there which "stuck" was the fabled opportunities for quick wealth in the West Indies. As a result, Thomas Sutpen would someday affect the West Indies as well [1827].

[44]

Though it is unclear who became The Man after the death of Ik-kemotubbe, and in fact there may have been no particular Man since the most predominant Indian name in the district during these years was that of his mother, Mohataha, there continued to be peace among the Chickasaws until the beginning of Andrew Jackson's presidency [1829]. During this decade the Chickasaws were to gain the reputation of being some of the greatest hunters among the North American Indians, a love and skill they passed on, tradition has proven, to their white brethren among whom they lived and to whom they were slowly giving everything away—or at least everything they had that the white man had any particular use for. One of the lesser bequests was a salve that one of the Indian women gave to Will Fall's grandmother this year {O}, a salve designed to cure skin disorders which would someday in fact cure one on Bayard Sartoris' face and net a Memphis specialist $50 to boot in the process [1919]. By this year also Jason Lycurgus Compson had built his fancy house on the square mile of land he had traded his mare to Doom for {F}.

To the south the Mississippi State Legislature had sent three commissioners to locate the site of Jackson, soon to be the state capital {N}.

But in the north, in the western part of Virginia, ordinary and commonplace if not happy events were taking place which, a few years hence, would affect our ancestors. Thomas Sutpen, still in his early teens, was ripped from his "home," whatever that might have been, in this place where he said the land belonged to no one, and dragged southward by his drunken and irresponsible father {A}. In the course of the move, his sister got pregnant and his father took ever more heavily to drink. He soon was getting himself laughed out of backwoods barrooms by both white trash and Negroes. This treatment, young Thomas was later to admit, did not escape his notice.

1821

Born: Child of Thomas Sutpen's sister

General Hinds and his party laid out Jackson according to Thomas Jefferson's plan [1804] {N}, and Mohataha officially deeded the square mile of Indian land (traded by Ikkemotubbe to his father) to Quentin Compson {M}. But truly meaningful events, no matter how meaningless they seemed, were still taking place somewhere to the north of us.

Thomas Sutpen's father, after a year or so of aimless wandering, job-seeking, and booze-swilling, finally settled down—probably in the Carolinas—to work for a rich white man who owned a big house, a lot of land, and countless slaves, one of whom he could even spare from the fields to fan him and bring him drinks on hot days {A}. Young Thomas was not jealous of this, but he was clearly confused by it—the principle behind such an arrangement totally eluded him. One day, while walking down the road with his sister, he was almost run down by this same man's coach. The man (according to Sutpen's later recollections) did not even bother to stop. Perhaps he was angered by *this,* but it seems more to have increased his inner turmoil about the right of one man to do such as this to another man, probably wondering most of all what the credentials were and how to gain them. The confusion was to continue to fester for two more years [1823].

1822

The first session of the State Legislature was convened in the new state house. It named its own county "Hinds" after the man who had laid out the city of Jackson {N}.

1823

Born: John Sartoris (d. 1873), in Carolina

In Carolina, Thomas Sutpen's father sent him with a message to the house of the rich man who employed them {A}. Having naively knocked at the front door of the huge, porticoed plantation house, Thomas was mortified when the Negro butler ordered him to go around to the back and never come to the front door again. Sutpen not only did not go to the front door again, he also never went to the back, even this time. Rather he went to the woods to think this over. After a hasty decision to shoot the rich man (and maybe his doorman, too), Sutpen thought better of it and instead ran away from his "home" forever, apparently never seeing any member of his family again. So, at sixteen, he went to live in the West Indies to acquire the fortune his single year of schooling had assured him was there for the white man who showed up to take it [1819].

This was the year of the Monroe Doctrine in which the United States promised not to meddle in European affairs nor tolerate European meddling in its own. So Thomas Sutpen went to the West Indies to meddle in theirs; and he would in a few decades have to permit (or at least accept) West Indian meddling in his [1859].

1824

In the vicinity of Yoknapatawpha, a Choctaw agency was established south of Jefferson, or what was soon to be called that anyway, at Yalo Busha {N}.

In Missouri, Calvin Burden, the first of two men by that name whom John Sartoris (himself only a yearling in 1824) was later to kill at the same time and place [1873], ran away from his home on a ship {L}. He journeyed around Cape Horn to California and there, in his Spanish surroundings, rejected his fundamentalist Protestantism in favor of a version of Roman Catholicism he apparently never understood.

THE PRESIDENCY OF JOHN QUINCY ADAMS, 1825–1829

1825

Born: William C. Falkner (d. 1889)

Born: Will Falls

Born: Jubal (d. 1865), the black slave servant of Saucier Weddel

Calvin Burden, still in California, lived this year and part of the next in a monastery {L}.

In Yoknapatawpha, a man named Ballenbaugh happened along this year and drove Wyott away from his ferryboat landing [1800] and turned the crossing into a roaring Gomorrah of wild men and loose women {R}, an identity and reputation it was to nurture and protect for the rest of the century [1886].

1827

Married: Thomas Sutpen and Eulalia Bon (in Haiti)

In Yoknapatawpha this year, the transition from the founding fathers of the County to the next generation of aristocrats was in abeyance. Ikkemotubbe and Dr. Habersham were both dead, though it is not clear when the latter passed on {N}. Alec Holston was old and crippled with arthritis, and Louis Grenier had moved a dozen or so miles south to build what would later be called the Old Frenchman's Place at a location which would still later be called Frenchman's Bend. Thus, with the McCaslins, the Sartorises, the

[47]

Sutpens, and the DeSpains yet to take control of the county's direction, the populace grouped itself around symbols rather than leaders. The Holston Lock was the oldest of these [1800], still a moral icon despite its uselessness otherwise [1810] and, for some people in some ways, its bothersomeness.

In Haiti, Thomas Sutpen, finding the pursuit of wealth something like his schoolbook had cracked it up to be but not entirely, was working this year for a large sugar planter named Bon {A}. When a Negro rebellion broke out, Sutpen and the Bon family were trapped for seven days in the plantation house. When the water ran out on the eighth, Sutpen, according to his own rendition of it later to General Compson anyway, stalked forth and almost single-handedly quashed the uprising, though he was badly wounded in whatever form the fight took and had to be dragged back to the house by old Bon and his daughter Eulalia. Through a cause/effect sequence which re-quires little imagination but which was to cause unimaginable tragedy for countless people later on, Thomas, twenty, married Eulalia in this same year [1863] [1865] [1869] [1884] [1909].

1828

The only records available for this year are commercial ones and have to do with the two stores which were, for several more decades, to be the district's main sources of supply. Jason Compson bought his way further into Ratcliffe's store {N}, and a man named Goodhue Coldfield arrived in Jeffer-son, or what was very soon to be Jefferson, with the makings of a small business packed in a wagon. He is said to have come from Tennessee, and it would have been better if he had gone right back {A}. He did not know that then, maybe never did, but his daughters would become very clear about it [1863] [1866].

THE PRESIDENCY OF ANDREW JACKSON, 1829–1837

1829

Born: Charles Sutpen (d. 1865), later called Charles Bon, in Haiti

The lull continued in Old Jefferson; but in Jackson the state Senate authorized the removal of the state capital to Clinton. This was later rejected by the House {N}.

1830

Born: Percival Brownlee, a slave, later to be fully emancipated

Born: Father of Gail Hightower (d. 1864)

Still trying to move the capital from Jackson, the legislature voted to displace it to Port Gibson, then changed its mind and favored Vicksburg {N}. Neither seems to have occurred, for the last time I went to the capital I was still going to Jackson.

In Yoknapatawpha, the end of Indian residency was near. Apparently Manless, for Mohataha was in full command if "command" is what it could be called, the Chickasaws had taken to hanging around the Ratcliffe-Compson store all day, wearing clothes they had bought inside and eating crackers and candy they must have gotten there too {N}. Mohataha herself was regularly seen doing something resembling loitering in town every Saturday, still wearing the purple dress Issetibbeha had brought her from Paris a long way back [1776].

1831

Married: Francis Weddel and his wife

Died: Ballenbaugh, the first of several

Though nobody knows for sure, and even he wasn't certain just when he did it, it was probably in this year that Thomas Sutpen, having discovered the trace of Negro blood in his wife's lineage (and therefore in his son's) and thinking the consequent material payments he had made them would be enough, deserted them in Haiti and left the island {A}. He initiated thereby the process of doom which would take almost thirty years to run him down [1859] and another ten after that to finish him off [1869].

If one single year could be chosen when the town of Jefferson became a community and not a settlement, and when Yoknapatawpha became a county and not a profane space buried in the woodland, 1831 would have to be that year {N}. Descendants of its forefathers pretty much agree that the Fourth of July that year was the moment of sacred consecration.

On Sunday, July 3rd, the state militia, after participating in the holiday preparations, got involved in a series of brawls with various townsmen. Bloodied and ejected, they settled for the night in Hurricane Bottom where the town could not get at them nor they at the town or maybe both. Also inhabiting the Bottom that night, however, were three members of the notorious Harpe gang, upon whose heads (or whatever other vital parts of their carcasses could verifiably be presented) rested a big reward. Sobering quickly, the militia took the three captive.

On the next day, Monday the Fourth, the militia brought the Harpes to town; the town, though, had no incarceration facilities worthy of criminals of so high an order. So they bored holes through the walls of their little mud-chinked jail [1800], inserted a chain through the door and wall, took the Holston Lock (still the town's symbol of morality [1810] [1827]) from the mailbag, and locked the Harpes inside—not so much to keep them in but to keep the holiday lynchers out, people Jason Compson had to hold at bay until the Harpes were secured within. The town then dispatched a rider to Natchez to report the capture and collect the reward and bring back some-body to take the Harpes away, preferably far away. While the townsmen held their own meeting to determine how the reward money should be spent, the lynchers and militiamen, the latter of whom felt entitled to the reward and the former of whom felt entitled to the Harpes, held their own boisterous gathering which threatened not only the necks of the Harpes but also the physical security of the town. Jason Compson once again defused the situa-tion by borrowing laudanum from Doc Peabody's bag, spiking their liquor (they were already too liquored up to know the difference), and rendering the entire mob comatose. All were shoved in jail with the Harpes, the lock was relocked, and the town went to bed.

On Tuesday the Fifth, however, the community awoke to find the lock gone from the jail, as well as the entire wall to which it was attached (though the inmates had neatly stacked the logs which had formerly comprised it to one side). Holston, very old now, cantankerously demanded his lock back; and Mohataha's braves were dispatched to find it and, all hoped, the Harpes too. A day-long search yielded nothing, so Compson recommended that the town pay Holston for the lock. Ratcliffe ventured a plan, moreover, which would bury its cost in the ledgers of the Indian agency. This accomplished, a more serious problem developed. Thomas Jefferson Pettigrew, the mail carrier, stepped forth to announce that, since holes had been slit in the mailbag to accommodate it [1810], the lock was now the property of the United States government and that the mailbag, more such property, had been illegally defaced from the start. He threatened action against the town fathers, action these same fathers attempted to deter by an outright bribe. Realizing that this was not what Pettigrew wanted, that he was a moralist plain and simple, they offered instead to name the town after him. His middle name, Jefferson, was selected, Pettigrew was satisfied, and Holston was offered $50 for the lock, though he accepted $15. Pettigrew then stunned everyone by stepping forward to show how other items—such as axle grease required by the Indians as they prepared their wagons for their about-to-be-

[50]

ordered trek to Oklahoma [1832]—could also be obscured in Ratcliffe's Indian-Agency books.

On Wednesday the Sixth and Thursday the Seventh, the town got down to rebuilding its jail. On the first day they set about throwing away the old materials and cleaning up the mess; on the second, the day when communal spirit first took over, they erected the sturdier though otherwise very similar building in its place. Louis Grenier brought his slaves from Frenchman's Bend to assist [1827], and Mohataha—already under threat of Jacksonian exile—brought some of her Chickasaw braves to help out as well. She supervised them from under her Parisian parasol. While Ratcliffe stewed inside his store over the $15 he had just bilked the Government out of, the other town fathers sat on the porch of his store planning a bigger, more substantial courthouse for the immediate future. At the end of this important day, Thursday, July 7th, 1831, the white men carried the old pirate's chest, which was the town's sole repository for important records, from the back room of Ratcliffe's trading post into the "new" courthouse.

Later this year, Francis Weddel, the titular chief of the Choctaws in the Yoknapatawpha district, made his celebrated journey to see President Jackson in Washington {"Lo!"}. The matter had to do with the crossing of the Tallahatchie River which Wyott had acquired from the Chickasaws in 1800 but which Ballenbaugh had turned into a bawdy house in 1825 and been charging toll to cross at ever since then. Wishing to acquire the crossing, Weddel's nephew had bet a hundred miles of land against Ballenbaugh's ford and booth in a horserace—and lost. During the night following the race, this young Weddel murdered the first Ballenbaugh in the county by splitting his skull. Francis Weddel hauled the nephew off to Washington where, confronting President Jackson, he demanded a full ceremonial trial and got it, or at least appeared to. Jackson apparently had to incant Petrarchan sonnets aloud in their original Italian before he could disperse the Indians and adjudge the accused nephew, it is supposed, guilty of justifiable homicide in the murder of the crooked tolltaker.

In this memorable year, several other events which would ultimately become meaningful were taking place, though not where anybody in the newly congealed community could know about them. Eulalia Bon began her several-year pursuit of the unfaithful and ruthless Thomas Sutpen across Texas and Missouri, though Sutpen himself, living at one time or another in either one or both of those states, was a sick man, suffering what General Compson later termed a "solitary furnace sickness" {A}. Having discovered the black blood which lurked in his wife's veins, and hence in his son's, Sutpen had to burn out the hate/agony which impeded his dream to be like the white man who turned him from his door (no, had his nigger do it!) eight years ago [1823] and, if possible, begin again. Possible it would eventually seem, but impossible it would ultimately turn out to be. But

[51]

Thomas Sutpen did not know this in 1831, nor did those still standing who were doomed to fall in the path of his trying.

1832

Born: Lucius Quintus Peabody, apparently the second, or at least the second of four doctors named this that we know about

Born: G. A. Fentry

Died: Eunice, wife of Thucydus, slave and mistress of Lucius Quintus Carothers McCaslin, mother of his child Tomasina—a suicide at Christmas

Died: Ballenbaugh's brother

Francis Weddel wrote President Jackson a letter in the autumn telling of a similar incident to the one last year [1831], though this time no split white skull was discovered: only the drowned body of another white man beaten, this time, in a swimming race with an Indian brave {"Lo!"}. Just coincidentally the victim's name this year was Ballenbaugh also. To prevent the reappearance of the Indians, Jackson issued a decree which henceforth prohibited any white man from actually owning the ford and sent out a cavalry unit to intercept Weddel and his tribesmen who were returning for yet another ceremonial trial.

Perhaps it is only coincidence as well, but this was the year of the Pontotoc Creek Treaty which sent the Choctaws and Chickasaws in straggling units off to Oklahoma for good, though they had known for a few years that they would have to go there. In Jefferson, Mohataha, still sitting under her purple parasol, rode into town one day in a loaded wagon. "Where is this Indian Territory?" she asked in defiant resignation {N}. Her horses were pointed west for her; and the wagonload of nine plus Mohataha, and including Habersham's son and his Indian wife, left Yoknapatawpha forever, more or less ending the Indian presence in the County.

This year ended tragically with the self-drowning of the McCaslin slave girl named Eunice {G}. No one knew why at the time, save for old. L. Q. C. himself; but Ike McCaslin was to discover, a half-century later [1881], that the cause was the revelation to her that her daughter by old Carothers, Tomasina, was also carrying a child of his.

Elsewhere in the state, the Legislature designated Jackson to remain the capital at least until 1850 {N}; and one of the state's first female academies was opened there, designed by a Parisian architect who was to show up in Jefferson, himself a slave even though he was white, a year later [1833].

1833

Born: Jeb Stuart (d. 1864)

Born: Terrel Beauchamp (d. 1888), "Tomey's Turl"

Died: Tomasina (b. 1810), half-black daughter to *and* mistress of Lucius Quintus Carothers McCaslin

Called in the McCaslin ledgers "the year the stars fell," because of the illegitimate, incestuous, morganatic birth of Tomey's Turl to Old Carothers McCaslin and his half-black daughter, Tomasina {G}, 1833 is rather more the year of Thomas Sutpen. After staying away from Yoknapatawpha for twenty-six years without even knowing he was doing it, Sutpen rode into Jefferson for the first time on a Sunday morning in June, bringing with him only the clothes on his back, the pistols in his holsters, and the horse between his legs {A}. It is hard to imagine why he did not just ride out the other side—which he could have done quickly because all Jefferson was then was the Holston House, the log courthouse, a blacksmith shop, and six stores (among them Ratcliffe-Compson's and Goodhue Coldfield's), a saloon, three churches, and some thirty houses. But he stopped, perhaps because he knew right away what the rest of the town knew in a matter of days—that he could shake down a departing Indian for a hundred square miles of virgin bottomland the red man no longer had use for and probably accepted junk for in return. He stayed four weeks at the Holston House, getting up early each morning and spending the entire day at an unknown destination. Three days after he arrived he demonstrated his shooting ability by riding his horse in a twenty-foot circle around a sapling, firing both pistols at a playing card pinioned to it, and hitting the card dead center every time. He refused all proffers of drink at this and every other time and seemed to those few who claimed to know him to be driven by a furious impatience.

One night in early July, Sutpen woke up the county recorder, flipped him a Haitian gold coin, and ordered his deed to the hundred miles of Indian land recorded in the courthouse. That same night he disappeared from town as mysteriously as he had turned up.

He was gone from Jefferson for two months but reappeared in September with the French architect [1832] and a wagonload of wild Negroes, the biggest brutes this slaveholding County had yet encountered. Two of these were women. But this time Sutpen didn't stop in Jefferson but rather rode straight through it and out the other side to the site of his deeded land twelve miles to the northwest. There was no particular arrogance in this—none of them had eaten in days and they were anxious to shoot a deer. On the following day, the two-year construction of Sutpen's plantation house, later to be called Sutpen's Hundred, was begun [1835]. Thomas, the architect, and the slaves lived at night body to body in a tent made out of the hood of their wagon, subsisting on a diet of evening venison and little else. They spoke to no one, though their activities attracted cartfuls of spectators each day.

But even as Sutpen's dream of lineage, dynasty, and empire was beginning to take shape after the fooled and wasted years in Haiti [1831], Eulalia Bon was in New Orleans retaining a lawyer and plotting how to use her four-year-old son to ruin his father [1859].

1834

Born: Clytemnestra Sutpen (d. 1909), half-black daughter of Thomas and one of the two slave women in his contingent

Furiously impatient, Sutpen, his architect, and his savages pounded away at the plantation house. And suddenly desiring acceptance into the community he had chosen and almost knew he was so greatly to affect, he began to bring his powerful Negroes into Jefferson on occasion to assist in the erection of the new, bigger, more permanent courthouse {N}. Perhaps it was no coincidence that his own house and the county building were to be, for a long time, the two largest structures for many miles in any direction. Both were surely bigger than their next rival, Grenier's plantation house to the south at Frenchman's Bend—Sutpen would have seen to that. The Parisian architect, who was later identified as a "slave" himself, taught the townsmen how to make bricks and even modified the design of the courthouse for them, all the while warning them mysteriously that "in fifty years you will be trying to change in the name of what you call progress; but you will fail; you will never be able to get away from it."

The architect proved himself unable to get away from anything either that summer {A}. He made his single escape try when the Hundred was about half-built. Immediately upon discovering his absence, Sutpen declared a holiday and set his wild cannibals and hounds and few white friends (the town fathers he was helping to build the courthouse) to running him down. On one occasion they were thrown off the trail by the architect's suspenders hanging in a tree, but they continued to pursue him (some say all the hunters including Sutpen were naked in the woods) for thirteen miles and ran him to ground in the late afternoon. There, in a cave under a river bank, he cowered like a trapped rat, his fancy Parisian clothes torn to shreds. Sutpen, apparently without wrath, stepped up to him and offered him a drink from his whisky bottle.

This pursuit was important in yet another way, for it was during the rest breaks that Sutpen revealed most of what we now know of his past life to his closest friend, General Jason Compson II, except that, being only seventeen, he wasn't yet a general.

1835

Sometime during this year and for most of the next three, Thomas Sutpen lived with his wild Negroes within the shell of his huge, just-completed plantation house {A}. To the best of anyone's knowledge, it had not a stick of furniture in it and, for certain, had not a pane of glass.

1836

Married: Calvin Burden I and Evangeline (in St. Louis)

Calvin Burden reached St. Louis this year, slowly terminating his long exile in the west [1824] and even more slowly approaching his predetermined doom in a Jefferson boarding house after the Civil War [1873] {L}. On his wedding night he rejected his Catholicism in a St. Louis saloon, censuring the members of his former faith as "frog-eating slaveholders." He bought a home later this year, also in St. Louis, and apparently settled in this border city for some years to come—but not forever [1842].

The nineteen-year-old Jason Compson II, still not the general he was later to become, lent Thomas Sutpen some seed to initiate his spring planting {A}. Still alone in his house save for his slaves, this year Sutpen began inviting men out from town to watch bloody cockfights, fights in which he used his big black men instead of birds and in which—it was rumored—Sutpen himself often participated.

In other parts of Mississippi, Andrew Jackson addressed the State Legislature in Jackson, the railroad from the North had been opened as far south as Vicksburg, and our neighboring city in Lafayette County—Oxford—was founded this year {N}.

THE PRESIDENCY OF MARTIN VAN BUREN, 1837–1841

1837

Born: Nathaniel Burden, son of Calvin, eventually father of Joanna Burden (an outsider who would be murdered by another outsider still a hundred years in the future)—in St. Louis

Born: Saucier Weddel (d. 1865), a white man with Indian blood

Born: Mother of Gail Hightower

Married: Jason "General" Compson and his wife

Died: Alec Holston, after many years of sickness and approaching senility

Died: Lucius Quintus Carothers McCaslin (b. 1772), after many years of land-grabbing, nigger-wenching, incest and miscegenation

Though this was primarily a year of McCaslins, Sutpen was maneuvering in ways the town barely noticed and, even if it had, would not at this point have understood {A}. He met the storeowner named Goodhue Coldfield at the Methodist Church and established an ambiguous relationship with him. Coldfield's life was modest and not at all congruent with Sutpen's grand designs [1838]; but what he had that Sutpen wanted was a marriageable daughter, something the town would finally come to understand Sutpen desperately needed.

One resident of Jefferson who did marry this year was Jason Compson II, though he married a girl from somewhere else who was for a time visibly ill at ease in this new environment {A}.

But, as I stated before, this was a year of McCaslins. The patriarch of the family, old Carothers McCaslin, died, bequeathing his land, his slaves, his money, and—connected with all of the aforesaid—his worries to his thirty-eight-year-old twin sons, Amodeus and Theophilus (or, as they were more familiarly known, Uncle Buck and Uncle Buddy) {G}. Much of the traceable history of Yoknapatawpha over the next decades is revealed in the ledgers they kept for the McCaslin plantation between 1837 and 1861. These were the same books their father had kept for many decades before this, the very ledgers which would later fall into the hands of Ike McCaslin [1881] and cause him to repudiate his inheritance and try at least to cleanse the present of the past of his ancestors.

Uncle Buck and Uncle Buddy were surprisingly enlightened men {U}, well in advance of their time despite their rudimentary formal education. Even before the Civil war [1840] they would be propounding a belief which sounded more than vaguely like socialism, but in 1837 they began voicing a theory that no land belonged to any man but rather all men belonged to the land {G}. In consequence of this, they thus had to hold that no man, white or black, could be owned by any other man; hence they were confronted immediately upon their father's death with the problem of what to do with the numerous blacks the old man had acquired and, at least once, had helped

[56]

to procreate. Realizing that the Negroes were too little educated and too naive in the ways of a world fast being controlled by immoral or at least amoral white men, Buck and Buddy apparently decided to initiate a very slow process of emancipation, making this more their lives' work than the profitable management of their father's vast holdings.

At first they dealt entirely in symbols. They moved all the slaves into old McCaslin's unfinished plantation house (which he had been building for some years but which had gone unnoticed because it was dwarfed by Sutpen's on the western side of the county). For themselves Buck and Buddy, without the help of even one Negro laborer, built and occupied a one-room cabin which over the years they added onto, again entirely by themselves. Next they attempted to free the oldest and wisest of their slaves, Roskus and Fibby, parents-in-law of the ill-fated Eunice and grandparents of the equally ill-fated Tomasina. But Roskus and Fibby were too old and too wise to go. Instead Buck and Buddy gave them ten acres of land outright, which they willed equally outright (probably as fast as he would take it off their hands) to their son Thucydus. Thucydus, already pushing sixty, also refused this inheritance, being old and wise enough to. So Buck and Buddy, frustrated that even symbols failed, tried to make him an alternative gift of $200, perhaps to teach him how to handle the white man's capital; but Thucydus refused this as well. So much for this year's efforts to emancipate the slaves, but they would try again and again over the years [1841] [1851] [1856] [1858] [1859]. Perhaps they should just have "proclaimed" it the easy way as Lincoln did in 1863.

What Buck and Buddy did accomplish, starting in this year and continuing until they officially lost ownership of all of them in 1865, was to teach the slaves a code of honor by locking them in the plantation house each night, except that they purposely left the front door ajar. The slaves were, by an agreement which could never have been anything more than tacit, allowed to prowl all night, provided they were back in the house by dawn. They always did and always were; this constituted a freedom they understood and appreciated. Meanwhile, for the next thirty-two years [1869], Uncle Buck ran the plantation and Uncle Buddy did the housekeeping. It is ironic that, a half-century later, Buck's son Ike would not fully appreciate his father's and uncle's efforts and repudiate the whole plantation, which was his inheritance, casting it into the far less competent hands of Cass Edmonds, his cousin [1888].

Two other events made 1837 important for Mississippi and Yoknapatawpha. The railroad opened its tracks from Vicksburg farther south to Natchez. And, the Indians gone forever, the white man began chopping down their forests to generate lumber to give these trains something to have to come to Mississippi to get {N}.

[57]

Born: Bayard Sartoris I (d. 1862), brother of John

Born: Tennie Beauchamp, ultimately to be the wife of Tomey's Turl

Married: Thomas Sutpen and Ellen Coldfield

If 1837 was a McCaslin year, 1838 was a Sutpen year. In January Thomas vanished again, this time for three or four months, returning in April with wagon loads of the fanciest furniture yet seen in the County, certainly surpassing anything down at Grenier's place in Frenchman's Bend {A}. Some of the more cosmopolitan members agreed that the style was very much like that found on the finest riverboats, and soon word was about town that Sutpen and his wild Negroes had highjacked one and looted it. Though this was never proven, and indeed no report of a knocked-over riverboat ever came to anyone's attention, a posse gathered—as if by spontaneous combustion—to arrest Sutpen at his now-completed, no-longer-unfurnished house.

While they were still journeying the twelve miles to the Hundred, however, Sutpen himself approached them and passed them, headed back toward Jefferson. The posse reeled about and chased him there, their anxiety to catch him now tempered by their curiosity about what he was up to. They stalled around the corner while he entered the Ratcliffe-Compson store, bought a new suit of clothes, and then emerged and pointed himself in the direction of Goodhue Coldfield's house. When he came back outside, he was officially engaged to Coldfield's daughter Ellen. He had not even attained their front gate, however, before the posse arrested him and threw him in the town's ever-more-impressive jail cell. That evening Coldfield and General Compson bailed him out.

Between April and June, Sutpen and Coldfield entered into some kind of business dealing which defies analysis to this day. Suffice it to say that, though he was lured far beyond the constraints of his hard-core morality, Coldfield did not wait longer than June to extricate himself from these machinations when he found some sort of bill of lading which revealed to him that the whole enterprise was probably crooked.

Still, in that same month of June, 1838, Thomas Sutpen and Ellen Coldfield married. Ellen, all reports agree, was hysterical at the rehearsal and weeping at the wedding. In the weeks before it, Sutpen and Ellen's aunt had managed to win a dispute with Ellen's father over the size of the affair—it was to be a lavish one. The invitation list was fully a hundred, extremely large considering the paucity of the white population of the County at the time, but only ten bothered to show up on the evening of the ceremony. Hate and jealousy and distrust of Sutpen himself partially explain this, no doubt; but the aunt's conduct earlier that day—she more or less dared the women of the town not to attend—must have done much in itself to dampen the affair. Of those so confronted, only Mrs. Compson appeared. As the newlyweds emerged from the church, he thirty-one but she only twenty, Sutpen's cannibals had to line the walkways outside, both to lend to the occasion what Sutpen must have considered class and to absorb as best they could the rotten vegetables being pelted at Thomas and Ellen by itinerant drovers and peddlers who were either put up to it by more reticent townsmen or just looking for some way to kill a Saturday night.

So Thomas and Ellen Sutpen, the latter totally unaware that her husband already had a nine-year-old son in New Orleans [1829], settled down at Sutpen's Hundred—finished and furnished—to await the conception and birth of *their* first male child. The wrestling matches in the stable, which had intrigued the men of the county for some years, continued unabated, with Sutpen himself usually wrestling the best slave each night in the grand finale.

1839

Born: Henry Sutpen (d. 1909) at Sutpen's Hundred

Died: Louis Grenier, the Old Frenchman

Thomas Sutpen had a male child within one year. And in this same year the first Sartoris—John, also the most important one—rode into Jefferson from Carolina. Still only sixteen, he attracted no special notice—then {N}. But he came with slaves and gear and quickly had his hands on some abandoned Indian land four miles straight north of town. Over the next few years he cleared its trees and built a house which, though a good ten miles from it and on a different road, was clearly meant to rival Sutpen's.

1840

Born: Virginia Sartoris (d. 1930), "Aunt Jenny," in Carolina

Born: Caroline Barr, a black who was beloved in the County

Born: Philip St. Just Backhouse (later, Backus)

In the decade of the 1840s, Yoknapatawpha County and the town of Jefferson and the State of Mississippi assumed the form that those who—consciously or not consciously, willingly or unwillingly—mythologize the antebellum period think they remember. The railroad which was to stretch from Memphis to the Atlantic, and to which John Sartoris was later to mate his, was under construction. Whatever Chickasaws there were who were still hanging on left to move west—these were mostly poor ones who followed reluctant suit with their brothers and sisters, but some were well-to-do slaveholding ones as well. One, for instance, owned ninety-five Negroes. Pettigrew's pony express was replaced by a monthly stage from Memphis, though such progress was no improvement since Old Pettigrew had shown up three times a month with the mail rather than just once {N}.

But it was now that the buildings grew up which the South had grown to identify as its own architecture, even though it was copied. Of course, Grenier's Old Frenchman's Place in the southeast corner and Sutpen's Hundred in the northwest were already legendary. But in Jefferson itself, the Benbow house was built in the late Tudor style which had the blessing of Queen Victoria herself. A hill man who somehow struck it rich quickly arrived from Frenchman's Bend and built what Aunt Jenny Du Pre was many years later [1919] to call "the finest house in Frenchman's Bend on the most beautiful lot in Jefferson" {S}.

Not the most imposing house, but certainly the most central, was the Compsons' {F}. The town of Jefferson had spread out from it ever since it was built (or started to be) in the previous decade and continued to spread until the idiot Benjy Compson burnt the house down in the 1930s [1935]. At first the house and the land around it were known as the "Compson Domain." Later, after the otherwise unassuming Quentin II got himself elected Governor in the 1850s it became known as the "Old Governor's Place," even after Jason II had become a general (albeit a losing one) in the Civil War. Somewhere around the turn of the Twentieth Century, though, it became known simply as the "Compson Mile."

In 1840 the Courthouse was finally completed with the arrival of eight marble columns on an Italian ship for the two four-columned porticoes on the front and back {N}. They were unloaded at New Orleans, steamboated up the Mississippi to the Tallahatchie and from there to the landing which Ikkemotubbe had once owned but which had passed on to Wyott and then passed on to Ballenbaugh and caused the two of them to simply pass on [1831] [1832]. Though another Ballenbaugh still operated it, and directed the unloading of the columns, the land was now actually the northern extremity of Sutpen's Hundred. From there the columns were moved to Jefferson on carts drawn by oxen.

People, as well as buildings, were important in 1840. Old Jason Lycurgus Compson, father of the governor and grandfather of the general [1811], was committed to an insane asylum for lining up rows of black children and shooting sweet potatoes off their heads {U}. Uncle Buck and Uncle Buddy continued to live in their now-two-roomed cabin with a dozen dogs to share it with them {U}. Having failed to emancipate the Negroes, they had somewhat better success with the poor, nonslave- or landholding whites, persuading them to pool whatever resources they had with the McCaslin plantation. No one ever knew exactly what the financial arrangements were, but everyone involved had food and shoes, which was more than they had before. Ellen Sutpen, though perhaps as hysterical internally as she had been at her wedding, was becoming the first lady of the County and acting it {A}; but Sutpen's first wife [1827] was already in the process of brainwashing her (and Sutpen's) eleven-year-old son in New Orleans, preparing him to work his (and her) revenge on Thomas, Ellen, and countless others whom Fate had connected to them [1859].

Still in St. Louis in this year was Calvin Burden—unable to read English, he was reading the Bible in Spanish to his son Nathaniel (and later to the three other children), teaching them to hate slaveholders and hell and foreordaining them and their offspring to suffer at the hands of the former and perhaps be consigned to the latter {L}.

THE PRESIDENCY OF WILLIAM HENRY HARRISON,
March 4, 1841–April 4, 1841

THE PRESIDENCY OF JOHN TYLER, 1841–1845

1841

Born: Judith Sutpen (d. 1884)

Died: Roskus, a McCaslin slave, father of Thucydus and, formerly, father-in-law of Eunice

Upon the death of his father, as if he had been holding out because of him, Thucydus finally accepted the $200 from Buck and Buddy [1837] and opened a blacksmith shop in Jefferson {G}. This was apparently the first slave these two gentlemen managed to free. Otherwise the year was uneventful, save for the fact that Henry Clay addressed the State Legislature in Jackson {N}.

1842

Born: Drusilla Hawk, later to be the second wife of John Sartoris

With nearly all the Indian woodland in Yoknapatawpha now felled (save for that on the McCaslin property in the northeast sector), cotton became the county's major source of income {N}. As a result, various northern functionaries—merchants, bankers, lawyers, and assorted others—began their mass migration into Jefferson.

In St. Louis this year Calvin Burden did what he could not resist doing forever no matter what his Spanish Bible taught him—he killed a man in an argument over slavery and had to flee the city with his family {L}. He was not fated for his final such argument in Yoknapatawpha yet [1873], but he was well on his way here, just as we are all well on our way somewhere that we surely don't even know of much before we show up there.

1844

The University of Mississippi was founded this year in the town of Oxford, to the east {A}.

THE PRESIDENCY OF JAMES KNOX POLK, 1845–1849

1845

Born: Rosa Coldfield (d. 1910)

Born: "Old" Anse MacCallum (d. 1920)

Died: Wife of Goodhue Coldfield, in childbirth

Goodhue Coldfield's wife died this year giving birth to her second child twenty-seven years after giving birth to her first [1818]. This one, Rosa, would never forgive her father for this, though no one who knew her would understand whether this was because she, Rosa, wished she hadn't been born herself (as she probably did) or whether she was furious that he had taken a life in the creation of one so useless as hers {A}.

In Mexico, John Sartoris, twenty-two, was making the acquaintance of the Scottish railroad engineer who was eventually to come to Jefferson to assist him in the building of his own line [1868] to connect with the main east-west tracks between Memphis and the ocean {S}.

1846

Born: Sarah Burden

Died: Francis Weddel, in Oklahoma

Rosa Coldfield, at one still toddling, began her sixteen-year gestation [1861] in her father's grim, tight little house, growing soon and secretly to hate the man, though she probably didn't know it {A}.

1847

Born: Lucius Quintus Carothers Priest I, later to be known as "Boss"

Born: Dr. Wyott (Ph.D.), son of the founder of the Jefferson Academy, later to be its president

Born: Beck (Rebecca?) Burden

Born: The woman who was to be the matron at the Little Rock orphanage where Joe Christmas matriculated

The plantations ran well and the cotton crop was huge. Almost all men prospered, the whites by their intelligence, their greed, and their desire to make a scratch on the face of oblivion and leave an heir to gouge a deeper one; the blacks by their strong backs and their ability to accept and endure. The Sartoris, Sutpen, Compson, McCaslin, and Grenier plantations did particularly well.

1848

Born: Oldest Daughter of John Sartoris

Born: Father of Mink Snopes's Wife, eventually to be a logging man

Born: Mr. Nightingale, a Baptist, who would never get over Columbus or the failure of Robert E. Lee

This is often called the year that changed the world. The potato famine had hit Ireland, but cotton billowed in Mississippi. Revolutions broke out in France, German, Austria-Hungary, Bohemia, and Italy; but tranquility was sustained in Yoknapatawpha. Francis Joseph emerged as the acknowledged ruler of Austria-Hungary, and Thomas Sutpen was surfacing as the un-acknowledged ruler of Yoknapatawpha County. The Taiping Rebellion started in China, but the slaves were quiet in America. Gold was discovered in California, but gold was growing in Mississippi. And this was the year the Germany I thought I loved in the first decades of the twentieth century {T} actually died, though I would not know it until long after I should have [1917].

Sutpen's grip on the county tightened this year. In an incident Rosa Coldfield would always stick to as her first recollection of the man {A}, Thomas, Ellen, Henry, and Judith arrived at church one morning with a wild Negro driving their buggy as fast as the mules could make it go. It seems that part of Sutpen's self-created image was to throw the fear of God into his neighbors by spinning dust in their faces (and all over their Sunday clothes) to prepare them for the oratory of the less intimidating minister (and the rules of a perhaps less intimidating God). After many weeks of this, the minister asked him to stop this "for the good of the ladies of the town." Sutpen complied by stopping both this and coming to church at all. Before long, however, the carriage was racing to church again, though this time it was Judith, seven, who ordered the driver to whip the mules, and then whip them again in the grove behind the church for "running away."

Judith, apparently, was always stronger, more daring, perhaps more masculine than Henry. On the single occasion when both of them secreted themselves in the stable to watch the Negro wrestling matches from the loft above, it was Henry who turned and vomited and Judith and her half-sister Clytie who watched in thrilled amazement. As a consequence of Sutpen's behavior as a whole, Rosa's aunt taught her, still only three, to look at Ellen as a woman who had vanished and the Sutpen breed as a lineage that ought to.

Two final notes are important to the Sutpen (and Yoknapatawpha) history this year. Sutpen, in an apparent display of power and influence, hired as an overseer the son of the very sheriff who had arrested him outside Coldfield's house ten years earlier [1838]. And in this year as well, Sutpen allowed a shiftless white vagrant to settle in a fishing camp on his property and live there for the next twenty years {"Wash"}. This man was Wash Jones, who would first idolize and then hate Thomas Sutpen, both intensely enough to have to kill him [1869].

THE PRESIDENCY OF ZACHARY TAYLOR, 1849–July 9, 1850

1849

Born: Bayard Sartoris II (d. 1919), later known as "Old Bayard," second child of John Sartoris

Died: Fibby, a McCaslin black, wife of Roskus, mother-in-law of Eunice

1850

Born: Carothers "Cass" Edmonds (d. 1897), to whom Ike McCaslin would hand over the McCaslin land in 1888

Born: Aunt Sally Wyatt

Born: Tom Tom Bird

Melicent Jones, a tramp like her father, moved in with Wash at the Fishing Camp on Sutpen's Hundred {A}. When she left no one knows, save that it was *after* she had blessed him with an unwanted bastard granddaughter in 1853 and *before* the Civil War, because by then she had been found dead in a Memphis brothel.

This year also marked the first appearance of Rosa Coldfield, five, at Sutpen's Hundred to visit her sister, Ellen, and her nine-year-old niece, Judith {A}. It was a summer Sunday, and what made the greatest impression on her was, she would later say, the sight of her aristocratic brother-in-law, Thomas, down in the scuppernong arbor drinking raucously with the white trash Jones.

A newcomer who attracted some attention in the county this year was the man named Farmer who became the Jefferson jailer and took up residence with his small daughter, Cecilia, in the old log hut which had served as the first jailhouse [1831] {N}.

1851

Born: Second daughter of John Sartoris, the youngest of his three children

Born: Vangie (Evangeline?) Burden

Died: First wife of John Sartoris, mother of his children, daughter of Rosa Millard; in childbirth

The county was shocked and saddened this year by the death of John Sartoris' wife, but otherwise plantation life continued to prosper for all the owners and most of their slaves. Buck and Buddy McCaslin, still trying their damnedest to free their Negroes, instigated a scheme whereby Tomey's Turl—illegitimately and incestuously and morganatically conceived son of

Lucius Quintus Carothers McCaslin [1833]—and each of his descendants would receive $1000 on the attainment of their twenty-first birthdays {G}. Having no mind nor desire for money, Turl declined his when the time came [1854], as would his first surviving child (Tennie's Jim) when his came in the 1880s [1885].

Two men who would be important to Yoknapatawpha in the future were quite active this year. In the next county, Gail Hightower's father was riding sixteen miles each Sunday to preach at a Presbyterian chapel in the hills {L}; and Nathaniel Burden, still only fourteen and of course not yet Joanna's father, fled from his own roughneck father's home, wherever that might have been in these years after he was run out of St. Louis [1842] {L}.

1852

Born: Will Varner

THE PRESIDENCY OF FRANKLIN PIERCE, 1853–1857

1853

Born: Milly Jones (d. 1869) to Wash Jones's promiscuous daughter, Melicent, and a never-identified white male beyond the age of puberty

Born: Sarah Edmonds, sister to Cass, future wife of Boss Priest

Born: Eupheus "Uncle Doc" Hines, maternal grandfather of Joe Christmas

1854

Born: Dennison Hawk

Born: Simon McEachern (d. 1913)

Born: Calvin Burden II (d. 1873), son of Nathaniel and half-brother of Joanna

Died: Thucydus (b. 1779), husband of Eunice, Old Carothers McCaslin's black mistress

And so came inevitably the event that started us toward the war the South would have to fight but even knew from the start it could not win. In this year the Kansas-Nebraska Act repealed the Missouri Compromise of 1820. That had been the first in a long series of crises about the extension of slaveholding rights into national territories, solved by allowing Missouri to enter the Union as a slave state if Maine entered as a free one, which it did. But the Compromise had further prohibited the holding of slaves in the territory of the Louisiana Purchase north of thirty-six degrees, thirty minutes latitude, roughly the Missouri-Arkansas border. Southerners in the 1850s, wanting no free territory west of Missouri, had already resisted four attempts before 1854 to incorporate Kansas and Nebraska into the Union as a single territory. Stephen A. Douglas generated this concession, the Kansas-Nebraska Act, to allow for two territories instead of one; and almost immediately a New England invention called the Emigrant Aid Company began shipping settlers to Kansas to populate the state with antislavery settlers so that Douglas' concept of "popular sovereignty" would force Kansas in as a free state. It had minimal success; but "bleeding Kansas"—many hundreds of miles from Mississippi—became a symbol of northern meddling in southern affairs.

The meddling, however, had no direct effect on Yoknapatawpha County as yet. Tomey's Turl officially cast off his inheritance this year on his twenty-first birthday {G}. Money meant nothing to him, and he continued to live in ritual bondage on the McCaslin estate under the beneficent eyes of Buck and Buddy.

1855

Born: Miss Emily Grierson (d. 1929)

Born: Miss Ballenbaugh

Born: Old Het, black woman, later a friend of Mrs. Hait's

Married: Rosa Coldfield's aunt and an unnamed horsetrader

The rumblings of impending war grew a bit louder this year. But the plantation economy continued to prosper, with the great owners paying it more attention than the war that would ruin them. Rosa Coldfield's aunt, who had so badly engineered Ellen's wedding many years earlier [1838], apparently got married herself; or at least she crept out a window one night and ran off with a horsetrader {A}. Rosa herself, ten now and still jammed into her father's little house and hating both it and him, began making her

[67]

once-a-year journey with him out to Sutpen's Hundred to visit her sister and her nephew and niece who were four and six years her senior. On four other occasions each year, between now and the start of the War, Ellen and the children would reciprocate with a visit to the Coldfield house in Jefferson. Thomas never came along, nor was much seen of him at the Hundred when the Coldfields visited there—that is, unless one ventured into the scuppernong arbor and could say anything coherent and, less likely still, get a response in kind from Sutpen or his drinking companion, Wash Jones.

In Frenchman's Bend this year a man named Trumbull became blacksmith and soon established himself as one of the most skillful in the County {H}. He held the job for fifty years until Flem Snopes found a way to run him out of it [1905].

1856

Born: First husband of Joan Heppleton

Married: Father and mother of Gail Hightower

Even though *Uncle Tom's Cabin* had been published four years ago, it began to attract interest only as the nation entered these final five years of intensifying squabbles between antislavery and proslavery forces. The campaign of 1856, in which Buchanan beat Fremont, called special attention to the book; and thereafter Buchanan had great difficulty keeping the two factions in balance and was resisted by extremists in both.

But if Buck and Buddy McCaslin had ever read Miss Stowe's book, and surely they hadn't because they could barely even spell, they would have had a good laugh, or perhaps a good cry, over it {G}. For some unexplainable reason they had even purchased a Negro this year from Bedford Forrest at Cold Water for $265. This slave, named Percival Brownlee, was a particularly useless one who could do nothing, or at least nothing right. It was not long before Buck and Buddy, far from imprisoning the man or torturing him, were seeking any available method to rid themselves of him. At first they tried to sell him to other slaveholders in the district, but they had no buyers. Brownlee's reputation had spread quickly and widely. Then they offered him—indeed ordered him to have—his outright freedom; but Brownlee (like the other Negroes Buck and Buddy had been dealing with) would not accept it. So they reluctantly tried to absorb him into their operation.

Later that year, the mule Josephine broke her leg, necessitating humane destruction. The job was assigned to the lackadaisical Brownlee, who, in his own sweet time and his accustomed amount of forethought, led the wrong mule out to the corral and shot it. Placing the value of the mule at $100, Buck and Buddy decided that they had now lost $365 on this deal—so at Christmas they changed his name to Spintrius and tried to market him again. Still there were no takers, and it would be quite a while yet before Brownlee would defiantly go on his own [1836] [1866].

Elsewhere, Gail Hightower's later-to-be-idolized grandfather moved out of his house when his son got married, giving the boy the house but taking his two faithful servants, Pomp and the unfortunately loquacious Cinthy, with him {L}.

THE PRESIDENCY OF JAMES BUCHANAN, 1857–1861

1857

Amazingly, in retrospect, life still proceeded on as if no war were coming. The Sutpen and Sartoris plantations, as well as their families, were thriving, as were, it seems, all the aristocrats in the county. Ellen, Henry, and Judith made their quarterly trips into Jefferson to visit with the two remaining Coldfields, and the Coldfields made their annual trip to the Hundred to see the available Sutpens {A}. Ellen and Judith, though, were now making extra trips to town each year to socialize with the more distinguished ladies who were fortunate enough to have distinguished husbands.

John Sartoris spun yarns around the cotton gin about his relatives, relatives who were to be the meat of the stories for the county for three-quarters of a century yet. His nineteen-year-old brother, Bayard I, still living in Carolina (and he never did live in Mississippi), had accidentally run his hounds through a rustic tabernacle where some Methodists were conducting a revival meeting; and, having apprehended the fox, he ran them through the ensuing indignation meeting a half-hour later {O}. John got this in a letter from his sister, Jenny (who *would* live in Yoknapatawpha and for a long time [1868]), and thought it was funny.

But 1857 is best known in Mississippi as the year of the Dred Scott decision, which our ancestors thought would help us but really wound up ruining us. Scott was a slave who had escaped his owner and been free for two years in a free territory. When he was recaptured he claimed this was enough to make him a free man, no longer a piece of chattel property. Judge Taney ruled on the Supreme Court that a Negro could not plead before the Court as a citizen, returned Scott to his owner, and handed the antislavery forces a considerable setback. Momentarily the South took heart. But soon it was besieged with all sorts of northerners looking to aid fugitive slaves, the same northerners who would feel entitled to the rest of its possessions as well after the War.

Married: Charles Bon and his octoroon wife

In June of this year Abe Lincoln, debating with Stephen Douglas for a senatorial seat in Illinois, uttered the words which were to prove all too true in seven years: "A house divided against itself cannot stand . . . it will become all one thing or all the other." Lincoln lost this election but revealed to us all what none of us was sure he wanted to know—that popular sovereignty among states was a sham and could no longer exist. But none listened yet.

In Yoknapatawpha, Tomey's Turl was bounding out the front door of the McCaslin plantation house to visit Hubert Beauchamp's slave girl Tennie, and Hubert often caught him and returned him in the middle of the night {G}. Buck and Buddy, at last seeing some independence in the black soul, pretended to sleep through it all.

In Baltimore, at a Christmas ball this year, Jenny Sartoris (soon to be Du Pre) danced with Jeb Stuart {S}; but she would not understand the true good fortune of her evening until the Civil War was well under way [1862].

1859

Born: Amodeus Beauchamp, the first child of Tomey's Turl and Tennie

Born: Charles Etienne de Saint Velery Bon, only child of Charles Bon and his octoroon wife

Married: Tomey's Turl and Tennie Beauchamp

Died: Amodeus Beauchamp, the same

The Civil War was almost upon us now, and one event in this year perhaps best symbolizes the southern order which was now so fragilely grounded and so soon to be lost. Tomey's Turl's escapes to visit his girlfriend Tennie at the Beauchamp plantation had become so blatant by now that Hubert was demanding that Buck and Buddy keep a tighter rein on their Othello-colored Lothario {G}. So Buck and young Cass Edmonds, nine, (but never Buddy) devised a ritual chase which ultimately resulted in the "recapture" of Turl, even though he would have been back home by dawn anyway. Buck would don a necktie and go to Hubert's where he would be wined and dined before having to nab Turl in Tennie's cabin. However, on one particular evening, Hubert, anxious to marry off his bothersome sister Sophonsiba to Uncle Buck, bet Buck $500 that Turl would be captured in Tennie's cabin after dark. Planning to win the bet by capturing Turl *before* dark, Buck accepted the challenge, only to be run over by the frightened Turl outside the cabin door at the moment of "capture." Without Tomey's Turl in hand, Hubert and Buck returned to the Beauchamp house for the night, Buck convinced that he had won the bet nonetheless because no capture had been made or would be either on this particular night. But he was wrong on that one, because he accidentally crawled into bed with Sophonsiba and thus was trapped (and himself captured) into an honor-saving marriage with her, much to Hubert's delight and, probably, in accordance with his plans. In an attempt to avoid the termination of his bachelorhood, Buck engaged Hubert in a card game in which the loser would end up possessing not only Sophonsiba (as a sister or a wife, whichever was appropriate) but *both* Negroes (as nuisances, which was for sure). Again Hubert won, and Buck went home to be a man harassed apparently forever—which could not be much longer now since he was already sixty.

However, Uncle Buddy, notoriously the best card shark in the county and perhaps the state, rescued his twin brother by engaging Hubert in a game for higher stakes. In that game Hubert actually passed up a possible straight for three trays, figuring nothing was going to beat Buddy. As a result, Buck went home a free man. All of this was partially for nought, however, since Buck eventually married Sophonsiba of his own volition anyway. Buddy also got Tennie without payment when she became part of the stakes as well. So the marriage which now ensued, before Buck and Sophonsiba, was that of Tomey's Turl and Tennie, initiating the long line of mixed-blood Beauchamps who inhabit the county to this day, though their first son, born this very year, did not survive for long after birth. Turl was only 25% Negro (being the son of a white man and that man's own half-black daughter), and Tennie was full-blooded—therefore their children, the most noteworthy of whom would be Lucas Beauchamp [1874], would all be 62.5% black, and their grandchildren would be of too many different shades to count. But, of course, all were officially Negroes, for some fraction of 1% was really all that was needed.

But if all that was the last vestiges of the southern order in full swing, what happened to the Sutpen family this year was the first clear sign of its impending destruction. In New Orleans, Eulalia Bon, Thomas Sutpen's jettisoned first wife [1831], was on the verge of bringing her plan to destroy him to fruition when she and her lawyer discovered to their horror that Charles, her son by Sutpen, had gotten married to an octoroon woman {A}. In a frenzy to keep their hopes alive by ending a relationship which could not assist them, they sent Charles packing in the fall for the reputationless University of Mississippi. They knew what they were up to, of course, for Henry Sutpen also set out, with horse and groom, for the same university this year. He also carried with him, it seems, a letter from this same New Orleans attorney which asked that he make the acquaintance of Charles Bon, a new student who would be older and somewhat out of place with the others. Without any doubt, Henry followed up quickly on this. Some feel he almost fell in love with the man and was soon writing his sister, Judith, letters which proposed that Charles would make her an excellent husband (and him an excellent brother-in-law). How much stock Judith put in such suggestions is uncertain, but it is clear that her mother began planning her trousseau long before either of them ever laid eyes on Bon. Meanwhile, back in Oxford Henry was aping everything the older man did and convincing him of his sister's desirability (which Henry was totally convinced of as well). The fact that Charles was his own half-brother, and therefore Judith's too, could not have occurred to him, for he knew nothing of this dimension of his father's past (or probably any other either). So in December of 1859, while the cosmopolites to the north pondered the implications of Charles Darwin's *Origin of the Species* which was published this same month, Charles Bon made his journey to Sutpen's Hundred and stayed twelve days, days in which he was apparently never alone with Judith. Yet somehow their betrothal became from then on a common assumption.

The Sartoris family, on the other hand, gathered for Christmas at Hawkhurst in Tennessee this year {U}. Knowing that upheaval was coming, they opened the family trunk for the last time before the war and committed to it those symbols of their order which they did not know would be torn from them but knew well enough would at least be held in abeyance for some years to come.

The year 1859 was also the year of John Brown's raid at Harper's Ferry in Virginia. To the southerners, the North seemed not only to be trying to steal their property but also to be equipping their human property with arms as well.

1860

Born: Pappy Thompson

Born: Ned McCaslin (d. 1934), a McCaslin slave child but not for long

Married: Theophilus "Uncle Buck" McCaslin and Sophonsiba Beauchamp

Died: Dennison Hawk, Sr., in Tennessee

Died: Melicent Jones, daughter of Wash, also in Tennessee, but in a Memphis brothel

It is not clear how or when he knew that Thomas Sutpen was his father—whether he had been told it before he left for the university the previous fall or whether he had been filled with enough hints and suggestions that they took hold when he first laid eyes on him last Christmas—but Charles Bon was clearly waiting for recognition from this outback land baron {A}. Surely the strongest chance he had was to allow the marriage plans to go forward, even though he probably had no romantic interest in Judith and would be—for so many traditional and biological reasons—an unacceptable husband for her.

But the plans for the Judith-Charles marriage went forward under an impetus of their own. That impetus resided mostly in Ellen who must have seen in Bon a chance for her own daughter to escape the crudities of Yoknapatawpha County for the better places like New Orleans and perhaps Europe with this young man who rendered her own son a hillbilly by comparison. So, in the early spring, Judith and Ellen dropped in on some town ladies to announce the wedding and then made their first trip to Memphis to buy items for her trousseau. Rosa Coldfield, now fifteen, was already stealing cloth from her father's store to sew for and, probably, live vicariously through her older niece.

In February, Henry Sutpen had transferred to the Law School at the university in a further attempt to ape Charles's present and future; and in June he brought him home for his second visit to the Hundred. But Charles stayed only two or three days this time, merely stopping over on his way home to New Orleans for the summer. Thomas himself, probably to Charles's distress, was not around (being in New Orleans himself to verify the thing he suspected about Charles and which turned out to be correct). And certainly to Ellen's distress, Charles departed on the third day without, as yet, even having given Judith an engagement ring. This did nothing to cool Ellen's wedding plans, however; and the trips to Memphis continued into the fall and even into the winter when the weather was so cold that their Negro driver had to keep stopping the carriage to heat bricks for them to thaw their feet on during the sixty- to seventy-mile journey.

Christmas came. On December 20th, of course, at a meeting of the state convention in Charleston, South Carolina, that body had solemnly voted that "the union now subsisting between South Carolina and other states under the name of the United States of America is hereby dissolved." Two days later, on Saturday, December 22nd, Charles Bon arrived for his third and second-last appearance at Sutpen's Hundred [1865], and the last from which he would depart alive.

He saw little of Thomas during this visit and apparently still gave no ring to Judith. On Monday the 24th, Christmas Eve, Henry and Thomas fell into a furious argument in the library; this was the occasion on which Thomas, buttressed by his research of the previous June, revealed to his son that

[73]

Charles was in fact Judith's half-brother and that any marriage between them would be incestuous. Henry was confounded; but his love for Bon was so great that, on the spot, he renounced his birthright to Sutpen's Hundred and rode off with his half-brother in the early hours of Christmas morning.

When Ellen discovered this, she was prostrate from the loss, though no one seems to have any recollection of Judith's reaction. Henry and Bon rode all Christmas day to the Mississippi River and boarded a steamboat for New Orleans. Through it all Charles must have wondered what effect it would have on Henry's blind loyalty when he found out, as ultimately he must, that he, Charles, already had an octoroon wife and by now even a son [1861].

The Sartoris family, once again the antithesis of Sutpen's, remained firm and close as war approached {U}. Granny Millard, John's mother-in-law, made her last prewar journey to Hawkhurst in the spring; and, on the very Christmas day on which Charles and Henry rode from Sutpen's Hundred, Sartoris' son Bayard, nine, encountered his first railway train during *his* last prewar visit to Hawkhurst. One of the Hawk Negroes took the time to demonstrate to him that when he drove a stick into the ground and sun cast a certain length of shadow from the stick, a railroad train would magically come pounding along the tracks. Bayard was enthralled by the power of it all and resolved to lord it over Ringo, his more worldly black companion back in Mississippi, that he had finally had an experience which the other had missed.

On this same Christmas Day, Gavin Breckbridge, fiancé of Drusilla Hawk, presented his wife-to-be with a beautiful horse named Bobolink, a mount Bayard would always admire {U}.

THE PRESIDENCY OF JEFFERSON DAVIS, 1861–1865

1861

Born: Boon Hogganbeck

Born: Foreman of the jury that would convict Mink Snopes of Jack Houston's murder in 1908

Married: Virginia "Jenny" Sartoris and Du Pre

JANUARY: Henry Sutpen and Charles Bon arrived in New Orleans, and Bon told Henry of his octoroon wife {A}. Henry must have spent a good amount of time walking the streets trying to get used to both this and what now would be an incestuous and even bigamous marriage. He probably got over the racial question because he himself had a half-Negro sister in Clytie—

[74]

his own father had had sex with a nonwhite woman. How they planned to cope with the bigamy was not clear, but it is hard to believe that they would have considered anything so simple as divorce. Incest seemed not to bother Henry. On another occasion, perhaps at Henry's instigation but probably on his own, Bon punched his mother's lawyer for chastising him for seeking recognition rather than money from Thomas Sutpen.

FEBRUARY: At Montgomery, Alabama, representatives of South Carolina, Georgia, Alabama, Mississippi, Louisiana, and Florida met to form the Confederate States of America {N}. On February 18th, Jefferson Davis was named provisional president, and he was made official the following year [1862]. Soon Texas, Arkansas, Tennessee, North Carolina, and Virginia joined the first six to make the total of secessionary states eleven. Back in Jefferson this month Ellen Sutpen took to her bed, ill from Judith's loss of Bon {A}. Thomas hardly noticed, for he was preparing to defend his land from the North, now that he had defended it, he thought, from his own earlier mistakes.

MARCH: Perhaps Yoknapatawpha County has had no more glorious moment in its history than March and April, 1861. From all parts of the district, men—too old, too young, and just right—flocked to Jefferson to join the regiment which was being formed there under the colonelcy of John Sartoris, "The Mississippi Second" {N}. Then, on a Sunday afternoon, Sartoris himself stood on the south portico balcony of the Jefferson Courthouse in the first Confederate uniform the town had ever seen. The four sides of the town square were lined with his soldiers, none yet with uniforms but all with whatever guns they could muster, while a Baptist minister prayed in their midst for the blessing of God on the Confederate cause. The best men in the area were later proud to say that they had fought with John Sartoris; and many of them quit with him when, over a year later [1862], men they considered Sartoris' inferiors (and their own) elected him out of the colonelcy. But now Doc Peabody came forward and volunteered his services as regimental surgeon. Another who joined him, though Sartoris could have done without him, was a man named Ab Snopes, a horse trader (or thief) whom Sartoris named his horse captain—which meant that he was to acquire horses by whatever means he could (and he had several) {"Barn Burning"} {"My Grandmother Millard"}.

One initial mistake that Sartoris made was preventing the enlistment of Uncle Buck and Uncle Buddy McCaslin in his regiment. Though spry, they were sixty-two now. As a consequence none of the white farmers who worked the land with the McCaslins would go to war with Sartoris, even though they had already signed up, unless one of the two men they idolized was allowed to go as well {U}. Colonel Sartoris was forced to capitulate: Buddy went to war after drawing lots with his brother, and Buck stayed home to work the plantation for as long as it remained possible to do so

[1862]. Buddy did not serve with Sartoris' regiment for long, though, becoming rather a sergeant in Tenant's brigade after they got to Virginia.

One of the most valiant officers and fighters the county produced was Major DeSpain, who remained faithful to the southern cause long after it had become a personal one for men like Sartoris and Sutpen {G}. Another such man who fought with the greatest devotion over the next four years for his homeland was "Anse" MacCallum who joined the Confederate Army at sixteen after walking all the way to Virginia to join Stonewall Jackson's regiment {"The Tall Men"}. He stayed with him until his commander was killed at Chancellorsville [1863] and remained with the same regiment until, in 1865, it was blocked by General Sheridan's army on the road to Appomattox. Anse then walked all the way back to Mississippi to spend the rest of his life farming a meager piece of land and to father a string of excellent sons.

APRIL: On Friday, April 12th, General Beauregard fired on Fort Sumter in Charleston harbor after Abe Lincoln tried to provision the Yankee forces holed up there. With this the Civil War officially started. On Sunday the 14th, a neighbor's slave road up to the porch of the Old Frenchman's Place and informed young Grenier about the bombardment. Grenier galloped the twelve miles into Jefferson, not only announcing the recent event but also proclaiming the eventual victory. The Sartoris regiment had already departed for South Carolina by then. And now Thomas Sutpen, still at home, gathered his gear, mounted Rob Roy, and tore off to catch up, leaving behind his sick wife, confused daughter, and doomed land {"Wash"}, all apparently in the hands of Clytie who, though a Negro, was the only one with the strength and sense needed to hold things together until he returned [1866]. Wash Jones went around telling the blacks that he was in charge of the plantation until the master returned; but they only laughed at him because they knew that he was not even allowed in the front door at the Hundred, whereas many of them were.

Also departing for war this month was Saucier Weddel, a Choctaw who was more white than red by now and son of Francis Weddel who was already dead and buried in Oklahoma {"Mountain Victory"}. Saucier had remained in the county on a small plantation he owned called Contalmaison; now he rode north like the rest, with his servant named Jubal, to try in vain to salvage it.

On Tuesday, April 16th, Cecilia Farmer, the teen-aged daughter of the local jailer, used a diamond ring to scratch this date in the window of the jailer's house, along with her name, as she peered through it to watch the young men ride out to the North {N}. She sat at the window endlessly for four years, waiting for them to come back. And then one did [1865].

One girl who was not allowed to watch the troops depart was Rosa Coldfield {A}. For months her father had refused to sell merchandise to anyone who favored secession or who planned to fight for the Confederacy; and so, as Sartoris' regiment was leaving town, some of his men broke into the store and looted it for supplies. Thereafter Rosa was blocked from any contact with the remaining soldiers or those who passed through, and her aunt was refused readmission to the house when her horse-trader husband went to war as well. Finally, out of sheer disgust with the material waste which the war was about to cause and out of a belief (generated probably by his associations with Thomas Sutpen) that the South was founded on principles of moral brigandage rather than on the high ideals he had always thought, Goodhue Coldfield put on his Sunday suit for the last time and retired to his attic, nailing the door shut and throwing the hammer out the window. For the next three years Rosa hoisted food to him through the same window, until one day (because he had died) he didn't take it [1864]. All the while she waited for Jefferson to be reinhabited by something other than old men, women, and (soon) wounded soldiers, and wrote heroic poetry about the fighting men of the Confederacy {N}.

Lastly, it was still April when the first Yankee scouting party passed through Jefferson; they found nothing to worry them, but they did find (and take) Mrs. Compson's silver despite the fact she had it hidden in the privy to keep it from them {"My Grandmother Millard"}.

MAY: The Union forces previously based in the South began to destroy anything they were forced to leave behind which the Confederacy could turn into war-making machinery. The arsenal at Harper's Ferry was burned down by its own commander, and the shipyards at Norfolk were dynamited and the ships sunk. But little was done to defend Washington save that the draw span on the Long Bridge across the Potomac was lifted at night. The South was just not ready with men or equipment to attack as yet, and Beauregard was still en route north from his victory at Fort Sumter. The Yankees, apparently more ready than the rebels but really not, raised the cry for a march on Richmond the minute Jefferson Davis moved the capital there. But war was still in the planning and not in the making.

Charles Bon, still in New Orleans, had decided to go to the fight, perhaps hoping to die before he would have to face his responsibilities, whatever they were, in the Sutpen matter {A}. But he claimed to have decided he would marry Judith when the war was over and wrote her a letter, preserved to this day, telling her so.

JUNE: Confederate troops moved into the vicinity of Fairfax, Virginia, for the first major battle of the war—just outside Washington. Among them was the Mississippi Second under John Sartoris, part of Stonewall Jackson's army {N}.

JULY: On the 20th, Beauregard finally got as many troops as he felt he needed to beat the Yankee army. He invited an attack, which he received on Sunday the 21st, near the crucial rail junction at Manassas. The Northern army under McDowell kicked up so much dust before crossing Bull Run at Sudley Springs Ford that their whole surprise attack was tipped off. But the North's superior numbers seemed as if they would carry the day nonetheless.

[77]

Sartoris and his men fought valiantly around the Henry House {U} (and in the process the colonel lost his copy of Dumas) {N}. Jackson's inspiration soon spread to the entire Confederate Army on the field. Then Jeff Davis showed up and, better still, six thousand reinforcements from the Shenandoah Valley. Suddenly the Yankee forces fell into retreat and then rout; and the South went home with its first victory, new vigor, and (as a prisoner) a New York congressman who had come out to spectate.

Almost killed at Bull Run from Sartoris' regiment was Brother Fortinbride. Though he was injured so badly that he had to return to Jefferson for the duration of the war {U}, he inspired folk back there with his story that it was Jesus Christ Himself who came along and told him to "rise up and live."

AUGUST: George B. McClellan was now commander of the Union forces, though his first decision was to stall the war through the winter till a large army could be mustered and weaponry increased. The Confederacy had similar problems and quietly acquiesced. After Bull Run, however, Henry Sutpen and Charles Bon left New Orleans and went to Oxford to join a company being formed there called the University Grays, creeping into it from the bushes as the entourage marched north {A}. In Yoknapatawpha, Granny Millard—managing the Sartoris plantation while her son-in-law fought—granted "freedom" to their slave named Lucius, who thought he wanted it but soon had enough of it and so came back {"My Grandmother Millard"}.

SEPTEMBER: The Confederate forces should have attacked the disarrayed Yankees now—in Washington; but they didn't and thus fell into winter quarters and soon boredom. John Sartoris came home this month, as he would every spring and fall, to care for his crop. He brought with him this time a captured Union musket which he hung on the wall {U}.

Other men who were to be important to Yoknapatawpha in the future were operating this year as well. Hiram Hightower began serving his four years as chaplain in Forrest's company and was one of its best fighters on any day but the sabbath {R}. His brother, however, the one who was to be Gail Hightower's father [1880], was a chaplain everyday and never fired a shot through the whole war {L}. Calvin Burden I lost his arm fighting for guerrilla outfits in Kansas {L}; and the man who was to kill John Sartoris, Redmond, had gone north to assist, and make money off, the Union army in Memphis {N} [1873].

1862

Born: Callina, second child of Tomey's Turl and Tennie Beauchamp

Married: Philip Backhouse (Backus) and Melisandre

Died: Bayard Sartoris 1 (b. 1838), before the Second Manassas

Died: Gavin Breckbridge, at Shiloh

Died: Callina, for want of proper food, almost immediately after her birth

The Union army for most of this year was under the command of General George B. McClellan who, it was said, always saw double when he looked southward. Perhaps it was because he was usually afraid to attack or because he invariably attacked at the wrong place at the wrong time; but the Confederate Army had tremendous success in the east in 1862. None of the Yoknapatawpha regiments fought in it, but McClellan was first repulsed in his Peninsula Campaign to take Richmond between April and July. A victim (he said) of mud and bad maps, he did manage to chase the rebel army from Yorktown through Mechanicsville and Fair Oaks. At the latter, however, he had the misfortune to wound the Confederate commanding general, Fightin' Joe Johnston, and have Robert E. Lee placed in his stead. Lee was joined by Stonewall Jackson at Malvern Hill outside Richmond on June 26th (and now some Yoknapatawphans were in it). On July 1st, they surrounded McClellan's army and, in effect, ended this drive on the Confederate capital. McClellan now sat around many months trying to figure out what to do next.

The glamor figure of the Confederacy this year, however, was Stonewall Jackson himself, under whom Sartoris' Second Mississippians were serving. He (and Sartoris) won a big victory at Kernstown in the Shanandoah Valley on March 23rd and then led a series of raids around the Valley, decimating Union forces and supplies at every turn. In early May he decided to press north to the Potomac and drive out every Yankee army in the district. He won victories at McDowell, Virginia, on the 8th of May, at Front Royal on the 23rd, at Winchester on the 25th, and finally reached Harper's Ferry on the Potomac on the 29th. Thereafter he won a major victory over General Banks at Cross Keys on June 8th before roaring off to join Lee in the defense of Richmond. Letters from Yoknapatawpha volunteers poured into the county gleefully predicting that the war would be over by Christmas. The Sartoris brigade was already anticipating a reception which would surpass the sendoff they had gotten on the town square just a year before.

Their expectations would not have been so high, though, had they been back home, for the Confederate army seldom had any success in the west (Tennessee and Mississippi) and was certainly having none now. In the course of ten days in mid-February, General Grant and Admiral Foote had brought down Forts Henry and Donelson, leaving the whole river system in the northern part of the state and central part of Tennessee in Union hands. In another ten days Admiral Farragut had captured New Orleans, and all the South had left on the Mississippi River was Vicksburg.

[79]

A number of different incidents can be recorded here to demonstrate the onset of fear and the refusal to yield in Mississippi, the state General Sherman called "the grand field of operations" even though he personally vented more grand wrath on the state of Georgia. In Frenchman's Bend, the Grenier family, hearing of Grant's February successes in Tennessee, began burying its gold all over the place on its huge plantation {Y}—gold which, legend has it, they never bothered (or had enough manpower left) to dig up after the war [1909]. Lots of people went looking for it anyway. In Memphis Uncle Buck, who went to war after all, though not with Sartoris, was serving with General Forrest's cavalry. One night, the story goes, he and the general's own brother rode on horseback into the lobby of the Gayoso Hotel and nearly captured one of the Yankee generals who was plotting the forthcoming siege of Vicksburg {R}. And in New Orleans, when he finally admitted Farragut into his city four days after it had fallen, the mayor perhaps voiced the sentiments of the South most clearly in his "welcoming speech" to his conqueror: "The city is yours by the power of brutal force, not by my choice or consent of its inhabitants. The people of New Orleans, while unable to resist your force, do not transfer their allegiance from the government of their choice. They yield the obedience which the conqueror is entitled to extort from the conquered." If any statement sums up the feeling most Southerners continue to have in the eighty years since the war, this one does. The loaded word is *obedience*. New Orleans spat in Union officers' faces, poured slop on Admiral Farragut's head, and hurled curses and jeers at General Butler, the Federal military commander of the city. Such as this would go on, too, for many decades to come.

In a sense, despite the glorious victories in Virginia, Yoknapatawphans were learning in 1862 that the glory of the Old South would hereafter be more symbolic and mythical for us than real. The county *imagined* John Sartoris atop Jupiter in a charge at Kernstown {F}, but it *saw* General Compson come home from Shiloh minus an arm {R}. It *heard* that men were behaving valiantly in a winning cause in Virginia, but it *knew* that either Charles Bon or Henry Sutpen had to drag the other nearly fatally wounded from the field at Shiloh {A}, less than a hundred miles away. It *suspected* that some of its own might have lost their lives at Malvern Hill and Cedar Mountain, but it had the option to *hope* otherwise. But it *could not deny* that the valiant Gavin Breckbridge, about to marry into the Sartoris family, was found dead, his lower jaw shot away, in the sunken road, again at Shiloh {U}. It *was told* that countians had fought furiously at Gaines Mill, but it was *appalled* to learn that one of their own—a man named Priest—was horribly emaciated when he was shot out of his saddle by a picket the following day. But maybe it was Shiloh that said to the Confederacy that the North would flounder and tease for a while, but eventually a man like Grant could (and would) throw six regiments (and six more if he had to) into the Confederate center and finally ruin them. But they defied, they fought, they chastised, they asked to die rather than have to surrender.

And yet there was Lee, who apparently could repel any attack the Yankees threw at him in Virginia and was even planning to launch some into the North, "the grandest figure on any field," for whom his men had "a proud admiration and personal devotion passing the love of a woman." And there was Stonewall Jackson who not only soundly defeated the cocky Pope at Cedar Mountain but who also chased him and trapped his entire army between the Rapidan and the Rappahannock. These men were demigods against the likes of McClellan, Burnside and Hooker. How could the South lose? Did we think we couldn't or did we know we would?

In late August, the Confederate Army won still another great victory in the Second Manassas; but, on a particular level, the seeds of our doom were already beginning to grow. In the days before the battle, John Sartoris' own brother—the first to be named Bayard—set out on a foolish raid, with none other than Jeb Stuart, on the kitchen tent of the gourmet General Pope, bent on having the anchovies he was known to covet. Actually, Stuart was probably just following other orders; it was just Bayard who wanted the delicacies. He rode right into the tent, jumped his horse over a breakfast table, grabbed the anchovies, and then got himself shot dead, right through the back by a cook wielding a derringer {S}. Such reckless bravado as this probably then won the battle which ensued, though even in that victory the losses of men and equipment were great.

After that battle, in the first annual election of officers, John Sartoris was elected out of his colonelcy, despite the support of Buck and Buddy's farmer volunteers, and replaced by a lesser man and an inferior soldier—Thomas Sutpen {"My Grandmother Millard"} {A}. The regiment would never again enjoy the success and glory it knew under Sartoris; and Sartoris, in an understandable fit of rage, jealousy, and self-pity, took those who voted for him, deserted the Mississippi Second, formed his own cavalry regiment, and rode west to fight with Bedford Forrest and Earl Van Dorn {U}. Before long his sole purpose became one of stealing horses, though the myth about him had already grown and even today most countians refuse to recall him as a horse thief.

Though there were many victories and staunch defenses yet to come, the Southern mythos began to crumble in September when Lee led his shabbily clad troops on his first invasion of the North. At a small rock bridge over Antietam Creek outside Sharpsburg, Maryland, the Union army under Mc-Clellan and Burnside drove the heretofore unbeatable Lee and the until now irresistible Jackson from the field with the greatest losses either army would ever suffer on any day of the war. The Mississippi Second, in its first battle under Sutpen's command and hardly able to afford any losses at all since Sartoris' desertion a few weeks before, was terribly mutilated. For several reasons, then, Sutpen's command of the regiment brought no distinction to it—but it was now down to about a quarter of its original size in just a year and one-half.

Yet Jeb Stuart's men not only crossed into Pennsylvania the next month, but they also captured (and then released) the town of Chambersburg. This was enough to cause Lincoln to remove McClellan as the Union commander and turn the job over to Ambrose Burnside who, by year's end, had made fools of himself and his army by trying to pontoon his way across the Rappahannock into Fredericksburg while Lee and Jackson lobbed shells on him from the heights behind the town.

Not all the work and suffering of the war was confined to the battlefield, and this is maybe the greatest hell that war has to offer. The Sutpen plantation, like others in the district, was being pillaged by Yankee troops, and food was consequently short {A}. Rosa Coldfield continued to hoist food to her father entombed in the attic [1861], but the quality of it was poorer by the month. Her aunt was trying to get through the Union lines to visit her husband, once a horse dealer enlisted by the rebel army but now a prisoner at the Rock Island Penitentiary in Illinois. The man who was to become Ike McCaslin's partner in a hardware business many years hence [1886] was now living in Charleston, working sixteen-hour days building blockade runners {G}. Percival Brownlee, the slave the McCaslins *tried to free* a few years back [1856], was now defiantly *waiting to be freed*. As he bided his time, he conducted revival meetings and delivered freedom sermons to county Negroes {G}. And a man who had lots to say about freeing the Negroes but who didn't bother to fight in the war for either side, Nathaniel Burden, killed a man in Mexico in an argument over a horse {L}.

Such was the situation in Yoknapatawpha County, in Mississippi, and in the South in 1862; but one lighter anecdote from this year remains to be told.

A dashing young Confederate officer named Lt. Philip Backhouse had fallen so desperately in love with Cousin Melisandre, who was living at the Sartoris plantation during the early part of the war, that he became incapable of clear-headed leadership in battle {"My Grandmother Millard"}. General Forrest and Granny Millard, the latter still managing the Sartoris land until John returned, decided that a marriage must take place immediately to restore Backhouse's men's confidence in him—but Melisandre, though she loved him, refused to endure the rest of her life with a last name so ugly as his. To set the situation aright, Forrest and Granny devised a mythical battle (Harrykin Creek) in which a general named Backhouse was killed and a lieutenant named Backus was given his commission. This allowed Backhouse to change his name and marry the perhaps too-sensitive Melisandre.

During all this Melisandre one day was forced to sit in the privy while the Yankees searched the plantation house for the Sartoris silver. They quickly found both her and it in the outhouse (since Mrs. Compson had hidden hers there and they had found that the year before); and it took Backus-Back-house's spectacular annihilation of the privy (without Cousin Melisandre inside it, of course) to save the silver from enemy hands.

As I read back over this I am aware that these incidents are silly and of much less magnitude than the others I have recounted for this year; but Melisandre and Philip Backus are my wife's parents and the only true connection I have with this war for independence I was born a half-century too late to fight in.

1863

Born: Third child of Tennie Beauchamp and Tomey's Turl

Died: Ellen Coldfield Sutpen (b. 1818)

Died: Du Pre, husband of Virginia Sartoris

Died: Third child of Tennie Beauchamp and Tomey's Turl, again almost immediately after birth from lack of nourishment

Died: Mother of Saucier Weddel

The Confederacy lasted into 1865, but it was as good as lost in 1863.

JANUARY: Despite a bad keynote when Braxton Bragg lost to the less incompetent Rosecrans at Murfreesboro, the year started well for the South. In the east Burnside finished himself off as commander of the Army of the Potomac with the famous and futile mud march to outflank Lee in northern Virginia; even more auspiciously, his command was given to the braggart and drinker, Fightin' Joe Hooker. Just north of Jefferson, Van Dorn's cavalry, with John Sartoris' renegades among it, destroyed Grant's supplies at Holly Springs. In Yoknapatawpha it became clear that the languishing Ellen Sutpen would die before the year was out. Also, with the issuance of the Emancipation Proclamation on January 1, Tennie Beauchamp packed her bags to leave the McCaslin plantation {G}. But, pregnant and homeless, she returned the next day.

FEBRUARY: Hooker's forces holed up at Aquia Creek, sending out only diversionary expeditions against Lee's bored and battle-hungry troops. In Tennessee an equally bored Yankee army tried to steal the horse Bobolink from Drusilla Hawk. She defiantly put a gun in its ear and threatened to shoot it rather than let them have her last remembrance of Gavin Breckbridge, dead ten months since Shiloh [1862]. Instead the Yankees burned Hawkhurst to the ground and left the Hawk family homeless {U}.

MARCH: Still trying to build confidence with derring-do and mythical reminiscences, the confederate troops managed to keep morale up in the west. Uncle Buck McCaslin, now serving with Sartoris himself (who earlier didn't want him), repeated his stunt of riding a horse through the lobby of the Gayoso Hotel in Memphis, this time solo [1862] {G}. Around the ruins of Hawkhurst a Confederate locomotive managed to outstrip a Yankee train in a race for a crucial rail junction. The Hawks and later the Sartorises considered this a great moral victory, even though the Yanks tore up the tracks, twisted the rails around some trees, and burnt the ties the next day. The South depended on "moral victories" such as these {U}.

APRIL: In the east Lee suffered a devastating blow when the Yankee general Stoneman destroyed his supplies, which were beginning to run low anyway. In the west, Grant moved his troops up below Vicksburg with the aid of gunboats; Mississippi awaited the inevitable fall of its last two river defenses, Vicksburg and Port Hudson.

MAY: Chancellorsville, a great Confederate victory in a battle it was to wish it had never fought. With the Union Army fortified against the Rappahannock, Stonewall Jackson's brigade, including Sutpen's Leftovers, charged Howard's division on the right side. The attack was so vicious that the Yanks reeled and, the next day, ran; and Hooker's tenure as commander of the Army of the Potomac ran out. But Stonewall Jackson, shot in the night by one of his own sentries who mistook him for an enemy, died a week later of pneumonia and an amputated arm. Sutpen's regiment then fell under the command of the one-legged general, Dick Ewell. In Mississippi Grant beat Pemberton at Big Black River to the south of Jefferson and planted himself squarely in front of Vicksburg.

JUNE: Things continued to go badly in the west—Bragg had been forced back to Chattanooga by Rosecrans, and Grant had dynamited some of the fortifications around Vicksburg. But the last ray of what still could be called hope shone in the east. An unknown general named Meade had replaced Hooker and seemed for the moment out of control of his responsibilities. Lee—taking advantage of this, using the confidence he had inspired in his men, and desperately needing food which his ravaged Virginia could no longer supply—invaded the North for the second time [1862]. By month's end he had advanced into southern Pennsylvania, a place Jeb Stuart had already proved it was not too hard to get to. In Yoknapatawpha this month, Saucier Weddel's mother contracted pneumonia while trying to bury her silver on a wet night {"Mountain Victory"}. The Yankees were already in Yoknapatawpha County looking for it when she died a few days later. Also dead at forty-five in this month was Ellen Sutpen of causes at once too simple and too complex to be described {A}.

JULY: On the 1st Lee encountered Buford's army outside Gettysburg and by the end of the day had repulsed the Yankees to Cemetery Hill where they were forced to await reinforcements from Meade. Sutpen, under Ewell, arrived late this day, dragging with him now two imported tombstones, one for his wife and one for himself. Known among the regiment as "Colonel" and "Mrs. Colonel," these two stones stood beside the battlefield for three days, symbolizing the final doom that would befall Sutpen and the South this weekend {A}. On the 2nd the Confederate forces almost outflanked the Northern army, and this would have ended the battle. But the heroism of certain New York and Maine detachments in scurrying to a defensive position on Little Round Top saved the day. On the fatal 3rd, Ewell fought Meade's extreme left, with Sutpen in tow, without success. In the afternoon Lee sent Pickett to break the center of the Yankee defenses in Ziegler's Grove.

The charge, as everyone knows, failed; and with it failed the Southern Ideal and the Southern Dream. At the very moment Pickett turned in retreat, our Past became irrecoverable, our Future intolerable. Lee's forces limped back to Virginia and got there. The Yanks were too weary and battle-scarred to give chase. Had it won at Gettysburg, the Confederate Army would have been to Harrisburg in a day, Washington in a week, and home in a month.

Gettysburg was lost on Friday the 3rd; Vicksburg fell to Grant the following day, the 4th of July. Port Hudson surrendered on the 7th. Now the Union had captured the entire Mississippi River; and on the 16th a federal supply boat passed from St. Louis to New Orleans without molestation, the first in over two years. The Confederacy was severed. Fearing the arrival of General Sherman, the state government fled from Jackson. With chaos impending, the citizens of the state were on their own to protect themselves and their belongings as best they could.

At the Sartoris plantation, such arrangements were hastily being made. With the Yankees in Corinth, John Sartoris himself materialized on the premises to rebuild the stockpen and bury the family trunk {U}. His son Bayard and his black companion Ringo saw so little of him on this occasion that they had to sneak downstairs at night to hear his larger-than-life tales of Van Dorn's cavalry raids. Evidently these managed to inspire the boys to a heroic defense of their home, for the day after Sartoris returned to Van Dorn they took a pot shot at a Yankee officer, shooting his horse out from under him. A sergeant chased them into the house, where they spent the next half-hour hiding beneath Granny Millard's skirts while the sergeant searched both for them and for anything of material value. In the midst of this the offended officer entered and—apparently a man of honor and decency—ordered the search halted even though he knew the boys' location. For their valor, Bayard and Ringo received a mouthful of soap for questioning the legitimacy of all Yankee births. But a larger problem that was developing was the rebelliousness of Ringo's uncle, Loosh, who had already announced to his wife, Philadelphy, that they should be prepared to leave soon for they were officially about to be "freed." Granny feared for their safety but said little.

During this tragic July, Tomey's Turl and Tennie Beauchamp gave birth to their third child (during the siege of Vicksburg) and, once again, lost it almost immediately to malnutrition {G}. Elsewhere the shortage of food brought permanent invalidism to Gail Hightower's mother as well {L}.

AUGUST: Bragg was forced to withdraw from Chattanooga and retreat to Chickamauga to await the reinforcements, under the command of Longstreet, which Lee had promised to send from Virginia. In Yoknapatawpha, after saying good-bye to Mrs. Compson, Granny Millard, Bayard, Ringo, and Joby made their first attempt to escape to Tennessee {U}. This was imperative because of the bounty the Yankees had placed on John Sartoris' head and, maybe, that of anyone related to him. They dug up the trunk they had buried the month before, passed some bivouacked Confederate troops along the northern road, and headed out of the county. On the fourth day, a Confederate officer along the way warned them to return, that Yankees were in control ahead, that John Sartoris himself had already headed back to Jefferson. On the road back, five strangers stole their mules in an act of piracy that was characteristic these days of Sartoris himself and entirely all too common in these desperate years. While in pursuit of the thieves, Bayard and Ringo stumbled upon Colonel Sartoris, and in turn they then all stumbled upon a lounging Yankee regiment. Being too few in number to capture them, they beat Ringo's one-eyed mule over the blind eye to make it run circles around the regiment, took the Yanks' pants and boots and weapons, and then let them sneak quietly away in the night. Then they raced back to Jefferson, barely ahead of the Union forces bent on terminating Sartoris' horse-stealing operation in the district, buried the trunk, and—again—fixed the stockpen. In the process, fifty Yankee troops rounded the bend in the drive and demanded to know where Sartoris was. Pretending to be someone else, Sartoris hobbled toward the house, swept up his gear, and galloped atop the mighty Jupiter into the distance with the Yankees firing shots at him as he rounded the barn. Though they lost their man, the detachment did walk off with the Sartoris trunk (after Loosh took it upon himself to lead them to its hiding place). Then he and Philadelphy announced that they had been freed and departed, Philadelphy reluctant but faithful to her husband. Before the Yankees themselves left, they burned the Sartoris house to the ground so that, in a few hours, only four brick chimneys stood amidst the smoldering rubble. Not that Bayard would ever have forgotten this day; but Will Falls, fifty years later [1919], would visit him in his office at the bank to tell it and retell it in the same way all of us told and retold things, as if we could make them turn out different from the way they did just by giving our tongues a chance to alter fate with a slip or a lie {S}.

Homeless, the Sartorises again made an attempt to reach Hawkhurst for shelter, apparently not knowing that the home of their relations was already itself a cinder with chimneys. They had lived in Joby's shack since the burning and were finding conditions intolerable. The scenes of devastation they encountered on the six-day journey into Tennessee were commonplace but indescribable—wounded and dazed soldiers, houses burnt as thoroughly as their own, homeless whites and Negroes wandering aimlessly. On the sixth day they encountered a group of freed slaves going toward "the River Jordan," which Yankee soldiers must have led them to believe was somewhere in the district. Granny tried to turn them in more practical directions; but, having been convinced to relish their deliverance from the individual Simon Legrees, they pushed onward toward the cleansing waters. When the Sartorises reached Hawkhurst, they found the Hawks living in Jingus' cabin as they themselves had been in Joby's, the railroad (which Ringo was desperate to see in person) ripped up, and Drusilla—desexed after her fiance's death at Shiloh—dressed as a man and acting like one. She announced that she planned to ride for the duration of the war with John Sartoris' outfit.

On the following day, August 14th, they found the Yankee army trying to disperse the Jordan-seeking Negroes. It seems they were about to blow up a bridge over the very river the blacks had decided was the one they wanted. Granny was instrumental in saving at least a hundred from flying debris, though Bayard lost a good deal of his hearing as a result of the explosion. Finding Colonel Dick, the same Yankee officer who had visited their home and lost his horse there a month before, Granny managed to get from him 110 mules, 122 Negroes, and ten trunks, even though she had actually sought only the four, two, and one respectively that belonged to the Sartorises. Dick also gave her a letter deeding all these to her, hoping, probably, never to see her again. Granny turned this into twelve more mules (for the dozen Negroes who were still on foot) from another Yankee outfit the next day. Under Granny's leadership, the family and 122 freed but now homeless slaves got back to the Sartoris plantation within a week.

SEPTEMBER: In a reversal of the usual trend, things crumbled in the east (Custer had captured a vast amount of Confederate artillery at Culpeper Courthouse) but shored up in the west (Bragg and Longstreet, but mainly Longstreet, had defeated the Yanks at Chickamauga despite the courageous resistance of General Thomas). In the county this month, Uncle Buck (home with Sartoris himself for the harvest) and his wife moved back into Old Carothers McCaslin's plantation house, kicking out the Negroes whom they no longer had to bother trying to free since they now automatically were so {G}. And John Sartoris, before he went back to Van Dorn's unit in Tennessee, spent his customary evening sitting around the hearth, fashioning his war myths {U}. Bayard, Ringo, and Joby were all eager listeners as usual. Joby had been Colonel Sartoris' body servant while he was still commander of the Mississippi Second [1861], but he was simply too old to keep up with his master's current renegade tactics. As a result his son Simon, Ringo's father— still in Tennessee on this occasion—now filled the position.

OCTOBER: In the east Lee destroyed hundreds of miles of railroad track to reduce Meade's mobility, but in the west Longstreet was unable to drive Hooker out of Chattanooga, a crucial position in that it was the Confederate rail center for sending men and supplies back and forth between the eastern and western fronts. Sartoris was back in command of his officially sanctioned horse thieves in Tennessee. On one occasion one of his men, named Zeb Fothergill, stole a horse from General Sherman's army which he felt sure could beat Jupiter in a match race {S}. Sartoris accepted the challenge, as he always did, and beat the northern nag by 300 yards going away. At the finish line, however, he stumbled upon still another company of unwanted Yankees, this time eating dinner. Again not wanting prisoners to slow him down, the Colonel pulled his shoes-pants-weapons seizure a second time; and again the Yanks crawled away in the night in their underwear.

NOVEMBER: Hooker and Phil Sheridan finally finished off Bragg, the most frequently beaten general in the Confederate Army, in the "battle above the clouds" at Lookout Mountain and Missionary Ridge. The Union forces were now in full control of Tennessee and northern Georgia; and General Sherman prepared to seek the sea. In the east Meade continued to dodge Lee while Lincoln cursed his general's cowardice.

DECEMBER: The two armies retired to winter quarters, the North with plenty to eat, the South with nearly nothing.

Sometime in 1863, Calvin Burden the elder heard only the second word in twelve years from his son Nathaniel [1851]—this time of a wife and child he had with him in Mexico {L}.

1864

Born: James Beauchamp, "Tennie's Jim," fourth child of Tomey's Turl and Tennie Beauchamp, the first to survive

Born: Sister of Major DeSpain

Died: Goodhue Coldfield

Died: Rosa Millard

Died: Jeb Stuart (b. 1833), at Yellow Tavern, Virginia

Died: Gail Hightower I, grandfather of Rev. Gail Hightower

Died: Pomp, his Negro body servant

Died: Mother of Lucius "Boss" Priest I

FEBRUARY: January was uneventful as the Confederacy entered its most ruinous but also most gallant and courageous year. In February Meade, clearly frightened of Lee, just jabbed at him at Raccoon and Morton's Fords. In Yoknapatawpha Drusilla Hawk officially joined the Sartoris regiment as a horse thief {U}, as did Grandpap Grier, though he was still too young to be a grandpap yet {"Shall Not Perish"}. One of the few big plantation houses left—the McCaslins', in which Uncle Buck now lived with his wife when he was not with John Sartoris—was burnt to the ground by General Grant's occupational forces in the County {G}. Also in this month was the strange episode in which Gail Hightower I, grandfather of the peculiar minister who would come to Jefferson in the early years of the next century [1903], was killed by an old woman with a shotgun while he was raiding her chickencoop {L}. The minister would somehow get this mixed up forty years later, believing (or wanting to) that his relative was actually participating in one of Van Dorn's daring raids on Grant's supplies in Jefferson. In any event, his disconsolate Negro body servant, Pomp, was also killed in Jefferson while trying to avenge his master's death on a Yankee officer.

MARCH: The Yankees made a daring raid on Richmond this month to free their prisoners of war, a raid which almost succeeded but in the long run didn't. In Mississippi Ab Snopes had by this time become detached from the Sartoris outfit and was thieving horses on his own. In this month he even tried to steal Sartoris' own horse, Jupiter, but received a shot in the heel from the Colonel instead {H} {"Barn Burning"}. Ab would limp from this for the rest of his life and even have to live in the hills [1865], for this and other reasons, for several years after the war [1868], until Sartoris finally got distracted by the railroad.

APRIL: The Jefferson business district was razed by Yankee torches this month {N}. They battered the courthouse badly but could not destroy it. Four miles north of town, around the Sartoris plantation, the Battle of Jefferson was fought and lost. The U.S. general had turned the jailhouse, the only building left on the square (save for the courthouse, of course) into his provost marshal's guardhouse, from whence the latter watched the smoke of battle itself with the jailer's daughter, Cecilia Farmer. In the main war in the east, Ulysses S. Grant was made supreme commander of the Union forces and launched his plan for all-out total warfare against us.

MAY: In Jefferson, the townspeople—now only women, children, and wounded soldiers—floundered in the rubble the Yanks had left them with. In the east the Battle of the Wilderness was fought indecisively, though both sides were badly damaged. Sutpen's Mississippi Second was nearly trapped in the forest fire that broke out, but it managed to escape and reappear the next week to assist in driving Hancock from Spotsylvania. Sutpen's numbers were very small by now, and his men rarely made much difference in any of the fighting. He was further reduced on the 19th in the trouncing Ewell's corps took from Tyler. In the Shenandoah Valley, Jubal Early and Mosby, who had picked up where Jackson had left off, managed to get into a position to threaten Washington; and it seemed as if the war had come full circle and gotten nowhere. But in Georgia the results were much worse. General Sherman had amassed the Army of the Tennessee, the Army of the Cumberland, and the Army of the Ohio and begun his savage march toward Atlanta. He attacked and beat Joe Johnston at Dalton, Tunnel Hill, Resaca (at which General Compson, now with one arm, apparently fought more savvily than he had at Shiloh [1862] {F}, and Etowah Bridge. But like Grant in the east, he was discovering that he could not beat the Rebs when they entrenched in earthworks.

JUNE: In a particularly dirty month of the war, Grant "The Butcher" was wasting thousands of Yankee and Confederate lives in indecisive battles. He lost at Cold Harbor and finally retreated across the James to try a new line of attack—the siege of Petersburg where the main body of Lee's army was securely entrenched. Unable to force Lee out, Grant sent Butler on fancy raids which secured nothing, let him build fancy fortifications which achieved nothing, and built himself an enormous headquarters at City Point, complete with a military railroad which he hoped would conquer the Virginia mud which had bogged down McClellan and others before him. Suddenly the whole eastern war reduced itself to two forts—Sedgwick (North) and Mahone (South), called also Forts Hell and Damnation—where the two armies commenced to stare one another down and, even, establish a code of honor which the rules of warfare tended to disparage: no shooting after sundown; time to gather in pickets, eat breakfast, and tidy up in the morning; the firing of a warning shot by one side or the other that it had completed its chores and was ready to fight; and then only occasional popping at anything which might look like an exposed head in the other fort only 300 yards away. But on the 27th, north of Atlanta, the Confederate Army won a surprising victory over Sherman at Kennesaw Mountain.

JULY: By the 5th, however, Sherman was already outflanking Johnston again and forcing him back upon Atlanta. General Compson, being from a family that was always better at backing up than at going forward, won some recognition for himself at this retreat {R}. In Virginia Jubal Early's threat to Washington was ended in his defeat at Fort Stevens. He, too, managed to back up, though; and, on the 30th, he burnt Chambersburg, Pennsylvania, to the ground. Grant then appointed Phil Sheridan, whose forces had just gotten through killing Jeb Stuart at Yellow Tavern, to clear Early out of the Shenandoah Valley and stifle his foraging raids into the northern states—which he did.

AUGUST: In Yoknapatawpha Goodhue Coldfield finally stopped accepting food hoisted into the attic [1861]. With the help of some neighbors, Rosa broke in and had his body removed and buried {A}. Out at Sartoris, in the temporary quarters in the few remaining Negro cabins that the Yankees didn't burn in the battle of Jefferson {U}, Granny Millard received a letter from Aunt Louisa Hawk which lamented Drusilla's loss of femininity in John

Sartoris' service. Meanwhile, Drusilla continued to perform with distinction and chose verbena, the only flower she could whiff above horse dung, as the symbol of her own feminine defiance and courage.

SEPTEMBER: On the first, General Hood was lured out of Atlanta to Jonesboro, and General Slocum captured the city for the North. In Virginia Sheridan beat Early badly at Winchester on the 19th and again at Fisher's Hill on the 22nd. He was also carrying out to the letter Grant's orders to devastate the Shenandoah Valley so thoroughly that it could not provide another winter's harvest for the Confederate troops.

OCTOBER: At Petersburg, the two armies had all but given up. They freely met each other for tobacco- and food-trading between the two lines of defense and talked among themselves of peace at any cost by Christmas. They were bored and miserable. On the 19th, after almost suffering a severe loss at Cedar Creek, Sheridan rallied his troops and literally disintegrated Jubal Early's Shenandoah Valley operation, ending all Confederate resistance there for good. In Georgia Sherman was bedeviled by Hood, Forrest, and Wheeler, but held Atlanta securely. The situation in Yoknapatawpha was as terrible as it was anywhere in the South, but people like Granny Millard were rallying their countrymen until the war would finally end {U}. In an arrangement that was clearly crooked but just as clearly necessary, she used her letter from Colonel Dick [1863] to requisition more and more mules, the most valuable animal in the war, from Yankee officers. Thereupon she would turn them over to Ab Snopes who would sell them back to the Yankees in Memphis. Knowing that Ab was cheating her on the financial returns, she found ways to cheat him as well—so all was probably even between them. Not that Granny was proud of herself—she publicly confessed her sins in Brother Fortinbride's church one Sunday, though she was not about to go and sin no more. Around this time, however, Ab Snopes arrived in town to announce that the war in Mississippi was over, that the Yankees had pulled out (except for Colonel Newberry's company in Mottstown), and that there would be no more market for mules, and no more mules to steal, and hence no more money for hungry Yoknapatawphans (which, of course, Ab did not give two hoots about anyway). Fearing that she would have nothing left with which to rebuild the Sartoris plantation either, Granny, understandably but foolishly, tried one more deal—with Newberry—and got caught at it. Newberry then left the state with all the mules she, Bayard, and Ringo still had left to turn over to Snopes. The tragic result of this was that she allowed Snopes to involve her in a horse-stealing deal (there was *always* big money in horses) with a loyaltyless pirate named Grumby who found his after-hours entertainment in terrorizing Negroes and women. On one occasion Granny rendezvoused with him at a cotton compress to negotiate a deal. When Grumby got what he wanted from her, however, he shot her dead. Bayard and Ringo, waiting a short distance away, ran to the compress and found there what

[91]

looked like a pile of sticks dressed in calico. From here on charity and good works would take a back seat in this county to revenge [1865]. The tears they hysterically shed for Granny were the last they would shed for anyone.

NOVEMBER: On the 15th, Sherman burned Atlanta and pulled out on his march to the sea. Before leaving he sent General Thomas north to finish off Hood and Confederate resistance in Tennessee. Things remained uneventful in Petersburg, Virginia; and Thomas Sutpen took the occasion to make his first appearance in Yoknapatawpha County, where his plantation house against all odds still stood, since April, 1861. With him were the two half-ton Italian gravestones he had been hauling with him since before Gettysburg [1863] {A}. He placed one on Ellen's grave and stashed the other, his own, in a hallway at the Hundred. To Buck McCaslin he told the harrowing tales of dragging them in a wagon through the Cumberland Gap, dodging Yankee patrols the whole way. He spoke with General Compson, who was again wounded and again home, and then returned to Virginia for what was to be the end for him in more ways than one, even though he would live through it.

DECEMBER: On the 9th and the 10th Sherman's ravaging army poured into Savannah and his march was over, culminating in a grand parade down Bay Street. He gave the city as a Christmas present to Abe Lincoln, and—in a seasonal greeting to his wife—said: "We have devoured the land; to realize what war is one should follow our tracks." But one could have realized what war is just by visiting almost anyplace in the South now, Yoknapatawpha County included. In this month Jefferson was already being rebuilt, though it was being done mostly by what we would later call carpetbaggers {N}. Among them was Ben Redmond who came back to share in whatever profits could be had from his neighbors' hardship. There was also a German black-smith who arrived in town this year whose daughters would eventually become matriarchs of a new aristocracy. Most memorably, however, Granny Millard was buried by Brother Fortinbride early this month {U}. Her coffin was borne by Uncle Buck McCaslin and others who knew all too well her service to the community in the last two years and what her loss would mean [1863]. Bayard and Ringo then set off in hot pursuit of Grumby, who was, according to his wife, now hiding in Alabama. At Christmas a letter addressed to Granny, from Aunt Louisa in Tennessee who still had not heard of her death, asked that the Sartorises be on the lookout for Drusilla who, Louisa was sure, must by now be fornicating in Cousin John's tent.

So the year ended, and the South waited for *The End*.

THE PRESIDENCY OF ANDREW JOHNSON, 1865–1869

1865

Married: John Sartoris and Drusilla Hawk

Married: Cecilia Farmer and a Confederate soldier no one had seen before or ever would again

Died: Charles Bon (b. 1829), murdered by Henry Sutpen, his own half-brother

Died: Grumby, murdered by Bayard Sartoris and Marengo Strother

Died: Saucier Weddel (b. 1837), murdered by a Union sympathizer in Tennessee

Died: Jubal (b. 1825), his body servant, murdered by the same Union sympathizer

Died: Hule, murdered by his own brother

JANUARY: His Georgia home thoroughly burned to the ground by Sherman, Lucius Priest, later to be known as "Boss," arrived in Yoknapatawpha County in search of his distant relatives, the McCaslins, whom, of course, he found here {R}. Charles Bon, now in North Carolina with Johnston, wrote Judith Sutpen a marital ultimatum [1861] this month, writing from a gutted mansion with the only ink he had—stove polish {A}. This letter, like the earlier one, wound up in Mrs. Compson's possessions (at Judith's wish). And Bayard Sartoris, Uncle Buck McCaslin, and Ringo were still out of the county in pursuit of Grumby.

FEBRUARY: Early this month they found him, though not without a brush with death beforehand {U}. As they sat at a fire one day a stranger rode up, himself claiming to be looking for Grumby, likewise to settle an old score. As he rode off, however, he turned and fired on them, hitting Uncle Buck in his rheumatic arm. The next day they found Ab Snopes also victimized, tied to a tree by his suspenders; so Buck, in need of medical attention, took him back to Jefferson, though Ab escaped en route to hide out in the hills for a dozen years [1877] before returning to the County to trade horses and, later, cause more trouble, this time with fire [1894]. Ringo and Bayard, after tracking Grumby in the rain for several more days, encountered yet more evidence of his activities—this time a dead Negro hanging from a tree with a warning note attached to any who would pursue him further. But pursue him they did nonetheless and finally gunned him down in a three-way crossfire among him, them, and two of his former allies. Then, in an act of savagery which was to become all too common among us, they returned him to the cotton compress where Granny was killed, nailed his body to the door, cut off his hand, and—upon their arrival back in Jefferson—nailed this hand to Granny's gravestone. Uncle Buck was particularly delighted and not ashamed of himself for being so either.

[93]

Elsewhere General Sherman was on the move north at the rate of thirteen miles a day through the South Carolina swamps, stringing corduroy road before him as he went. Wade Hampton was sent out to stop his advance but failed miserably. On the 17th Sherman arrived in Columbia and burned two-thirds of it to the ground. A quote of Sherman's on this occasion is relevant to Bayard Sartoris' activities this month: "My aim was to whip the rebels, to humble their pride, to follow them to their inmost recesses, and make them fear and dread us. Fear is the beginning of wisdom." If what Bayard did from dread and fear was wisdom, all too much of this sort of wisdom was soon to break out all over the South.

MARCH: Lincoln's approach might have been better, but Lincoln had only a month to live: "I want submission and no more bloodshed," he told Grant. "Let them have their horses to plow with and, if you like, their guns to shoot crows with. I want no one punished; treat them liberally all around. We want those people to return to their allegiance to the Union and submit to the laws." Sheridan had joined Grant at City Point, inflation was rampant in Richmond ($1500 for a barrel of flour), and Lee had diseased troops in the trenches at Petersburg. The end of the South was at hand. Symbolically this played itself out in North Carolina where Sutpen's Second Mississippi and the one to which Henry and Bon were now attached (the University Grays had been wiped out at Shiloh) [1862] had joined forces under Johnston {A}. Henry met his father in his tent here one night and told him that, despite the fact that it would be incestuous, he was prepared to let Charles Bon marry his sister, Judith. But at this moment, it seems, Sutpen played his trump card: he told Henry that Bon had Negro blood in his veins. Stunned, Henry returned to Charles and, probably reluctantly but definitely forcefully, forbade the marriage. Charles refused to accept this and told Henry to kill him on the spot—which Henry, because of his great and curious love for this man, could not do yet.

APRIL: On the first, the Union cavalry attacked Lee's far right flank at Five Forks, beat it, and began to surround Lee's trenches at Petersburg. On the second the entire Confederate army fled, and on the third the Yanks moved their wagon trains into the long-besieged city. Lee's only recourse was to retreat to North Carolina and join Johnston's army; so he spent the week fighting his Union pursuers (with the inevitable Sheridan at their front) off his trail at Jetersville, then Sayler's Creek, then Farmville. But, as Lee stopped each time to fight, General George Armstrong Custer circled around behind him and beat him to the vital rail junction at Appomattox Station on the eighth. Now thoroughly trapped, Lee, in his most gallant uniform, surrendered to the gizzled and mud-splattered Grant in the parlor of Wilmer McLean's house on the morning of the ninth, without the approval or permission of President Davis. On the twelfth, the Confederate soldiers, many of them clutching their flags in tears, officially turned over their weapons and guidons to the Union soldiers. Then they went home, though were about to find that they no longer had any.

In Jefferson, Appomattox probably went unnoticed {N}.

MAY: In a flight of his own, Charles Bon arrived at Sutpen's Hundred before Henry. He placed a picture of his octoroon wife and child in his coat and awaited his half-brother at the gates to the home which should have been both of theirs but soon would be neither's. Henry arrived, shot Charles dead, told his sister, then left the county for forty years [1905]. Later that day Wash Jones rode into Jefferson and up to Rosa Coldfield's back door to announce Bon's death. Rosa went immediately to the Hundred, started up the stairs to view Bon's body, but was blocked by the monkeylike Clytie [1909]. Apparently, then, Rosa Coldfield never did lay eyes on the man her niece was to marry. As she, Judith, and Clytie ate lunch in the kitchen, Wash and another man sawed away in the yard on Bon's coffin, carried it upstairs, loaded him in it and then—all together—they carried it downstairs. Judith went first and bore most of its (and so his) weight. In the funeral at the Cedar Grove, Uncle Buck McCaslin, seeking some tribute to pay this unfortunate, misused, and unwanted young man, gave forth with three piercing rebel yells. From then on Rosa Coldfield took up residence at the Hundred, out of need for kin, food, and shelter as they awaited the return of their one remaining man from North Carolina, not because they needed him but because he, they felt, needed them. He would not arrive until the following January [1866]; so the three women spent their time taking care of the straggling soldiers who daily stumbled past their door. One of these was Anse MacCallum who walked back defeated from Appomattox, just as he had walked to Richmond four years before [1861], already defeated even then but requiring four years of proof to know it {"The Tall Men"}.

In this month, in Tennessee (probably the least sincere of all the states which seceded), Saucier Weddel—the quarter-Choctaw son of Francis Weddel—and his servant Jubal unknowingly sought shelter in the home of a family of South-hating hillbillies. Warned to leave that night by a boy named Hule and his sister, Weddel was forced to stay over because Jubal had gotten too drunk to travel {"Mountain Victory"}. In the morning Weddel and Jubal were ambushed on the road by Hule's brother Vatch and killed, along with Hule himself who was shot trying to protect this dapper soldier whose name and bearing had so intrigued his sister.

While Bon was being murdered at Sutpen's Hundred and Weddel was being murdered in Tennessee, the Sartoris family was trying to rectify a situation which, they felt, was sapping their noble name of its last shred of dignity {U}. They were sure that Colonel John and Cousin Drusilla were sleeping together, though in reality—even if John wanted to—it is unlikely that Drusilla had any interest in it. Sartoris fumed, but the ladies continued the important work of trying to return femininity and sexual innocence (or at

[95]

least the appearance of it) to Drusilla, who had ridden with men so long now that she must have smelled like one [1863]. While Miss Habersham shielded Bayard from this corruption, Aunt Louisa bluntly forced the marriage between John and Drusilla, which the two acquiesced in since they had no particular objection to it. After a skirmish in town with the first of many troublesome northerners [1873], John and Drusilla were married, to the relief of the Sartoris females and those who associated with them.

SUMMER: Jefferson soldiers, the ones who survived the war, continued to straggle home. Few were as lucky as Ballenbaugh's son who arrived with a large amount of uncut dollar bills that no one knew where he got {R}. Most returned to their devastated lands and tried to make something grow again—anything at all, probably, because they had not eaten well in at least a year. Some found themselves displaced from their land or shops by carpetbaggers who had arrived first {N}. One young man who didn't belong here rode home from war with a stocking full of corn seed, paused with us only long enough to lure Cecilia Farmer from the jailer's house, marry her, trade his horse for a mule, and depart with her for a new start (for both of them) in Alabama.

AUTUMN: Judith Sutpen, stoic and tearless, made two trips to Charles Bon's grave to rake the fallen leaves from it {A}. She waited still for her father's return, knowing by now that her brother couldn't or at least wouldn't. In Jefferson this fall, despite John Sartoris' continuing efforts, a black man was appointed town marshal through the intercession of the occupying federal troops {G}. Known only as Sickymo, the man had gotten his name and reputation when, as a slave before the war, he repeatedly stole his master's alcohol, diluted it with water, and peddled it from a cache under the big sycamore tree behind the drugstore. The position of marshal, though, was honorary—the soldiers were the "law."

At Jackson, the Mississippi state government returned from exile this year {N}. And in Charleston the man who would eventually be Ike's partner in the hardware store was beginning a twenty-one-year tour as a ship's carpenter {G} [1886].

1866

Born: Judge Allison (d. 1931)

Born: Judge Dunkinfield (d. 1929)

Born: Stonewall Jackson Fentry

Married: Anse MacCallum and his wife

Married: Nathaniel Burden and Juana

By the first of the year Jefferson had made great strides in its own recovery. The town square was already in pretty good shape; and Redmond, working from the same plans Sutpen's architect drew thirty years ago [1834], had begun the restoration of the courthouse {N}. But much of this activity was simply a veneer which distracted the eye from the moral rot which had already infested too many of us. The Sutpen family, perhaps, is the clearest example.

Thomas returned in January and was greeted by Judith, who by now had given way to her too long repressed tears {A}. To support himself and his family, he and Wash and another man labored furiously to restore his ravaged land. At night he and Wash would sit together and drink just as furiously, Wash often having to carry him home to Clytie even as the sun rose on the next day. In March he was confronted one night by the county's first pack of Ku Klux Klansmen, led by none other than John Sartoris. They demanded to know if he was with them or against them in their fight against blacks and carpetbagging Northerners. Never on good terms with Sartoris in the first place, Sutpen ordered them off his land, snarling at them that the South could be great again if men would spend their time reviving their lands as he was doing rather than riding around spooking people as they were. In April, Thomas, now fifty-nine but still seeking an heir, became engaged to Rosa Coldfield, still only twenty-one but already an old woman. The engagement lasted only two months, however, for in June he managed to insult her irrevocably by demanding that she prove she could bear him a male heir before he would marry her. The Sutpen innocence and hubris, all in one statement! She broke the engagement on the spot and quit the Sutpen property, never to return there again until she went there late one night some forty years later with Quentin Compson, General Compson's grandson [1909].

Without food or money or, now, dignity, Rosa in her own way went crazy. Though the town—accustomed in these years to sharing what it had—would have given her food, she insisted on foraging through fences to steal it from their gardens. Judge Benbow himself took to leaving her baskets of food on her doorstep, baskets she would replace there the next morning without even bothering to wash the dishes. She was behaving just as her father had without bothering to nail herself in the attic. Benbow, to ease her plight, helped her sell her father's store; but, knowing that she had no use for money and would waste it, he kept the profits and used them, for the next thirty-eight years, to buy her food and clothing [1904]. When the money started to run low years

[97]

later, he began betting it at a Memphis horse track to try to increase it. When the horses lost, he replaced the losings with his own money; when they won he put the winnings in her account. Rosa, of course, knew nothing of any of this, and the town did not either until his folio of records was discovered in his papers when he died in 1904. All the while, Rosa lived in her father's small house, blinds drawn, emerging only on Sundays for church and Wednesdays for prayer meetings.

Without an intended upon whom to father a son, Sutpen turned to Wash Jones for help; or did Wash turn to him in their delirious drinking bouts in the scuppernong arbor? Wash had managed in his inveterate hero-worship to restore Sutpen's ego in other matters; and now he had a granddaughter who—if not ripe enough yet—would be in a year or so [1867]. So Thomas began to send her trinkets snatched off the shelves of the store he was soon to become manager of, gifts which were intended to effect—and eventually would—the sort of potluck eugenics he had already suggested to Rosa Coldfield.

Some of the county's original aristocrats began, each in his own way, to recover from the war. Major DeSpain acquired the title to the hunting lands on the McCaslin property; Buck and Buddy were apparently all too happy to give up something they didn't believe they owned anyway {R}. General Compson, without ready cash, took out the first mortgage the Compson land ever had attached to it, though he was forced to bargain on this with the only folk in town who had any spare money, a group of New England carpetbaggers {F}. Since he would never again be financially solvent, Compson was able to make payments on the mortgage only by selling off more and more chunks of his land. He was still doing so when he died at the hunting camp at the Tallahatchie River Bottom over thirty years later [1900]. Anse MacCallum, on the other hand, got married within a year after his return and built the house in the northeast reaches of the county which he was to occupy and continue to own until his death in 1920 {S}.

The county's less desirables were retrenching as well. Percival Brownlee, the useless slave the McCaslins had tried to free a hundred different ways except that he never wanted to go (or at least wouldn't bother to) {G} [1856] [1863], passed through Jefferson one day in the company of an Army paymaster who was seeking out regiments of the occupying army. When Brownlee spotted old Uncle Buck on the square, he jumped out of the wagon, flashed him that manufactured grin of the freed Negro, gestured at him defiantly, and fled down a back street. (Buck cursed the irony of this until the day he died.) Finally, in Kansas, the long-lost Nathaniel Burden caught up with his mother and father after months of looking for them and finally "married his wife of thirteen years" [1853] {L}. The ring was borne at the ceremony by his twelve-year-old son Calvin. Order, of a sort, was slowly being restored.

Born: Isaac McCaslin (d. 1947)

Born: Jackson MacCallum

President Johnson was trying to deal moderately with the South, as Lincoln himself had promised to do; but congressional radicals like Thaddeus Stevens insisted upon pouring it on. The Fourteenth and Fifteenth Amendments became law, carpetbaggers and scalawags continued to operate, and Johnson himself was almost thrown out of office. In reaction the Ku Klux Klan had continued to amass greater numbers and had moved up from ghostly visitations to whippings, tarrings, featherings, and soon to killings. Amidst all this and alongside the expenditure made by the United States to acquire Alaska rather than reacquire the South, Yoknapatawpha struggled to rebuild.

But amidst all this as well one of the most decent men the county had ever produced (or ever would either) was born—Isaac McCaslin, later to be "Uncle Ike" to the whole County {G}. The first and only child of Uncle Buck and Sophonsiba Beauchamp McCaslin, he would spend the greater portion of his life trying to right the wrongs done by his forbears to the Negroes. On the day of his birth, his Uncle Hubert Beauchamp, Sophonsiba's brother, placed fifty pieces of gold in a silver cup, to be presented to Ike on his twenty-first birthday [1888]. This, in view of the times, was an exorbitant amount of money; and, before very long, Hubert was forced to borrow on the bequest. Within six years he had taken the whole thing, including the cup, and left Ike only a coffeepot filled with IOUs. At the Sutpen plantation, Thomas could no longer devote all his energies to rebuilding and farming—food and money were depleted {A}. Therefore, he assumed management of a small crossroads store at which he sold mostly calico, beads, plowshares, kerosene, and ribbons to freed Negroes. During this time he and Wash apparently agreed that, upon the attainment of her sixteenth birthday, Milly, Wash's granddaughter, was to be Sutpen's next helpmate in his quest of an heir who would be male, would be white, and would behave himself to boot {"Wash"}. To prepare the way, he continued to send her, via her grandfather, the trinkets off his store shelf which even the Negroes wouldn't buy. To keep the situation intact, he continued to drink with Wash and do him favors of whatever sort he could—such as lend him a scythe which Wash took home, used, failed to return, and let rust on his back porch for two years until he found a use for it again [1869] {A}.

In Jefferson, Dr. Wyott, president of the Jefferson Academy, became a declared and practicing atheist {T}. Elsewhere in Mississippi, Calvin Burden the elder and his son Nathaniel crossed into the state {L}. Shiftless and carpetbagging themselves, they had found employment with the U.S. Government; their job was to "help out" the freed Negroes in the South—which meant more getting them registered to vote than feeding their stomachs or clothing their nakedness.

1868

Born: Jason Compson III (d. 1912)

Died: Father of Lucius Priest I, in critical condition since the war

John Sartoris and Redmond, a man who was Sartoris' antithesis in every way but now necessary, put together every cent they could muster and began building their railroad to join Jefferson and other Mississippi towns to the main east-west line between Memphis and the Atlantic {U}. Work was short in these years and workers plentiful, so Sartoris and his cohort could afford to pay the men late on every occasion, always at the last moment before whatever pride the men had left would have driven them from the rail gang.

With John apparently about to reachieve some measure of success, though it was to be industrial rather than agrarian now, Aunt Jenny Du Pre, widowed and made lonely by the war, arrived from South Carolina [1862]. Bayard and Ringo drove north to Tennessee Junction to pick her up, though neither had ever met her. When she detrained she was carrying with her two bottles of sherry, two jasmine cuttings (which she planted in the Sartoris garden and today are enormous bushes), and a piece of colored glass from a window in the house in which she and John were born {"There Was a Queen"}. From this January day forward, Jenny Du Pre, twenty-eight, became a moral mainstay of Yoknapatawpha County, her courage being all that many had to cling to in the desperate years ahead. She was, after the example of Granny Millard, to be another superlative Sartoris woman.

Less superlative was Milly Jones who, either by compulsion or by desire, did not wait for sixteen years of age to become pregnant; in November she already was by Thomas Sutpen, though few later believed that this was the first time he ever tried {A}. She, Sutpen, and Wash anxiously awaited the results next May would bring.

In Jackson, Buzzard Egglestone used troops to drive Governor Humphries from office and prepared to make his own war on the northern intruders {N}.

1869

Born: Henry MacCallum

Born: Willy Christian (d. 1934)

Born: Wesley Pritchel (d. 1940)

Born: Sophonsiba Beauchamp, fifth child of Tomey's Turl and Tennie, second to survive

Born: Daughter of Thomas Sutpen and Milly Jones

Married: Lucius Quintus Carothers "Boss" Priest and Sarah Edmonds

Died: Daughter of Thomas Sutpen and Milly Jones, killed by her great-grandfather

Died: Thomas Sutpen (b. 1807), killed by Wash Jones

Died: Milly Jones (b. 1853), killed by her grandfather

Died: Wash Jones, killed by Major DeSpain

Died: Theophilus "Uncle Buck" McCaslin (b. 1799)

Died: Amodeus "Uncle Buddy" McCaslin (b. 1799)

Both for the nation and for Yoknapatawpha County, this was a big year in railroading. On May 19th, the Golden Spike was driven, connecting the Union Pacific and Central Pacific railroads and, at the same time, connecting the Atlantic and the Pacific by two chains of parallel steel bars. In Yoknapatawpha John Sartoris' railroad, with the help now of the Scottish engineer John had met in Mexico in the '40s [1845], was making grand progress; and, at year's end, the Scotsman was the family's guest at a Christmas celebration during which Aunt Jenny entertained, and perhaps occasionally bored, the company with tales of Jeb Stuart's and her brother Bayard's exploits during the war [1862] {S}.

If a new Sartoris dynasty was about to emerge, the Sutpen one was ended for good this same year {A}. Through the spring Wash and Sutpen continued to drink furiously in the scuppernong arbor while they awaited Milly's delivery. Then, on a night in May, Milly and one of Thomas' mares "foaled" on the same night. In the morning Sutpen arrived at the barn where both females had labored, checked the foal, and then inquired as to his own offspring. Upon discovering it to be a girl, he chastised Milly and returned to his mare. In a frenzy of disappointment, mostly over the fact that Sutpen did not measure up to the image he had of Southern landholders and military aristocracy, Wash Jones lunged at the now legendary Thomas Sutpen and killed him with the very scythe he borrowed from him two years before [1867] {"Wash"}. Then he spent the rest of his day tending to his grand-daughter and her baby.

When Sutpen failed to arrive home for dinner, Judith sent one of the black boys who hung around the house for handouts to find him {A}. The boy discovered Sutpen's body at the barn and saw Jones hiding inside. Within an hour or so, Major DeSpain, currently serving as sheriff, arrived at Jones' house and ordered him out. A cornered rat with human emotions mixed with animal instinct, Wash killed his granddaughter and her baby both, set fire to the house, and rushed outside, running directly at DeSpain with the bloody scythe upraised. In self-defense DeSpain killed Jones. The day's carnage was ended and with it a heroically energetic but tragically futile attempt by Thomas Sutpen to become a man no Negro butler would think of turning away from the front door and sending around to the back one [1823].

On the day of Sutpen's funeral, his coffin fell off the back of the wagon which was carrying it to the cedar grove, ironically because the mules were driven too fast by, perhaps, the same black giant who had driven them to church just as fast twenty years ago [1848]. It rolled into a ditch, but Judith bravely had it extricated and brought to the grove where Charles Bon, her intended husband, and Ellen, her misused mother, already lay. There his daughter, who had endured so much suffering because of him, conducted her own private service and then returned to what was left of the Hundred (very little) and of her family (only a half-black half-sister).

In Jackson, Tougaloo College for Negroes was founded this year {N}; and in Cambridge, Massachusetts, a black man known as Deacon assumed his role as official welcomer for all Southern Harvard freshmen who got off the train there {F}. He would welcome two Yoknapatawphans as well some forty years hence: me [1907] and Quentin Compson [1909].

1870

Born: Maury Priest

Born: Eunice Habersham

Born: Belle Worsham

With their natural animosities finally getting the better of them [1868], the Sartoris-Redmond partnership dissolved because the latter could no longer withstand the dictatorial methods of the former and because the former could no longer bear working with a man who had collaborated (or at least toyed) with the North during the war when he should have been fighting for the South {U}. It was Judge Benbow who arranged for the dissolution; and he was probably deceived into believing, as Redmond himself was, that the low price Sartoris offered for his partner's shares was all he could afford. It was not until later that either man knew that Sartoris, because of federal grants and other sources of revenue, was much better heeled than he had claimed.

The death of Sutpen did not go unnoticed by the Sartoris family {U}. On a walk in the garden one day, Drusilla rationalized for Bayard until she found a difference between the two men—Sartoris and Sutpen—who were so similar in many ways. Sutpen's dream was, she said, a dream to gain profit for himself; Sartoris' was one to rehabilitate the South. This was clearly a shallow reading of both men.

Near the Hundred Judith and Clytie ran Sutpen's store until they could find a buyer for it {A}. During this period they never really opened the store but only responded to flagging from the road when a prospective black customer happened along. When it was finally purchased, they used the small profit to buy a tombstone for Bon [1865] and, later, another for his son [1884].

That son they met for the first time when Bon's octoroon wife showed up at the Hundred with him, apparently at the invitation of Judith herself, to cry over his grave. They were welcomed in and stayed at the Hundred for a week, though they made only two visits to the grave. The boy, Charles Etienne de Saint Velery Bon, was now eleven and spoke almost no English. During the visit he spent most of his time in the library and was regularly tended to by the giant Negress who accompanied them from New Orleans. And when the week was up the three returned there.

The Sartoris railroad was almost complete by the end of 1870; and many of the workers, among them a man known as Uncle Doc Hines, were being let go {L}. In Jefferson Sickymo was still town marshal [1865], a fact about which he liked to brag well into the next century, even amidst the destitution which had by then befallen him {N}.

1871

Born: Negro mistress of Jack Houston

Married: Eldest daughter of John Sartoris and her husband

Married: Will Varner and his first wife

Died: Octoroon wife of Charles Bon

Died: Hill man shot by John Sartoris

Having laid his track, John Sartoris was now in need of a locomotive and borrowed some money from a group of northern businessmen to buy it {U}.

Sartoris was involved in another incident this year which created some sensation in Jefferson and, maybe, a catharsis in Sartoris. Stepping out his door one night he saw a hill man standing in his drive. We don't know if there was an exchange of words, but we do know that Sartoris shot him dead with his derringer within the course of about a minute. Sartoris claimed self-defense, that the man was a robber; and he was freed for lack of evidence, though neither did he have any evidence to support his own contentions either. Feeling guilty afterwards, Sartoris sent some money to the man's family. Several days later the man's wife walked uninvited through the Sartoris front door and, while he was eating his dinner, flung the money in his face and stalked out without speaking. Perhaps he reflected then on the number of men he had killed in his life; but, if he did, it was not enough to prevent his killing again [1873] {L}.

Some of the war returnees managed to redirect their tendencies to kill to the hunting camp on the McCaslin land. General Compson, for instance, shot an enormous buck there one day this year {G}. Yet on another occasion he, Major DeSpain, Cass Edmonds, and Walter Ewell—in one of the early versions of their hunting parties which were later to become seasonal rituals—protected a small, half-grown bear who had been scared up a tree by the tooting whistle of the tiny lumber train which was already threading its way in the county's woodland. These four men actually stood guard around the tree for thirty-six hours so the bear could get down safely and scamper off into the woods when its fear of the machinery finally wore off.

Judge Benbow took a trip to Barbados this year and returned with lantana in a hatbox {S}. From Frenchman's Bend, Will Varner and his new wife honeymooned in St. Louis {H}. And from Sutpen's Hundred Clytie journeyed to New Orleans to bring Charles Bon's now-orphaned son back to Yoknapatawpha after his mother suddenly took ill and died {A}. They travelled northward in the cold of December, living among Negroes on the freight deck of a steamboat.

In the North this year, Chicago burned to the ground, just as Richmond, Columbia, and Atlanta had [1865], though this fire was started by a cow rather than by what anthropologists would have no choice but to refer to as humans.

1872

Born: Miss Atkins, later to become a dietitian in Joe Christmas' orphanage

Married: Dennison Hawk and his wife

In the heat of midsummer, the Sartoris railroad finally opened {U}. The first train, decorated with flowers, pounded through Jefferson with John Sartoris in the cab furiously blowing the whistle all the way and even more furiously when he passed the home of Redmond, the man with whom he began this venture [1886] and the man whom he later drove out of it [1870].

In Frenchman's Bend, Will Varner began buying up every parcel of land he could lay his hands on, including Grenier's now-abandoned Old Frenchman's place {H}.

At Sutpen's Hundred sometime this year, Charles Etienne Bon was first informed of his Negro blood, blood which made him by Mississippi standards a full Negro, even though it amounted to only nine percent {A}.

1873

Born: Captain Strutterbuck, later to be a war veteran twice and a Memphis whoremonger many times

Died: Calvin Burden I (b. 1812), shot by Sartoris

Died: Calvin Burden II (b. 1854), shot by Sartoris

Died: John Sartoris (b. 1823), shot by Redmond

This was the year in which John Sartoris killed Calvin Burden I and his grandson Calvin Burden II, two carpetbaggers who had been at work for a few years in nearby districts registering Negro voters [1867] {L}. Fact and legend blur on this event. One version has it that this was one of the Colonel's first acts when he returned from the war in 1865, but as far as I can tell the Burdens were still far away then in Kansas {U}. Moreover, the younger one would have been too young then, eleven, to be registering Negroes or at least too young to be shot for doing it, even by Sartoris. So 1873 must have been the year, and it must have been one of Sartoris' last acts before he got shot himself. The first version says it happened in the Holston House, but it is doubtful that the Burdens would have put up there or even would have been allowed to. The other version has it that it occurred in Mrs. Winterbottom's boarding house, that three shots were fired in uncertain sequence (though two had to have been from the Colonel's lethal derringer) and that, as he strode away, Sartoris apologized to Mrs. Winterbottom for messing up her premises {S}. In any event he did it because they were trying to get a Negro, Cassius Q. Benbow, *elected* town marshal of Jefferson; and the county was to mythologize the event, a process which makes it more timeless and symbolic than historical anyway.

Nathaniel Burden, son of one Calvin and father of the other, buried them and hid their graves so that Yankee-haters could not violate them {L}. Some wondered why Nathaniel never retaliated against Sartoris, though others have explained it away by his pacifistic French heritage and his deterministic belief that what men do is a product of their geographical region, not of their conscious minds. A third version would be, simply, that Redmond beat him to it.

In the midst of all this Sartoris and Redmond were in vicious competition for a vacant seat in the state legislature {U}. It was clear from the start that the war, the railroad, and then the Burdens would make Sartoris the easy winner—which he was. Nevertheless he took the opportunity the campaign offered to defame Redmond's character beyond reclamation; and, on the night of his victory, he took the further opportunity to open a bottle of fine wine and drink to his heritage and damn Redmond's. On this same occasion he presented his sister, Jenny, with a silver railroad oil can with a train, a wreath, and the date "August 9th, 1873" engraved upon it {S}.

Meanwhile, Redmond bristled and wound up challenging Sartoris to a duel {U}. The Colonel, however, declined the invitation, telling Bayard that it was time to stop killing and do some what he called "moral housecleaning." Perhaps that *was* the reason; or maybe Sartoris had just gotten too used to shooting men without giving them time to prepare for it. At any rate, when the Colonel eventually confronted Redmond in the latter's office, he had the trusty old derringer concealed in his cuff, though he never got to fire it because Redmond fired first. And, like Sutpen a few years before him [1869], so ended Sartoris, killed by a pseudofriend he had turned on and used.

This was in September, and Bayard had already returned to his senior year of studies at the University of Mississippi. Notified of his father's death by Professor Wilkins, Bayard returned with Ringo to Jefferson that night, unsure of what course to take but being pushed toward classical revenge by everyone around him. George Wyatt and Ringo were particularly adamant, but most of all so was Drusilla. Earlier that year Bayard had been confused by her attempt to make romantic overtures toward him in the garden and had staved them off because she was his father's wife. Now, dressed in her yellow ballgown, she handed him two duelling pistols and a sprig of verbena, saying that she would give him the latter once he had done what she said was his fated task. But a look into Bayard's eye revealed to her that he would not do it, and she broke into a fit of hysterical screaming. Meanwhile, Aunt Jenny, displaying the common sense which had become her trademark in the county, supported Bayard in his preference not to act. The next morning, flanked by Ringo and Wyatt, Bayard approached Redmond's office and entered alone. Almost immediately Redmond fired two shots but had purposely aimed them away from the young man he was sure had come to kill

[106]

him. Bayard did not fire back. With this settled, Redmond stood, donned his coat and hat, walked out of the office, boarded the southbound train without baggage, and left Jefferson forever. As Bayard emerged from the office, Wyatt and Ringo acquiesced in his decision to end the bloodletting; and when he returned home he found the sprig of verbena on his pillow nonetheless. Apparently Drusilla had accepted his choice as well, but she had already left, perhaps on the same train with Redmond—to live the rest of her life with her brother Denny who was reading law in Montgomery, Alabama.

Meanwhile, at Sutpen's Hundred, Clytie and Judith found a shard of mirror under Charles Etienne Bon's pillow {A}. The boy, it seemed, had been searching his face in the privacy of his room for the 9% of blackness he had been told was there. And at the McCaslin plantation, or at least what was left of it, Hubert Beauchamp finished his borrowing from Ike's bequest [1867], taking the silver cup as the last hockable item and stuffing all his IOUs into a coffee pot in its place {G}.

Finally a new black man showed up in Jefferson this year. Known as Tom Tom Bird, he was employed to fire various of the town's boilers in its city installations {T}. Later he would become one of the very few among us to be able to outsmart, at least once, the otherwise unoutsmartable Flem Snopes. [1914]

1874

Born: Zachary "Zack" Edmonds (d. 1921)

Born: V. K. Ratliff

Born: Jack Houston (d. 1907)

Born: Anse Bundren

Born: Lucas Beauchamp, sixth and last child of Tomey's Turl and Tennie, third to survive

Born: Molly Worsham, later to be the wife of Lucas Beauchamp

Married: Uncle Doc Hines and his wife

Married: Bayard Sartoris II and his wife

The hunting parties had by now established themselves as a ritual [1871]. Twice a year, Major DeSpain, General Compson, Sam Fathers, and the others went out to DeSpain's camp on the Tallahatchie River to shoot deer and, once a year, pursue a giant bear called "Old Ben." This was the first year that, to the best of his recollection, Ike McCaslin, only seven, resented being left behind. Yet Sam Fathers, the old part-Indian, part-Negro woodsman, had already noticed the boy's interest and spirit and had begun to teach him about the woods {G}.

Teaching of a grimmer sort was going on at Sutpen's Hundred: Clytie had begun to teach Bon's son to do physical labor despite the hindrances of his slight build and weak constitution {A}. A rumor was abroad that Sutpen himself had fathered him on Clytie, but Clytie was just acting out of her own semiconscious realization of what the boy's black blood implied for the remainder of his life. But in the 1870's *most* people were working hard with their backs—there was still too much reconstruction to be done. Lt. Backhouse [1862], now known as Backus, was working a small farm in the county and drinking cold toddies and reading Roman poets in his spare time {K}. Some had *less* work to do now: for example, the Ballenbaughs, whose ferry had been rendered virtually impotent by the arrival of Sartoris' railroad [1873] {R}. Moreover, since law enforcement was still in the hands of occupying federal troops and their appointed toadies, the ferry landing became before long a den of thieves [1876].

1875

Born: John Sartoris II (d. 1901)

Born: Stuart McCallum

Born: Raphael Semmes "Rafe" MacCallum, twin brother of Stuart

Born: Addie Bundren (d. 1930)

Born: Milly Hines (d. 1893)

Born: A blind Negro who spent much time on Jefferson streets in his later years playing a mouth organ and a guitar

An uneventful year by all indications, but its sheer uneventfulness reflected its return to stability and order after a volatile postwar decade. Ike McCaslin, at eight, was still learning the law of the woods from Sam Fathers {G} [1889]. Dr. Peabody began courting the wife it would take him fourteen years to court sufficiently. And Mrs. Compson, always doing her best for freed Negroes, gave an old resident of the local poorhouse called "Old Het" her not-so-old coat, a coat Het wore well into the twentieth century [1926]

{T}. In Frenchman's Bend, Will Varner, who now owned most of the land in the district and was renting it out to sharecroppers, took the opportunity to establish the only cotton gin thereabouts and thereby managed to get his hand also into the part of the crops the sharecroppers shared in {H}. Elsewhere, Uncle Doc Hines and his long-suffering wife gave birth to their only child, Milly; and Uncle Doc (it was said later) was thrown in jail for brawling the very night she was born {L}.

1876

Died: Jobaker (Joseph Baker), a hermit, a friend of Sam Fathers

The one-hundredth birthday of the United States but only the 96th insofar as the Mississippi count was concerned. A hugh Centennial was held in Philadelphia, and northern industrialists paraded forth their newest inventions which would, ultimately, make horses, mules, and probably even men and ground obsolete. And, as if fate had waited for this celebratory year to spring it, the Presidential election wound up with Rutherford B. Hayes the contested winner after his own Republican party gave all the contested votes of South Carolina, Louisiana, Florida, and Oregon to him instead of to Samuel J. Tilden, to whom they probably belonged. And in Montana, a Yankee general named Custer, the one who cornered Robert E. Lee at Appomattox, was massacred by six thousand Indians.

In Yoknapatawpha, Jobaker, a hermit and friend of Sam Fathers, was found dead in his forest cabin {G}. This is insignificant in itself, save that Sam holed up in his hut and shot at the Negroes who approached to remove his body. When he had frightened everybody away, Sam burnt the hut, with Jobaker in it, to the ground. Meanwhile, Ike McCaslin, still awaiting his chance to hunt, took up reading the ledgers that Buck and Buddy had kept, and Old Carothers McCaslin had kept before them. These ledgers, though a mystery to him this year, would reveal enough about the corruption of his family and his race to cause Ike to give up his claim to the McCaslin land a dozen years hence [1888].

Elsewhere in the County, the current Ballenbaugh had fully succeeded in turning the now-useless ferry landing into a nighttime haven for cattle thieves {N}. Reports were that he distilled whisky too. And one day a federal agent was found shot to death in the vicinity of where everyone else presumed Ballenbaugh's still to be. Ballenbaugh was never troubled about this, for, while the county (now governing itself again) did not like Ballenbaugh, it liked federal agents even less.

On the lighter side, one of Yoknapatawpha's most often-traded horses, a nag known to us only as "Beasley Kemp's horse," was swapped by one of the best-known horsetraders in the state, Pat Stamper, to Herman Short for a mule and a buggy {H}. If the horse itself was no good, as it was to prove itself to be many more times [1880] [1881], you can bet the buggy and mule either died or petrified or corroded within a week after Stamper managed to unload them on someone else.

THE PRESIDENCY OF RUTHERFORD B. HAYES, 1877–1881

1877

Died: Sophonsiba Beauchamp McCaslin, wife of Uncle Buck, mother of Ike

With the death of Jobaker, Sam Fathers announced (not asked) that he would live in the Big Bottom alone now {G}. Even though he paid Sam a salary for undefined work, Cass Edmonds permitted this because he knew he could not stop it. This was in March.

Boon Hogganbeck, sixteen now, borrowed $4.75 from somebody to buy a Texas paint pony somewhere and brought it home one day wired between two gentle mares. When he reached Jefferson, however, it managed to break loose and drag him through the dust on his stomach down the main street of Jefferson. After he finally freed himself it took him two days and seven miles to catch it, which is less time anyway than the people of Frenchman's Bend were to spend a few years hence [1908] on their own wild horses {H}. People in this county were, and still are, natural born fools about horses.

When Sophonsiba Beauchamp McCaslin died this year, Ike was left an orphan at ten {G}. Some of the Edmondses suggested that he should open his bequest from Uncle Hubert early, the one which no one knew yet was not even there [1873]. But Ike refused to violate the spirit of the "gift." He had finally outgrown rabbits and possums, and he was allowed to go on his first November hunt with DeSpain, General Compson, Walter Ewell, Sam Fathers and the others. Because of his lack of seniority, he was given the poorest deer stand and caught nothing. As he waited in vain, however, he acquired a sense of his own fragility and impotence against Nature and sensed all about him the awesome presence of the Bear Old Ben, though he never saw him. He also became accustomed to the sense of ritual which surrounded these hunts—everything from killing honorably and well, to hunting Old Ben only on the last day, to Major DeSpain's annual admonition to the old black man Uncle Ash not to wrap the reins around the brake of the mule buggy—and Ash's yearly defiance (or just disregard) of it.

In Frenchman's Bend, Vynie Snopes, Ab's wife, decided she needed a milk separator and began to save for four years to buy one [1881] {H}.

1878

Born: Amanda Workitt

Born: Labove

Born: Sidney Herbert Head

Cass Edmonds gave his younger cousin Ike McCaslin a gun this year, a gun Ike was to use for the next seventy years, though the only part of it which would last the whole seventy was the silver trigger with his and Cass's initials on it {G}. On the November hunt, Boon Hogganbeck, seventeen, wandered into the DeSpain camp and was accepted as a member of the hunting party because, in some ways, he was needed {R}.

1879

Born: Lucy Pate, later Houston (d. 1903)

Boon Hogganbeck got into some kind of squabble on the main street of Jefferson with a Negro man this year and fired five shots at the man as he fled from Boon's brute strength {G}. Never able to shoot a gun and hit what he aimed at, Boon caught a Negro woman in the leg with one of the shots and smashed a $45 plate glass window with another. Cass Edmonds paid for the window and DeSpain for the woman's hospitalization; and Boon was re leased in their custody. Given twenty-six more years, Boon would find occasion to do this again [1905] {R}.

The November hunt was eventful this year {G}. Uncle Ash insisted on shooting and not just cooking this time, so he was allowed one shot at a bear with an old pump gun and some shells General Compson had given him as a souvenir a few years back. As good a marksman as Boon, Ash missed the bear but became intrigued by the expended cartridge on the ground. He laid the gun against a log while he went over to pick up the shell; but the gun chose to fire into the air of its own accord while Ash was doing so, scaring the entire party enough that they never let Ash shoot again. Cass Edmonds, on the other hand, shot a big bear this year; and Ike, locating a buck's bedding place and staying patiently in it to await its return, killed his first deer. After he did so, Sam Fathers slit the buck open, dipped his hands in the hot, smoking blood, and smeared it on Ike's face. On this day, the last one of this year's hunt, Ike at twelve became a man. The hunt was composed in 1879 of General Compson, Major DeSpain, Cass Edmonds, Walter Ewell, Ike, Sam Fathers, Boon Hogganbeck, Tennie's Jim, and, of course, Uncle Ash. Ewell shot one of the biggest bucks he ever killed, so this year was particularly memorable for him as well.

A court trial captured some interest in Jefferson this year. Charles Etienne Bon, now twenty and still confused about the Negro blood he was told he had but could not see or feel, attended a Negro dance at which he started a fight and whipped out a knife {A}. He got the worst of the brawl and appeared in court in handcuffs and bandages. General Compson paid his fine and got him off by using his influence with Justice Jim Hamblett. Compson took him into the judge's chambers and advised him to go North, for there he would be white enough to live as a white man. Bon went [1881].

Since the U.S. government had not figured out yet that it could shake income tax out of its citizens' pockets just by ordering them under penalty of jail to pay it, it was not illegal when Doc Peabody quit keeping financial records on his practice this year, something he had promised himself he would do when he attained a theoretical worth of $10,000 {O}. Elsewhere in the County, Ab Snopes, apparently finding it safe to roam around now with John Sartoris dead and Bayard mellowed, took up residence on Anse Holland's land where V. K. Ratliff, five, and his father were also working a small portion of ground {H}. Uncle Doc Hines, who used to lay track for Sartoris, was now working as a foreman at a sawmill in the next county but was probably already programmed by irrevocable fate to return to Yoknapatawpha in fifty more years [1930] {L}. Also programmed by fate fifteen or twenty years ago, the Ku Klux Klan was in its heyday in the county, though no one knew for sure who was a member and who was not {G}. Those who were would not have been respected for it, but neither would they have been blamed.

1880

Born: Lee MacCallum

Born: Jody Varner

Born: Gail Hightower II

Born: Bobbie Allen

Died: Sophia Allison

General Compson gave Boon a gun for this year's November hunt, but Boon missed five shots in a row when he fired at his first deer {R}. Walter Ewell, however, killed a six-point buck from the caboose of a lumber train he was riding to a nearby settlement to buy supplies {G}. Ike killed his first bear this year; and the dog Lion, who was to be trained for eventual battle with Old Ben, tangled with and killed a doe and a fawn [1883].

In the Frenchman's Bend area, Grenier's once imposing mansion (The Old Frenchman's Place) began to be pulled apart for firewood by neighboring residents {Y}. Beasley Kemp bought the horse which Herman Short had traded Pat Stamper for four years ago from Herman for eight dollars [1876] {H}. Though it has been mythologized as Beasley Kemp's horse, this is the first time Beasley ever owned it. And he didn't own it for long either, for he soon traded it to Ab Snopes for straight stock and an old sorghum mill which Ab had "borrowed" from Anse Holland. This trade would have Ab burning barns before too much longer [1894].

In the North, Charles Etienne Bon was travelling from place to place, starting fights over his Negro blood and getting into them over his coalblack girlfriend {A}.

Finally, a controversy arose over some wording on John Sartoris' tombstone [1873]. Redmond's family objected to the words "By Man's Ingratitude He Died," feeling that this reflected libelously on Redmond, who was, by now, dead himself {S}. Bayard, about thirty now, agreed and had the wording changed to read "Fell at the Hand of Redmond."

THE PRESIDENCY OF JAMES GARFIELD, March–September, 1881

THE PRESIDENCY OF CHESTER ALAN ARTHUR, 1881–1885

1881

Married: Charles Etienne de Saint Velery Bon and a coalblack Negro woman

Having poured over his ancestors' legends for some years now and having progressively learned a different code of conduct in the woods, Ike McCaslin began to realize and partially understand the wrong and the shame of the South {G}. At fourteen still too young to act on his accruing wisdom, he took to reading the Old Testament intensely, and to hunting probably just as intensely. For the first time he was invited along on General Compson's June birthday celebration hunt to shoot raccoons and turkeys for two weeks. One day, at Sam Fathers' urging, he went out to stalk Old Ben and was gone for eighteen hours, nine out and nine back. Frustrated during the day at not seeing the bear, Ike laid his gun, compass, and watch on a rock and proceeded farther into the woods. Finally Old Ben, as if a mystical vision, rose up and showed himself, stared at young Ike for a moment, and then ran off into the woods. When Ike returned to camp and told Cass Edmonds and Walter Ewell of his experience, Cass could not understand why Ike had not shot the animal at his first sighting. But this was the difference between Cass and Ike.

In the spring, the wild yellow dog, Lion, had killed one of Major De-Spain's new colts, and DeSpain decided to bait him with the colt's carcass to capture him. Lion was soon a prisoner in DeSpain's corncrib where he kept throwing himself at the door until he became weak enough for Sam Fathers to touch him. All during the summer, as President Garfield lay dying from Guiteau's bullet in Washington, Sam and the others tried to bring Lion under their power by a cycle of feeding and starving him until he became dependent upon them. By November a special relationship had been established between Boon and Lion; and the whole party agreed that, if they were ever to have a dog worthy of stalking Old Ben, Lion would have to be it. And it was on this year's hunt that General Compson, one-armed, became the first of the party to draw blood from Old Ben, though the bear got away and healed for another year [1883].

In Frenchman's Bend, honor was generally of a more commercial sort, though domestic frugality and horse-trading instinct came into severe conflict this year {H}. Vynie Snopes, after four years of painful saving [1877] had gotten together enough money to buy her coveted milk-separator and sent Ab and young V. K. Ratliff to Jefferson to pick it up. But Ab, being the unfortunate present owner of Beasley Kemp's horse, was destined to become the victim of three different trades with the notorious Pat Stamper before the day was out. As soon as Ab spotted Stamper on the road to Jefferson, he sent V. K. into Whiteleaf's store for saltpeter, tar, and a fish hook. The two of them then painted the horse, fed him the saltpeter, and stuck the hook under his hide; and suddenly Ab became the owner of a very spirited horse indeed. As a result, Ab was able to swap Stamper Beasley Kemp's horse and his own mule for a pair of matched mules. Back on the road to Jefferson, the gloating Ab quickly discovered that the mules were too weak to pull the wagon; and he and Ratliff wound up pushing it and them into town. When a crowd gathered around shouting that this was "Stamper's team" and laughing at Ab, he bought a pint of liquor and consumed it in two gulps. Then he and the boy picked up their separator and pushed their wagon and mules sheepishly back out of town. Encountering Stamper again, Ab negotiated a trade in which he gave up the matched team and the milk separator for his own mule and a fat horse, which was all that Stamper would offer or take. On the way home, chagrined already at the loss of the separator, they watched the fat horse change color in a rainstorm and, then, shrink. It was, of course, none other than Beasley Kemp's horse painted and inflated with a bicycle valve. So at this point the day's trading had Ab down one separator. Vynie, of course, was furious when they arrived home; but, with the help of Cliff Odum, she took their mule and Beasley Kemp's horse back to Stamper to trade for the milk separator. This turned out not to be enough, however, and she was forced to throw in their cow as well, the one which was giving the milk she was bent on separating. Total Snopes loss: one mule, one cow, and Beasley Kemp's horse, not to mention four years of saving up for the separator. As a result, Ab became, in Ratliff's words, "soured on life" forever. Ab left the district and V. K. would not see him again for thirteen years [1894].

And there is another animal story that belongs to this year. Ned McCaslin, a Negro who had assumed the surname of the family who had owned his forebears, "borrowed" Cass Edmonds' mare and mated her with the farm jackass to create a mule monstrosity which the county has not seen the likes of since {R}. Edmonds decided to punish Ned by making him pay for the use of his animals at the rate of ten cents a week for the next three years [1884]. But Ned was easily able to do this since he was entering his freak in every mule race for miles around and winning every one of them by luring it home with a handful of sardines [1905].

Charles Etienne Bon returned to Yoknapatawpha County after a two-year absence [1879], married now to the coalblack woman and father of the child with which she was pregnant {A}. He settled on Sutpen's Hundred to farm a small portion of it. He kept to himself and was seen in Jefferson on only three occasions.

1882

Born: Jim Bond

Born: Flem Snopes (d. 1946)

Married: Ab and Lennie Snopes

Died: Vynie Snopes

Uneventful in Yoknapatawpha County. It would someday be meaningful to countians that Germany, Austria-Hungary, and Italy formed the Triple Alliance in Europe [1914]; but it mustn't have seemed so now. Within the McCaslin-DeSpain alliance, however, Ike began raising a filly; and the others continued to ready Lion for his ultimate combat with Old Ben {G}. People drifted into the DeSpain camp now just to get a peek at this much-touted dog; and in November Lion pursued the bear for the first time—but into a river, and Ben managed to swim to safety several miles downstream. This November also was the first time that Boon Hogganbeck was officially "in charge" of General Compson who, at sixty-five, had made a somewhat sudden turn in the direction of senility, though he was to endure for nearly twenty years longer [1900] {R}. He continued to hunt with enthusiasm until the end.

Flem Snopes was born this year.

1883

Born: Mink Snopes

Born: Eck Snopes (d. 1918)

Born: Net Snopes and her twin sister, to Ab and Lennie Snopes

Born: Negro companion of Hoake McCarron

Married: Alison Hoake and McCarron

Died: Sam Fathers (b. 1803)

It was apparent to the hunting party and all others alike that this was to be the year that Lion became ready to fight Old Ben on his own terms {G}. On the final day of the November hunting trip, the day traditionally devoted to the pursuit of the bear, Lion *did* trap Old Ben about five miles from the Tallahatchie River. He held the big fellow at bay long enough for Boon to get five shots at him; but, as always, Boon missed all five and the bear got away. Boon felt unworthy to sleep alongside Lion that night. But the party resolved not to wait another year for its next try, however, and extended the hunting trip by four days. Boon and Ike were sent to Memphis for more liquor and supplies and got there by riding the caboose of a logging train to Hoak's Junction, a combination sawmill and commissary and from there hoboing along the main track to Memphis. In the city Boon got drunk to drown his misery and caused them to miss their return train. By the time they did get back to the camp, five more Jeffersonians had joined the party for what all perceived to be the final showdown with the long-sought Ben: Jason Compson III, fifteen; Bayard Sartoris, now thirty-four; his son John II, about eight, and two others. After breakfast, twelve more arrived. The party set out around 9 A.M. and quickly crossed the river to the other side because Lion seemed to sense that Ben had done the same. He was correct; he overtook the bear on the other side and pounced on his neck until Boon could catch up for another try. Then, while Ben and Lion grappled furiously on the ground, each bent on killing the other, Boon jumped on Ben and stabbed him repeatedly with his knife until he finally, almost incredibly, lay dead. But at the very moment Boon succeeded, as if there were some mysterious connection between his life lines and the bear's, Sam Fathers collapsed and fell face first into the mud. Boon, torn and exhausted, hoisted Lion on his back while the others carried Sam Fathers to his cabin. Tennie's Jim went to get Doc Crawford at Hoak's. When Crawford arrived, he assured them that Sam would be okay, that Lion's innards could be sewn back inside him, and that Boon's cuts would heal. Boon, knowing better, sensed that Sam, at least, had given up and wanted to die; but it turned out to be Lion that did so first.

Fifty townsmen actually attended the animal's funeral. They held lighted pine knots during the ceremony in the woods. Perhaps what they really wanted to see was the dead carcass of Old Ben, but most of them found him too scary to look at for long. So all departed for home except Ike and Boon, and they stayed behind to watch over Sam Fathers. Sometime that same night apparently Sam told Ike and Boon to build him an Indian funeral platform, kill him, and burn his body. By the dawn the first and last of these had been accomplished, but none ever knew for sure whether Boon killed Sam or whether the old woodsman passed on naturally. When Cass Edmonds later demanded to know, all the while admitting that he himself would have killed him if Sam had asked him to, Boon refused to answer; and young Ike ordered his cousin to "leave him alone." Each would carry this secret to the grave.

Though the deaths of man and beast at the DeSpain camp were the most important events of 1883 in the county, several others are worth mentioning. Ike turned once again to his reading of the McCaslin ledgers and vowed to make restitution for the inhumanity and disgrace he saw recorded there [1879]. At Sutpen's Hundred, Judith, echoing General Compson's advice of a few years ago, told Charles Etienne Bon to go north, that she would take care of his wife and son; but this time, unlike the last, he simply refused {A}. On the McCaslin land young Lucas Beauchamp, later to be known as "the most uppity nigger in the county" but now only nine, began saving coins and knotting them in a rag {G}. He stored them in the old dispatch box of his white grandfather, Lucius Quintus Carothers McCaslin. At Hoak's, some-time earlier than when Ike and Boon passed through there, Alison Hoake had jumped out a window into the arms of a man named McCarron and disap-peared {H}. Her father awaited their return, sitting on the front porch of the commissary with a shotgun on his lap for ten solid days; but when they came back they were married and about to be the progenitors of one of the great male sex symbols of Yoknapatawpha County [1884], though it would be some twenty years yet before he would have the opportunity to demonstrate and prove that [1907].

Also this year, the Sartoris railroad was taken over by a national syndicate, and Bayard used the profits to open a bank in Jefferson {S}.

In New York the Brooklyn Bridge was opened.

All of this happened in the Year of the Bear, a year which marked the zenith

[117]

of the Yoknapatawpha wilderness and, necessarily and by definition, the beginning of the end of it.

1884

Born: Henry "Hawkshaw" Stribling

Born: Col. Sartoris "Sarty" Snopes, youngest child of Ab and Lennie

Born: Hoake McCarron

Born: Alice, a friend of Joe Christmas at the orphanage

Born: Harriss

Born: Tomey's Turl Beauchamp II

Died: Charles Etienne de Saint Velery Bon (b. 1859)

Died: Judith Sutpen (b. 1841)

Died: Juana Burden

The Yoknapatawpha wilderness began to die because northern logging companies started to cut it down at a faster pace. Ike was to go to DeSpain's hunting camp one more time [1885], but the Major himself never went again {G}. In January and February, General Compson and Walter Ewell suggested to DeSpain that they start a hunting club and lease hunting privileges, but he flatly refused. In June the hunt which annually marked General Compson's birthday was not held; and in November no one showed up either. A few of the old party did hunt that fall, but they went out of the county to a site forty miles farther away. Old Ben, Lion, and Sam Fathers were all dead by now; and all the rest seemed less alive [1883].

In Jefferson there was a yellow fever scare in January when the county medical officer diagnosed it in Charles Etienne Bon. But Judith Sutpen had already contracted it and, on the 12th of February, was the first to die {A}. Before she passed away she enlisted General Compson to buy a tombstone for Charles who she knew would die later that year (and did). When Judith went, Rosa approached her benefactor, Judge Benbow, and ordered him to secure a stone for Judith's grave as well [1866]. Benbow, as always, did what he was ordered. With both gone, Clytie and Jim Bond became the only residents of the once grandiose Sutpen's Hundred; and this half-black monkey bravely took over the raising of this half-crazy boy. For the next twelve years she also assumed the payments for Bon's tombstone as well [1896].

Evidently no epidemic did, in fact, break out. Miss Emily Grierson was sick for two years around this time [1886], but I doubt this can be attributed to yellow fever {"A Rose for Emily"}. The real disease the county had at this time was one called "Ballenbaugh"—the roadhouse on the northwest route out of the County, not too far from Sutpen's Hundred, had by now acquired a reputation which brought the scum of the south, and the lower reaches of the North, from every corner [1825] {R}. Political candidates campaigned and got elected on this one issue alone—that they could and would rid the county of the place—but none was able to live up to it.

This was the year Anse Holland moved up to Jefferson from Frenchman's Bend {K} and the one in which Sally Wyatt was conducting her one-sided courtship of Judge Benbow's son, Will {S}. In Frenchman's Bend also, Jack Houston should have been going to school but wasn't, staying home instead to learn his father's farming business {H}. In Jackson, Jackson College for Negroes was founded {N}; and Jefferson Davis made his last public speech in the State House, though he was to live five more years [1889].

THE FIRST PRESIDENCY OF GROVER CLEVELAND, 1885–1889

1885

Married: Nathaniel Burden and a woman from New Hampshire

Died: Father of Emily Grierson

In the spring of this year Major DeSpain sold his woodland to a lumber company which was already timbering the lands to the north of his {G}. In June Ike McCaslin and his cousin Cass Edmonds went to DeSpain to request one last hunt before the woods were cut down. DeSpain agreed, though he refused to participate himself. Ike then went to Hoak's, where Boon had been serving as town marshal since January, to bring him back for this final outing. He was not there, however, so Ike, playing a hunch, returned to the site of Lion's and Sam Fathers' graves, the place where Old Ben's paw hung in an axle grease box above them. As he approached he heard a clanking noise, which he discovered in a few minutes to be Boon beating on the barrel of his disassembled gun with the stock. Squirrels chased helter-skelter on the tree behind him. When he heard the approach of what he knew to be another man, Boon, without looking up to see who it was, screamed out in hysterical

[119]

defiance "Get out of here, they're all mine." Somehow Ike brought Boon to his senses, though how is unknown.

On December 29th, James Beauchamp (Tennie's Jim) vanished from the County on the night of his 21st birthday without claiming the $1000 bequest from Old Carothers McCaslin [1833] {G}. Since Jim was the first (besides his father) of the part-white McCaslins to live long enough to be entitled to it, Ike set out to Jackson, Tennessee, to give it to him, resolving to start now to undo the wrong and shame of his ancestors. He never found Jim, though, and was forced, on the 12th of January, 1886, to return the money to Cass Edmonds in trust.

Two of the town's eccentric ladies were briefly noticed this year. General Compson discovered a folder of Rosa Coldfield's poems, over a thousand of them, poems she had written at the rate of one a day during the war but which no one until now knew about {A}. Miss Emily Grierson's father died this year, and for three days she refused either to accept that fact or to have him buried {"A Rose for Emily"}. Finally some townswomen imposed upon her; then some men came in and took the reeking corpse to an already-dug grave and filled it in quickly.

With his father, his son [1873], and his wife [1884] now dead, Nathaniel Burden sent a letter to his relatives in New England, asking that they find him a good moral woman and ship her to him immediately to be his wife {L}. Late in the year he married a woman from New Hampshire, the woman who was to be the mother of the ill-fated Joanna Burden shortly thereafter [1930].

1886

Born: Horace Benbow

Born: Hope "Hub" Hampton

Born: Allison, daughter of Major DeSpain's sister

Born: Tug Nightingale

Born: McWillie

Born: Bobo Beauchamp

Married: Sophonsiba Beauchamp and a preacher

As it had for several years, the complicatedly intermixed lineage of Mc-Caslin-Edmonds-Beauchamp continued to dominate the activities of the County in 1886. Sophonsiba Beauchamp, seventeen, fifth child of Tennie and Tomey's Turl and second to survive birth, went to Cass Edmonds and announced that she planned to marry a preacher man {G}. Cass accepted this and wished them well, though it is not certain whether he informed her of the money that would be due her from her white grandfather's will in four years. Ike McCaslin entered the hardware business, this in partnership with the Charlestonian who had built blockade runners during the war [1861] and ships since then [1865] but who had by now moved to Jefferson. Percival Brownlee, the most useless of all McCaslin slaves before the war [1856], was now reported, by a countian who had just returned from there, to be quite financially secure in his new position as proprietor of a select New Orleans brothel.

Progress came to Yoknapatawpha this year in two different forms. First, the town council appropriated money to have sidewalks laid along several of the main streets, and a man named Homer Barron arrived from the North to supervise the project [1887] {"A Rose for Emily"}. Before long it became known that he had entered into an affair with the heretofore beauless Miss Emily Grierson [1929]. Second, the Ballenbaugh mess was finally cleared up, not by law or edict, but by a strapping Baptist minister who had learned to fight in the war—Hiram Hightower {R}. He cleaned out everything—booze, whores, gambling, thieves, and probably a couple of killers—simply by walking in, laying his Bible on the table, and then beating them up one by one, and soon two by two, with his bare fists, all this in the duration of an hour or so on a summer night. This done, the Ballenbaugh building was converted by Ballenbaugh's daughter into a store and hotel and the land around it into a farm.

Out at Hoak's, where Boon Hogganbeck was still marshal, Hoake McCarron and his Negro companion were growing up together, sleeping in the same room, as they would for the next eight years [1894] {H}.

In the North, the AFL was organized, but hard workers remained pretty much independent of each other in Yoknapatawpha for a long time to come [1938].

1887

Born: Joanna Burden (d. 1930)

Married: "Old Anse" Holland and Cornelia Mardis

Died: Homer Barron

A murder was committed in Jefferson this year that no one would know about for forty-two more years [1929]. Homer Barron had laid his last

[121]

sidewalk and, to put it perhaps too crudely, had done the same to Miss Emily Grierson {"A Rose for Emily"}. It was time for him to move on, leaving Emily with only the affair and not the marriage she had thought would come of it. So she went to the local druggist, bought some arsenic, poisoned him, and stashed his corpse in her bedroom. Since Barron was due to leave town anyway, no one connected the fact of the bad smell they began to notice around Miss Emily's with the other fact that maybe he hadn't. Whether she committed this crime to avenge her honor or to practice some impossible form of reverse necrophilia (or maybe do both) we were never quite sure.

Ike McCaslin, unsuccessful at finding Tennie's Jim to give him his share of the McCaslin bequest [1885], now set out for Arkansas and the more findable home of Sophonsiba Beauchamp and her preacher husband {G}. Though they had little money, they refused the thousand dollars Ike handed them because they "wanted to be free." Ike respected their wishes but, to quell his own conscience, placed the money in a trust at a local bank to be sent to her at the rate of $3 a month for the next twenty-eight years [1915].

In Frenchman's Bend, Will Varner bought up what was left of the Old Frenchman's Place {H}. In Jefferson a former resident of the Bend, Old Anse Holland, married Cornelia Mardis and moved into her father's home {K}. And in Jackson, the townspeople sponsored a three-day Kermis Ball to raise money to build the now well-known monument to the Confederate dead {N}.

Like the rest of the country, Yoknapatawpha County had, for some time, been fighting the evils of railroad monopolies, for even the Sartoris line was now part of the Illinois Central. With the Interstate Commerce Commission Act, passed this year, countians believed that President Cleveland had ended the high freight prices they were being charged to ship their crops to market. But, like most other acts of the U.S. government, it was a piece of paper that did nothing for us or for anyone else. Resentment against the centralized federal government, festering to begin with, greatly intensified during this and ensuing years.

1888

Born: Spoade, in South Carolina

Died: Terrel Beauchamp, "Tomey's Turl" (b. 1833)

At long last the restoration of Jefferson Courthouse was completed and no evidence of the severe pounding it took two dozen years ago [1864] survived. It now had a roof and a four-faced clock {N}.

Ike McCaslin, now twenty-one, after many years of reading the McCaslin ledgers, at last repudiated his ownership of the McCaslin land [1876] {G}. He was the only white male grandchild of Old Carothers McCaslin; so by fate the land had fallen to him. On the occasion that he did this, he declared that Sam Fathers had freed him from everything but the land, so now he was freeing himself from that. He believed this to be, moreover, only a symbolic gesture, for—as he told Cass—he was in accord with his father's and uncle's philosophy that the land owns the people and the people cannot own the land [1837]. In the act of placing the land in Cass's care, Ike voiced the opinion—held by many of us today—that things went wrong in the county when Ikkemotubbe realized that the land could be sold for money [1813]. God, Ike professed, wanted Old Carothers McCaslin to have it because the Indians had misused it. Failing in his role as God's instrument, however, McCaslin and men like him caused the Civil War, the suffering by which God always reminds man to abide by His Law. Ike still felt, though, that the South was God's chosen land despite the fact He had allowed it to be ravaged, that He loved the southerners because they loved the land and were courageous in its defense. After discoursing like this for some time, Ike opened his bequest from his Uncle Hubert [1867], only to find—in the place of the silver cup and the gold pieces—a coffee pot stuffed with IOUs [1873].

After he left the land, Ike received offers from Old General Compson and Major DeSpain to live with either of them, but he refused to and moved instead into an old house in Jefferson. He ran his hardware store and lived off its meager profits and off the $30 a month Cass would pay him for the land for the rest of his own life (which now only had nine years left in it) [1897].

In Frenchman's Bend Jack Houston, still only fourteen, was beginning to attract notice. It was well known in the district (as everything gets well known if one hangs around Varner's store long enough, which almost everyone who was male did) that Jack was already using whisky and had a Negro mistress a year older than he. Also, having put off school by every device he could, he was finally forced to enter the first grade. Big even for fourteen, the six-year-olds surrounded him like Lilliputians. A girl named Lucy Pate assisted him in his studies (and in his fights against those who made fun of him) [1903]. She was the star pupil of the second grade in the one-room schoolhouse. When it became clear late in the school year that Houston was going to fail the first grade, Lucy made sure she failed the second. During the summer, Houston was one of those who worked in the erection of what became known as Tull's bridge, a bridge that was to be of service to the district for over forty years until it was washed away in the flood of 1930 {D}.

Elsewhere in the state, Gail Hightower, eight, discovered the trunk in the attic which contained his grandfather's military jacket {L}. From now on the ghost of the man he believed was a hero (but who really wasn't because he did not die fighting Grant but rather raiding an old woman's chickencoop

[123]

[1864]) haunted him. Before long he resolved to get to Jefferson some day to live on the spot of his relative's demise [1903]. He was to get there and suffer his own demise as well. This was assigned to him by Fate at the age of eight.

THE PRESIDENCY OF BENJAMIN HARRISON, 1889–1893

1889

Born: Margaret Stevens, later Mallison

Born: Gavin Stevens, her twin brother

Born: Eula Varner (d. 1927)

Born: Anselm "Young Anse" Holland

Born: Virginius Holland, his twin brother

Born: McKinley Grove, brother of Lena, in Alabama

Married: Dr. Peabody and his wife

Married: Jason Compson III and Caroline Bascomb

Died: William C. Falkner (b. 1825)

In late May word reached Yoknapatawpha County of the Johnstown flood. It is doubtful that it caused too much excitement in Mississippi, and lots of folks probably felt the state of Pennsylvania was getting what it deserved. But one black man named Hatcher was sufficiently disturbed to clean his lantern, gather up his wife and meager possessions, and assume a position on the highest knoll in town, the one behind the graveyard {F}. They descended only after several days of waiting for the flood waters to drift down this way. Hatcher was so mortified he never cleaned his lantern again, lest some irrevocable process of association make a fool of him the second time.

Down at the Bend Will Varner's wife had taken to lying naked in the moonlight in order that her seventeenth child, with which she was now pregnant, might be a girl (her first). It was and the Varners named the child Eula. Will redrew his will, bestowing upon her a quarter (instead of a seventeenth) share and gave each of his sons 4⅔% shares {T}. For the next three years, the Varners pushed Eula about the town in the first perambulator

Frenchman's Bend had ever seen [1892]. She would outgrow the perambulator long before she would learn to walk.

Dr. Peabody finally succeeded in marrying the girl he had courted for
fourteen years [1875] {S}, and Willy Christian took over management of the
drugstore his father had founded in Jefferson in the 1850s. {"Uncle Willy"}.

1890

Born: Lucius Peabody, IV

Born: Minnie Cooper

Born: Otis, nephew of Corrie Hogganbeck

Idle gossip. North of Jefferson the DeSpain hunting camp was disassembled by the logging company; but the old hunting party—consisting of
many of the same but also some different members—resumed the November
expeditions after a lapse of some six or seven years [1884] {G}. At Hoak's,
young Hoake McCarron beat his Negro companion in a fair fist fight {H}.
Near Frenchman's Bend to the south, Jack Houston, at the age of sixteen,
failed first grade for the second time; so he went home, got a pistol, and left
the county to join a railroad gang in Oklahoma—not so much to free himself
from school as to get away from Lucy Pate who was purposely flunking along
with him just to bolster his ego. Addie Bundren, a fifteen-year-old less-than-
attractive farm girl, bemoaned the fact at Varner's Store one day that her
outlook on life was being poisoned by her fatalist father's repetitive statements that people are only born to live a short time to get ready to be dead a
long time {D}. V. K. Ratliff, only sixteen himself, mused otherwise to her;
but he had a near contact with death himself this year. His old grandfather
contracted some problem with his leg—perhaps a shotgun shell might have
been what he contracted—and Doc Peabody had to amputate it {S}. V. K.,
the women, and the other children were told to hide behind the barn to save
their pristine ears. Although the old fellow lived for several more years,
Ratliff never forgot the furious cursing he heard from the house while the old
guy drank whiskey through the severing. Nearby, Mink Snopes was growing
up with a father who continually beat Mink's stepmother, so much so that
Mink went out one day and shot her a squirrel which they then both cooked
and savored together. A tender scene of which most countians would have
considered Mink incapable {M}.

In Jackson, the Mississippi State Convention drew up our present constitution {N}.

[125]

Born: Quentin Compson (d. 1910)

Born: Shreve McCannon, in Canada

Born: Tommy (d. 1929), an innocent who was to be come involved with big
time bootleggers.

Nathaniel Burden led his four-year-old daughter Joanna out to the cedar grove in which the graves of her grandfather and brother were hidden [1873] {L}. There he made a wild and haunting speech to her about how the Negro was the white man's curse and doom, that no white could go to heaven until the black man had been lifted out of his earthly subjugation. He concluded with finality that no white man could ever accomplish this; and so all whites, including Joanna, were cursed, damned and doomed, marked for Hell from their births forward. Joanna never forgot this moment and spent her entire adult life trying to resist this fate and was cursed, damned, and doomed simply because she bothered to try [1930].

At Hoak's, young McCarron was steering a middle course in such matters by paying his Negro companion an agreed-upon sum to allow him to beat him with a riding crop at periodic intervals {H}. Cass Edmonds, a McCaslin if even only on the distaff side, was trying in his own way to raise up his Negroes as well {G}. In this year he presented the most liberatable of all the Yoknapatawpha blacks, Lucas Beauchamp, with a handmade beaver hat. Lucas, seventeen, accepted it, as he did most things that were offered to him, though not all [1936].

A circus came to Jefferson this year, a rather unspectacular one, and the only thing anybody was to recall of it later was a toothless tiger which gave nightmares to young children like five-year-old Horace Benbow {O}. And, lastly, Stonewall Jackson Fentry left his father's farm in this year to take a job at the sawmill near Frenchman's Bend {K}.

1892

Born: Candace "Caddy" Compson

Born: Melissa Meek

Born: Vaiden Wyott

Born: Gerald Bland

Born: Joan Heppleton, sister of Belle Mitchell

Died: Father of Joe Christmas

Forced out of her perambulator, not by the fact that at three she could finally walk, because she couldn't, but by the fact that her sheer mass of hip and pelvis could no longer fit through the opening comfortably or otherwise, Eula Varner was now planted in a chair, a piece of furniture she was removed from only when the exigencies of housekeeping (and probably nature) forced that she be {H}. Yet already the residents of Frenchman's Bend recognized that this was a feminine force to be dealt with, in not as many years to come as most would suspect [1898].

At the McCaslin land Lucas Beauchamp and Zack Edmonds both reached eighteen this year; and, since they had—though black and white—virtually grown up together, a sort of joint party was thrown to celebrate what in Yoknapatawpha was recognized as the attainment of manhood {G}.

Elsewhere, in the small Arkansas town where Doc Hines was currently working, a circus caravan had managed to get itself bogged down on a muddy road during a severe rainstorm {L}. Some of the circus folk went to the nearest house, Hines', to get some block and tackle equipment to extricate themselves; but one of them—a dark-skinned man, perhaps mulatto, perhaps Spanish—stayed behind to seduce Uncle Doc's daughter Milly. With the circus still stuck the next day, Milly went off with the man a second time; and, when she returned, her father beat both her and, symbolically, all "bitchery and abomination" in the world. He then went out in the dark, ran down the man he supposed to be his daughter's violator, and killed him, not at all sure in his own mind that he had gotten the right man. But Uncle Doc dealt in symbols and to this extent he was satisfied. Milly had conceived a child by this man, however, a child who would be almost logically determined to arrive in Jefferson in 1927 and be killed here in 1930.

In Jackson, Millsaps College opened this year {N}.

THE SECOND PRESIDENCY OF GROVER CLEVELAND, 1893–1897

1893

Born: Bayard Sartoris III, "Young Bayard" (d. 1920)

Born: John Sartoris III (d. 1918), his twin brother

Born: Narcissa Benbow

[127]

Born: Jason Compson IV

Born: Joe Christmas (d. 1930), in Arkansas

Married: Ike McCaslin and his wife

Died: Milly Hines (b. 1875)

Died: Mardis

Died: Old Man Hoake

The South felt some spinoff this year from the Federal bungling in gold and silver and suffered somewhat more than the rest of the country in the Panic that occurred in August; but it had come to accept such things by now, if for no other reason than that there was nothing it could do about it. In Jefferson electricity was being introduced into some of the more well-to-do homes (like my own), and streetlights were being erected {T}. Tom Tom Bird, the town's best-known burner-firer, was hired to fire the burners at the electric plant [1873]. Jefferson could not match, nor did it want to, the electrical displays it read of at the World's Fair in Chicago, however.

The most relevant news for Yoknapatawpha, not now but in the future, was occurring in Arkansas {L}. That summer Milly Hines gave birth to the child later known as Joe Christmas [1930], and in fact she died in childbirth when her father refused to get her a doctor. Uncle Doc Hines then attempted, unsuccessfully, to place Joe in a Little Rock orphanage in the first few days of his life. In November, Hines took a job in another orphanage; and, on December 23rd, while his wife was chopping the wood she maybe should have been, Hines crept into the house and stole Joe away to place him in the same orphanage in which he worked as a janitor. He accomplished this by setting him on the doorstep the next day, allowing him to be found there by a young intern.

Ike McCaslin was wed this year to a nondescript woman he should not have married {G}. They went to live in a cheap frame bungalow dowried on Ike by the woman's father, but the woman had great designs. Though he would never admit it, Ike was apparently confronted on his wedding night and offered his wife's maidenhead—if, indeed, she still had it to offer—in return for his reacquisition of the McCaslin land from his cousin, Cass Edmonds [1888]. He made a half-hearted promise to do so; but even then the woman knew he never would and cried herself to sleep. It was said later by some that Ike never saw his wife naked a second time and realized right then that he would never have the son that he had probably married to get in the first place.

If Ike was trying to stay clear of land in 1893, Anse Holland inherited a good chunk of it when his father-in-law, Mardis, died {K}. And a young man named Odlethrop committed a murder this year and fled the County, though the repercussions of this were still to come [1903] {K}.

1894

Born: Lucius Quintus Priest II, known as "Loosh"

Born: Buck Thorpe (d. 1917), also known as "Jackson and Longstreet Fentry" and as "Ripsnorter"

Born: Joel Flint

Married: Judge Allison and his wife

Married: Stonewall Jackson Fentry and Miss Thorpe

Died: Mrs. Fentry (Miss Thorpe)

Died: Mr. McCarron, father of Hoake

From this point on in this chronicle information and accuracy will increase significantly, for it was in this year that V. K. Ratliff became an itinerant sewing machine salesman who travelled over four counties and committed to memory everything he heard {H}. I was five years old myself and still hearing more than I retained, I fear.

One event Ratliff remembers vividly is the return of Ab Snopes to the county for the first time since Pat Stamper whipped him three times on the same weekend a dozen or so years before [1881]. Apparently he got kicked out of Grenier County for squabbling with a man named Harris and, it seems, burning down his barn to settle the argument he had already lost with words {"Barn Burning"}. On the day after the hearing in which this happened to him, Ab arrived on Major DeSpain's property to work some of his land; and, to set things straight from the start, he invited himself through the front door of DeSpain's house and trompled on Miss Lula's imported white rug after first tromping in some homemade droppings from DeSpain's domestic white horse. (Sarty's brother Flem did not go along, perhaps even then able to foretell that this would someday be *his* house [1927] and, therefore, a house into which horse dung ought not to be tracked.) That afternoon a Negro bearing the rug for cleaning was sent to Ab's camp. Ab and his two daughters cleaned it so well that they shredded all the fur off it;

[129]

and then Ab and his ten-year-old son, Sarty, flung it on Major DeSpain's front porch. DeSpain, furious, brought Ab before the justice in Jefferson for his second trial in a week. Fined ten bushels of corn, far less than DeSpain demanded, Ab resolved to burn DeSpain's barn to the ground as he had Harris' and probably others'. In the midst of the preparations, however, young Sarty became disillusioned, for his father had heretofore always sent a nigger to warn the barn owner what might happen if he did not see things Ab's way. But no Negro was sent on this occasion, the code of barn-burning honor was about to be broken, and Sarty tried to break away to warn DeSpain. Restrained for a time by his brother, Flem, and his two sisters, he got away but arrived too late at DeSpain's to prevent the fire. Sarty, though, disappeared from his family and the County forever. DeSpain was unable to prove that Ab had burned the barn, and Ab cancelled his contract with DeSpain because he felt the two of them "would not get along" {H}.

The seeds of tragedy were sown in Stonewall Jackson Fentry's life this year {K}. Preacher Whitfield married him to a Bend woman named Thorpe, even though Fentry knew she was already expecting another man's baby. Late in the year she died in childbirth, leaving Fentry to raise her son alone. Though he gave him his name and raised him conscientiously for several years, he would lose his "son" some years hence when the Thorpes would come forward to "claim kin" [1897] {K}.

In Jefferson, Bayard Sartoris, in his forties now and known as "Colonel" just because his father was one, was elected mayor and quickly confronted by a stink raised by Miss Emily Grierson (and she rose several stinks of various sorts over the years she lived here [1885] [1887] [1929]) over the payment of taxes, an item which she, like many, did not comprehend {"A Rose for Emily"}. Eventually Sartoris, never able to cope with a strong-willed woman anyway, exonerated her from these or any future taxes, claiming that her father had loaned money to the town and this was the town's way of repaying it.

At Hoak's, young McCarron felt ready to set out in the world this year after his mother brought his father, found dead in a Memphis gambling house, home for burial {H}. It would be a few more years before Eula Varner would be ready for him, however [1907]. Elsewhere Doc Hines took up residence near the orphanage in which he worked and had placed Joe Christmas, to watch him grow up to be God's instrument against womanfilth and lust {L}.

1895

Born: Maury (later Benjy) Compson (d. 1935), an idiot from birth

Born: Byron Bunch

Born: T. P. Gibson, a Compson servant because his mother was

An important year for the Compsons, or at least a landmark for Jason III's wife, Caroline (Bascomb), with the birth of the idiot son, Maury, who would have to be renamed Benjy later [1900] to protect his no-account uncle's ego {F}. The familial doom she had been anticipating almost since the day of her marriage began to take shape [1890]. Compson blood was not, she felt, of the quality of Bascomb blood, though no one hereabouts had any other samplings of Bascomb blood except Uncle Maury's and his blood didn't seem all that good.

On March 17th, Lucas Beauchamp became twenty-one years old; and, unlike the others, Ike did not have to trace this dark-skinned grandson down to give him his $1000 bequest {G} [1885] [1887]. Lucas showed up for it this very day and insisted upon being taken down to the bank where the teller counted it out before his suspicious eyes. Lucas then told him to put it back, which certainly did not mean "give it away."

In this year Jack Houston began living with the woman he picked up in a Galveston brothel, a woman he was absolutely faithful to for the next seven years {H} [1902]. It was fortunate that he did not continue in the Frenchman's Bend school [1890], for the new teacher there was a woman named Miss Addie {D}. Permeated by her father's misanthropy [1890], she took no small pleasure in whipping her students and scorning their petty hopes and desires. One day Anse Bundren wandered by and, before long and for some reason, proposed marriage. Having no better offers, she took him.

In Jefferson, Emily Grierson began giving china painting lessons to local ladies. None, of course, knew what she had in her bedroom {"A Rose for Emily"} [1887].

1896

Born: Oldest daughter of Henry Armstid

Married: Anse Bundren and Addie

Married: Lucas Beauchamp and Molly Worsham

I was seven in this year and by now I was receiving and recalling if not understanding what was happening about me. If Benjy Compson signalled his family's doom, certainly young Jason, spoiled terribly by his grandmother (whom the children called Damuddy), was the clearest evidence of it {F}. At three, he was operating like a Snopes at thirty. His acquisitive instincts were already finely honed.

[131]

Lucas Beauchamp took a wife this year; and Cass Edmonds, holding land to which he was not entitled [1888], tried as he often did to relieve his McCaslin guilt by building the newlyweds a house and giving them a portion of the McCaslin fields to cultivate {G}. Lucas took this, of course, as his due, for Edmonds was only a distaff McCaslin whereas Lucas was straight out of the male side. Ike McCaslin, guilt-ridden as well, gave Lucas and Molly a walnut bureau that he had made himself as a wedding present.

Anse MacCallum showed up in town one day with two Texas horses which, unlike most of the horses from Texas which would leak (or run) into this County [1908], worked well for him for the next ten years {H}. He had traded fourteen rifle cartridges for them, their former owner probably figuring he would have gotten the best of the deal if he had only gotten half as many. Ab Snopes left the County once again this year [1894], his incendiary activities now too well known to allow him further employment [1902].

At Joe Christmas' orphanage, his single friend, a twelve-year-old girl named Alice, was adopted and taken away {L}. Joe was left to fend for himself under the watchful eye of the old janitor he could not have known was really his grandfather.

Gold was discovered in Alaska, it was heard, but no countian went to find any and certainly none ever *got* any.

THE PRESIDENCY OF WILLIAM McKINLEY, 1897–1901

1897

Born: Cash Bundren

Married: Zachary Edmonds and Louisa

Died: Cass Edmonds (b. 1850)

One of those personal tragedies that only a Fate conscious of what it was up to could even have invented happened this year. Stonewall Jackson Fentry, three years a widower after being only a few months a husband [1894], attentively raising the boy who was not even his own but came along as a liability of his wife's (and whom he had named Jackson and Longstreet Fentry), was forced to turn the boy over to his wife's brothers {K}. The Thorpes, after three years, had come to "claim kin"; and there was legally nothing that Jackson could really do about it, though he had long since considered the boy his own. Unable to bear the loss, Fentry left the County.

One day he would return [1903] and, in unfortunate circumstances, encounter the boy again [1917].

If a dead horse can be thought of as doomed, the Compson doom continued—Nancy fell in a ditch and Roskus had to shoot her {F}. For several days thereafter buzzards stripped away the mare's carcass before the amazed eyes of at least three of the Compson children.

At the orphanage early this year, Joe Christmas first became aware, much in the manner Charles Etienne Bon had, of the confusion of identities caused by the supposedly Negro blood which waited in his veins {L}. Joe had the misfortune to call the gardener a nigger, and the man replied that nobody but God would ever know what Joe was. Later this year he was caught stealing toothpaste from a medicine cabinet and was severely reprimanded—which did not, unfortunately, cure his love for the taste [1898].

1898

Born: Carothers "Roth" Edmonds

Born: Forrest Gowrie

Born: Henry Beauchamp

Died: Damuddy Bascomb

Died: Louisa Edmonds

Died: Sis Beulah Clay

Evidence, perhaps, that some of the North-South animosities had been alleviated in the course of three decades was the fact that many countians went to fight this year in the Spanish-American War {S}. John Sartoris II was one of these and Manfred DeSpain was another {T}. Son of the Major and a West Pointer, Manfred served as a second lieutenant under a captain named Strutterbuck. He came through the Battle of San Juan Hill unscathed; but, after Cuba was occupied, he was wounded in an altercation with a sergeant in a dice game {M}. Manfred later said the scar on his face came from a Spanish bayonet, and it took most of us a long time to know any differently. Frankly, most of us thought the fact that the sergeant fought him with an axe more sensational and would have stuck to that story ourselves {T}.

Young Quentin Compson started school this year; he was very bright {F}. I knew this because we were in the same room despite the fact that he was a couple of grades behind me. But he was a strange, contemplative boy who had a close relationship with no one save his sister, Caddy, with whom he used to sit for hours on end chatting tirelessly and reading picture books. That summer their grandmother, Damuddy, died; and Quentin became very upset, as I recall, but not at that. On the day it happened all the Compson children, having been sent outside to play, chose to go wading in the creek which ran by the Compson land. Caddy slipped and got her dress wet, and the Negro servant Versh helped her take it off. But Quentin got furious and slapped her, causing her to fall and get her underpants all muddy. When they got home, Jason, of course, "told" on them, but neither mother nor father was particularly interested in the midst of the funeral preparations. Caddy went on to take charge at the supper table. After dinner they went out to play with lightning bugs with Frony and T. P., two of Dilsey's children; but, noticing all the lights on in the house, Caddy climbed the well-used tree beside the Compson house [1928] to take a peek at what she thought was a party. Dilsey made her get down and take the children in the house for bed. All this while, though, young Quentin, only seven, sat in the barn by himself, musing on Caddy's behavior and her threat that she would run away because he had hit her. That night Caddy and Benjy slept in the same bed in the spare bedroom, while Quentin and Jason slept in the other. If Quentin's relationship with his sister was close before this day, it was to become rather perversely protective after it.

Earlier this year, in March, Lucas Beauchamp had to do some protecting as well {G}. He and Molly had their first child in January. In March, the big flood of 1898 swelled the creeks in the northern part of the County; and in the same month Roth Edmonds was born, son of Zack and Louisa. But Louisa did not survive the birth. Thus, despite the fact she had her own two-month-old son to worry about, Zack asked Molly, shortly after Henry's baptism (at which Miss Habersham was godmother {I}), to come to nurse young Roth {G}. Molly did so and stayed six months until September. So at about the same moment Quentin Compson seemed first concerned about his sister's six-year-old maidenhead, Lucas had decided to kill Zack for sleeping with his wife, though this was purely an assumption on his part. He ordered Molly home, told Zack he would have to come to his house from now on if he wanted Roth suckled, and then waited—razor in hand—for him to show up. But Zack never did, so Lucas went to the Edmonds' farm, entered the house, and accused Zack of feeling able to fool around with another man's wife because he was white and the other man was black. Zack was further dumbfounded when Lucas whipped out the razor and told Zack to get his pistol. Zack did not want any part of this, but Lucas had questioned his courage enough that he could not do other than comply. In the fight that ensued, Lucas and Zack wrestled furiously on Zack's bed for the pistol which had been tossed in the middle of it, Lucas eventually muscling the nose of it

[134]

to Zack's chest and firing. But it misfired, and both men sobered and stopped fighting. Later that day Lucas returned to plowing his field, unable to figure out why the gun did not go off; and Molly returned to nursing Roth Edmonds—at Zack's. How much of this county's history hangs on guns which failed to fire? [1907] [1930] [1946].

Also this summer some events were occurring in and around Frenchman's Bend which were ultimately to mean something. Addie Bundren had quit as schoolmarm shortly after she married Anse, and her replacement—an older man—simply could not keep order [1896] {D} {H}. Will Varner, by now in charge of most things in the area, was quietly on the lookout for still another, particularly since his daughter, Eula, was starting school in the coming session [1899]. Though Will would not find out about him for another year, there was a man known only as Labove attending the summer session at the University of Mississippi and, after that, working at a sawmill to get enough money together to go back in the fall. In September the college football coach, recognizing a certain multipurpose athletic ability in the man, talked Labove into playing for him and got him several part-time jobs to earn some cash. Through the fall Labove played football, a game he quickly and intensely hated; what he had decided, however, is that he was entitled to one pair of football cleats for each game his team won. These shoes he would send home to his impoverished and heretofore shoeless family, five pairs in all since the year's record was 5–1–1.

While Labove played football and pilfered shoes, Eula Varner entered the one-room school in Frenchman's Bend, not by her own desire or even her father's, but by Jody's decision that this pulsating mass of feminine tissue (heavy-breasted and well beyond puberty at nine) was likely to become the receptacle of every spare drop of human semen in the northern part of the state unless she got herself otherwise occupied. Yet Jody could not even get her to school and then pick her up again without every male in and around the Bend panting in the manure-strewn tracks of the horse he carried her on. If he speeded up, she began to bounce; the studs behind would break into low whines and begin to run faster. If he rode slowly her dress climbed a quarter-inch up her thigh with each clip-clop of the horse's feet. Jody was hysterically eager to have this stopped but insofar as I know never succeeded.

Not at all interested in sex or womanhood was Joe Christmas, five now and still in his orphanage. In October, while Quentin stewed, Labove broke tackles, and Eula bounced, Joe was still indulging in his one simple pleasure, nursing furiously at the nipple of a tube of toothpaste {L}. One day, however, he took too much and threw up in the very room where the orphanage dietician, Miss Atkins, and an intern were making love. Miss Atkins assumed he was spying on them and called him a "nigger bastard" but later wound up giving him money to be silent about something he really did not even understand or know was going on. Since she knew the janitor (Doc Hines)

[135]

hated Joe as much as she did, she enlisted his help to have him adopted. But Hines merely shrieked at her that Joe was God's instrument against fornicators and womansin. With nothing left to do, the dietitian went to the matron of the orphanage, revealed Joe's heritage (or what she believed it to be), and convinced her that Joe should be removed from the premises as soon as possible. Two months later, Joe was adopted by a man named Simon McEachern and had his name changed to Joe McEachern. It seems that Doc Hines also got instructions from God at this time to kill Joe so that this little nigger bastard, product of womansin himself, would not ruin the face of the earth; but the boy was gone before Hines could effect His Will. He would try again some thirty-odd years later [1930]. Having no further reason to stay at the orphanage, Hines quit and moved himself and his wife to Mottstown, just to the south of the County line from Jefferson.

Jack Houston moved from Galveston to El Paso during the year {H}, still with the woman he picked up a while back in a brothel there [1895]. Mink Snopes, the man who was to kill Houston but still had never met nor heard of him [1907], quit going to church, seeing nothing in any churchgoer he wished to emulate once nor hearing anything from any preacher he wished to listen to twice {M}.

Finally, Campbell College for Negroes was moved from Vicksburg to Jackson this year {N}.

1899

Born: Buddy MacCallum

Born: Darl Bundren

Born: Montgomery Ward Snopes

Born: Bart Kohl (d. 1937)

Died: Cornelia Mardis Holland

The first half of this year was uneventful with the exception of one peculiar incident. Some strangers moving eastward from Arkansas picked the place the Sutpens used as their graveyard to camp in one night and were run out by a something they could articulate only sparsely and understand not at all {A}. None in the town ever knew exactly what happened, though some theorized it was some spooking device cooked up by Clytie to rid herself of unwanted neighbors. Or could it have been Jim Bond himself, already crazy enough to spook anybody without even meaning to?

Otherwise perhaps the most ultimately significant event was the opening of school. I was in the fourth grade this year, Quentin Compson in the second, and his sister Caddy was in the first {F}, along with Melissa Meek (eventually to be the town librarian [1943]), and, of course, the Sartoris twins, John and Bayard. On the first day some of the older boys challenged them to a fight over their long curly hair, a fight they took up quickly and before long won {S}. On ensuing days larger groups containing larger boys threw down the gauntlet again and again, but the Sartorises beat all comers. They were getting themselves badly scarred, though, and usually went home with their clothing in shreds; so old Simon cut off their hair one day and the fights stopped, to everyone's relief.

This was the year Labove became schoolmaster in Frenchman's Bend, though he was never seen in Jefferson until a basketball tournament the following year {H} [1900]. In January he returned home from his football season with a sweater bearing a big red "M." This was appropriated by his grandmother, as one pair of cleats had also been earlier in the season. The other four pairs were shared around among the rest of the family, depending on who needed them on a given day. On a muggy one in July, Will Varner visited Labove's father, who rented land from him, and noticed the old woman walking around the house in football cleats and a letter sweater. Upon curious inquiry, he learned of the son's education and, since the previous schoolmaster was gone entirely now, offered him the job, explaining to him how he could pursue his studies, play football, and work, all at the same time. Labove accepted. In October he opened the school and rode every Friday night to Oxford, played football the next afternoon, slept Saturday night in Oxford, then returned to the Bend on Sunday. During the week he spent his nights reading and his days teaching—in the same classroom—students who ranged in age from six to nineteen, including Eula Varner, who was ten now. In his "spare" time, he set to fixing up the old run-down school building.

Hoake McCarron, Labove's antithesis in every way, including his appeal for Eula [1907], began studying in a military boarding school. Mink Snopes, at sixteen, went whoring in Memphis for the first time, but he would return there for the same purpose many times after that {M}. Another resident of the Bend, Addie Bundren, gave birth to her second son, Darl, this year and made Anse promise to bury her in Jefferson whenever she happened to die {D}. Anse would later regret this [1930].

People who weren't in our County yet but coming toward us, in time if not in space, were active in this last year of the nineteenth century. Herbert Head, to marry Caddy Compson [1910], was thrown out of his club at Harvard for cheating at cards and then out of Harvard altogether for cheating on exams {F}. Gail Hightower began his three-year courtship of his wife {L} [1903]; and a man named Van Tosch moved from Chicago to Memphis to breed racehorses {R}. He would later hire Jefferson's Bobo Beauchamp as a stable boy.

1900

Born: Gowan Stevens

Born: Daughter of Odum Bookwright

Born: Crawford Gowrie (d. 1940)

Born: Ruby LaMarr

Born: Popeye Vitelli (d. 1930)

Born: Grandson of Toby Sutterfield (d. 1918)

Married: Vitelli and his Wife

Died: Jason Compson II, "General Compson" (b. 1817)

Died: Julia Benbow

Natural gas and oil were discovered in Mississippi, especially in the vicinity of Jackson, and a great influx of population from Texas and Oklahoma ensued to grab up the wealth before it was depleted {N}. But none was found around Jefferson, and it continued to be a town which never fully made the shift between the agrarianism it was used to and the industrialism it wasn't. A case in point is General Compson who died in senility at eighty-three this year and was still paying off the mortgage he took out on his land in 1866 by selling off portions of it for ready cash. The Compson Mile had been virtually cut to a pasture, which he willed to his idiot grandson, Benjy. His son Jason, however, now drinking heavily and writing satiric eulogies about his townsmen in their postwar milieu, would before many more years sell off even that to the local golf club [1909]. But Jason III was a good, kindhearted, gentle man who had a little too much of those three virtues to fit well among what the turn of the century had reduced most people to being.

The Compson family endured several other trying events this year. When Dilsey became deathly ill, they got another younger Negress to do their housekeeping {"That Evening Sun"}. This woman, Nancy, had been having (as they later found out) sexual relations for pay with Mr. Stovall who was both cashier in the bank and deacon in the Baptist church. When she asked

[138]

him in public one day for overdue payment, he beat her, kicking out some of her teeth. Now pregnant by either Stovall or her husband, Jesus, she was usually afraid to go home for fear that, because of the now infamous altercation in town, Jesus would kill her. Often she slept in the Compson home after doing Dilsey's duties. But one night, when she was compelled to return home in the dark, she lured Quentin, Caddy, and Jason to go with her for protection, promising them popcorn on the other end. Quentin and Caddy were eager for this and for the Negro ghost stories she always told them, but Jason was recalcitrant and threatened continually to "tell" on them, something he spent most of his childhood doing. Later Mr. Compson came to fetch the children and spent some time comforting Nancy, but to no avail. As he led the children home, Nancy, sure that Jesus was lurking outside, took up singing and moaning in funereal fashion. As far as I know, this Jesus at least never got her.

In November, despite the protestations of Caddy and Dilsey, the youngest Compson boy—the idiot—had his name changed by his mother from Maury to Benjy to salvage the last shard of self-pride Uncle Maury, after whom he was named, managed to have {F}. Benjy, whose sense of order was continually being ruptured by his mother in such ways as this, howled through the entire occasion on which this was revealed to him, despite the efforts of Caddy and her father to comfort him. Quentin just watched the whole proceedings with grim passivity. That very day he had been in a fight at school with a boy who put a frog in Caddy's desk; and, once the current scene was ended, he retired quietly to his room to study. Like Damuddy's death two years before [1898], this change of name and his mother's behavior were symbolic to Quentin of the disintegration he sensed in his family, in his southern heritage, and in his own inner self.

If the Compsons were crumbling, the Sartorises were trying to hold their name and their tradition together {S}. On March 16th, the twins, John and Bayard, were given inscribed Bibles as presents from their mother. On Sunday, June 10th, Jenny Du Pre unveiled the monument to the Confederate soldier on the town square; but the statue, which was supposed to have faced defiantly North, was pointed accidentally South. This was never corrected {N}. At the unveiling, tottering former Confederate officers, some of whom had already sacrificed sons in blue uniforms during the Spanish-American War, wore their old grey colors and fired their shotguns in the air. And it was about this year as well that old Will Falls began walking into town from the county poor farm eight to ten times a year for visits with Old Bayard to tell and retell stories of the heroism of John Sartoris and all those like him {S}. Each time the story was embellished and the myth grew larger, but the Sartoris family unified itself around these very legends. Since Bayard had been hard of hearing ever since the bridge explosion of 1863 and heard little of what Falls said anyway, he would pretend that the old man was somewhat of a bother to him; but he gave him tobacco and peppermint every time he came and bought him a new suit of clothes every year for the next nineteen.

In Frenchman's Bend now, the second greatest force at work, behind Will Varner himself, was Labove {H}. Though he had already begun to notice the eleven-year-old blob of sexuality in front of him, she had not gotten the best of him—yet. In January he was gone for a week while he took his final examinations in Oxford. When he returned, he and some town boys cleared land for a basketball court; and for the next year and a half [1901], playing without shoes, they beat every team in the district, including the one I was on at the Jefferson school [1906]. Meanwhile, Hoake McCarron, the rival he never even knew about, philandered away a year at his military school [1907].

Boon Hogganbeck returned to the district this year [1885], surrendering his position as marshal at Hoak's {R}. He moved into the Commercial Hotel in Jefferson, built to be—but never succeeding at it—the rival of the Holston House. He lived there except on those occasions when Zack Edmonds was gone from his land at night. When this happened, he moved in with Zack's young child, Roth, to protect him and see to his needs.

Mink Snopes ordered a gun this year, the one he would kill Jack Houston with in the future [1907] {H}. And Miss Habersham bought the famous round black hat which would hereafter become her trademark and which she wore for the rest of her life {I}.

In Mottstown, Uncle Doc Hines, crazier than ever and now out of a job because he was, spent most of his time visiting various Negro congregations and preaching white supremacy {L}. Ironically, the same Negroes who heard him would make gifts of food to the Hineses because they knew that Doc was flat broke [1905]. In Memphis, Lucius Binford became Miss Reba's faithful lover and helped her manage her whorehouse [1929] {R}. In Pensacola, a strikebreaker impregnated a woman (whom he later married) with a child who was to come here before thirty more years would be up and commit a murder {Y} [1929]. This county has woven enough bad fate for itself without having the sexual needs of a syphilitic Florida work-scab embroidering on it as well.

THE PRESIDENCY OF THEODORE ROOSEVELT, 1901–1909

1901

Born: Sebastian Gauldres, in Argentina

Born: Clarence Egglestone Snopes

Died: John Sartoris II (b. 1875)

Yellow fever was back in the county this year and took, among others, the life of John Sartoris II, grandson of the Colonel, son of Old Bayard, father of Young Bayard and Johnny [1884] {S}. Doc Peabody said it was complicated by an old Spanish bullet from the last war [1898].

Manfred DeSpain, another veteran of that war, brought his red EMF racer to town this year, to the best of anyone's recollection the first automobile ever to penetrate the town of Jefferson and one of the most annoying that ever would {R}. Labove's basketball team from Frenchman's Bend traveled to St. Louis for a tournament and, playing in bare feet and overalls, beat all comers [1900] {H}. Old Het entered the employment of Mrs. Hait [1875] {T}. Aunt Sally Wyatt, finally forced to realize that she would be forever husbandless, shut off her memories this year and became another one of our many eccentric women around here [1884] {O}.

So it was certainly not an important year in the county's history. The chief piece of gossip going around was that Maury Bascomb, parasitical brother-in-law of Jason Compson III, had an affair going with Mrs. Patterson; and it was the idiot, Benjy, who let the town in on the secret {F}. On the last day of school before Christmas, December 23rd, Benjy howled all day to go out. When Caddy came home, she took Benjy with her on her regular and unwitting delivery of one of Maury's lascivious notes to his mistress. On the way back, however, Benjy got caught crawling under a fence and wailed all the while Caddy was trying to unsnag him. Perhaps this is the first time anybody, especially Mr. Patterson, really noticed what was going on. Maury, of course, was furious and soon would be in pain as well [1902].

1902

Born: Melisandre Backus, eventually to be, by a circuitous route, my wife

Born: Louis Grenier, also known as Lonnie Grinnup (d. 1938)

Born: Wallstreet Panic Snopes, to own a chain of grocery stores

Born: Frankie, girlfriend of Belle Mitchell

Born: The tall convict, unrecognized hero of the great flood of 1927

Married: Gail Hightower and his wife

Died: Father of Jack Houston

[141]

Died: First wife of Eck Snopes

Old Bayard Sartoris founded the second bank in Jefferson this year, and Manfred DeSpain became a major stockholder {T}. On opening day Aunt Jenny put a big rubber plant in the lobby, a plant which still stands there today and is more intimidating than ever.

The Maury Bascomb–Mrs. Patterson affair ended this spring with a bang which unfortunately landed on Maury's eye and was placed there by Mr. Patterson's fist [1901] {F}. Maury, it seems, had foolishly taken to letting Benjy deliver the messages for him, and Mr. Patterson had intercepted one while hoeing in his garden. Jason Compson was particularly angry to find out about all this and taunted his wife about the vaunted qualities of her family. Maury himself refused to leave his room until the eye healed and had Versh deliver all his meals to him in bed.

In Frenchman's Bend, Labove graduated from the University of Mississippi, with both an M.A. and an L.L.B., and was admitted to the state bar all in one year {H}. On the night of his graduation he visited an Oxford brothel to celebrate; but then, oddly enough, instead of going out to practice law he returned to his puny job at the Frenchman's Bend school. At first it was thought that he was drawn back by his championship basketball team, but later some people began to realize that it was simply because of his animal attraction to Eula Varner who daily spread her thirteen-year-old legs lackadaisically before him [1906]. Elsewhere, Hoake McCarron, who was to succeed with Eula where neither Labove nor I ever would [1907], had graduated in three years from his military boarding school and was sent by his widowed mother to an agricultural school downstate. Though the standards of the school were low to begin with, Hoake messed around most of the time and did very poorly. Perhaps that is why Labove and I failed with Eula—we worked and studied too hard and forgot how to "mess around," the only thing Eula would understand for a long time to come.

Another resident of Frenchman's Bend, or at least a former one, Jack Houston, ended his twelve-year exile in Texas and came back [1890] [1895] {H}. His father had died this year and left him his land; so Jack split up his savings and gave half to his mistress. After waiting long enough to make sure she was not pregnant, he said goodbye to her and, despite her pleadings to go with him and merely live near him, left her behind in El Paso.

The nearest big city to Jefferson is Memphis; and, with the invention of the automobile, it got nearer than ever {R}. A Memphis man drove his car into town one day but left it here because he could not drive it back over the muddy roads. Mr. Buffaloe, the mechanical genius who kept the steam-driven electric plant running, and Boon Hogganbeck, a genius at nothing mechanical, stared at it in amazement for days before eventually being just compelled to take it apart and see what made it run. They had it back

[142]

together before its owner returned for it, but Buffaloe had already resolved to build one for himself.

Perhaps by car, by wagon, or by foot—but somehow—Bobo Beauchamp got himself to Memphis as well this year and entered the employment of Mr. Van Tosch, though he was generally set on having more fun than he was planning to do work to support [1905]. Another who went to Memphis this year, on one of his whoring trips, was Mink Snopes {M}. But this was the last time Mink would see this city for forty-four more years, and by then his own daughter would be one of its whores [1946].

Elsewhere, Joe Christmas, now eight, was living with his stepfather, Simon McEachern {L}. Each morning before breakfast he was forced to learn and recite his catechism, often with his pants down to his knees so Simon could beat him if the results were not quick or complete enough. On one particular day Joe was beaten so hard he was knocked cold; and, on the next day, his beating had, out of charity, to be withheld till afternoon. On another day, a Sunday, McEachern actually became ashamed of himself for whipping the boy on the sabbath; so he knelt down with Joe and they prayed together. All through this Mrs. McEachern tried to console Joe, but by now Joe only understood brute force and distrusted all such demonstrations of humane feeling, especially when they came from a woman [1898].

Gail Hightower, now in the seminary to study for the ministry, was confronted this year by the girl he had been courting for three years, herself a minister's daughter [1899] {L}. She demanded savagely that he marry her, and he did so.

In Pensacola, after two years of marriage, Vitelli deserted his wife and sickly two-year-old son {Y}.

1903

Born: Howard Allison (d. 1913)

Born: Stonewall Jackson "Monk" Odlethrop (d. 1933)

Born: Matt Levitt

Born: Isom Strother

Married: Mink Snopes and Yettie

Married: Jack Houston and Lucy Pate

Died: Lucy Pate Houston (b. 1879)

Died: Grandmother of Popeye Vitelli

I started high school this year and so automatically decided it was time I started smoking as well, which I never thereafter quit doing {K}. I begin now to have very clear recollection of the people I knew then and, of course, the fates which befell them. Jason Compson IV, later one of the biggest capitalists in the county save that he never got the money to go with his instincts, was hanging around with the Patterson boy (both were ten) {F}. He was spending his spare time making kites with which to deprive the rest of us of the money we earned cutting grass, carrying trash, raking leaves, and filling cisterns. I always identified more with his twelve-year-old brother, Quentin, though, because, like me, he was very interested in the history of the county, the glory of the southern past, and the war which ended it. We often sat around and listened to Indian tales, such as the ones about how Ikkemotubbe took over the Manship from Issetibbeha and various assorted relatives [1803] {"A Justice"}. These were told by an old part-Choctaw man who liked to call himself Sam Fathers even though the real Sam had been dead and immortalized for twenty years now [1883]. On other occasions we would scout out history on our own. Always fascinated by it, Quentin, his black friend Luster, and some other boys went with me one day to see Sutpen's Hundred, now dilapidated for want of a sane male to care for it or any money to do so even if there had been one {A}. We dared each other to go inside and Quentin was about to do it—not out of bravado but out of sheer need to see and feel and know what till then had only been heard about—when we saw Jim Bond howling and slobbering in the yard. As we stood amazed, the monkey-like mulatto woman named Clytie, the very daughter of Thomas Sutpen himself!, ran us off. Most of us were scared enough to never go back, but Quentin one day would have to [1909].

Horace Benbow, the County's best known college student until Quentin and I went, began his freshman year at Sewanee, where his father had gone before him {O}. He was quickly an honors student, and word was about that he planned to be a lawyer. Perhaps I decided at this point to be a lawyer as well, thinking perhaps that that was what you had to be if you went to college.

Mr. Buffaloe built his homemade car this year and had the misfortune, on the very first occasion that he drove it through Jefferson's business district, to scare Old Bayard Sartoris' buggy horses and cause them to run through town smashing the empty wagon into or through whatever got in their way {T}. Bayard had been mayor of Jefferson, so it took him no longer than the next night to have an ordinance passed and recorded which prohibited cars on the streets of Jefferson, a law still on the books and framed in the courthouse today [1904] {R}.

On the subject of less mechanical forms of transportation and speed, Ned

[144]

McCaslin's half-mule–half-horse died at the age of twenty-two [1881], never beaten by mule or horse in any race, and he had raced against anything anyone had wanted him to at any time {R}. He was buried by Ned with great pomp and circumstance, and Ned spent the rest of the year in mourning.

Another man in mourning in 1903 was Jack Houston. Having returned from Texas and taken up the management of his father's land, he married Lucy Pate, the childhood sweetheart who had waited a dozen years for him to get back from wherever it was he was headed the day he left in 1890. Jack found himself madly in love with her; perhaps he always had been {H}. But in June, only a few months after their wedding, Lucy was killed by the stallion Jack had bought himself as a wedding present. Happening upon the scene of her trampling, Houston flung himself on the stallion's neck and tried to stab it to death with his penknife before gaining enough control of himself to back off and shoot it. Jack would mourn for four years without cessation, and even then it would take his own death to stop him [1907].

In this year, Mink Snopes, the man who would kill Houston, was working in a lumbercamp, despite the fact he had left home supposedly to go to sea {H}. Here he fell in love, if that is what Mink exactly could fall into, with the daughter of the camp's owner. She was also the camp's prostitute. Things seemed to boom here, for the owner had free convict labor from the penitentiary, not to mention a free gold-toothed quadroon mistress; but before the year was out the business had collapsed. Mink and Yettie, out on their own now, were married by a Justice of the Peace who held a wad of chewing tobacco in his left hand while he performed the ceremony with his right one. Then they came to Yoknapatawpha County to reside on a poor farm in the vicinity of Frenchman's Bend. Other Snopeses had already preceded them here, of course. Ab's family was currently living on the McCaslin property, and Ab was working Ike's land. His son Flem, always more prone to let money itself do the laboring, had managed to get into a small financial deal with his idiot cousin Ike, who himself was lurking about the Bend telling everyone he was "Ike H'mope."

The most notable arrival in Yoknapatawpha this year, however, was the new minister at the Presbyterian church, Gail Hightower {L}. Though we didn't learn of it till years later, he had arrived here with his wife on the heels of a wild train ride during which he embarrassed her by talking at the top of his lungs about his grandfather's heroism in Jefferson during the war [1864] and how God had predestined him to spend the rest of his life here on the same soil where his grandfather was killed. Hightower must have known by this time that the man was killed raiding a chicken coop, but his conscious mind could not replace the image of heroic raids it preferred to house. Anyway, for the next couple of years, Hightower horrified his congregation with wild sermons in which he interspersed the Bible and the Civil War cavalry legends, surely to the detriment of both [1905]. Yet I always thought

[145]

the man was basically good and decent, for he gave most of his spare cash to charitable causes, such as a home somewhere for delinquent girls, and later would shame himself trying to save a lesser man's life [1930].

Others came back and went away in 1903. A man named Odlethrop, who had left the County some years ago (1893), returned here with a city woman in a smart automobile {K}. He left again before long, and it wasn't till several months later that we discovered that he had left a baby behind which had to be taken in by Odlethrop's mother, an old hermit woman. Jackson Fentry returned to the County to work his father's land again [1897] {K}. And Mr. Boyd, six months after his wife gave birth to their son, Howard, deserted her and left the County {"The Brooch"}. For a while gossip bandied Boyd about, but years later [1930] we were all sure that any man in his right mind would have left, though most men would have taken young Howard out of there as well.

If there is anything that a chronicle of this or any county reveals it is that children are the undefended and undefendable victims of their parents' fantasies and sins. Young Boyd is an example (or would be); but Joe Christmas, Gail Hightower, Quentin Compson, and others were so, just as much. So was the Vitelli boy, a long way off from the county still and not yet known as Popeye {Y}. In this year his grandmother moved in with him and his mother, for the grandmother herself had been deserted by her husband and left penniless. Popeye himself became sick this year with stomach problems which were to plague him until his death [1930]. For whatever reason, his grandmother one day gave him to a Negro chauffeur waiting outside a store, and then she burned down the Vitelli house so his mother would think he perished. Though he was taken to a better home now, he was already predetermined to do what he would do in Yoknapatawpha twenty-six years hence [1929].

Lastly, 1903 was the year in which the new capitol building in Jackson was completed and capped with a golden dome {N}.

1904

Born: Bryan Gowrie

Born: Older daughter of Mink Snopes

Born: Girlfriend of the tall convict

Died: Judge Francis Benbow

One's schoolyears tend to blur. I remember Quentin Compson being reprimanded by the teacher this year for counting down the last fifteen minutes of class every afternoon, but this is all I remember {F}.

[146]

Judge Benbow died this year; and for the first time the town knew what he had been doing to keep Rosa Coldfield solvent when the Judge's son, Percy, found the folio of her account [1886] {A}. By this time the judge had accumulated enough winnings at the Memphis horsetrack to see her through to the end of her life, which surely would have to waste away soon now [1910].

But most of all, 1904 was the year in which the automobile—despite the law against it [1903]—infiltrated Jefferson like ants into an antproof cupboard. Till now only Manfred DeSpain's and Mr. Buffaloe's autos were owned as well as operated here, and this year DeSpain's managed to do the same thing to Old Bayard's buggy horses that Buffaloe's had done the year before [1903] {T}. Bayard tried to invoke the antiautomobile law against DeSpain, but DeSpain retaliated by entering the mayoral election against the Sartoris puppet, Mayor Adams. Cars were the issue, the only issue. Throughout the campaign, DeSpain raced from personal appearance to personal appearance as fast as he could and with the cutout open. The town was behind him even though Mayor Adams and his son Theron tried to invoke the Cuban axe story [1898] to undermine Manfred's candidacy. During a debate one day, Manfred looked straight at Theron on the platform and told him to go get an axe if he wanted to see how well he could fight with one. The crowd loved it and elected DeSpain mayor by a lopsided majority. He continued to drive fast through town, though he dropped the cutout after the election; but the motor age had officially been born in Jefferson. For being the other automobile pioneer in town, Mr. Buffaloe was named city electrician [1903]. DeSpain opened the first garage, gas station, and auto agency. And, as mayor, rather than have the Sartoris law repealed, he had it framed and hung in the courthouse for the public to scorn. The only retaliation Bayard could make was to refuse to lend money at his bank for autos, so people like Luke Provine had to concoct crazy notes to buy their Model Ts.

In the spring of this year, none other than fifty-seven-year old Boss Priest himself, who ran the rival bank to Sartoris', bought a Winton Flyer, not because he wanted one but because he wanted to show up Sartoris {R}. Boon Hogganbeck and Mr. Wordwin, cashier at the Bank of Jefferson, were sent to Memphis to pick it up and, on the way back, had to pay $2 to get towed out of the mud at Hell Creek Bottom [1905]. Boon, though, was crushed to find out that Boss was planning to leave the car in the garage and never use it; but he finally managed to convince him that the car should be driven once a week to keep it from rusting. So, all in goggles and dusters, the entire family would ride with Boon every Saturday afternoon in the spring, and *every* afternoon in the summer. Boon realized what he had in his hands and honored his responsibilities to carriage drivers, assisting both them and their horses in their adaptation to the sound and behavior of the automobile. These afternoon jaunts were almost ended one afternoon, however, when Boss Priest, sitting in front, covered Grandma, sitting in back, with tobacco spittle. Grandma ordered the car home without even wiping off the slop; but by the next day Alison, Boss's daughter-in-law, had created a handshield she could raise every time she saw Boss about to expectorate. Ned McCaslin was the only member of the Priest household who would not ride; everyone else loved it, especially Boon and young Lucius Priest, Boss's grandson.

Meanwhile a bad situation was getting worse at Hightower's church. His wild sermons continued, and Mrs. Hightower began to sit in church (and walk the town) with a stony, embittered look on her face {L}. One week she exploded in church during the sermon, and the congregation raised some money to help the minister send her to a sanitarium for a few months. Hightower went to visit her every two weeks while she was there and went to bring her home in the fall. For a while she seemed better.

Down at Frenchman's Bend, Ab Snopes, having quit Ike McCaslin's, moved back into the vicinity with his wife in April, along with Flem, his two daughters, and a widowed sister-in-law {H}. Jody Varner made the mistake of renting him a farm before he heard about Ab's barn-burning activities some ten years earlier [1894]. Realizing that his guarded pleas not to burn down any of the Varner barns were not getting through to Ab, Jody hired Flem as clerk in the Varner store, even though most people were used to just putting their money on the counter for anything they needed when no Varner was around to collect it from them. But Flem was fire insurance. He did his job very efficiently and even made Will Varner himself pay for his tobacco on one occasion. Flem first became the Flem we came to know and hate on another occasion, however—the time when he lent five dollars to a Negro at Quick's sawmill on the condition that the man pay him ten cents a week for the rest of his life.

The second half of the year was more auspicious down at the Bend. While V. K. Ratliff, our main source of information on doings down there, was in Tennessee selling sewing machines, Flem somehow displaced Jody in Will's favor and by September was given the more important position of tending the cotton gin while Jody had to watch the store. And by October Flem was lending money usuriously to more people than just Quick's Negro. In November, when Ratliff returned, he found Flem already living in a boarding house in town, now too important to hang around on the farm with his no-account father and bovine sisters.

Three other events are significant in the Bend this year. The Armstids, a couple who typified the sort of hard-working people Flem was to ruin, had one of their mules die on them during the spring ground-breaking; so each took turns in the traces with the other mule until the job was done [1908] {H}. Also, in the later part of the year, Addie Bundren, Anse's wife, had an affair with none other than the Reverend Whitfield and conceived her son Jewel {D}. Apparently the affair had been over for two months before she

[148]

confirmed her pregnancy. In the outlying district, Hoake McCarron had returned to be overseer of his mother's farm after being forced to leave college following a short-lived affair with the wife of one of his instructors {H}.

In Memphis Bobo Beauchamp was busy being Bobo and getting into more trouble by the day [1902] {R}. He had begun dabbling in horse-race betting with a white gambler and, by year's end, owed him more than a hundred dollars which, of course, he had not a prayer of being able to pay. But a small band of Yoknapatawphans would be along to aid him the next year [1905].

And this was the year Quentin Compson began being regularly reprimanded for his clock-watching at the end of the school day {F}.

1905

Born: Jewel Bundren, really the illegitimate son of Reverend Whitfield

Born: Younger daughter of Mink Snopes, to be a prostitute

Married: Boon Hogganbeck and Everbe Corinthia

Died: Maggie Dandridge Stevens

Died: Grandfather Lessep

Died: Wife of Gail Hightower, in Memphis

Died: Sophie Starnes, in Division

Forty years ago Henry Sutpen had shot Charles Bon at the gates to Sutpen's Hundred and run away [1865] {A}. This year he crept home, at sixty-six very ill, and returned to the bedroom he had slept in as a boy innocent of the future to which time, fate, and his father had doomed him. No one in town would know he was back for four more years, and by then he would be almost dead [1909].

In the Compson household a certain indefinable tension had been building for some years which was having, as its public manifestation, a deep devotion of both the pensive Quentin and the howling Benjy to their sister, Caddy {F}. In turn, the third brother, Jason, seemed to hate her more each year. For example, Benjy one night howled so loudly on the upper floor of the Compson house that neighbors for blocks away could hear it. It was later explained that he was reacting to some perfume Caddy had begun using, probably to make herself alluring to some of the local lads, and which for Benjy signalled some sort of doom. Quentin on the other hand was known to be having a quite physical relationship with a neighborhood girl named Natalie, though this was probably only to make his sister jealous. One afternoon she all but told Natalie to stay away from Quentin; but later she spied them rolling around together on the floor of the Compson barn, whither Caddy had gone to get out of a driving rainstorm. Upon seeing this, she ran out crying; and Quentin pursued her to the creek. They both fell into it and began smearing each other with mud, Quentin all the while demanding of her "Do you care now?" Later, after settling themselves down, they sat in the creek to clean themselves up [1898]. It was repaired for the moment, but there was an alliance between brother and sister which most of their friends recognized as strange but which few ventured to talk about. To those of us who, like myself at a wise sixteen, tried to understand it, the whole thing seemed less incestuous than it was a desire on the part of Quentin and Benjy to substitute Caddy's love for the coldness, the bitterness, and the constant complaining of their mother.

May of this year was the occasion that Boon Hogganbeck had been waiting for for over a year—when Boss Priest would leave his car unattended and, also, leave town. It came about this way {R}. On Tuesday, the 2nd, Ludus, one of the Negro hands at Boss Priest's Livery Stable, appropriated one of the wagons to go on a six-mile pursuit of a new girlfriend and wound up keeping the mules out all night. When he returned, his foreman—Boon— was furious at him, not so much for stealing and damaging the wagon as for failing to purchase some first class liquor from Uncle Calvin Bookwright which Boon had given him $2 to get. Instead Ludus had brought him a dribble of rotgut, which Boon detected in no time. Boon's boss, Mr. Ballott, laid Ludus off for a week; but this did not quash Boon's anger. On Saturday, the 6th, Boon came rushing through Maury Priest's office demanding a gun. Maury refused it to him, however, so Boon ran down John Powell who carried a pistol *pro forma* as a symbol of manhood. He snatched the gun and, on the main street of Jefferson, fired five shots at Ludus, all of which missed Ludus, though one did crease the buttocks of a Negro girl and another smashed the window of Ike McCaslin's hardware store [1879]. The incident was very similar to another one Boon was implicated in years ago; but this time there was no General Compson left to bail Boon and Ludus out, so Maury Priest had to post the bond for both.

This had pretty much quieted down when, a week later on Saturday, the 13th, Boss Priest and the whole family had to travel by train to Bay St. Louis for Grandfather Lessep's funeral. Young Lucius, eleven, contrived not to have to go and pretended to his family to go to Zack Edmonds' to stay until they got back. What he really did, though, is hop in Grandfather Boss's car,

[150]

once Boss was out of town and his own moral compunctions were out of steam, and set out with the car-crazy Boon for a joy ride to Memphis. They left at 5:30 that afternoon and decided to drive to Ballenbaugh's for the night, though before they got there they discovered that Ned McCaslin had stowed away in the back and resigned themselves to taking him along. When they reached Ballenbaugh's, no longer so riotous a place since Miss Ballenbaugh had taken it over [1886], they gave her and some of the black farmers thereabouts rides in the car. Then they put up for the night.

On Sunday, the 14th, Boon got the car mired, the second such incident in thirteen months, in the mud at Hell Creek Bottom and had to be towed out of it by the same man with two mules who had towed him out of it the previous year [1904]—the differences being that this year the man had deliberately plowed up the road to make crossing impossible and was also charging six dollars instead of two to extricate a car. Without much choice, they paid and finally reached Memphis in twenty-three and one-half hours, a new record despite it all. Since Ned was black he could not stay at Miss Reba's brothel with Boon and Lucius; but he was told to be back at 8 a.m. the next morning or he would be left behind. Only by leaving then could they possibly beat Boss Priest back from Bay St. Louis. Before this day ended, however, Ned had run into the debt-laden Bobo Beauchamp [1904], given the Priest auto to a gambler to settle Bobo's debt, borrowed a horse named Coppermine from Mr. Van Tosch (the breeder who employed Bobo), and returned to the dumbfounded Boon with a plan for winning back the car despite the fact that Coppermine had never won a race in his life. Again without a choice, Boon and Lucius enlisted one of Miss Reba's customers—a railroad man—to get the horse to Parsham, the scene of the race and, probably, of their own deaths if Coppermine lost.

On Monday, the 15th, the group arrived at Parsham and made plans to use Miss Corrie's unethical runt nephew, Otis, to ride the horse. (Miss Corrie, by the way, was one of Miss Reba's employees, a favorite of Boon's.) However, Lucius himself wound up having to do it when Otis refused any payment under twenty dollars. Meanwhile, word about the impending race was getting around and potential betters, and the sheriff, began showing up at the track. During all this Miss Corrie was taking a great liking to Lucius, at Boon's expense, because Lucius continually defended her honor as a woman against all those who saw her only as a whore, a concept of femininity Lucius would not have understood anyway.

On Tuesday, the 16th, Coppermine, running under the name "Forked Lightning," lost the first of three scheduled heats against a horse named Acheron. But this was exactly as Ned had planned it. Before the second heat could be run, however, Boon was locked up for brawling with the sheriff and Ned for stealing a horse—but Ned promised the crowd that the final two heats would be run the next day nonetheless. Lucius spent that night with an old darkie named Uncle Possum while his friends were boarded at the Parsham jailhouse.

On Wednesday, the 17th, everyone was out of jail because Miss Corrie had given herself to the sheriff to arrange it, though Boon hit her for this and Lucius hit Boon for hitting Miss Corrie. Back at the track, the second heat was declared a tie when Acheron, a highly nervous and uncontrollable animal to begin with, smashed through the fence after accidentally being swatted with Lucius' whip, and ran the whole race on the outside of the track. The betting crowd agreed to let all stakes stand on the third heat alone. So they were off once again. As the two horses entered the stretch of the final heat, Coppermine was clearly losing; but Ned was also standing in the middle of the track holding something in his hand. Suddenly Coppermine surged forward and pounded home, winning the race going away. Ned had used the same trick he had used for twenty-two years to get his half-horse half-mule to win every race it entered [1881]: he simply gave the animal a whiff of "sour deens" (sardines) which apparently no horse nor mule either can resist and will run like hell to catch up with and get every time. In the midst of this last heat, however, Boss Priest (having discovered his car missing and well knowing where Boon would go with it) showed up. Ned, though, had by this time won enough money both to bail out Bobo and buy the car back from the white gambler who could not have unloaded it because it was stolen and, in 1905 anyway, would be easily traced.

On Thursday, the 18th, an extra heat was run between Acheron and Coppermine, with all bets on the latter, including Boss Priest's and Mr. Van Tosch's. All except one, that is—Ned's. In retrospect, then, it is not surprising that Ned brought no sour deens to the finish line and Acheron was the easy winner. Or, rather, Ned was.

On Friday, the 19th, they were all back in Jefferson—with the auto; and Lucius was about to take the whipping from his father he knew he deserved. However, Boss interceded and said that Lucius would best be punished by living with the network of lies he had had to spin to get himself into and then out of his week's troubles. Eventually Boon married Miss Corrie, and they moved to Jefferson. Everyone hoped that this would be enough to settle Boon down, for the whole idea of a "network of lies" was as incomprehensible to him as any mechanical device with more than one moving part.

A week or so after the Lucius-Boon trip to Memphis, Gail Hightower's wife took one there as well, perhaps only one of many, and was there by a woman from her husband's congregation {L}. Throughout the summer Mrs. Hightower was never in church; and, after a service packed with his usual cavalry-galloping sermons, Hightower would tell those parishioners who bothered to inquire that she was using the weekends to visit her people. But then, in the late summer, she was found dead on a Memphis sidewalk, fallen from the window of a hotel in which she was registered as another man's wife. The following day Hightower courageously showed up to conduct his Sunday service, only to find reporters all over the church lawn. Though the church was packed when he got there, it began to empty out during the sermon which was, perhaps, the most hysterical he had ever delivered. Leaving the church afterwards, he tried to hide his face from photographers with a hymnbook; but one of them got a picture from the side—Hightower seemed to be laughing. The next day, Hightower buried his wife, conducting the sermon himself until another minister suddenly stepped forward in the middle of it and humanely conducted it for him. The congregation was less understanding, though, for they asked Hightower to resign before the week was out. When he refused, he found himself locked out of his church the following Sunday. He then quit as he was asked.

This was also the summer when Roth Edmonds, who had grown up for seven years with Henry Beauchamp, began to recognize their racial differences [1898] {G}. As diplomatically as he could he began to sleep in a different bed, eat at a different table, hunt with different people. In the early fall, by then having overcome many of these difficulties, he showed up at Molly Beauchamp's door and suggested that he eat with them that night, as he used to. However, Henry refused; and Roth, at seven, was forced to accept the heritage that had been bequeathed to him.

In Frenchman's Bend, the modern bequest was taking shape. V. K. Ratliff was out of circulation this year and spent many months recuperating from an operation in Memphis {H}. I always thought that it was his absence from the Bend during this period which allowed Snopesism to get forever out of control down there and eventually here. Flem had bought a herd of Hereford cows, was pasturing them on Will Varner's land, and selling them at an enormous profit. He bought the blacksmith shop from Varner and replaced old man Trumble, who had been shoeing horses there for fifty years [1855], with I. O. Snopes, who then turned around and hired Eck Snopes as blacksmith. Trumbull had no choice but to pack his bags and leave town forever. But Eck could not shoe horses, and Jack Houston got angry enough about this one day to toss Eck into the drinking trough. At the same time, Eula Varner was being stalked by an ever-increasing number of males of every sort; and, though she went on a lot of picnics this summer, she still had no favorites among those who were trying to court her. Meanwhile, Labove's desire for her was becoming uncontrollable as well [1906]. But none of this matters, for a Snopes would eventually have her, too [1907]. In the fall I. O. married a daughter of Flem's landlady, though he was presumed to have been married before because he had a five- or six-year-old boy with him since he showed up in town. The Snopeses were entrenching.

Four young men of Jefferson were growing up this summer as well, though some more so than others. John Sartoris at twelve killed his first bear

[153]

in the river bottom near MacCallum's {O}. Luke Provine, rambunctious leader of a gang of young crazies, and his group raided a Negro church picnic and, for laughs, set fire to the men's celluloid collars {"A Bear Hunt"}. Among these men, however, was old Uncle Ash, who, because he was wearing a very special collar, vowed revenge when he could get it [1925]. Young Anse Holland, taking with him only a team of mules, ran away from home this year after a dispute with his father over his share of the Holland property, a dispute in which his brother Virginius took Old Anse's side [1929] {K}. And finally Hawkshaw Stribling, eventually to be the best barber in Jefferson but not living here yet, planned to get married; but, by year's end, his intended—Sophie Starnes, from Division on the Mississippi-Alabama border—had died. Later, we in Jefferson found out that Hawkshaw had promised, in her memory, to take care of her family and, later, to pay off all their considerable debts [1917] [1930] {"Hair"}.

In Mottstown, Doc Hines quit doing work of any sort and, now, the Negroes quit bringing him food {L}. In Pensacola, the sickly Popeye Vitelli had, at five, finally learned to walk {Y}.

1906

Born: Lucius "Luke" Hogganbeck

Born: Vardaman Snopes, son of I. O.

Born: Bilbo Snopes, his twin brother

Born: Nancy Mannigoe (d. 1937), a Negro woman to be executed for the murder of a white child

The pressure to acknowledge only her brothers as males continued on Caddy Compson {F}. When Benjy came upon her in a swing one day kissing her current boyfriend, Charlie, he howled so loudly and so continuously that she ran from Charlie and into the house to wash her mouth off. She probably promised Benjy, to whatever extent she felt he could understand it, never to do this again, which meant of course that she would try to be more discreet about where and when she did it. Quentin caught her kissing another boy on another occasion and wound up rubbing her face in the grass, Caddy all the while defending herself by screaming "At least I didn't kiss a dirty girl like Natalie" [1905]. There was no young man that Caddy ever showed interest in of whom, to my knowledge, Quentin ever approved. He particularly disliked a pimple-covered young man who took her to the county fair this year. When Quentin broke his leg in the autumn, he actually sat in a chair outside the house and flung coal at any boy, pimpled or otherwise, who approached the house to see her.

A thousand miles away, while Quentin was pelting his sister's boyfriends, a man named Spoade was entering the freshman class at Harvard. Spoade was later to be a friend of Quentin's [1909] and was known around the Yard as a student who never missed his early class but also never got there on time nor fully dressed.

The Reverend Hightower, now without a church [1905], was asked to leave town for good {L}. He refused, of course, even though his former congregation had raised money for him to do so.

At the Priest household, Boss traded in the Winton Flyer that had caused so much trouble the year before and bought a White Steamer instead—it seems that Grandmother Priest could not stand the gas fumes {R}. The proudest member of the family this year, though, was young Lucius, after whom Boon and Corrie Hogganbeck had named their first son.

In Frenchman's Bend the year was one in which several matters which had been cooking for years finally got overdone {H}. In January, Labove could control his lust for Eula no longer. Alone with her after school one day, he pounced on her, holding her tightly enough to keep him with her but loosely enough to feel her great feminine mammalian mass jiggle up and down against him. She demonstrated surprising strength, however, and knocked the former football star to the floor, warning him to "stop pawing me, you old headless horseman Ichabod Crane." She then stalked off and Labove waited to literally be killed by her brother Jody who would by now be outside to pick her up. But Jody never came after him because Eula never told Jody what had happened because what had happened was not significant enough to Eula for her to bother telling anybody about. When poor Labove realized this, he walked down to Varner's store, bought a nail, drove it into the schoolhouse door, hung the key on it, and left town forever.

Though Jody never knew about Labove's attack on Eula, he knew somebody would have to move soon; so he made her wear corsets to protect the virginity he hoped she still had. At seventeen, she was now being followed by hordes of young men eighteen, nineteen, and twenty, all of whom—while they waited for her to make her choice—banded together to keep outsiders away [1907].

In March V. K. Ratliff was back in the Bend after his operation. While selling Mink Snopes a sewing machine one day, he discovered the extent to which Flem had penetrated the finances of his relatives and fellow townsmen (if Flem could ever have a "fellow" anything) and resolved to conduct a financial offensive that would run Flem from the district. Though he did manage to sell Flem fifty goats at a profit to himself, somehow V. K. came out on the losing end of the deal, which Flem so ensnarled in red tape that Ratliff could no longer follow it. Flem had also gotten himself appointed legal guardian of his idiot cousin, Ike, and thus had control of Ike's small financial resources. By September Flem was also the chief collector and settler of all of Will Varner's accounts; and by November he and Will were riding around together in a buggy, foreclosing (or threatening to) as a team now.

And an argument which would result in a fatality got started near the Bend this year {M}. Mink Snopes had paid a local Negro a dollar to let his yearling mate with the Negro's scrub bull. When no pregnancy occurred, Mink could not afford another dollar and so let the cow wander into Jack Houston's field to feed there for the winter and also be serviced by Houston's bull. Late in November Houston noticed the cow chewing away and began to consider what action he would take against Mink.

In Pensacola, Popeye Vitelli, six, grew the first hair his head ever produced {Y}.

1907

Born: Virgil Beard

Married: Flem Snopes and Eula Varner

Married: Eustace Grimm and the Doshey girl

Died: Jack Houston (b. 1874)

In the North this year they panicked on Wall Street because securities were losing value; but few in the county, save for young Jason Compson, even knew enough about what securities were to worry about it.

Horace Benbow graduated an honors student and Rhodes Scholar from Sewanee this year and was off to the other Oxford {S}. I myself departed for Harvard {M} and was immediately befriended, as are all southern students, by old Deacon, a black man who knew what a rebel white boy needed to be happy [1869] {F}. I was the first countian to ever go to Harvard, though I would be followed there in two years by Quentin Compson [1909]. It wasn't so much that I was brilliant that I got to go. Even I would have to admit that I got a little too much involved with some town young ladies during the previous year or so, and my father decided to get me where I couldn't spend all my time "fumbling beneath skirts" {I}. So I went to where there were few skirts around and no time to fumble beneath the ones that were.

One skirt I never fumbled under was Caddy Compson's, but evidently by now others had been {F}. Mrs. Compson started wearing black this year, claiming that her little daughter had died when she started kissing boys. Mr. Compson, probably in a dual attempt to get away from his wife for a while and to try to straighten Quentin out about his sister's maidenhead, began to take his son on hunting trips that were laden with man-to-man talks. One rainy day they stumbled into the cedar grove with the five Sutpen tombstones in it and mused for a while about the family ruin {A}. When they signalled Luster to drive the wagon over to pick them up, though, Luster recalled the time [1903] when he and the other boys had been chased away from the Sutpen property by Clytie; so he would come no closer. Within two years Quentin would have to come back, but that time it would be with an old woman instead of two men [1909].

Meanwhile, Gail Hightower continued to bear the brunt of the County's worst instincts {L}. When he refused to leave, the town tried to force him out with various wild rumors—one had it that he had his wife heavily insured [1905] and then drove her to suicide; another that he had been having sexual relations with his Negro cook since the death; another that he was a homosexual, this because he had not (obviously) satisfied his wife and that he had hired a male cook to replace the female one that had already been whispered out of his employ. The Ku Klux Klan made several overt threats against Hightower himself and one night beat the cook as he returned home. But the minister would not leave.

In Frenchman's Bend, Jack Houston still grieved desperately for his wife, now dead four years [1903] {H}. Perhaps this in itself caused him to over-react to Mink Snopes's heifer [1906]. One day, just before the spring planting, he sent a rather haughty black servant to Mink with orders to remove the cow {M}. Mink said it was no longer his, that he had sold it last summer to the Gowries. Later he retracted this and tried to buy the cow back for $16, a deal Houston refused because the cow had eaten more in food than that and been topped by his bull to boot. Things became so tense between the two men that it was actually Houston who first suggested bloodshed over the whole thing—one day he put his gun on a fence post and suggested that he and Mink run at it to see who could kill the other first. But Will Varner settled it in court, where, of course, he was the local Justice of the Peace. He agreed that Mink owed Jack $37.50 but that the two should split it down the middle. Houston agreed to let Mink work his $18.75 off digging post holes and stringing fence wire for fifty cents a day for the next thirty-seven and one-half days. Mink agreed, though, to keep Varner from running him off his land for failing to plant it, he had to dig for Houston by night and plow his own fields by day. Mink did this. On the 38th day, however, he did not pick the cow up by noon but left it until later when the Negro would feed it. As a result Houston charged him an extra one dollar pound fee, the going rate. So Mink, now in a fury, dug for two more days or, more accurately, nights—and then led the cow home.

What he did then was to get his $5 emergency money from behind the brick in his house and hitch a ride to Jefferson to buy shotgun shells at Ike

McCaslin's hardware store. He was rolled for his money on the way up here, however, and never got to find out that Ike would never have sold him the shells in the first place. So he returned to the Bend the next day and somehow managed to scrounge up two hunting shells. He loaded his gun, which he hadn't fired in years [1903], went to a bridge that he knew Houston was in the habit of crossing, and waited three days. Finally Houston came by, and Mink raised his gun. The first barrel failed to fire, the second killed Houston instantly {H} {M} [1946].

Mink went home and washed his gun; in the distance he could hear Houston's hound baving over his master's body {H}. Mink returned, removed the body from the ditch in which he had left it, and—after a terrible tussle over it with the dog—stuffed it in a pinoak. He then threw his gun in a slough and went into hiding for three more days. During this period his cousin Lancelot "Lump" Snopes, who had replaced Flem as Varner's clerk, put two and two together and decided that Mink had killed Houston to get the $50 he, Lump, knew Houston had in his pocket that day. Lump stalked Mink hoping that Mink would lead him to the body, but Mink knocked him out before pulling Houston's body from the pinoak and dragging it toward the river, again having to fight off the loyal hound. Just as he was about to throw it in the Yoknapatawpha River, he was captured by the deputy sheriff and taken to the Jefferson jail. Before getting there, however, Mink tried to jump the wagon, whether to escape or to commit suicide no one was sure, but failed in both. As he awaited trial in the jailhouse, he continually tried to get local boys to go, for a dollar, to Frenchman's Bend to bring Flem to him. Flem, of course, never would have come and never did {T}. Meanwhile, V. K. Ratliff kept Mink's two daughters in his room while Yettie went out to work during the day.

Snopeses were all over the district now {H}. Flem had built a new blacksmith shop early this year and sold the building, for a profit, to Will Varner. And throughout the spring, before he was murdered, Jack Houston had been bothered by the idiot Ike Snopes who had become romantically involved with one of Houston's own cows, a cow Houston eventually gave Ike as a present in order to free himself from the sodomistic embarrassment he regularly encountered in his very own field. This action merely transferred the activities to Mrs. Littlejohn's back yard, however, where Lump Snopes began charging admission to those hungry to see a man, even if an idiot, fornicate with an animal. It was Ratliff who put a stop to it all, convincing I. O. and Eck to buy the cow from Mrs. Littlejohn (the nearest thing to an owner it had) in order to save the Snopes name. Eck, never a true Snopes where money was concerned, wound up paying $15, while I. O., definitely a true Snopes, paid $1.80—all this before the righteous eye of the less-than-righteous Reverend Whitfield.

1907 was the predestined year for Eula, unbelievably eighteen now, to surrender her virginity {H}. Like teams fighting through an elimination tournament for a gold cup, all the young men in the district had narrowed down to the final five: a Tull, a Bookwright, a Quick, a Turpin, and a Binford. Each waited for one to surface among them {M}, and they continued to act as a gang to keep a sixth one from intruding. When a travelling salesman took Eula to a dance one night, she was escorted home by someone else and no one ever heard what became of the drummer {H}. But one day the fate-ordained male passed through the Bend—Hoake McCarron saw Eula and the life force began to take hold. As soon as they knew what Hoake's intentions were, the final five warned him to stay away, if only because he had not participated in the elimination rounds, by tacking a notice to his door in the middle of the night. McCarron sent his Negro back with five separate refusals to conform, and the five beat up the nigger. Then, on the night of McCarron's first date with Eula, they ambushed the couple at Tull's bridge and an epic fight ensued. Theron Quick was hit over the head with a buggy whip wielded by Eula, and the other four—who compared to McCarron as four goats compare to a stallion—were badly bloodied. Then, on that very spot, even though he knew he had fractured an arm from the fight, Hoake took the maidenhead that Jody Varner had tried so hard and so long to preserve and Labove and others so hard and so long to take [1906]. And at the moment of climax his broken arm actually telescoped one bone into the other! Will Varner, a veterinarian in addition to being everything else, set the arm that night—it wasn't till later, when Eula turned up pregnant, that poor Will finally understood what caused the first telescoped bone he had ever seen.

When it was known that Eula was with child, McCarron and two others scurried out of town, the first because he knew who was the father, the other two because they liked to think they could have been or, maybe, have the Bend think they were. Jody was bent on revenge; but, instead, Will got Eula married to Flem Snopes, who, as far as anyone knew, was sexually impotent. But she would at least give birth within the boundaries of wedlock rather than outside them. Will bought them their license and gave them the Old Frenchman's Place as part of Eula's dowry {T}, though Flem accepted this on option, having the privilege to return it for cash unless he could sell it [1908]. He sold it alright. In the fall McCarron sent a note to Eula from Jefferson but it was never answered nor, probably, received either—Eula and Flem were on their honeymoon, which meant for Flem a business trip [1936] {M}.

With Flem gone for a while, Varner evicted his father, Ab, for failure to pay his rent for the past two years {T}. It is odd to think that Will felt Flem would have objected to this.

Finally, Eck Snopes, one of the few honorable Snopeses, gained some notoriety when he saved a Negro's life this year {T}. As he and the Negro were lifting a heavy log on Eck's farm, the log slipped and Eck propped it

[159]

entirely on his own back until help could arrive to drag the black man out from under it [1918]. As a result, Eck would have to wear a neck brace for the rest of his life, though his cousin Flem would comfort him in his pain by letting him clerk in a restaurant Flem was soon to acquire [1908].

1908

Born: Percy Grimm

Born: Linda Snopes

Born: Admiral Dewey Snopes

Married: Tom Tom Bird and his fourth wife

Died: Will Benbow

This was the year that Snopesism moved from its hatchery in Frenchman's Bend to its maturity in Jefferson. Perhaps the greatest irony of this is that it was the most persistent of all Snopes fighters, V. K. Ratliff, who—by a strategic error—helped to bring it here. I was in my second year at Harvard now, but the events back home were the ones which would truly shape what my life would henceforth have to be.

On March 9th, Ratliff met Bookwright in V. K.'s Jefferson hash house to catch up on the winter's shifting around of Snopeses. {H}. Eula, now Flem's wife, had returned from her honeymoon in Texas without him. And Eck, taking pity on the now cowless Ike, bought him a small statue of one so he could linger in whatever memories his feeble mind could conjure up. And I. O., married to Mrs. Tull's sister's niece for less than three years, deserted her and moved to Jefferson when his first wife, a big gray woman whom he had never bothered to divorce, showed up for some reason to claim him. She brought a child with her as well. I. O., we all thought, was a divorced man or a widower; but he was really a bigamist, though this did not bother him very much.

Flem himself came back in April with a stranger named Buck Hipps and a string of wild ponies {H} {"Spotted Horses"}. V. K. did his damnedest to prevent what he knew was coming—he ran through town and warned everyone to leave as quickly as he could so he wouldn't wind up owning a horse he wouldn't want. But, fools about horses that they were, they not only didn't go but also hung around the corral the next day to see what Buck and Flem would try to pull. For a while they were silent, for Buck did not know how to move them into buying as yet. Finally he offered one free to Eck

Snopes if Eck would start the bidding on the second one. This did it. Eck wound up with two and almost everyone else around had at least one of the critters by the end of the day. Even Flem himself traded a buggy for the last three. Henry Armstid spent his last five dollars on one of them, though Hipps took pity on his wife and tried to return her the money through Flem. Flem must have pocketed it, though, because she never got it back.

So, in the late afternoon, everybody entered the corral to claim his horse; but the horses—seeing the gate open for the first time all day—suddenly came to life and broke at a dead run in all directions. The fray was on. One of Eck's actually ran through Mrs. Littlejohn's boarding house and chased Ratliff out the back door in his underwear. Eck's second one ran across the bridge on the outskirts of town and right over the top of Tull's wagon, knocking out Tull and scaring the life out of his wife and daughters. Armstid, still a horse-owner at this point, was trampled in the corral trying to rope his and had to be carried to Will Varner's for treatment. Two days later, while Bookwright and Quick and many others were still chasing theirs down, Eck had actually caught one of his, though the other died of a broken neck when it ran dead on into a rope that had been strung across the road to slow it down. Meanwhile, Armstid, still semiconscious in Mrs. Littlejohn's, was receiving attention from his long suffering wife. His oldest daughter had to watch the other children out at the house, where she slept at night with an axe in bed in case the crazy horses managed to show up there. When Mrs. Armstid later asked Flem for the five dollars, Flem denied that Buck ever gave it to him but presented her with a bag of candy from the store to make her feel better. No one was more disgusted by all this than Ratliff, who now publicly vowed to give up trying to help these people beat Flem at anything.

The repercussions of this incident were several, though Ratliff's decision to fend for himself would ultimately be the most meaningful. Lon Quick, one of the few who caught up with his purchase, used it for many years as a stud to breed horses which were almost as wild; and careful folks came to have to ask if a given horse had any of Lon Quick's in its bloodline {D}. Two trials were held in Whiteleaf's store over it as well {H}. In the first, Mrs. Armstid versus Flem for the missing five dollars, Flem never showed up and Lump committed perjury to protect him. Mrs. Armstid lost the case. In the second, Mrs. Tull versus Eck Snopes for her husband's injuries and damage to the wagon, the sterling Eck requested that he be allowed to pay for all damages without a trial—but the judge, unable to determine that Eck really owned the horse in the first place (since no papers were issued on any of them), ruled that Eck did not own the animal and should not pay the damages. Mrs. Tull lost her case and vowed revenge she never got.

In this same month of May, a trial of greater magnitude was taking place in Jefferson. Mink Snopes, defended by a one-year graduate of the law school at the state university, was convicted of the murder of Jack Houston; as the trial closed he swore revenge on Flem for not showing up to get him off, a revenge he most certainly *did* get, though he would have to wait almost forty years for it [1946]. Mink was sentenced to life imprisonment, though his lawyer told him privately that he could get out in twenty years on good behavior {M}. When Mink asked to have this written down, the lawyer returned to the judge and the district attorney and asked to have Mink retried on insanity charges rather than criminal ones. When the three returned to Mink's cell to suggest this to him, Mink beat up the lawyer for calling him crazy. And so he was shipped to Parchman in June.

In August, back at the Bend, Ratliff made that error of strategy that would cost all of us so much {H}. He, Armstid (back on his feet now), and Bookwright became aware that Flem was going out to the Old Frenchman's Place, which he owned as part of Eula's dowry [1907], and digging every night for two weeks. Sure that Flem was on to the location of the long-lost Grenier silver (which the family hid from the Yankees nearly a half a century ago at the beginning of the Civil War [1862]), these three got Uncle Dick Bolivar, a local fortune teller, to lead them onto the property with a divining rod and, eventually, to a bag of silver coins. Thrilled, the three of them made an offer on the land; and, after some hard bargaining, made the purchase the next day through Flem's agent, Eustace Grimm. Ratliff, claiming he wanted to turn it into a goat ranch, paid for his share with the half-ownership he had in the Jefferson restaurant (this was his big mistake), Armstid with a mortgage on his farm, and Bookwright with straight cash. For the next three nights they lived at the Old Frenchman's Place, digging furiously all night long—until it dawned on Ratliff to look at the dates on the coins in the bag they had found. All were postwar coins and they realized—or at least V. K. and Bookwright did—that the bag had been salted by Flem to make them buy the useless property from him at a higher figure than he could have gotten if he had just dealt it back to Varner as his wedding contract allowed him to. Armstid refused to believe that he had been beaten by Flem again and continued to dig night and day, too crazed by now to listen to the pleas of his wife and friends.

In September, Flem packed up his belongings. He and Eula, who by now was lugging her baby daughter around in her arms, moved to Jefferson to operate their half of the cafe Flem had done Ratliff out of. As they drove out of the Bend, they stopped to watch Armstid dig for a while; and, after spitting in the dust, Flem pulled out. When they got to Jefferson, they pitched a tent behind the restaurant and took up residence in it.

It was in this very month, just before I was to leave to go back for the fall semester at Harvard, that I personally first encountered Eula's overwhelming femininity {T}. Even though I had never met her, I remarked to her one day on the street that she was beautiful; and she simply replied "Yes, of course." Such beauty, however, could no longer waste itself on Flem, a man who was impotent and would have preferred money to sex even if he weren't {M}. So, before the year was out, the notorious affair between Eula and Mayor Manfred DeSpain was under way [1927] {T}.

In the same year, Caddy Compson, at sixteen younger than Eula, was still the object of her brothers' curious affections {F}. Since Benjy was now thirteen, she could no longer sleep in the same bed with him; but it took months of her lying with him until he fell asleep before she could totally separate from him into her own room. Benjy had been moved into Uncle Maury's old one, its former tenant having already disappeared from town sometime before this. Meanwhile, Quentin was in his last year of high school now; and his father sold the last portion of the Compson Mile, a pasture earmarked for Benjy because he loved it, but now to be the Municipal Golf Course, in order to be able to send Quentin to Harvard and, as it turned out, pay off Caddy's wedding which would occur sooner than anybody wanted it to [1910].

Into town this year came Joanna Burden, twenty-one-year-old grand-daughter and sister of the two Calvin Burdens murdered by John Sartoris some three dozen years back {L} [1873]. She was immediately an outcast, a pariah because of her name and her northern heritage, and lived alone in an old house on a large piece of land on the northern extremities of town. Here she would wait twenty years to become the mistress of [1927] and then to be killed by Joe Christmas [1930], who at this time was being introduced to sex, somewhere else, at the age of fifteen. Some of his friends had comandeered a Negro girl into a sawmill shed to let them take turns with her. When Joe's chance came, however, he was so repulsed that he started kicking her and was, in turn, dragged out by the other boys and beaten up. When he got back to McEachern's, Simon admired his bloody face because he thought the boy had been out waging war on fornication and fornicators.

Horace Benbow was on his way home from England this year when his father, Will, died [1907] {O}. The family wired him in New York to tell him to hurry back for the funeral. Two days after it, he reopened his father's law offices, though he told us later that he had planned to become an Episcopal minister until this event changed his course. Horace was always a romantic, however, and he probably wouldn't have done it or made much of a minister if he had.

THE PRESIDENCY OF WILLIAM HOWARD TAFT, 1909–1913

1909

Died: Clytemnestra Sutpen (b. 1834)

Died: Henry Sutpen (b. 1839)

While I entered my third year at Harvard this year, spending most of my time with a comical young man named Spoade {M}, Jefferson entered the ten-year period in which it was literally inundated with Snopses {Y}. Though they were at first encouraged by Flem, he would later have to do all he could to get rid of most of them. But Flem at this point was only a restaurant operator and would be for the next four years {T} [1913]. He had torn up the Bend, and poor Henry Armstid was in an asylum; but now Flem was on the "bottom" again, living with his wife and a baby that wasn't his in a tent. Within six months of his arrival, though, he had managed to buy out, or at least get rid of, the other partner in the restaurant and had installed Eck Snopes behind the counter in place of himself. Eck was fired pretty soon thereafter, though, when he began openly admitting to customers that there was no meat in the hamburgers. I. O., on the run from his second wife, replaced him. Eck, his neck still in a brace and still always followed around by his son, Wallstreet Panic, was out of work for a time; but he soon became night watchman at Renfrow's oil tank, a job he got through Will Varner's connections with the Jefferson Masons [1918]. Beginning this summer also, Flem sent Eula and the baby away on a vacation; and pretty soon the town knew that Manfred DeSpain was going on yearly vacations, too—to the same place at the same time [1927].

This spring, Gail Hightower, the minister who refused to leave a town where no one wanted him, was found beaten up in the woods outside of town {L}. It seems the Klan had thrown a brick through his window the day before, and it bore a note which warned him to leave town before sundown. When he refused, they came at night to make him wish he had.

But the significant events of 1909 center around the Compson family {F}. Jason, at sixteen, was worried about money; so he quit school and took a job at a local store, hoarding like a miser whatever he could out of his niggardly earnings. Quentin was worried about time, so his father, perhaps foolishly, gave him a watch, a family heirloom [1910]. But Mrs. Compson was worried about Caddy and set Jason, probably for a fee, to spying on her. Mr. Compson and Quentin were furious about this and were about to get it stopped when Caddy did what everyone, save perhaps for her father, feared— she gave herself to a man, a stranger in town, named Dalton Ames. Benjy, it is said, knew this when he smelled her one night; so he howled. Quentin probably just knew it by instinct; but he followed her when, at Benjy's proddings, she ran down to the creek and sat in it to cleanse herself for her brothers once again [1898] [1905]. Hysterical, Quentin first threatened to kill Ames, then to steal his own college money, then to enter into a suicide pact with Caddy. Later Caddy offered herself to him, or so he implied to me on the train to Harvard that September. In the midst of it all Quentin rousted

Ames out of the barbershop one day and told the man to meet him on the bridge over the creek. Ames did so and turned away Quentin's threat to kill him if he didn't leave town by demonstrating his expertise with a pistol. Quentin then flailed out at him, but Ames just held his arms till the boy fainted. Mortified, Quentin went home and told his father that he and his sister had committed incest and that he was contemplating suicide. Compson believed none of it, of course. He suggested that the boy leave for the North early, to spend a month in Maine while Caddy and her mother were vacationing (and apparently husband-hunting) at French Lick [1899]. Quentin did not take the advice, but Caddy (not yet pregnant but on her way to getting so) did meet Herbert Head on her jaunt [1910].

Quentin was hardly in control of this when, about a week before he and I left for Cambridge, he was contacted by Miss Rosa Coldfield and asked to come to her "office" {A}. The woman was never seen by anyone except at religious services on Sunday and Wednesday; but it was on a Saturday, September 4th, that Quentin reluctantly went to see this strange old lady. Through the hot, muggy Mississippi afternoon, he listened to her rant about Thomas Sutpen, the man who proposed marriage to her over forty years ago [1866] but wanted her to prove she could bear a male heir before he would make good on his promise. She claimed to be telling him this so Quentin could publish it when, after college, he became a writer. She then asked him to accompany her to Sutpen's Hundred (where Quentin had been twice before and didn't like it either time [1903] [1907])—there was something in the old house she said she wanted to find out about [1905]. During the early evening Quentin's father filled him in on the rest of the legend, much of which has already found its way into this chronicle. Around dark the boy and the raving old woman journeyed in her buggy out to the house twelve miles along the northwest road. There they climbed the porch, and Rosa told Quentin to take the hatchet she handed him and break in the door of the darkened building. Instead—amidst the ghostly echoes of niggers wrestling niggers, father arguing with son, and brother shooting brother—he climbed through a window and let Rosa in. And then both were confronted by the candle-lit and shriveled Clytie. Clytie, Quentin told me, begged him not to let Rosa go upstairs [1865]; but Rosa knocked her down and started up in a bolt. In her excitement she must have collapsed and somehow been returned to her carriage by the idiot, Jim Bond—Quentin was not sure. Quentin himself, though frightened, moved on upstairs, no longer obeying a will that was his own. There, in a room at the head of the stairs, Quentin saw an old man in bed. Incredibly, it was Henry Sutpen, the murderer of Charles Bon [1865], who revealed now to Quentin that he had come home four years ago to die [1905]. Though it is surprising to think so now, it was only on this single occasion that the secret behind Bon's murder was ever revealed—that Bon, according to Henry, had Negro blood in his veins and had to be stopped from marrying Judith Sutpen. It was Quentin, then, who solved the mystery the county had given up trying to. Quentin now scurried in horror out of the room and the house, ran back to the buggy, and drove it home as quickly as it would go—which wasn't very fast or at least fast enough. He dropped Miss Rosa, herself weak and stunned, at her house, ran home, and—sweating profusely—threw himself on his bed. While Benjy sawed blissfully away in the next room, Quentin lay awake all night, the words "Jesus, Jesus, Jesus" scraping staccato through his parched mouth.

Why Rosa waited three more months is unclear. But on Wednesday, the 22nd of December, she took an ambulance out to the Hundred to bring Henry in for hospitalization. Thinking Rosa was coming with the police to take Henry in for the murder of Bon, Clytie set fire to the old structure and burnt it to the ground. Only Jim Bond escaped; Clytie and Henry perished in the ashes of their shared-father's dream [1833]. Rosa left the scene in the ambulance, already in a coma. She never regained consciousness and died shortly after the new year [1910].

On the very day Sutpen's Hundred went up in smoke, Quentin himself was on his way home for Christmas, guardedly anticipating his return to the South which he was no longer sure whether he loved or hated {F}. As the train stopped at a Virginia crossroad, he spotted a Negro on a mule. Quentin hurled up the window, addressed the man as "Uncle," and flipped him a quarter as a Christmas present. He must have loved it—the Old South that is—the South he was told had once been but which he had never seen nor ever would see.

1910

Born: Quentin Compson IV, a girl

Born: Vardaman Gowrie

Born: Bilbo Gowrie, his twin brother

Born: Lena Grove

Born: Luster, a Compson black, second of that name

Married: Candace "Caddy" Compson and Sidney Herbert Head

Married: Joan Heppleton and her first husband

Died: Quentin Compson III (b. 1891), by his own hand

[166]

Died: Rosa Coldfield (b. 1845)

Died: Mrs. Odlethrop

Quentin Compson and I returned to Cambridge on the 3rd of January and Miss Rosa succumbed in her coma on the 5th, was buried on the 8th, and was largely forgotten by the 10th, since few in town had known her to speak to {A}. I recall that on Friday night the 14th Quentin and his roommate Shreve McCannon, a Canadian, lay awake most of the night piecing together the Sutpen story pretty much as we now know it. Fueled in their discussion by a letter, written on the 10th by Mr. Compson, their vapory breaths penetrated the darkness of the cold room as they considered the reasons for and the consequences of men such as Sutpen. Shreve told Quentin that the Jim Bonds—half-white, half-black idiots of no particular color or mentality— would inherit the earth; he also accused Quentin of hating the South, which Quentin vigorously if not altogether convincingly denied.

In February sometime, back in Jefferson, Caddy turned up pregnant by a man she could probably not, by this time, even identify {F}. In March Quentin received what he knew was coming—an announcement of the impending marriage between Caddy and Herbert Head, the man her mother had managed to recruit the previous summer at French Lick [1909]. I received one too, but only Quentin returned for the ceremony late in April. When he got there on the 22nd, he found that Head had already given Caddy an automobile as a present, making her, according to her mother, the first woman in Jefferson to drive. He had also promised Jason, the family's financial wizard and budding miser, a job in the bank in which he worked in another city. What Head did not know was that Quentin, the only member of the family he had not met by the weekend of the wedding, had done some research on him at Harvard, which Head himself had once attended [1899]. Almost immediately upon their introduction, Quentin revealed to him that he knew that Head had been kicked out of his club and even out of Harvard itself for cheating. Herbert tried to bribe Quentin to keep this information from his sister, but Quentin found himself compelled to tell her that the man she was to marry was a blackguard.

On the 23rd Quentin and Caddy apparently had a long talk in which she admitted her pregnancy and refused his plea for her to run away with him. She took responsibility for her father's increasing alcohol consumption, though she shouldn't have, for that belonged to his wife. Caddy asked Quentin to finish school, to take care of their father, and to keep Benjy out of the Jackson asylum, whither there was growing pressure from mother and brother alike to send him. Unlike the past, however, Caddy did not permit Quentin to touch her at all during this, their last private encounter.

The wedding took place on the 24th and was marred by, among other

[167]

things, Benjy and his black attendant, T. P., getting drunk on "sasparilla" in the cellar and Benjy cracking his head on the ground after falling off a box he was standing on to peer through the window at the festivities. Caddy embraced him to stop his howling, and Quentin pounded T. P. into the pig trough until he sobered up. Mr. Compson, too, got very drunk.

When he arrived back at Harvard a few days later, I am quite certain that he had already decided to commit suicide but had resolved to wait until the end of the school year so that the money from the sale of Benjy's pasture would not be wasted [1908]. I saw very little of him during these last five or six weeks, though on one occasion he told me that, with Caddy gone, Benjy had taken to running up and down along the fence howling at the schoolgirls who walked home along the street and who had learned after a while to cross it before passing the Compson property.

Finally, on June 2nd, Quentin Compson killed himself by throwing himself into the Charles River with a flatiron in either pocket. His mind was surely a muddle of hysterical associations of Caddy, the family, time, and the South past and present; but all we could reconstruct about his activities on his last day are the following:

1. He awoke late enough that Shreve had to warn him about being tardy for class;

2. He broke his watch and cut his finger around 8 A.M.;

3. He packed his trunk and mailed the key to his father;

4. He ate breakfast with the Parkers;

5. He purchased the flatirons sometime during the morning;

6. He saw Gerald Bland rowing on the Charles before noon;

7. He saw Deacon around noon [1869] [1907] and gave him a note to give Shreve the next day (a note which willed Deacon some of his clothing);

8. He was arrested in the afternoon for following and "assaulting" a minor girl, though the girl later admitted that Quentin was trying to help her escape a charge by a bakery owner that she stole a bun and that she, not he, had done the "following and the assaulting" after that;

9. He picnicked with Gerald Bland, Bland's mother, and some friends during the afternoon and wound up picking a fight with Gerald and getting badly beaten;

10. He was taken to a farmhouse by Shreve and Spoade to clean him up;

11. He returned by streetcar to Cambridge where he cleaned some clothing with gasoline and left his watch in the dresser drawer for Shreve;

12. Before going out to meet his destiny, he brushed his teeth and put on his hat.

School being over a few days later, I accompanied Quentin's body back to Jefferson. The family, with Mr. Compson on the bottle and Caddy gone, had come completely apart. Even the Negroes now were complaining about the evil fate which stalked the Compsons. Only when their maid, Dilsey, took control was order restored. As she said of her own children to Roskus, her husband—who was complaining about ill luck while trying to milk a cow with his single unrheumatic hand—Versh was working, Frony was married, and T. P. was old enough to help out with the chores. Everyone died sometime, she said; and it was up to each of us to stay alive until that time came [1943].

If the Compson family went downward in 1910, the Snopes family went upward {T}. Probably because he was committing adultery with Flem's wife, Mayor Manfred DeSpain appointed him to the newly created job of superintendent of the city's power plant, a job that hardly needed to be done since Tomey's Turl II could be counted on to fire the burners at night as Tom Tom Bird did during the day. But Flem now had additional income to supplement that from his restaurant business and various investments; so, saving even more money by using Eula as his counterwoman, Flem could afford to move his wife and two-year-old stepdaughter out of their tent and into a small, rented, back-street house {M}. Hearing that his son was starting to get ahead, old Ab Snopes, in his seventies now, moved into a house two miles outside Jefferson and, like Mink, awaited favors that would never be done.

Two more local boys went off to school: Roth Edmonds, twelve, to a boarding school {G} and Eustace Graham to the state university where, for the next five years [1915], he would gamble his way through on his way to a law degree he would later misuse [1929] {Y}.

At McEachern's farm, Joe Christmas' life took a different turn this year, though it is hard to claim that this was the one which pointed him toward Jefferson as yet {L}. In retrospect, everything he ever did or had done to him had probably pointed him here for his finish twenty years hence [1930]. In town one day to do errands, Joe and McEachern stopped at a cafe for coffee; and there Joe was attracted to a smallish waitress named Bobbie Allen. Though she took no notice of him now, she would. Perhaps sensing this, his stepfather told him it was a bad place, to stay away. Joe didn't.

When Mrs. Odlethrop died in Jefferson this year, no one knew it until the stink of her body brought people into her house to look {K}. Her grandson, Monk, only seven at the time, was guarding it, perhaps not knowing what else to do with it. When the authorities tried to take him in to find him another home, Monk would have none of it and wound up living with a well-known whiskymaker in the district named Fraser. He would stay here, helping him brew his corn, for the next eleven years of his life [1921].

Finally, to the north of us in the next county, the lumber company which was also stripping the McCaslin land established a factory and caused a great influx of population {O}. In about a decade [1919], Horace Benbow and his wife would have to be part of this new town of Kinston, but right now Horace was fairly successful in his father's law practice.

1911

Born: Temple Drake

Born: Titania "Little Belle" Mitchell

Born: J. C. Goodyhay

Born: Pete, brother of Alabama Red

Died: Miss Carruthers, organist at the Presbyterian church

Once again a year of hope and upward movement for the Snopeses but generally downward or sideways for the rest of the county, especially for the Compsons.

The only cornered Snopes, Mink, evidently didn't consider himself so, for he responded to a letter from Yettie which asked if she should bring the two girls to visit him by saying "no" because he didn't expect to have to be in Parchman much longer {M}. The warden was astonished at this, for even life sentences took the better part of one to get over with [1946].

Meanwhile, the rest of the Snopeses were either entrenching, as Flem had shown them how to do, or establishing a degree of *snobisme,* which Flem was about to show them how to do {T}. I. O.'s wife (the first one, who came back), for instance, considered herself superior to Eck and his wife and consequently would not talk to them [1908]. Flem had bought his way into the Commercial Hotel, which he renamed the Snopes Hotel, and moved his restaurant out of Ratliff's old building into this one. Eck's wife was appointed manager since Eck's branch of the family was the only one Flem could trust to keep their hands out of the till. Another Snopes, who had not been here before and would not be here again—Wesley "Actual Schoolmaster" Snopes—showed up in June, stayed the summer, but was run out (some say at Flem's instigation) after being caught in a cotton house fooling around with a fourteen-year-old girl. But Snopeses increase, they do not decrease—he left behind him his two sons, Virgil and Byron. Byron had a particularly good sense of money; so Old Bayard Sartoris gathered him to his breast quickly and sent him off to business college in Memphis where he learned both to handle books and compose mash notes [1919], on the promise that Byron would accept a job in the Sartoris bank when he finished. This was also the year that Bayard sent his two grandsons off to the University of Virginia for their freshman years, thinking that fine old institution would find some way to tame them; but Johnny and Bayard continued to be Johnny and Bayard, studying little and raising general hell {S}.

In the Compson family, troubles got worse {F}. Quentin's suicide was still traumatic [1910] when Caddy Compson Head gave birth to her daughter, named Quentin, at the end of 1910; and somewhere early in 1911 Herbert must have started counting months and realized that, at best, he had a seven-month baby or, at worst, somebody had Caddy two months before he ever did. Correctly assuming the latter, he divorced her, reneged on his promise of a bank job for Jason, and was probably all too glad on the whole to detach himself from the Compsons. Mr. Compson, now in the last year of his life, went to wherever it was they had been living, got the baby, and brought her back to Jefferson. Caddy went into exile. Mrs. Compson, on the occasion of the child's arrival, forbade anyone to ever mention Caddy's name in the child's presence.

Before the year was over, things worsened. Benjy, now in his own private hysteria to replace the sister he needed, continued to howl at little girls walking home from school; and, when someone left the gate open one day, he ran out and caught the Burgess girl. He affectionately roughed her up before Versh could subdue him. Jason, now eighteen, renewed his campaign to have Benjy committed to the asylum in Jackson, if that could even be done before Mr. Burgess shot him. Instead, failing to understand why it was that Benjy pursued little girls, the family had him castrated; and now he became known to his embittered brother as "The Great American Gelding." He also transferred his interest from little girls to caddies on the neighboring golf course, though it was the name of their profession he loved and not their gender.

Also eighteen this year was Joe Christmas {L}. He had been given a heifer by McEachern, but he had traded it for a new suit with which to impress Bobby Allen. McEachern, of course, beat him for this; but for the first time Joe threatened retaliation. He also kept a sharp eye on a loose board in the attic where he knew his stepmother was stowing spare cash. Though he generally disliked women, Joe's interest in Bobbie stemmed from the fact that she was gruffly kind to him when those around her would tend to scorn him. He must have associated her with Alice, the girl in the orphanage who so frequently protected him and whose first name, actually *only* name, sounded like Bobbie's last one. Yet he still could not cope with her femininity because the whole concept of sexual intercourse virtually nauseated him, not to mention the attendant matter of menstruation. He apparently heard of the latter for the very first time this year; he threw up and later went out in a field to kill a sheep and wash his hands in its blood. Yet, after a time, a masochistic affair with Bobbie blossomed nonetheless.

Otherwise the year's events were trivial—those quiet moments when fate is hard at work but has not produced a finished product as yet. Lucas Beauchamp wandered into the McCaslin commissary one day and opened a charge account—which Zack Edmonds granted him even though he knew, and would later remind Roth, that Lucas would never pay up on it because he

[171]

would outlive Zack, Roth, and even the very books in which his records were kept {G}. But Lucas would not have taken no for an answer, and thus nobody would ever try to hand him one. Miss Vaiden Wyott became the second grade teacher at Jefferson school in 1911, a fact I stress because she would later help us, without fully realizing how, in our efforts to de-Snopes ourselves [1915] {T}. To the north the lumber business boomed; and Kinston in particular was beginning to erect row upon row of identical frame houses with garages to match—this is the first encounter we had with what was later to be known as the tract house, the subdivision, the housing project, or whatever it is you call it in the place you come from {S}. Fake affluence which would be tomorrow's slum.

In Honolulu, Joan Heppleton, whom we had not met yet, deserted her husband and fled to Australia with an Englishman and assumed his name {O}.

1912

Born: Vinson Gowrie (d. 1940)

Born: Doris Snopes, a boy, younger child of I. O.

Born: A St. Louis salesman who would deal here in gold-divining machines one day

Died: Jason Compson III (b. 1868)

In these days you could get a bachelor's degree and a law degree both at Harvard in five years. So I got both and returned to Jefferson, with no intention of staying here longer than I had to {T}. I already had dreams of going for a Ph.D. at Heidelberg, though that would have to wait a bit [1914]. I opened up a small law office and, at twenty-three, went to work to support myself for the first time in my life.

The first thing I encountered when I returned was the final ruin of Mr. Compson {F}. He was never seen in the business district now; if you needed to see him you could find him at any hour on his front porch, still in the nightshirt he had not taken off from the night before (or perhaps many nights before), drinking continually until he was too drunk to refill his decanter. Then, T. P. would do it for him. He had even given up writing his satiric eulogies and seemed only to be waiting for the end he was entitled to have as soon as possible, even if he couldn't bring himself to do it Quentin's way. Then he died. I went by the house to give consolation if I could, but mainly to show my face. I found Mrs. Compson crying, Dilsey moaning, and

Benjy howling more loudly than ever, with the old dog Dan keeping up a steady harmony with him. To get this under control, Dilsey sent Benjy and the girl Quentin down to Frony's to play with Luster, though they spent most of their time bickering over spools. On the day of the funeral, T. P. restrained Benjy until the carriages left the drive; but then, carrying Quentin and leading the apelike Benjy, he ran down to the corner, crying, to watch the cortege go by. T. P. was black and a Gibson; but in this household that was almost the same as being white and a Compson.

I was totally amazed to find the missing Caddy herself at her father's funeral. She wore a dark cloak and had just finished placing flowers on Quentin's grave when the procession drove up. She stood to the rear throughout and was given no recognition by her mother or Jason, but she stopped Jason afterward and arranged what I later found out was a deal in which, for an advance payment of $100, Jason would bring her daughter to her so she could see her child before she returned to wherever it was she was headed. So Jason got Mink, one of the funeral hack drivers, to take him home. He got the girl, still less than two, and had Mink race the carriage by Caddy as she stood expectantly at the depot. As soon as they had passed her, Jason held the baby up in the back window and Caddy's peek at her baby amounted to about two seconds worth. Caddy came to see him at the store the next day, but Jason showed no sympathy, being—as he still is today—totally unsympathetic to any human difficulty but his own. Caddy then went to Dilsey to arrange a more substantial encounter with her daughter, but Jason threatened to fire the woman and have Benjy committed to the state asylum if Caddy pursued this. Her final attempt was to offer Jason $1000 if she could get the child away from Mrs. Compson; but Jason, intuiting that Caddy would send Quentin money until she was grown, refused, knowing there was much more cash to be had by holding her for this ransom. He convinced Caddy to leave town lest he not allow her daughter to enjoy what other girls did as they grew up. Then, for the next sixteen years, Jason stole and hoarded nearly every cent Caddy would send for Quentin's well-being, though the girl would ultimately find a way to get a lot of it back [1928].

Meanwhile, Joe Christmas' affair with Bobbie Allen was at its zenith {I.}. He had also taken up smoking and drinking at the dances they attended. He seemed not to understand until late this year, when he caught her in her room with another man, that Bobbie was a whore. Until this time he had been paying her fifty cents (not for any particular favors but just as a gift) every week out of Mrs. McEachern's attic trove [1911]. Her employers, Max and Mame Confrey, scorned her for "doing it" for such small pay; but Bobbie seemed really to love Joe, insofar, that is, as a whore can really "love" any man. Even when he told her that he thought he had nigger blood in his veins, it apparently meant nothing to her. Even when Bobbie was "sick" (and Joe had vomited the first time she ever told him she was), Joe was able to

[173]

overcome his previous repugnance to "womanfilth" and love her, insofar as Joe would ever be able to "love" any woman.

In the Sartoris family, Old Bayard finally decided that his twin grandsons would have to be separated from each other for his and their own good, so he yanked Johnny out of Virginia and sent him to Princeton, leaving Young Bayard behind to calm down at Virginia {S}. And Old Bayard's friend Judge Dunkinfield was made chancellor of the Yoknapatawpha County Court this year [1929] {K}.

Events elsewhere simply accrued. Joan Heppleton was divorced by the husband she deserted in Honolulu {O}. In Pensacola, the rich woman with whom Popeye Vitelli was left by his grandmother started to throw frequent parties for him in an effort to force normality upon this strange child and gain him friends {Y}. The effort was to prove a waste [1913].

Lastly, 1912 contained the best horse race story since several countians indulged in the sport seven years ago [1905]. An Argentinian horse entered the country at New Orleans under the guardianship of a man named Mr. Harry {B}. He was met there by a black groom named Tobe Sutterfield and his grandson who represented the rich Kentuckian who had bought the horse. The three brought the horse northward; but in Mississippi a trestle broke beneath their train and plunged the horse and the three grooms into the river below. They managed to save the horse, but it had a badly fractured leg. Knowing that this would mean stud pasture for one of the fastest horses in the world, they hid out in a swamp until the leg healed. Then, despite the hot pursuit of the Kentuckian and no fewer than five agencies he had hired to find them, they raced the horse at tracks from Texas to Iowa to Ohio, winning everything despite the fact that the horse ran on only three legs. People everywhere became so fired up to see the horse run that they purposely sent the agents on wild goose chases so the races could go off as scheduled. In one town the residents battered the agents' car apart while they were inside the sheriff's office—when they demanded $2000 restitution, the sheriff himself adjudged the damage as only being $50 and passed his hat through the crowd to get it. By year's end, the horse was still winning, but the agents were ready to quit the search [1913].

THE PRESIDENCY OF WOODROW WILSON, 1913–1921

1913

Born: Dewey Dell Bundren

Born: Cedric Nunnery

Born: Susan Reed

Born: Boy who was Uncle Willy Christian's best friend

Died: Simon McEachern

Died: Howard Allison (b. 1903)

Mr. Harry, Tobe Sutterfield, and his grandson were still on the lam with their horse this year [1912] {B}. We were intrigued even by the sparse accounts we read of the events in the paper. The agents had quit, pure and simple. They could not even be bribed to stay on this case—it was just too difficult and too dangerous. But when the owner offered a reward too high to be matched by mere bets on this (now) low-odds horse, the three men and their champion were finally run to ground by a pack of Missouri hillbillies. Before they were taken, though, Harry shot the horse and managed to escape. Sutterfield and his grandson, however, were captured and, for a while, held. The three would be back together in France during the war five years hence.

During the summers when I was home from Harvard, I used to help my father be City Attorney {T}. So this year I more or less took the job on as a sideshow to my not-very-big law practice. Perhaps predictably and even symbolically, my first pursuit of evidence was against Flem Snopes, whom I was anxious to run to ground on principle but never quite could. Flem had pretty much given up the restaurant and hotel business now and had taken over the job as manager of the city water and light plant full time [1914]. The service was spreading out as more and more buildings were becoming plumbed and electrified, but it was not big enough yet to prevent Flem from having too much time to be scheming and not working. What I later discovered was that he was currently stealing brass from the waterworks and making Tom Tom Bird, his daytime engine operator, store it on his property. I knew he was up to something, but it would take me a while to find out just what. What I *did* know was that Flem had a gorgeous wife who was exactly my age and not at all happy living with Flem. I knew that she and Mayor Manfred DeSpain had had an affair on the side, but DeSpain seemed to be little better for someone like Eula [1908]. Perhaps the first person to recognize how interested I was in her, perhaps even before I knew it myself, was my thirteen-year-old cousin Gowan, who was about to go away to private prep school in Washington this year where he could do something besides play football, fire burners, and peep at DeSpain and me in pursuit of Eula. At the Cotillion Ball at Christmas, I even went so far as to send her a corsage to honor her womanhood; but word of it got out ahead of time, via Gowan, and had the adverse effect of having half the town chasing after corsages at

[175]

the last minute. At the Ball I managed to keep Manfred and Eula apart most of the evening, though Manfred beat me up in the alley for it later. And this started a run on chivalrous fights that evening as well—Grenier Weddel sent Sally Hampton Parsons a corsage, and her husband, Maury, gave Grenier a black eye for doing it and Sally one for taking it.

That was not the only run-in I had with Manfred that year, nor the only one he bungled. During the summer he had been roaring through town in his latest car with the cutout open (he had gone back to doing this [1904]), making an infernal racket all day every day. Finally Gowan and Top tried to stop it by scattering tacks on the road near our house, which failed; then by putting a rake there, which also failed; and finally a sharpened rake—which didn't fail but which had Gowan and Top working awfully hard changing tires while DeSpain lounged in our parlor sipping coffee. Later that summer I figured Manfred must also have been behind the missing brass at the power plant and tried to have him impeached for malfeasance. Judge Dunkinfield transferred the case to my father, however; and it was more or less dropped to get both of us out of a tough spot. By year's end it was still not evident to me that I was wasting my time going after DeSpain, a harmless hotshot, and that I should have been after Flem, not harmless and not a hotshot.

Death seemed to be leaving the Compson family alone now, but the remembrance of it was still too fresh to control. The family, whites and blacks alike, made frequent trips to the cemetery to put flowers on Quentin's and his father's graves {F}. Everyone went except Jason, that is, though they would always stop at the store to invite him and he would always refuse.

Joe Christmas apparently committed his first murder this year, though the second one would be more immediately meaningful to the county {L} [1930]. McEachern had long suspected that Joe was hanging around with loose women, so he followed him and Bobbie Allen to a dance hall one night and confronted them. He screamed at Bobbie and called her a Jezebel, whereupon Joe clobbered him over the head with a chair and surely killed him. He then grabbed Simon's horse, rode out to the house, unloaded all of Mrs. McEachern's stored-up money right before her eyes, and raced back to town to pick up Bobbie for their escape. But, if Bobbie could handle a half-Negro boyfriend who paid her only fifty cents a throw, she could *not* handle one of these who was also a murderer. When Joe demanded she go with him, he was badly beaten up by Max Confrey; when he awoke, Bobbie and the Confreys had cleared town.

So, at twenty, Joe went on the road, resentful against the world but especially against women, religious fanatics, and racists, all of whom had perverted his younger life [1927]. At various times over the next fourteen years, he worked as a laborer, miner, prospector, and gambler in such far-flung places as Oklahoma, Missouri, Mexico, Chicago, Detroit, and finally Mississippi. He moved about by freight trains, trucks, wagons, and later by general hitchhiking in ever-more-plentiful private cars. He went to bed with every white woman he could coax between the sheets, punishing their gender by announcing, climactically, that they had made love with a nigger. The one who refused to be shocked by this he beat up, probably as a thoroughgoing surrogate for Bobbie. At sometime during these fourteen years, he was badly sick with VD for two of them.

And then there were several other scattered happenings in Jefferson which are worthy of mention. Ten-year-old Howard Allison, son of the judge, who owned a pony and loved to ride it, was found dragging from the stirrup one day, dead {"Beyond"}. Virginius Holland was forced out of his home after an argument with his father, just like his brother Anse had been before him [1905] {K}. He went to live with Granby Dodge [1929].

Elsewhere Joan Heppleton was deserted by her English boyfriend in Bombay [1911] {O}. In Pensacola Popeye Vitelli killed two lovebirds at one of his stepmother's parties, a cat three months later, and finally was committed to a home for incorrigible children [1918] {Y}. He would be let out later and be allowed to get to Jefferson [1929].

1914

Born: Colonel DeVries

Born: Samuel "Butch" Beauchamp (d. 1940), grandson of Lucas and Molly

Married: Heppleton and Joan

Died: Roskus Gibson, black servant of the Compsons

On June 28th, Archduke Franz Ferdinand was assassinated at Sarajevo, and on August 4th the First World War started in earnest. It looked like a foreign affair, but before long we would all have to go to it or worry about those who had [1917]. In January I was appointed interim County Attorney for Yoknapatawpha {K}, so I officially started out after Flem Snopes. But Flem beat me again; so by year's end I had decided to go to Heidelberg.

In January, I had the water plant audited and found out that brass pipes valued at $218.52 were missing. Audaciously, I had Flem billed for them {T}. Flem went to Tomey's Turl and told him that Tom Tom Bird, the daytime burner operator, had been stealing the pipes and storing them on his property. Flem told Turl to find them under pain of losing his job, which is the exact same reason he told Tom Tom to be putting them there in the first place. So Turl would leave the night shift each morning and wearily go out to scrounge around Tom Tom's land; before long, though, he was also scrounging in bed with Tom Tom's young wife {"Centaur in Brass"}. Well, Tom Tom caught him at it one day and chased him crazily over a several-mile route before he jumped him and caused them both to fall over a cliff. Somewhere in the midst of this brawl both men stopped fighting simultaneously when they realized that Flem was manipulating both of them. So they must have decided to blackmail Flem somehow, for the whole incident quieted down for a while and they kept their jobs. But one day—whether for spite or fun or justice—they carried the pipes secretly to the top of the town water tank and dropped them in {T}. After a few days, everybody in the town was complaining about the taste of the water, and eventually the tank had to be condemned. Flem was forced to resign as superintendent and sat the whole summer on his back porch staring at the tank, which Ratliff later called a "Memorial to Flem." I do not know when it finally dawned on me that the missing pipes must be in the tank, but when it did I ordered the tank drained. It was pointed out to me, however, that the pipes, if found therein, were still on city property and that—while they were not where they were supposed to have been—they could not be considered stolen. I wrestled with this, though even Flem and Manfred DeSpain were not sure that this would float in court.

It was at this point that Flem's wife, Eula, came to me, almost surely at Flem's direction, and offered herself to me if I would drop the suit. Whether from legal ethics or some idealized concept I had of Eula, I declined; but I never did pin the theft on Flem either, even though everybody knew he had done it. Cornered, I demanded once again that Manfred resign from office, as Flem had; and he told me he would if I would just say "please" to him. I wouldn't, so DeSpain didn't. So I left Mottstown, Memphis, and New York for Heidelberg, prematurely gray at twenty-five and ready to romanticize a different, non-Snopes-ridden land.

Meanwhile, two of Eck Snopes's sons by two different wives—Wallstreet Panic and Admiral Dewey—both entered kindergarten this year. The significant fact here is that, while Admiral Dewey was an acceptable six, Wallstreet was twelve.

Another death at the Compsons' this year—this time it was Roskus, Dilsey's husband {F}. Benjy howled for days, as did the new Compson dog, Blue (Dan had died by now, too). To cut down the commotion surrounding the funeral, Dilsey told Luster to take Benjy and young Quentin down to the barn to play; but Luster refused, claiming to have seen his grandfather's (Roskus') ghost down there the night before.

Having tried two years of college and not liking it, especially the year they spent apart at two different ones [1913], the Sartoris twins were back in town and preparing to be wilder than ever {O}. John spent most of his time hunting, and all sorts of crazy stories surround this. Once, while fox hunting with the MacCallums, he cut across Sampson's Bridge ahead of the dogs. A short time later the MacCallums saw him riding downstream on a log singing to the fox—who was riding on the other end. What they did this year was tamer than what they would do next; but Narcissa Benbow—though never one to admire daredevilry—became interested in Bayard and began a five-year chase to nail him down {"There Was a Queen"}. Granby Dodge started paying Old Anse Holland's taxes anonymously this year, income tax (which we had by now) and otherwise. The town thought that Virginius, Anse's estranged son, was doing it; but it later turned up that Granby was, with money he had borrowed from Virginius {K}. During the year also Granby and Virginius made the mutual-deed-of-trust wills that were to solve a legal case I had to get into many years later [1929].

A new face in the county this year was a man named Tommy whom few would notice until he turned up murdered here fifteen years later [1929] {Y}. Lee Goodwin, the man whose employ he would be in when that happened, was currently a cavalry sergeant on the Mexican border and didn't even know him yet.

There were further developments on the Sutterfield horse story [1913] {B}. In April, the lawyer appointed to defend him claimed the arrest was illegal; and, in reverse of what they usually do in a southern Missouri town when they have a black man stewing in a jail cell, the townspeople gathered outside and demanded that he be set free, claiming that they "did not like rich niggers around here" to cover whatever their real motive might have been at this moment. The local authorities acquiesced; and before Sutterfield and his grandson left town they made the most startling revelation of all in this strange story of the three-legged horse: that they had only bet enough on him to keep themselves fed and clothed. They had run him out of admiration for his courage and not out of a craving for easy cash. I personally wondered how this horse and Ned McCaslin's mule would have done pitted against one another [1881].

1915

Born: First child of the country family adopted by Narcissa Benbow

A year of loose ends as the County came to understand that another war was headed its way. The *Lusitania* was torpedoed off the coast of Ireland in May, and 114 Americans lost their lives to the Germans. Henry Ford went to Europe to make peace but came home to tell the country that the war would have to run its course. He seemed to imply that we might have to help it do that. I was still in Heidelberg, of course, keeping my mouth shut; and I only got scattered bits of news from home from my mother, V. K. Ratliff, and a few others who remembered to write. My younger sister wrote me of exchanging friendship rings with her girlfriends from the Jefferson Academy, one of whom was Melisandre Backus who was one day, by a circuitous route, to be my wife [1942] {I}.

Flem Snopes spent most of the year still staring at the water tank, trying to figure out how to get the brass pipes out of it before it was demolished {T}. Wallstreet Panic Snopes had advanced from kindergarten to the second grade by spring and was tutored through the third grade work during the summer by Miss Vaiden Wyott, who also advised him to change his name to Wall Snopes and forget both the thoroughfare and the commotion which once took place on it [1911]. Not only was he learning quickly, it seemed as if he were working energetically at odd jobs as well. During the summer he acquired a delivery route for a Memphis newspaper and, by the fall, now in the fourth grade, had gotten one for a Jackson paper and given the Memphis one to Admiral Dewey. The Jackson route was so vast that he had to hire two other boys to work for him. Such was the news of the Snopeses.

The most exciting news, as always these days, was about the Sartoris boys. They were, of course, still hunting with the MacCallums and generally helling around. One day, when there was supposed to be a balloon exhibition in town, John made the ascent himself when the travelling aeronaut got sick and the gathered crowd was about to be disappointed {S}. He came down hard in a briar patch three miles away, but he returned cheerfully to town in a Negro's wagon despite much torn skin and clothing {O}. Not to be outdone, Bayard on another occasion attached a rope to the top of Flem Snopes's ninety-foot water tower and swung on it from the roof of a building across fifty yards worth of piled lumber and freight cars, letting go at the end of the arc and plunging downward into a narrow concrete swimming pool while the crowd which had gathered to watch *this* gaped in horror. Particularly frightened were Narcissa Benbow, who feared losing Bayard, and Aunt Jenny Du Pre, who feared for the Sartoris name. Later this year, after working a few months as a flying instructor in Memphis, Bayard decided to officially register his bravado and joined the Royal Air Force, winding up in the same unit as Gerald Bland, a Rhodes Scholar whom Quentin and I had known without relish at Harvard {"Ad Astra"}.

Other than that, from all appearances things in Jefferson were calm. Ike McCaslin received a notice from the Arkansas bank that the $1000 it was sending at $3 a month to Sophonsiba Beauchamp had finally exhausted itself and advised him to send more if he wanted the payments continued [1887] {G}. Young Anse Holland returned from his exile to Jefferson, but continued a self-imposed one, living as a hermit in a one-room, dirt-floor cabin [1905] [1929] {K}. Buck Thorpe, who was once Jackson and Longstreet Fentry before the Thorpes claimed him back [1897] and who was now known around town simply as "Ripsnorter," was involved in activities less sensational but definitely more illegal than the Sartorises—such as stealing unbranded cattle and herding them down the main road to Memphis, distilling illegal whisky that was known as the worst in the county, and generally beating up every other young man in the district as well as fooling around with Herman Bookwright's daughter on the side [1917]. The best student in town this year and for several following was Virgil Beard, whose mother owned the boarding house [1919] {S}. Another student, young Loosh Peabody, was off at medical school in New York but returned once or twice a year to see his father.

One of the county's biggest bootlegging operations would eventually be run by Lee Goodwin and his common-law wife, Ruby LaMarr [1929] {Y}. During this year Lee was in the Philippines, though he got sent home to Leavenworth after killing a soldier in a fight over a black woman. Ruby was still living with her volatile father and, at some point in this year, was forced to watch in horror as he gunned down her lover.

In Alabama, Doane's Mill, which would one day send us Lena Grove, opened for business this year [1930] {L}. In Memphis, among some friends of ours, Lucius Binford was officially appointed landlord at Miss Reba's whorehouse, word of which leaked back to Jefferson through Boon Hogganbeck's wife, who used to work there [1905] {Y}. Joan Heppleton, after only a year of marriage [1914], divorced her husband and went underground until she showed up in Jefferson four years later [1919] {O}.

1916

Born: Second child of the country family adopted by Narcissa Benbow

Died: Mrs. Will Starnes

In 1916 we got ready to go to war again, though certainly not with the relish our forefathers apparently got ready to go to their war with. I came home from Heidelberg this summer, knowing I would soon have to return to Europe for a different purpose {T}. I did so later in the year when I worked as a stretcher-bearer in the American Field Service in France until I got pneumonia and had to be sent home the following year [1917] {T} {M} {K}. Buddy MacCallum joined the U.S. Army and waited patiently for us to get into the war {S}. Too impatient for that, though, was John Sartoris who went to England and caught up with his twin brother who was already flying there.

Back home things were quiet this year, and such quiet years usually meant that Flem Snopes had moved up to the next level of the social strata {S}. So he managed to become Vice President of the Sartoris Bank by buying up enough shares over the years to vote himself in [1927]. Hawkshaw Stribling, a barber who would soon get to Jefferson [1918] [1930], made his eleventh annual trip to Division to clean Mrs. Starnes' house for her, though this year she died while he was still there, eleven years after the death of her daughter whom Hawkshaw had loved {"Hair"}. Doc Peabody warned Old Bayard Sartoris that he had a heart condition, but Bayard was not prone to pay much attention [1919]. And Belle Mitchell, according to her anyway, made a poet out of the son of a local carpenter and paid his way to New Orleans where he got arrested as a draft-dodging conscientious objector and narrowly missed going to prison {T} {O}. Instead, according to a letter Belle got from him, he fled New Orleans and wound up in Texas, taking over a newspaper job which had been vacated by a man who had enlisted in the Marines. Lastly, Judge Allison, still not over his son's death a few years back [1913], was—to Jefferson's horror—becoming great friends with the town atheist [1913] {"Beyond"}.

Elsewhere, Ruby LaMarr fled from her murderous father and went to Leavenworth to try to get Lee Goodwin out of prison {Y}. She gave herself to a lawyer to get him to help her, only to discover afterward that he had no jurisdiction to do so.

1917

Born: Spoot Rider (d. 1941)

Born: Third child of the country family adopted by Narcissa Benbow

Married: Bayard Sartoris III and Caroline White

Died: Mr. Nightingale (b. 1848)

Died: Buck Thorpe (b. 1894), also known as Jackson and Longstreet Fentry and Ripsnorter

Though some other things happened that I will tell you about, 1917 was a year in which to study the varying reactions of human beings to war—going to it, trying to serve even if not allowed by age or gender to go to it, or trying not to go to it—that is, stay out of it. From April 6th on you could observe the entire spectrum.

On that date the only countians actively going at it as yet were John and Bayard Sartoris in the Royal Air Force [1916]. So in April, having recovered from my pneumonia and having gotten my nose in too much county business on the side, I departed with the first American troops, though I was to be a noncombatant in charge of running a YMCA installation in France {T}. I took Montgomery Ward Snopes with me, pretty much as a source of information and to protect him from having to go any other way, which he wouldn't have. This was to prove a great mistake on my part. Many Jefferson boys (since I was twenty-eight I couldn't go with them) joined Jackson McLendon's Sartoris Rifles. My cousin Gowan wanted to go to, but at seventeen he was prevented from enlisting and had to live with the Mallisons until his folks could get the State Department to let them out of China where his father was on a diplomatic mission. Byron Snopes didn't sign up for anything and thus got a draft notice instead {S}. So he went to Memphis for his physical and was back at work at the Sartoris Bank in twenty-three days, having failed it by strapping a piece of chewing tobacco under his left armpit to speed up his heart beat. Byron would, as a result, become one of those so-called "men" who messed around, or tried to, with other men's wives while they themselves were being wounded overseas. His cousin Montgomery Ward was just as bad; no sooner had he planted himself in France than he and a French girl had set something up in the back room of the YMCA canteen that was obviously more intriguing to the soldiers than what was going on in the front one {T}.

There were others as well who went. Buddy MacCallum, now rejected by his father for joining the "Yankee" army, was shipped overseas from New Jersey after getting in a fight with a man who insisted upon calling him "Virge" {S}. Darl Bundren was in France and must have fought well, though he was better known around the camps for his famous peek-a-boo telescope {D}. The Sartoris black named Caspey Strother was drafted for a labor battalion and worked on the docks at St. Sulpice where, he later claimed, he freely defied white officers' orders in order to do what he pleased {S} {O}. Tug Nightingale, who like Buddy MacCallum had a father who threw him out of the house for "fighting in blue" (even though it was brown now), joined McLendon's regiment because he felt Germans had to be taught "to stop mistreating folks" {M}. Ironically, he was detached from the Rifles during its training in Texas and reassigned elsewhere as a cook. Lee Goodwin, out of Leavenworth to fight in a convicts' brigade, fought extremely bravely and had received two medals before 1917 was over {Y}. Joe Christmas enlisted in the army, served four months, and then deserted just before his outfit was to go overseas. He was never caught. And finally Jackson McLendon was decorated for valor this year {"Dry September"} [1929].

Perhaps for the first time in 140 years, World War I made Northerners and Southerners feel like they had a common purpose. And it made both more cosmopolitan, all gaining friends and acquaintances they would remember, and sometimes reencounter, years later. In England, for instance, a British Captain Warren and an American named Ginsfarb made an acquaintance which would be renewed a decade hence in Jefferson [1928] {"Death Drag"}. The Reverend Tobe Sutterfield arrived to represent an International Peace Organization but was spurned by Mr. Harry, the man with whom he raced the three-legged horse and who was now a British sentry [1912] [1913] {B}.

[183]

Another man some Jeffersonians would meet again in the future, in the lobby of Miss Reba's whorehouse in Memphis, was Captain Strutterbuck [1898] [1922] {M}. Fate had thrown together a million men, and the entangling was to last long after the Great War for those who survived it.

Women in Yoknapatawpha served in other ways. Narcissa Benbow worked for the Red Cross and a number of other organizations {O}. She adopted a country family consisting of a man, his pregnant wife, and two infants. She assisted them in the birth of their third child, kept their house, and once a month wrote letters for the family to the husband who had gone to Europe to fight. Ruby LaMarr, hoping for Goodwin to return a free man, worked in a munitions plant in New York. In Jefferson, Judge Dunkinfield's daughter was home, driven from Europe by the war; she brought her father a brass box as a memento of the Europe which was about to be ravaged beyond recognition, just as the South had been [1929] {K}. Down the street Harry Mitchell did not bother to go to war at all {O}.

Before April, however, other things happened in the county that are worth remembering. Buck Thorpe, "Ripsnorter" as he was called, was killed by Herman Bookwright for running off with his daughter down in Frenchman's Bend {K}. Bookwright then turned himself in to Will Varner, still the justice of the peace there. Bookwright's family came to me just before I left for France, and I agreed to defend him. In one of my better summaries, which some always thought worthy of Darrow himself in content and conviction, I argued that Bookwright, like all of us, was so ensnarled in history and fate that he could not help himself in what he did, that Thorpe did enough to provoke any man to extreme action. The jury was out an intolerable amount of time and came back hung when a juryman named Fentry refused to go along with the will of the other eleven to acquit Bookwright. Another lawyer got Bookwright off in the next term, but I was immediately curious as to why Fentry was so adamant in his desire to see Thorpe vindicated by Bookwright's conviction. I went to speak with him at his run-down home but was run off by a shotgun blast. Later Rufus Pruitt and his mother told me the missing piece of information when I talked with them at Varner's Store that same day—Buck Thorpe was really Jackson and Longstreet Fentry, whom old man Fentry had raised as a small child for several years until his relatives came to claim kin [1894] [1897]. Fentry could not forgive Bookwright, who he felt had murdered his own son, even though Thorpe wasn't his son and hadn't even seen old Fentry since the day he was taken away.

The war did not do much to hamper love-making in the county this year. Bayard returned from England to marry Caroline White in Memphis {O}. Aunt Jenny Du Pre went up for the occasion, though she later admitted to being mortified when some of the students Bayard had taught at the Memphis Flying School flew overhead during the ceremony and dropped roses, most of which landed on rooftops rather than on the wedding party, and when the whole thing was conducted with rented swords and all sorts of other military trappings. Caroline managed to get pregnant before Bayard went back to war and decided to name her baby John the minute she knew she would have one {S}. Also, just before he departed—himself to a YMCA position in Europe—Horace Benbow became attracted to Belle Mitchell, though the romance would have to be held in abeyance for about sixteen months [1919]. A woman named Minnie Cooper had a boyfriend this year, too, with a car, the first male companion she had managed to retain and she was twenty-seven {"Dry September"}. It was a torrid romance, according to town gossip, but it did not survive the war—the man, a cashier at the other bank, went away [1929]. And Hawkshaw Stribling, with Sophie Starnes dead a dozen years now [1905] and her mother one [1916], took over the mortgage payments for the remainder of the Starnes family—$200 a year, always paid on April 16th (to commemorate Sophie's death). He did this for the next sixteen years until the house was paid for [1933] {"Hair"}.

Finally, two Finns escaped from Russia this year when the Bolshevik Revolution broke out—they would later find their way to Jefferson to become two of the town's most efficient capitalists, even though they would call themselves socialists [1919] [1922] [1938] {M}.

1918

Born: John Sartoris IV (d. 1918)

Died: Caroline White Sartoris, in childbirth

Died: John Sartoris IV (b. 1918), shortly thereafter

Died: John Sartoris III (b. 1893), shot down in Europe

Died: Lemuel "Judge" Stevens II, father of Gavin Stevens and Margaret Stevens Mallison

Died: Eck Snopes (b. 1881)

Died: Reverend Tobe Sutterfield

Died: Grandson of Reverend Sutterfield

Died: Mr. Harry

Carnage. Antigny, Chateau Thierry. Belleau Wood. Soissons. St. Mihiel. The Argonne Forest. Finally it ended, though not without taking its toll on the county. Several Yoknapatawphans lost their lives, most notably Johnny Sartoris.

Johnny was not originally assigned to the unit that got him killed but was only transferred there when he and his commander, a British officer named Spoomer, could no longer endure each other's presence. Unfortunately, both were interested in the same woman, a French girl named 'Toinette, and they would stop at nothing to do each other out of her {"All the Dead Pilots"}. It was only too bad that Spoomer was in charge of the flying schedules, for this allowed him to have Johnny in the air at precisely the hours, usually the prime ones, that he wished to have 'Toinette in bed. So Johnny was, for a while, confined to symbolic acts of retaliation, such as strafing Spoomer's dog. But finally, in a trick quite reminiscent of his grandfather in the other war, Johnny got back at him by stealing his clothes while he was in the back room of a cafe making love to the girl during an enemy attack [1863]. Spoomer had to return to the base in a woman's skirt, and from there to England with a demotion and a reassignment. But Johnny was demoted and reassigned, too, to the outfit in which he got killed.

The only version we have of Johnny's death is young Bayard's, since he was the only one flying with him that day that was close enough to watch it {S}. In a vicious dogfight against a pilot Bayard liked to refer to simply as "The Hun," Johnny kept zigzagging all over the sky in pursuit of him, often coming between Bayard's guns and the German plane, causing Bayard not to fire or, if firing already, to dive to steer his bullets away. I personally have often wondered whose guns did Johnny in, whether Bayard accidentally downed his own brother's plane because of his daredevil flying. Anyway, suddenly the chuteless Johnny bailed out of his plane, after first thumbing his nose at Bayard and flipping his hand at The Hun, and sprawled out flat in the air, doing a gutbuster (as Bayard described it) on a cloud. But after he passed through the cloud Bayard never saw him again, despite flying downward faster than Johnny's plane was crashing to try to rescue him in some inconceivable way. Twice Bayard was almost hit by his brother's flaming plane, almost as if the two were doomed to go together. Bayard wished later that they had.

This was in July. And, as the story goes, Bayard flew alone for eight days until he finally shot down a German aircraft that he could manage to convince himself belonged to The Hun {"Ad Astra"}. Meanwhile, Johnny had been buried in an anonymous grave in a cemetery just north of St. Vaast.

Other countians were heroes, too. Buddy MacCallum won a medal on the German front when he tried to jump a machine gun position in a wheatfield, got badly wounded, and wound up in a field hospital {"The Tall Men"}. So home came Buddy MacCallum bearing a luger he took from a German soldier in France {S}. Not knowing, of course, how dangerous it could be to do so, Buddy traded it to Crawford Gowrie for a brace of foxhounds; this, I suppose, left Buddy free to do what he preferred above killing and Crawford free to do what he preferred above hunting. The Grier family's Uncle Marsh was wounded in France as well {"Two Soldiers"}.

Through all this I was a noncombatant, at times happily, at others reluctantly, and—more often than not—ashamedly. I kept the YMCA canteen in Paris going, despite Montgomery Ward Snopes and things he did to sabotage it, and I even found time to fall in love with a Russian girl until the war was over {K}.

Also in Paris at this time was the Reverend Tobe Sutterfield, associated several years before with his grandson and the Sentry Harry in the three-legged horse incident and now head of an American peace mission [1912] {B}. In an incident provoked by a mutinous and pacifistic corporal named Stefan, the Reverend Sutterfield, his grandson, Harry, and several others stepped out of the trenches on a French battlefield and walked toward the German lines. Their purpose, apparently, was to embrace their enemies and demonstrate to their military superiors that the enlisted men on both sides no longer wanted to fight. The Germans rushed out to meet them, to declare their collective separate peace. However, batteries from both the Allied and the German sides gunned the entire peace party down; among the dead were Sutterfield, his grandson, and Harry.

Nor was this Yoknapatawpha's only connection, however roundabout, with this bizarre incident. For having allowed the incident to occur in the first place, General Charles Gragnon was relieved of his command and, for a multitude of other reasons, marked for execution. One of the three American soldiers sent to his cell to finish him off clandestinely was Philip Mannigault Beauchamp, a distant relative of Lucas Beauchamp and Nancy Mannigoe. Philip had been studying to be an undertaker after the war. On this occasion he was ordered to use his talents to plug an errant bullet hole on Gragnon's body, lest the world recognize his death to be murder rather than the justifiable act of self-defense it was being claimed to be. Such stories as this were not uncommon during The Great War.

But in November it ended. In Paris there was a celebration for the Supreme Commander on the Champs Elysées after the surrender of Germany {B}. On that very evening Bayard Sartoris, Gerald Bland, and Buck Monaghan—also in Paris—took a German aviator that Monaghan had shot down to a French cafe and, before long, incited a riot when Monaghan began chastising the pacifistic German {"Ad Astra"}. This was broken up, however, and all were thrown out. So they set out for a brothel. Bayard later told me that, as he walked, he cried all the way for his dead wife, his son, and his twin brother Johnny. He recalled also a remark made by a subadar who was in their company: "All this generation who fought in the war are dead tonight, but we do not yet know it." But I think Bayard *did* know it.

And so the course of fate, which had been momentarily interrupted and permanently altered by the war, began to weave its labyrinthine path again. Lee Goodwin was shipped home from the war posthaste and returned, without thanks, to his cell at Leavenworth {Y}. Popeye Vitelli, the man for whom he would in the future die, was set free this year from the home he had grown up in [1913] and began his yearly visits to his invalid mother in Pensacola.

Since men like Stefan could not get the war stopped, people back in Jefferson tried to get on as best they could until it was over. For most of the Snopeses (Montgomery Ward being the only one who bothered to show up in Europe during the war and he was not there either to fight or to win), the war did not even amount to a nuisance. Clarence Snopes, later a state senator [1921], was commanding a gang of roughnecks which specialized in beating up Negroes and terrifying women and children {M}. Byron Snopes wrote mash letters to Narcissa Benbow {S} {"There Was a Queen"}. Flem got himself further into the Sartoris Bank stocks while Old Bayard himself worried about his nephews, who, by July, had become singular and not plural. Eck Snopes, who, because of the neck brace he wore from saving a Negro from a log several years before [1907], could not have gone to war if he had wanted to, lost his life at home instead. When Cedric Nunnery, a local youngster got lost one night, Eck climbed to the top of one of the gas tanks he was paid to guard and lit a match to see if the boy was hiding inside {T}. The tank blew up, of course, and no trace of Eck was ever found, save for the neck brace itself which Tom Tom Bird found wrapped around a tree the next morning. The gas company gave $1000 to Eck's wife, and she in turn gave it to their son Wall to open a grocery business, in which she served for a while as his partner.

While my nephew, Gowan, was in Washington for his last year of prep school, his parents finally were released from China {T} [1917]. In the second half of the year the Negro church burned down; and the chief Sartoris black, Simon Strother, was appointed treasurer for the rebuilding funds {S}. None of his fellow churchgoers knew for quite some time, however, that Simon was lending out the money they collected to a black hairdresser and probable whore, Meloney Harris. None ever suspected what Simon was up to, since he was easily in his seventies; but Simon justified the loss of the money Meloney left town with by citing his boss's occupation—that is, Bayard's—as amounting to pretty much the same thing: handing out other people's money without their knowing who had it. In trouble also this year was Crawford Gowrie who was drafted on his 18th birthday on November 2nd but decided to desert rather than go to war {I}. He did so on November 10th, not knowing that the war would end on the following day. For the next eighteen months, still not knowing it, he lived in a cave fifteen miles from Jefferson, stalked by the authorities to be drafted for a war which by then had ended [1920].

Horace Benbow was one of the last of us to get to war, failing to leave home or show up until February of this year. He too was a noncombatant. His sister, Narcissa, renewed her interest in Bayard when he came home from the war briefly to attend the funerals of his wife and son, both dead in childbirth [1914]; and she, like others, patiently sat through the renderings of his brother's death and stories of alternative bravado, such as the occasion when he knocked two teeth out (or claimed to have) of an Australian major's mouth for talking to the woman he was with at the Leicester Lounge in London {S}.

V. K. Ratliff traded in his horse cart for a Model T {D}. Late this year a man named Samson started trading with Stuart MacCallum whom he had known since Stuart, now forty-four, was a boy but whose name he could never recall. And just as the war was ending, Hawkshaw Stribling came to Jefferson from Porterfield to work in Maxey's barbershop {"Hair"}. He quickly fell for a five-year-old girl named Susan Reed and bought her a Christmas present this year and every year thereafter [1930].

These are just a few of the things that happened at home before the Courthouse bells were rung furiously on November 11th to celebrate the Armistice. With this, some quickly and some much more slowly, all of us started home, though I was to remain there only two weeks before going to Washington to work for the rehabilitation bureau which was getting ready to put the Europe we had just destroyed back together again {T}. During the several months I worked there, I took up translating the Old Testament into classical Greek, a project that my nephew Chick would one day love to chide me for {G}.

1919

Born: Son of Young Major DeSpain (d. 1942)

Born: Vardaman Bundren

Born: Second wife of Will Varner

Married: Bayard Sartoris III and Narcissa Benbow

Married: Horace Benbow and Belle Carpenter Mitchell

Married: Melisandre Backus and Harriss

Married: Ruby LaMarr and Lee Goodwin (common law)

Died: Bayard Sartoris II, "Old Bayard" (b. 1838)

Died: Yettie Snopes, wife of Mink

This was the "year of the boy," the year the boys came home men or less than men because they had seen too much to be able to think very much of being part of the human race anymore. Tug Nightingale was one of the last to return and one of the first to be taunted by the likes of Skeets McGowan who never left the back of his drugstore counter in 1917 or 1918 yet still felt compelled, indeed obliged and credentialed, to challenge the veracity of those who told their real or imagined stories of horror {M}. The imagined ones, though, were just as real as the real ones because the imagined ones were invented before the fact, for the most part, rather than after. Perhaps because of this none of us felt too bad the night Tug laid McGowan out cold and sent him for a few days in the county hospital. Luckily he was out of sight there during the visit of the only local woman war hero, a nurse who was the relative of a Jefferson citizen who had been stationed near the guns of Montedidier, closer than I ever managed or wanted to get to live ammunition while I was over there. Also back was Darl Bundren who was picked up at the Jefferson station by his father, Anse, and neither of them was seen in town again for over eleven more years, until one day they brought their wife-mother here to bury her [1930] {D}. Finally, one of the last to arrive was Horace Benbow, fresh from a close postwar scrape with death when he almost started a fire on board ship with his infamous glass-blowing machine {O}.

Also arriving "home" this year were a number of people who had never called it that before—like the last of the great influx of Snopeses, among them Montgomery Ward, himself a "war veteran"—and the two Finns who had finally made it from Russia to Jefferson [1917] {M}. One, a cobbler, took over Mr. Nightingale's shop; the other, a tinsmith, founded his own business.

At the age of thirty, I returned as well, though not for long. During the spring I began dating, then fell in love with, then became engaged to Melisandre Backus, once a friend of my sister's at the Jefferson Academy [1915] {K}. Besides this I did very little else, except for an occasional leftover case I worked on for my late father [1918]. By the fall, I decided, with my father's bequest, to return to Heidelberg to finish my Ph.D., still not sure that small-town county-attorneying was a sufficient goal in life to pursue [1942]. I would marry Melisandre the next year when I returned; but, before I could even manage to get home, I took up dating a Russian girl in Germany and writing to her after she went home. Ultimately I managed to cross letters and envelopes, and she and Melisandre both dropped me in classic epistolary fashion. So, during the fall, I was only half-surprised when Margaret notified me that Melisandre was now engaged to a New Orleans bootlegger named Harriss (more than twice her age, Margaret told me.) Then, in less than another week, I received a second letter announcing that they had already been married, that Harriss had stayed in Yoknapatawpha for about two weeks after the ceremonies, then had returned, *sans* Melisandre, to New Orleans and was not to come back here until the Christmas holidays. When he did so he proved to be even richer than the town (or probably Melisandre) remembered him. But other states than Mississippi were dry now that Prohibition had begun, so men like Harriss found money, friendship, and even respect among those who would continue to be intolerant of law-breakers of any other sort at all, perhaps excepting those who lynched Negroes in the name of the community.

But if Yoknapatawphans today recall 1919 for anything at all, it will always be for the fact that it marked the more or less final and more than less long-awaited demise of the ancient Sartoris family, whose progenitor had led our troops to the Civil War [1861] (only to be rebuked by them a year later [1862]) and whose lineage had provided cannon fodder for several more wars thereafter, where all American soldiers fought for the blue rather than any at all for the grey. On a day in the spring of this year, Old Bayard, still president of the Sartoris bank at seventy-one, was informed by his Negro chauffeur, Simon, that Young Bayard had himself returned from war, though not as a Sartoris and not as a hero, but as a tramp, jumping off a speeding freight train north of town. He finally showed up at the Sartoris back porch around nightfall. The whole town was soon to know that Young Bayard could not survive here long, and Old Bayard probably knew it from the first moment he spoke to him or, perhaps, even heard he was back. His conversation was a maze of confused detail about his lost brother, Johnny, who had been shot down in the war [1918], and his dead wife, who had died in childbirth the same year. So, while other war veterans tried to settle down to normality as best they could, save perhaps for the Sartoris black who had gotten "liberated" during the war and was not prepared to do any more menial work around the old plantation, Young Bayard went off to Memphis to buy himself a fast car and soon became the terror of Yoknapatawpha roadways as he sped up and down them with his Aunt Jenny in the seat beside him. (Nobody was ever prepared to decide whether Aunt Jenny went to tame him down or because she got a kick out of the speed herself.) Soon Old Bayard, too, had taken up the riding habit, but there was no doubt at all about his reasons [1903].

So there was a general consensus among Old Bayard, Aunt Jenny, and even Simon (because by now Isom had been helling around in the car as well) that this youngest of the remaining Sartorises ought to get married; and Narcissa Benbow was selected, almost by tacit agreement among herself and young Bayard's guardians, to be the mate. At twenty-six she was the only granddaughter of Judge Francis Benbow, only daughter of Will Benbow, sister of Horace Benbow—who was a lawyer, graduate of Sewanee and Oxford—the blood lines, in short, were right. But she had a strange attachment to her brother, though perhaps luckily for both of them he had an even stranger attachment to Belle Mitchell, wife of Harry Mitchell and about to fly the coop. So, with Horace himself showing signs of quick departure after his own recent return from the war (where he, like me, had been a noncombatant), Narcissa was prone to agree, again tacitly, that she should be united in wedlock to this strange young man, Young Bayard, whose mind was still flying planes while his body drove a car, whose name was Sartoris but might as well—as far as he was concerned—be Smith, and whose remaining time on earth was limited, though only he knew that and even that was to be too long for him. Yet Narcissa had another problem: few knew, though her Aunt Jenny was among those who did, that she was regularly receiving mash notes from an unknown source; and it was not for some years that we connected them to Byron Snopes. The handwriting turned out to be Virgil Beard's, but he was paid off for this service with a long-coveted air gun.

But there was the matter too of a proposal—Young Bayard had not made any yet. Rather, he was more interested in nighttime carousing with his men friends, in wild driving, and even in wild stallion riding, and (as an offshoot) frequent visits to Old Doc Peabody for bandaging. Finally in June, while Byron continued to write his mash notes, while Horace continued to work at a glass-blowing machine he had set up in his basement {O} and play tennis at the Mitchells' in the afternoon, while Narcissa continued to pine in the confusing threeway, multifaceted triangle of Byron-Horace-Bayard, and while Aunt Jenny continued to nag Old Bayard about having a wen she believed to be cancerous removed from his face—amidst all this loud, noiseless clamor, Young Bayard drove his car off a bridge into a creek bed and nearly killed himself. And he probably would have if a Negro named John Henry had not resisted his father's urgings to leave hands off and hauled Bayard into Peabody, who threw a cast on him and put him right where Jenny and his grandfather needed him to be—laid up in a bed {S}. So this was how the proposal they sought was to come about, for Narcissa was imported to read to him, though he probably heard not a word she said as his psyche was still in the European skies watching his twin brother plunge chuteless through the clouds after bailing out of his plane [1918]. Finally, he even told her about it, and both he and she knew that no one—not even she—would ever be able to share in the horror the moment held for him.

In July Old Bayard went to Memphis to have his wen removed and wound up with a fifty dollar bill for the treatment, even though it apparently fell off on its own in the doctor's outer office, the result of an ancient ointment Old Man Falls had smeared on it some weeks before [1820]. In July as well, Belle Mitchell left Harry for good and took Little Belle away from her singing and dancing lessons to Reno, Nevada, to acquire the quick divorce she needed to marry Horace, who was himself making plans to leave Jefferson and the scandal that was likely to ensue. One which was brewing already, however, concerned the mismanagement of the Negro church funds by Simon Strother {S}. Meloney Harris had long since spent whatever amount Simon gave her (probably the gross total); and now Simon blatantly attempted to make, and totally succeeded in making, Old Bayard feel it was his white man's burden to bail him out. Bayard fumed; but the Sartoris and Strother names were cleared, and Simon was invited back into the congregation.

In August several matters began to come to a head. Young Bayard was now out of his cast, had had his car repaired in Memphis, and was once again on Yoknapatawpha roadways and Jefferson streets, though he was going more slowly now and had Narcissa rather than Jenny or Old Bayard in the seat beside him. But one day he had to try it again and took Narcissa for the wild ride that she was under the mistaken impression he had promised never to take her or him on again. Both they and the car survived it this time, however; and perhaps it was then, after she really made him promise to give it up, that the engagement, if one were really ever formalized, occurred. By the end of the month they had gotten married. On the evening of their wedding, however, the disappointed Byron Snopes broke into Narcissa's room, re-trieved his mash letters, apparently fondled some of her underpants against his cheek, and lay in her bed. As he did so, Bayard and Narcissa pulled up in the driveway, and Byron was forced to exit through a window and cut himself badly as he fell to the ground {"There Was a Queen"}. As far as we could tell, he crept home to his room at his cousin I. O.'s (where he had moved from Mrs. Beard's boarding house in a futile attempt to escape the materialistic Virgil who stood ever anxious, eager, and ready to write more craven letters for him), bandaged himself as well as he could, went to the Sartoris bank (where he had left the appropriate door ajar), stole some money, and left town with a hired Negro driver right under the nose of Buck, the night marshal {O} {S} He reached Frenchman's Bend around 2 A.M., passed Will Varner's store [1905], the blacksmith shop (which had a gas pump in front of it now), Mrs. Littlejohn's huge unpainted boarding house where several of his relatives had either lived or made money off those who did, and on out into the country to the home of a girl named Minnie Sue {O}. In desperation over Narcissa's marriage, he awakened Minnie Sue from her bed and began to paw furiously under her nightgown until she managed to shove him away, weakened as he was from loss of blood, and told him to come back the next day when he was out of heat. But Byron limped to the car, started the engine, and left the county forever. The only remaining contact we would have with him would be some years later when he mailed four children he had fathered on an Apache squaw to Flem, who would in turn mail them rather quickly back [1929] {T}. The money he stole was never recovered; and Flem, then vice president of the very bank he had robbed, moved his own money to Boss Priest's bank, trusting no institution which someone as essentially stupid as Byron was able to break into.

With the marriage of Horace and Belle Mitchell imminent, Belle's family sent its other daughter, one Joan Heppleton, into Jefferson to get a look at her sister's future mate [1915] {O}. The town saw Horace and Joan driving together a lot, and apparently they fell into an affair together while Belle was off in Reno establishing six weeks' residence. But by late fall Joan had gone, whether or not she had filed her report as yet. Horace was ducking around town to avoid contact with Harry Mitchell and finally nailed down the windows of his now-empty house to move to Kinston, where he had chosen to have them live because of its recently acquired and clearly sham affluence [1911] {Y}. (I was there once some years later; it was one of those places where all the trees have been felled and identical frame houses with garages to match have been built in symmetrical rows) {O}. Flem Snopes would go there some years later when he was seeking an economical layout for Eula Acres after the next World War [1945].

Through the fall the marriage between Narcissa and Young Bayard was going well enough on the surface {S}. They were often seen hunting together, at other times hugging passionately in unlikely locations. But the ghost of Johnny was between them, and Narcissa knew it. Events were largo, yet time seemed to be moving allegro. Then, in December, ten days before Christmas, the coda, the crescendo—though he was probably driving as carefully as he could, Bayard skidded his car to avoid another on an icy road; and, with his grandfather in the seat beside him, he careened down an embankment and, after some anxious moments, came to a safe rest at the bottom of a ravine. But, somewhere between the road and the resting place, Old Bayard suffered the heart attack Doc Peabody had been warning him about all year. At seventy-one, this man who had fought with his legendary father in skirmishes on the western front in the Civil War [1863], who had slain the murderer of his grandmother [1865], who had gone to college and then refused to slay the man who had killed his father [1873], who had established and then become president of the county's biggest bank [1902], who had outlived most of the next three generations of his own family—this man was dead.

Young Bayard could not go home. He had a local Negro bring him his horse, Perry, then rode to the MacCallum house many miles to the northeast where he lived for the next week and a half, hunting, brooding, watching the harmony of family life for which the MacCallums, genealogy-less, were widely known. They had not been to town and so had not heard of his accident or of his grandfather's death. Finally, on Christmas eve, he departed—they thought for home—but he knew not where. Lost, he housed himself in a reluctant Negro's barn for the night, shared Christmas breakfast with them and then, for ten dollars, convinced one of them to drive him to the railhead. Here Young Bayard Sartoris boarded a train jammed with Christmas merrymakers and left Yoknapatawpha County, his home, and his pregnant wife forever [1920].

With the death of Old Bayard, a new bank president had to be chosen. Upon examination of the stock holdings, it was discovered that Will Varner and Manfred DeSpain were the biggest holders, with Flem Snopes still running a fairly distant third {T}. However, his votes plus Will's would have been enough to have Flem elected president, had not Flem devised a plan whereby he would vote his own and Will's stock in Manfred's favor if DeSpain would agree to replace out of his own pocket all the money that Byron had stolen. DeSpain agreed, but he had to mortgage his home—the old DeSpain property—to Will Varner to come up with the needed cash. So the bank books were in order once again, and Flem knew he was holding the trump card he needed—Manfred's long-lasting and well-publicized affair with his wife [1908]—to become president himself whenever he felt he was ready. But Flem had some more relatives to clear out of town, some more respectability to establish before he would, within a decade, claim both DeSpain's job and his mansion [1927]. By then, too, the new mortgage on it would be repaid as well.

But, as in other years, events were occurring beyond county boundaries that would, nonetheless, determine and shape our lives in the not-too-distant future. Philip Beauchamp, home from the war after his messy involvement in the Corporal Stefan matter [1918], did not really come home but established himself as an undertaker in Chicago {B}. Ruby LaMarr finally got Lee Goodwin out of Leavenworth by using a shrewd lawyer whom she paid with money and with sex {Y}. The tall convict at Parchman, whom we would later know as the hero of the 1927 flood, was not in there yet but was on his way—down near the Bend he tried to take up drinking this year (but got into fights before he could get fully drunk) and so took to reading paperback detective tales to pass his time instead. There he learned the techniques with which he bungled his only robbery attempt a couple of years later [1921] {W}.

And so ended the "Year of the Boy," the year when the boys became men and discovered that manhood, if they had been lucky enough to survive to attain it, was not what they thought it would be. Young Bayard Sartoris, unwilling to live, tried his best to get himself killed at home (since the war had failed him) and, within the next six months, would succeed on an Ohio airfield {S}. Horace Benbow, prepared to substitute art for reality when he escaped the horrors of war, found himself instead entering upon a futile and debilitating marriage about which the county would hear much over the next decade or so [1929] {Y}. Montgomery Ward Snopes, finding that the war had changed morality as he understood it, if not practiced it, prepared to open a peep show in Jefferson similar to the one he operated in France

[195]

behind my back in the back room of the YMCA canteen in Paris [1920] [1923] {T}.

And I just decided to become County Attorney after I returned from Europe and, in whatever ways that office would allow, resolved to try to hold Yoknapatawpha County together in the face of a modernity it could not, a decade ago, ever have conceived of.

1920

Born: Benbow "Bory" Sartoris

Born: Max Harriss

Married: Caddy Compson and a motion-picture magnate, in California

Died: Bayard Sartoris III, "Young Bayard" (b. 1893)

Died: Anse MacCallum, "Old Anse" (b. 1845)

Died: Simon Strother, a Sartoris black, once body servant to Colonel John Sartoris

With the exception of Aunt Jenny DuPre, the Sartoris influence and power in Yoknapatawpha County ended this year, and with it went the last vestiges of the southern ideal which so many of us, despite its inherent flaws, spent so much of our lives trying to recoup without knowing exactly how to define it. Young Bayard never had the chance to return to see his son, Benbow or "Bory" as he was called, a son who would himself quit the county after the next war. In January we heard that Bayard was in Tampico, in February in Mexico City, in April in Rio, and early in June in San Francisco. The following week, on the 10th, he turned up in Chicago {S}. Harry Mitchell, whose former wife was already remarried to Horace Benbow and living in Kinston, saw Bayard in a bar there on the same night Harry had his prized diamond stickpin stolen by a bar girl.

Bayard died on June 11th in Dayton, Ohio, lured there (though it probably did not take much luring) by a fly-by-night airplane builder to test-fly his latest model, a model which came apart in the air and, ironically, plummeted Bayard to a death very similar to that of his twin brother, Johnny [1918]. On the next day Aunt Jenny was in the process of trying to wire him to come home when Doc Peabody showed her a newspaper story describing his death. As she had had to so often, she firmly accepted this, knowing it was to have to come before long, somehow, anyway. But the household suffered another death this month, one not so expected. Simon Strother was found murdered one day in Meloney Harris' cabin, perhaps in a showdown over the money he had given her or perhaps in just trying to give her more [1919]. Hence went the last man in the county, with the exception of old Doc Peabody, to know, love, and serve Colonel John Sartoris himself. So Aunt Jenny retired to bed for a while, weary and sick but with another decade left to her yet; but soon she was well enough again to take walks through the cemetery and muse upon the complex and foreordained fate of her family. As if to break that fate by ending the string of Johns and Bayards who were devoured by it, Narcissa christened her son Benbow instead of John as was intended; but Aunt Jenny was of the opinion that changing a name could not change a destiny.

And what of the destiny Narcissa was trying to change it to {O}? Horace Benbow, the last in the county to retain *that* surname, had moved his glass-blowing machine to Kinston, there to be badgered by his new wife for not having enough money to entertain her with, as he had implied he had. His sole regular duty seemed to be to walk down to the railroad station every Friday afternoon to pick up Belle's mail-order shrimp.

If the old names of Benbow and Sartoris had followed the paths of Sutpen and McCaslin and Compson, the replacement name was Snopes. With Washington and Heidelberg out of my system now, I was home for good and got myself elected posthaste as County Attorney, deciding that I needed such office if Snopesism were to advance no farther [1919] {T}. But it did. Byron was already gone from town with a good deal of its money in his pocket. Flem was still vice president of the bank from which he stole it and was about to set out on his own course of pilfering which, ironically, for the most part could be called "legal." Manfred DeSpain, still carrying on a torrid affair with Flem's wife, Eula [1908], was now the president of the Sartoris bank; and, in accord with stipulations Flem set down when he assumed office, he repaid out of his own pocket all the money Byron had swiped, resigned his office as mayor, and sold his auto agency. Montgomery Ward Snopes, who I knew from firsthand experience had to be watched closely [1917], opened an artsy-craftsy photography shop—the Atelier Monty—on the town square and invited lots of town ladies for tea on opening day. For the next three years he changed the displays in his window frequently; so I was deceived and it took me, and Flem as well, all that time to find out what was really going on in there [1923].

Surely the most sensational event of the year, however, was the capture in May of Crawford Gowrie, the draft-dodger who had been hiding in a cave nearby since the day before the war ended 18 months ago [1918] {I}. The man actually fought a thirty-hour pitched battle against Hub Hampton and his deputies with no other weapon than the German luger he traded Buddy MacCallum his foxhounds for. He finally ran out of ammunition, though;

[197]

and they took him in for trial where he got off, surprisingly, with only a year in the State Penitentiary for desertion. Meanwhile, his more respectable brother, Forrest, was off in Vicksburg, where he became manager of a delta cotton plantation this year.

Also off to the pen for eight months was young Anse Holland, who was arrested for making whisky almost before Prohibition had started, though liquor had always been prohibited, if not particularly hard to get, in Mississippi {K}. His twin brother, Virginius, came to court and offered to pay his fine, but Anse insisted on the pen. He got out quickly for good behavior. Elsewhere in the state, beyond the Bend, a tall man was getting ready to be a convict himself, drinking bootleg whisky and performing Al-Capone-like stunts for his girlfriend, who got some sort of thrill out of running stoplights and getting chased by police cars [1921] [1927] {W}.

A few other events and incidents that happened this year were these: Young Loosh Peabody finished medical school but decided to work in New York with a Dr. Straud who was experimenting with electricity and medicine {S}; Jewel Bundren, down at Frenchman's Bend, worked the entire summer and part of the fall plowing Lon Quick's field at night so Lon would give him the offspring of the spotted pony he bought a dozen years ago from Flem Snopes [1908] {D}; the town heard that Caddy Compson had remarried in California to someone in the motion picture business {F}; and Harriss returned during the summer in the biggest, shiniest car the town had ever seen {K}. He hired a Negro governess for the impending birth of his child by Melisandre Backus—a son named Max. But he was gone once more before the birth and did not see his son or wife again until Christmas, when he returned in the same car.

THE PRESIDENCY OF WARREN G. HARDING, 1921–1923

1921

Born: Daughter of Harriss and Melisandre Backus

Died: Zachary "Zack" Edmonds (b. 1874)

Died: Wife of Isaac McCaslin

Died: Mr. Backus

Died: Fraser, a county whiskymaker

[198]

The Snopeses were active again this year, but it was a year of paperwork and undercover dealings which would not come to light for a while. So I had some time to return to my Old Testament translation, which I attempted briefly three years ago but was unable to start on steadily till now [1918]. For the next twenty years, I would spend several nights a week working on it.

Wall Snopes, the decent one, bought out his partner in the grocery business this year, and he and his mother took it on themselves {T}. In June Wall graduated from high school at nineteen, only seven years after he had started kindergarten [1914]. He also proposed to Miss Vaiden Wyott, the second grade teacher who had pushed him through to the end, but was declined [1915]. She was already engaged apparently, but she did introduce him to the woman who would be his wife and who, though her married name would be Snopes, fought Snopesism as hard as anyone [1922] [1923].

And, still not dead, Ab Snopes, who must have been a minimum of eighty by now, with years of horse-stealing and barn-burning behind him, moved into Jefferson for the first time in his life, at least insofar as any of us knew or could remember. Nor did we ever see Flem acknowledge his presence, but the old man supported himself by selling watermelons he grew in his garden. It was not long, however, before his fifteen-year-old nephews, Vardaman and Bilbo, spotted some boys stealing the melons and told Ab about it. Thereafter, even when they didn't see any boys, the two would rile Ab up anyway just for the kick of seeing him run out into the patch with his shotgun. Clarence Snopes, formerly leader of a gang of young hoodlums [1918], was now town constable. Though often conscientious and effective, Clarence had a propensity for losing his temper in the administration of justice and injuring innocent people in his furor {M}. On one occasion a man pressed charges against him for pistol-whipping him. To clear this up and keep the Snopes name as clean as possible, Will Varner, himself an old but vigorous man now, got Flem and Manfred DeSpain to get Clarence elected to the state legislature—which meant buying and stealing votes. Before the year was out, Clarence was so elected and was frequenting the Gayoso district in Memphis instead of beating up on civilians in Jefferson.

In the McCaslin family, Ike's unloved and unloving wife died this year, willing the small bungalow her father gave her to Ike [1893] {G}. Also dead was Zack Edmonds, so the land that Ike had given up passed to Zack's twenty-three-year-old son, Roth, who vowed to manage it exactly as Cass and Zack had. But he was quick to discover that he was fated to have a similar problem to the one they had as well—Lucas Beauchamp, who began this year distilling corn liquor somewhere on the McCaslin land [1941]. Roth decided to leave well enough alone for as long as he could, and he could for a while.

Old Man Backus, who would have been my father-in-law if I had married his daughter sooner than I did [1942], died doing what he had done everyday for the last forty-seven years—working his farm, reading Roman poets, and drinking cold toddies on his porch [1874] {K}. He left the plantation to Melisandre, who was already about to give birth, in September, to her second child—a girl. Harriss did not come back until Christmas this year either, at which point he took over the administration of the Backus land and arranged to have Negro tenants do the farming.

The county had another young man, this time Howard Boyd, go away to a fancy college this year, the University of Virginia [1903]; and his possessive mother went along to run a boarding house in Charlottesville {"The Brooch"} [1930]. Someone else who went away was the cashier from whom Minnie Cooper had spent four futile years awaiting a proposal of marriage {"Dry September"}. Minnie was thirty-one now and looking older. Another young man in town, Percy Grimm, made it widely known that he was furious with his parents for letting him be born too late to get into the last war {L}. And still another, Monk Odlethrop, the idiot, was brought into Jefferson when his foster-father, Fraser, the still operator, died, probably from over-work {K}.

Monk found employment at a filling station where he occupied himself ostensibly, pumping gas and sweeping, but where his real job was keeping an eye on the half-pint bottles of hooch the owner had stashed in a nearby ditch.

Prohibition was, of course, in full swing now, and so was the gangster resistance to it. Harriss was shipping lots of imported stuff north out of New Orleans {K}. And Crawford Gowrie, now out of Parchman, became a liquor runner (perhaps for Harriss, perhaps not) from New Orleans to Memphis for the next nine years [1930] {I}. And into Parchman went the tall young man from near the Bend who had spent the last couple of years impressing his girlfriend with gangland stunts {W}. He was finally caught sticking up a train with a gun that could not have fired and was given fifteen years, though this was to be extended by ten, until 1946, because he supposedly tried to escape during the flood of 1927. His girlfriend visited him in prison, once, three months later, but she was already wearing unfamiliar earrings and never came back a second time.

Crime seemed to have become a national profession in the years after the War. Some of it was because of Prohibition, which made many who were otherwise respectable buy and hide crummy gin. But it was more the result of a certain shiftlessness that set in, a loss of purpose, which the subadar back in Paris had told Bayard Sartoris was to be the equivalent of being dead without knowing it [1918]. Buck Monaghan, for example, was now a wing-walker in a flying show—not that he wanted to be one, he just didn't know what else to be {"Honor"}. At night he was having an affair with the wife of his pilot, though he supposedly swore her off when the pilot—named Rogers—saved him one day when Buck made a mistake which nearly cost him his life [1928]. Later Buck was to become a used car salesman, which he did not want to be either.

[200]

1922

Born: Son of Howard and Mildred Rogers

Married: Wall Snopes and his wife

Died: Mother of Lena Grove

Died: Father of Lena Grove

The Atelier Monty, Montgomery Ward Snopes' photography shop, suddenly became the scene of a lot of late-night activity this year; Hub Hampton and I asked Grover Cleveland Winbush, the night marshal to keep an eye on it {T}. He later assured us that nothing illegal was going on there, we believed him, and so it got away from us for yet another year [1923]. Flem, meanwhile, made the overture we all knew he would have to make sooner or later—he tried to buy his way into Wall Snopes' grocery business and Wall almost let him except that his new wife refused to allow it. She clearly knew Flem better than Wall did. And there was a new Snopes on the streets this year, or at least one none of us had noticed before. This was Linda, Eula's fourteen-year-old daughter by Hoake McCarron [1908]. If I had been harboring any thoughts of doing with Eula what Manfred DeSpain had been doing for thirteen years now, the devotion I would soon feel for this young girl would all but prohibit it from now on.

Other Snopeses that all of us *did* know about were all over the place as usual {M}. Clarence Snopes, now a state senator, did the county the "service" of reactivating the Ku Klux Klan and appointing himself the Dragon or Kleagle or whatever they call it. Virgil Snopes went off to Memphis with Fonzo Winbush in search of employment and wound up rooming at Miss Reba's, which they mistakenly thought was a legitimate boarding house [1905]. It did not take very long before they knew what was going on there though, and Virgil in particular became a nightly participant {M}. When Clarence would either get off his legislative seat or take off his hood for the weekend, he too would show up. He soon came to understand, from the gossip around the house, that Virgil could satisfy a whole string of women on any given evening. No thoroughgoing Snopes, of course, could resist making money off something such as this, so Clarence started taking bets on Virgil's performance, bets he would win nine out of every ten times. Meanwhile, back in Jefferson, Flem bought the black felt hat that he would wear for the rest of his life. More than anything else it was a symbol of the respectable appearance he wished all those with a similar last name to his would strive for.

Harriss, up to as much as Flem but at least up to it elsewhere, visited his wife and children in Jefferson this summer and stayed two months, the longest he ever did, while electric lights and water pipes were being installed at the Backus plantation {K}. Then he left in August and returned as usual at Christmas. Rumors continued to circulate about what he really did in New Orleans, and I was just as glad that it was not in my jurisdiction to find out or even to have to wonder. What *was* in my jurisdiction, however, was Will Provine's still which Hub Hampton accidentally uncovered {T}. Judge Long sentenced him to an incredibly long term of five years, one for *having* the still and four for making his wife carry water a mile and a half to it several times a day.

Elsewhere the Tall Convict in Parchman received a postcard with the picture of a Birmingham hotel on it this year; she had circled the room where she was honeymooning as the new Mrs. Vernon Waldrip [1921] {W}. Also in Parchman, of course, was Mink Snopes, still behaving himself and with only six years to go before his twenty were up [1907] {M}. Surely Flem must have been counting as well and beginning to think about what he was going to do about it. Elsewhere, Howard and Mildred Rogers, back together after Mildred's affair with Buck Monaghan, had a son this year and named Buck to be the godfather {"Honor"} [1923].

Finally, fourteen-year-old Percy Grimm, ever more angry that he had been born too late to go to any war, was becoming the superpatriot he would always admire himself for being {L}. This year he got himself into a bloody street brawl with a man who claimed he hated Frenchmen so much that he would fight with the Germans against them in the next war, which included fighting against Americans if they aligned themselves with the French. Percy fought him, only to be beaten to within an inch of his life, as surely he knew he would be. Percy would eventually have his day in defense of what he perceived to be American values [1930].

THE PRESIDENCY OF CALVIN COOLIDGE, 1923–1929

1923

Born: Nat Beauchamp

Born: Pete Grier (d. 1942)

Died: Lonzo Hait

Wall Snopes' wife had to be on her toes again this year—and was [1922] {T}. It seems that Wall needed to borrow some money and walked into the

Sartoris Bank, of which Flem was still vice president, to do just that. His wife intercepted him just in time, and Flem was foiled once again. Wall then secured his loan from V. K. Ratliff, who was made a partner in the business. When I suggested to V. K. that I might like to invest in Wall myself, he simply told me that I would have to find my way around Wall's wife first. I never bothered to try. Wall used the money to buy the store next to his, connected the two buildings, and made it into his warehouse and stockroom.

We finally found out this year just what was going on in the Atelier Monty [1920]. One night Willy Christian's drug store was broken into and robbed of some narcotics, probably Willy's personal supply. Winbush, the night marshal, never saw nor heard it despite the fact he was paid to patrol the square. So Sheriff Hampton and I presumed he must have been somewhere else doing something he wasn't paid to do. It turned out that he was in the back room of Montgomery Ward's photo shop, where the latter staged nightly viewings of some French postcards he had converted into slides and projected on a hung-up sheet. Since we could find no one in town willing to admit he had been there to testify to this, we had to lock Montgomery Ward up on Bayard Sartoris' old automobile law (he owned one) until we could get something better on him [1903].

Now, as it turned out, Montgomery Ward was not making a bundle of money on his theater—he was merely waiting for Flem to offer to buy him out {M}. Flem, though, wanted no part of such obviously unrespectable shenanigans and even came to me to try to bribe me to send his cousin to prison with or without evidence {T}. I declined the offer, so Flem did it another way. He drove out to the Gowries in Beat Four, bought some corn liquor from them, then dumped it in his cousin's developing trays {M}. Then he made a phone call to Jack Crenshaw, the county liquor agent. When Crenshaw showed up and pointed the stuff out to Hub Hampton, the sheriff was appalled that he had overlooked it {T}. I had my suspicions, and Hub probably did too, so I asked Flem if he might not have been in on this; he quickly, though privately, admitted he had, but only for the "good of Jefferson," lest such an unsavory scoundrel as his cousin be allowed to prowl the town for lack of evidence.

But there was another reason Flem did not want him prowling the town and that was because he needed him in Parchman. Not Atlanta, the federal penitentiary, but Parchman, where Mink was {M}. When Montgomery Ward balked at the idea and even at the idea of taking $10,000 to make it worth his while to take the longer stay in Parchman (for the purpose of neutering Mink's chances for a twenty-year term on good behavior), Flem had one of his cousin's obscene pictures sent through the mails in one of the Atelier Monty's printed envelopes and, next, threatened to get his cousin in the trouble with the post-office department. Montgomery Ward, helpless, assented to the Parchman scheme. So, after a few days at Miss Reba's while out on bail with Senator Clarence Snopes, he was off to serve a two-year term in Parchman for possessing illegal liquor. He carried with him a set of women's clothing that Mink was to use as a disguise in his escape attempt. Bent on revenge against Flem, Mink, dressed as a grandmother, made the try but was caught immediately by five dumbfounded guards even before he got near the gate. This happened on Saturday, September 8th, 1923. Flem's plan had succeeded to the utmost, for now, instead of being eligible for parole in 1928, Mink would not be considered until 1948. Flem, however, never had to worry about having Mink's term extended to 1968 [1946].

Though Ratliff and I did not understand at the time why it was so important for Montgomery Ward to go to Parchman, we did now, and for the time being just had to content ourselves with just being amazed at the things Snopeses will cook up against anybody, even each other. Then another example presented itself. Lonzo Hait was killed by a passing freight train one day, and we found out afterward that he had been working for I. O. Snopes planting mules on the tracks so that I. O. could collect the insurance money from the railroad, money he split with Lonzo {"Mule in the Yard"}. But, even if the plan backfired on poor Lonzo, it also did on I. O.; a week later Hait's wife, Mannie, collected $8500 from the railroad on Lonzo. I. O., naturally, felt entitled to share in this; but Mannie, another Snopes fighter of the first magnitude, never gave him any {T}. As later events would prove, this would not be the only Snopes she would bring to his knees [1926].

During the summer Harriss came up from New Orleans as usual to see Melisandre and the two children, both of whom were walking now {K}. It was on this occasion that he chose to rent the entire Backus plantation to a Memphis farmer who came in on a weekly basis and lived in a Negro cabin while on the premises. Only the main house was withheld for the Harriss family's own use.

Other things went on this year as well. The Finn who was the cobbler tried to organize the Jefferson Proletariat, as he called the townsmen who did any kind of manual labor, even though he did not know enough English to convince them of what he was saying or even make them understand the first thing about it [1917] {M}. The tinsmith Finn tried to organize the blacks, but they made it known they wanted no part of him. In Ohio, Matt Levitt won the Golden Gloves championship but unfortunately brought his pugilistic skills back here to use on others not so ready to defend themselves [1924] {T}. And a new man arrived in town, a quiet, unassuming young fellow named Byron Bunch {L}. He got a job at the sawmill; but, except for the fact that he worked six full days a week and went off into the hills for a prayer meeting each Sunday, we knew little about him. He seemed to do most of his talking to the still-present Reverend Hightower, which, of course, earned him some public scorn.

Born: Charles "Chick" Mallison, Jr.

Melisandre Harriss was in Paris this year, as was I on a European vacation which had as its primary purpose a chance to go back to Heidelberg. I did not cross paths with her. It seems that she suddenly up and left the Backus property and came, with her children and Negro servants, to Europe, leaving her renovated house a mausoleum of water pipes and electric lights [1922] {K}. I suspected trouble in her marriage but did not have any facts. During the time she was in Paris I sent her a message asking why she did not wait for me in the year of our courtship, but she replied only by saying that she didn't think I really wanted her [1919]. I suppose this was all the response I deserved. So she was to stay in Paris for the next fourteen years, as it turned out, keeping in touch with Yoknapatawpha only through the seasonal cards she sent my sister and the four other school chums with whom she maintained contact [1938]. Never did she mention the places she had been, only the growth and development of her children.

With Melisandre behind me, or at least I thought she was, I found myself, when I returned to Jefferson, being drawn ever closer to Linda Snopes {T}. I never really knew whether I loved her or just wanted to save her from her father; but something drove me to see her as much as possible. I bought her ice cream at Willy Christian's drug store, gave her books to read, and invited her to dinner with my family. Before long, though, Matt Levitt, Golden Gloves golden boy [1923] and definitely interested in Linda, began to take exception to my attentions and manifested this by racing his car through town with its cutout open while Linda and I were in the drugstore. Caught in the middle, Linda started not showing up each afternoon, so I got a young friend of mine to deliver the books to her, as well as a few harmless but encouraging messages. The next time I did see her, Matt came boldly forward and punched me in the face, though Linda then belted Matt over the head with an umbrella. Linda sent Matt away and embraced me for the first time; and before I knew it I had proposed marriage. And before she knew it she had accepted, though she quickly withdrew by saying that, though she loved me, she didn't want to marry me. I understood this because it was exactly the way I felt about her mother. The romance cooled quickly, though, because my face was so badly damaged that I had to stay under cover for the next six months to quell town gossip. Once again I was forced to use an intermediary to deliver books and notes.

Clarence Snopes cleverly got himself re-elected to the state legislature this year, though Ratliff even more cleverly would head him off another time [1945] {M}. He was running a nip-and-tuck race against another man who, like himself, was possessed of inferior abilities, so that the swing votes would have to come from those who—like V. K. and I—considered ourselves liberals and distrusted both of their red necks. Then, just before the election, Snopes disavowed his association with the KKK in the County [1922] and even took steps to disband it, which he could pretty easily do since he was the Kleagle and didn't have all that many followers in the first place. So Ratliff and I wound up, incredibly in retrospect, voting for this white-suited liar who, it turned out, was not learning to be a good legislator so much as he was biding his time while he learned to be as opportunistic as his cousin Flem.

Old Ab Snopes was still growing and selling his watermelons this year, though I had to have him in for a hearing after he pumped young John Wesley Roebuck full of squirrel shot for stealing from his patch {T}. Ab was so old and jaded that all we could really do was fine and warn him. He did not accept the warning nor did he, to the best of my knowledge, ever pay the fine.

Down in Frenchman's Bend, where not much ever happened now that all the Snopeses had moved to Jefferson, Hub Hampton got into a row which almost cost him his job. A certain lady down there lost a baking contest to the wife of one of the county's more notorious still operators {I}. This woman then approached Hampton, announced the location of the still (which Hub knew anyway), and demanded that he break it up. When he expressed his reluctance (because like many of us he was getting some of his favorite rotgut there as well), she threatened to turn him into the governor (who might have been getting some of his best stuff there also). So Hub went to the still and found a Negro man attending it. He sat down with him and the two got progressively drunk until Hub fell asleep. The Negro and the still owner then got a quilt and a pillow from Will Varner's store, tucked Hampton in to keep him from catching cold, and trucked the still away. Hub was off the hook.

Finally, Jefferson took a special census this year and found its population to number exactly 3000 {T}.

1925

Born: Essie Meadowfill

I continued my efforts this year to break Linda Snopes free from her father and send her out into the world to be the surrogate of her mother, whose life Flem had not so much ruined as misdirected for the second half of it. First of all, Matt Levitt had to be disposed of—and he was, with a fight {T}. In fact, Matt was fighting all comers now and even some that wouldn't come—so he went to them. One of his most eager opponents was young Anse MacCallum, who invariably got pummelled within an inch of his life each time and had to have that last inch saved for him by his brother Buddy. Matt would fight with his car now, too; one day he almost ran Otis Harker down in the middle of Main Street at high noon. Because of this and probably an accumulation of other things as well, he was fired from his garage job and, on another occasion, got arrested for running his cutout open in town, which had a law against automobiles, period, much less cutouts [1903]. So finally Hub Hampton got rid of him—he made him a deal that he could run his cutout absolutely wide open just once if he would continue driving out of town when he did so and never return. Jobless, spurned by Linda, and hated by every man of fighting age in town, he opened it wider than anyone imagined it could open as he thunder-droned past Linda's house for the final time.

In February Linda took up dating athletes, but this turned out not to pose any real problem; so my next move had to be to get her to leave Jefferson forever. I inundated her with catalogues from eastern colleges, all of which she read as if she were choosing one. She was to be class valedictorian, selected over Virgil Beard [1919] who must now have yet another reason to dislike Snopeses. I bought her a green suitcase as a graduation present, but in late May she informed me that she was not going to be allowed by her "father" to attend any school but the Jefferson Academy. I went to Eula to try to plead her case and found out something I had not understood till now—if Linda went away and perhaps got married, Flem would not get Eula's share of Will Varner's inheritance because Eula would have no reason not to run off with Manfred DeSpain or at least away from Flem. Flem it seemed had been heaping all sorts of gifts on Linda all spring to lure her into staying, but finally it took a direct order to attend the Jefferson Academy. Eula, standing in the midst of the living room which Flem had furnished to look respectable in the most traditional sense of the word, begged me to marry Linda, clearly to free both her and her mother from Flem. But I already knew Linda's feeling on the subject and thus knew the solution would not work. So Linda started at the Jefferson Academy in the fall.

Meanwhile, the Snopes who got away from Flem—Wall—had rented the last livery stable in Jefferson to be his warehouse and converted his other facility into the first self-service grocery store in Jefferson. He also bought the lot next door for a parking lot. His wife and mother continued to assist him as his business grew, honestly and surely.

The DeSpain hunting camp was about to be destroyed by the lumber company, which had already cut all the trees up to its edge {R}; so some of the townsmen—with names which were not the same as those of the men who used to go fifty years ago—decided to stage one last hunt there before it was razed. V. K. Ratliff went out just to see what was going on, I suppose, knowing a momentous event when he saw one. When he got there he found one of the men, Luke Provine, suffering from twenty-four-hours-worth of hiccups {"A Bear Hunt"}. Since he had tried every other remedy, he accepted

[207]

Ratliff's advice to visit John Basket, supposedly a witch doctor, at the Indian mound five miles away. The next day, Luke returned and beat Ratliff up, for no apparent reason since the hiccups were gone. As it turned out, Old Man Ash, finally getting revenge for the celluloid collar he had lost to Luke and his gang of thugs twenty years ago, had put the Indians up to a scare tactic that managed to snuff out the bravado even in the likes of Luke [1905]. So Ratliff drove back to town, all bruised and bloodied, because Old Man Ash lost a celluloid collar to Luke Provine twenty years ago at a church picnic that poor V. K. didn't even know was held.

Other happenings this year: Howard Boyd graduated from the University of Virginia, with his mother in tow [1921]; she had lived up in Charlottes-ville with him the whole time {"The Brooch"}. Out on the Backus land, with Melisandre in Europe, Harriss began importing pedigree stallions and stab-ling them there {K}. Aunt Jenny DuPre was after Narcissa Benbow to remarry now, though Narcissa had a secret that was causing her more immediate problems [1929] {"There was a Queen"}. This year Uncle Pete Gombault became U.S. marshal in Jefferson for the next decade or so, a position he obtained as a political sinecure {N}. It was an intolerable appoint-ment, for Uncle Pete was known to all of us simply as Mulberry, named so after the tree under which he stashed and tended his still at the expense of law enforcement in the district. Speaking of law enforcement, I personally had the real pleasure of ordering the Governor of Mississippi confined to the Jefferson jailhouse for thirty days for refusing to testify in a paternity suit brought against one of his lieutenants. Through Melissa Meek, the town librarian, we learned that Caddy Compson had divorced her husband [1920], by mutual agreement, in Mexico {F}. And in Detroit, Joe Christmas got married this year to the blackest woman he could get his hands on {L}— much like Charles Etienne Bon forty years back [1881], he was trying to breathe blackness into himself and find identity in the race to which the white one had exiled him or, more properly, to which he had exiled himself. And at Parchman the warden offered the Tall Convict the position of "trusty" so he would not have to plow fields anymore but rather could guard the other men with a gun. Feeling he had already handled a gun one too many times, however, he declined {W}.

1926

Died: Amanda Workitt Gowrie (b. 1878)

Lee Goodwin finally got to the County in 1926, after years of checking the squares in and out of the prison that would get him here [1919] {Y}. He set up not so much a still as a full-scale business down on the Old Frenchman's

Place, where any countian who had the cold cash could buy some of the best booze available during Prohibition. His operation was limited in this year, though my cousin Gowan was one of the first to find him and become a regular customer [1929].

I had only one encounter with the Snopeses this year, which automatically meant that the next year would be active—and it was. It was another situation where Flem had to pay out a lot of cash to protect himself from his just-as-crooked but not-just-as-smart relatives. One of I. O.'s mules wandered into Mrs. Hait's yard one day and was discovered there by Old Het. Reminiscent of the Jack Houston–Mink Snopes yearling problem twenty years ago [1907], an argument ensued between I. O. and Mrs. Hait in which the cost of the mule was hotly debated {"Mule in the Yard"}. There was bad blood between these two anyway because I. O. thought Mrs. Hait still owed him some of Lonzo's insurance money [1923]. The whole thing became very complicated and nasty, and somehow I got called in to witness all of it. What eventuated, however, was that Flem paid $150 each for I. O.'s mules, one of which had caused Mrs. Hait's house to burn down in the process, on the condition that I. O. would return to Frenchman's Bend and never show up in Jefferson again. In exchange for the money, I. O. agreed. Then Flem paid off Mrs. Hait's mortgage. As V. K. always said, Flem would pay any money to protect his respectability, but not much for anything else.

This was the year I was involved in the drainage canal business and could not watch very closely the Snopeses who were otherwise in action {T}. Linda began her second year at the Jefferson Academy, Wall's business thrived, and Eula took her last vacation with Manfred DeSpain.

Elsewhere in town the Reverend Hightower made a rare semi-public appearance when he went, at her husband's plea, to help a negro woman give birth {L}. After he had called the doctor and gone to the scene, Hightower discovered the woman had gotten out of bed and killed the child, half-born, in the process. He apparently did all he could, but soon a new rumor was abroad which had it that the child was Hightower's bastard and that *he*, therefore, had killed it on purpose.

Mrs. Boyd was paralyzed by a stroke this year, though she still managed to run her son's life from her bed [1930] {"The Brooch"}. Harriss rebuilt the Backus house during the spring and summer until it was five times as big and five times as "southern" as it used to be, modelling it apparently on a motion picture version of an ante-bellum plantation {K}. Melisandre was still in Europe with no plans to return, though I never heard that this particularly bothered Harriss. Down at the sawmill where Byron Bunch still worked his six-day shift, a white man named Birdsong opened up his crooked dice game with which he fleeced the mill Negroes of their paychecks before they could get them home {G}. This game would go on for many years until one of them would have to kill him [1941]. Susan Reed, a young girl who was a particular favorite of Hawkshaw Stribling's, began wearing make-up, skipping school, and—probably—becoming a harlot {"Hair"}.

In all a quiet year in Yoknapatawpha County, but the next one would be tragic.

1927

Born: Child of Howard and Amy Boyd (d. 1928)

Born: Georgie, nephew of Uncle Rodney

Born: Child of the woman saved by the Tall Convict during the Great Flood

Died: Eula Varner Snopes (b. 1889), by her own hand

Died: Lucius Binford, in Memphis

As I read back over the years I have written so far, I am always reimpressed by the fact that we are all the victims of currents we did not initiate or wish for yet are forced to endure. Some can direct those currents to useful ends; but most of us can only see them swelling into tidal waves to inundate us enough so we can no longer swim with, much less against, them. If Quentin Compson, now dead seventeen years, was the supreme example of the latter sort [1910], surely Flem Snopes was representative of the former. The year 1927 was the climax of all Flem had worked for, at least from the day he discovered Jody Varner was scared of losing some of his father's precious barns [1904], but probably even from the day when, much younger, he realized that his brother Sarty's rejection of barn-burning was as futile and merely symbolic as Ab's burning them was [1894]. So, though he had suffered a momentary setback here and there—like having to pay for all the brass that never did come out of the town water tank [1914] or having to buy all of I. O.'s mules and pay Mrs. Hait's mortgage as well [1926]—1927 was the year in which Flem showed how effectively he had tied all the ends together simply by biding his time, understanding how and why people did and would do the things that they did, watching, acting always at the right moment, never too soon, never too late. Except for one string, Flem had tied a beautiful knot—that one string was Mink, festering in Parchman [1908] [1923]; but Flem still had, he thought, twenty-one years left to tie that one too [1946].

In January Will Varner appointed me trustee of Linda's inheritance; I thought they had beaten Flem to the draw, but Flem must have known they were coming from the Bend that day {M}. In a series of swift moves, he allowed Linda to transfer from the Jefferson Academy, where she had completed a year and a half, to the University of Mississippi; in return for this privilege, he demanded that she turn over her share of the Varner money to him {T}. Then in April, vice president of the Sartoris bank long enough [1908], Flem played the trump card that he had held for eighteen years. Paying V. K. fifty cents a mile for the six miles V. K. had to deviate from his normal sales route, Flem went to Frenchman's Bend and announced in his bland way to poor old Mrs. Varner that her only daughter, her life's greatest blessing and joy, had been shacking up with Manfred DeSpain for most of the last two decades [1907]. Mrs. Varner dispatched Jody, who had worked harder than anybody at keeping Eula's maidenhead in one piece before Hoake McCarron finally took it, to go get Will; and Will departed for Jefferson at 2 A.M. the next morning. He arrived in town amidst a polio scare that closed the school down for most of the next two days when the Ridell boy apparently contracted it. But the town seemed almost more concerned about what Will would do—some hoped he would let his violent temper unhinge to rid us of our eighteen-year-old Flem Snopes plague, but others felt that anyone who openly admitted it now would expose the town's real inner depravity for having tolerated it. Flem and Will negotiated in Flem's office at the bank, the final deal being that Flem would trade Eula to DeSpain in return for the opportunity to purchase the bank stock DeSpain held and which allowed him to be president {M}. On Wednesday Eula went to the beauty parlor for the first time in her life and afterwards arranged a meeting with me in order to plead that I marry Linda if all of this took place. Once again I knew that my promise would mean nothing insofar as Linda was concerned.

On Thursday morning the town awoke to learn that Eula Varner Snopes—the "supreme primal uterus" as she was known in the Bend and the most beautiful woman to ever set foot in Jefferson, who had been pursued by every white male in the county who was potent and then had been "won" by Flem, one of the few who wasn't—had ended her life with a gunshot to the right temple {T}. So my sister Margaret and I went to Oxford that day to bring Linda home; and, while we were gone, DeSpain resigned as bank president, sold his stock to Flem, and announced that he would go west right after the funeral. On the day of his wife's death, Flem installed himself as president of the Sartoris bank and, perhaps, walked down the street and gathered up his own money from where it still lay secure in the vault of the Priest bank [1919].

The town had amassed four ministers to conduct Eula's funeral; but I insisted on doing it by myself, with the sole assistance of the minister from the Bend who had baptized her thirty-eight years ago. Manfred DeSpain was there, but this was the last day we would ever see him—and so died as well another mythic name in Yoknapatawpha County. After the ceremonies,

[211]

Linda asked me to swear that Flem was her real father, which I did; but she didn't believe me (and right there probably vowed to destroy him as he had destroyed her mother) [1946]. Together we took the best photo we had of Eula, taken at the Atelier Monty (no less) five or six years ago, and sent it to Italy to have her image forged into a gold medallion. Meanwhile, Flem began moving himself into the DeSpain mansion, the very same one his father had tracked horse manure into about thirty-five years ago [1894], and began making plans to have it renovated into the sort of antebellum plantation house Harriss had already turned the Backus place into.

A month or so after Eula's funeral, fate deposited Joe Christmas in Jefferson, the final destination it had, for some reason, been aiming him toward since the day he was ill-conceived in an Arkansas town because a circus caravan had gotten stuck in the mud {L}. The day Joe got here he climbed through an empty window at Miss Joanna Burden's gloomy old house and helped himself to some food. And then Joanna confronted him and told him he could have all he wanted. Never one to comprehend feminine motives for anything, Joe took up indefinite residence on her property, and soon inside her house as well, and got himself a job at the Jefferson planing mill working among Byron Bunch, Birdsong, and a score of others, but talking to none of them.

Also this year, Harriss began reappearing in the County more often—perhaps four or five times a year—always with some friends to lounge around in his converted mansion. Tyler Ballenbaugh bought a $5000 insurance policy on poor, simple Lonnie Grinnup (really Louis Grenier) and paid the premiums for the next eleven years [1938], at which point I would be confronted with having to determine why he might have bought it in the first place. And Nancy Mannigoe, a black woman who worked in the employ of several households in town, was kicked in the stomach at a Negro picnic and lost the baby with which she was six months pregnant—she claimed not to know if the man who kicked her was the baby's father or not [1936] {N}.

The forces I spoke about briefly a moment ago: one can, as Flem did, try to manipulate them; or he or she can, as Eula did, try to endure them. But heroism can be of two sorts—the sheer symbolic bravado of an Ab Snopes burning down a barn or the will to preserve life just on the assumption that we were born here for some purpose. Perhaps Eula exemplified the latter sort, as did Linda and Ratliff, and (I hope) I.

I think the Tall Convict did as well, the one from down near the Bend who had gotten himself into Parchman a few years back for trying to rob a train [1921] {W}. In the days immediately following Eula's death in April, tremendous rains hit Mississippi, and various river communities were being threatened by rising waters. The Tall Convict was one of a group of twenty convicts sent to Mounts Landing to fortify the levees. Before long he was dispatched in a boat to rescue a woman from a cypress tree and a man from the roof of a cottonhouse. He reached the woman, who turned out to be on the verge of

[212]

delivering a child, but he never found the man. Trying desperately to return to his starting point at Mounds Landing, the Convict found his boat drifting helplessly on the river, past Vicksburg. Twice they were almost picked up—once by some people in a shanty boat who would take the woman but not the Convict, a second time by a group of people on land who were about to pull them in until they saw what he was and so machine-gunned them instead. Finally, south of Baton Rouge, they drifted to high ground, whereupon the woman delivered the baby and the Convict officiated with the only tool he had—the lid of a tin can.

Throughout this ordeal, the Convict had only one purpose—to get the woman home so he could get back to his comfortable prison cell. But the forces did not have this in mind, so they were dragged farther south by a ship that, though it rescued them, was planning to take them to New Orleans. So they were put ashore at Carnarvon where the Convict, to earn some money, entered into an alligator-hunting partnership with a French-speaking cajun. The cajun did it with a gun; but, knowing no better, the Convict subdued his first alligator by wrestling it to death, to the cajun's wild delight. On the tenth day here, however, the cajun ran into the shack and quickly gathered up his things, shouting "Boom, Boom, Boom" all the while and gesturing wildly upward with his arms. After he had gone, a motor launch pulled up and ordered the Convict, the woman, and her baby off the ground because the levee was about to be dynamited. They were taken to a nearby town, housed in an armory for flood victims, and then "captured" by a deputy sheriff who was campaigning to unseat his boss, though, in reality, the Convict had freely turned himself in. Thrilled at the possibility of finally returning to prison, the Convict told the deputy, "Here's the woman, yonder's your boat, but I never did find that bastard on the cottonhouse."

There is one final irony to all this. Because of administrative foul-ups which caused prison officials to declare the Convict dead, the warden had to cover his staff by having the Convict tried and convicted of attempting to escape—the Convict had, like Mink Snopes, ten years added to his sentence, though Mink had gotten twenty. One of his friends bemoaned that he would now be ten more years without a woman; but the Tall Convict, savoring a cigar, was glad to be dry and rid of that whole half of the human race.

1928

Born: Child of Lee Goodwin and Ruby LaMarr

Died: The Boyd child (b. 1927)

In this year before most capitalists got turned loose from their money, two young women in Jefferson got turned loose from their capitalists: Linda Snopes and the eighteen-year-old girl named Quentin Compson.

[213]

Flem had, of course, bought a car upon becoming president of the bank; and, of course, he did not drive it but had himself a Negro chauffeur to do it for him {T} {M}. Its first trip beyond the county, or maybe even beyond Jefferson, was to drive Linda to Memphis to catch the train for New York where she was, at my advice, to take up residence in Greenwich Village. On the way out of town, Flem had her driven, first, past the renovated DeSpain mansion and, second, to the cemetery to visit her mother's grave where she saw, for the first time, the gravestone that Flem had placed there. The inscription read: "Eula Varner Snopes, 1889–1927—A Virtuous Wife Is a Crown to Her Husband. Her Child Shall Rise and Call Her Blessed." Flem was now a deacon in the Baptist Church and had composed the inscription himself. So, with this memory, Linda went to the Village.

Meanwhile, the DeSpain mansion was nearly completed for the town to look at the outside of, for no one was ever invited to see the inside {M}. A distant relative of Flem's, Watkins Products Snopes, had done most of the interior work, included in which was the essential ledge attached to the fireplace for Flem to rest his feet on. And, like anyone who has succeeded in terms understood by the greatest number of people—money and position— Flem became an object of jealousy within his family from this year forward. Senator Clarence Egglestone Snopes, for example, devised a plan, which would reach fruition next year [1929], whereby the nine-years-absent Byron Snopes [1919] would mail him, from Texas, the four semi-savage children he had fathered there upon an Apache squaw.

Less successful in monetary matters but still trying was Jason Compson, thirty-five now and still brooding about being done out of the bank job by Caddy's indiscretions [1911], the product of one of which was now his ward {F}. Since his first employment in 1909, Jason had managed to save about $3000 out of his niggardly earnings, plus an undisclosed amount, but certainly larger, that he had siphoned off the $100 a month Caddy faithfully sent to support her daughter, Quentin. Economic and personal matters at long last came to a head in the Compson household on Easter weekend.

On April 6th, Good Friday, Jason suspected that Quentin was about to skip the family which, of course, would deprive him of any further funding from Caddy. He chewed her out at breakfast for running around the house with her robe flapping open, for skipping school, for signing her own report cards, and for spending her book money on things other than books. After much struggling he got her to school that morning, though not before she noticed the portentous erection of a show tent in the lot next to Mrs. Beard's boarding house. Jason then went on to his own job, which he did desultorily at best and often just walked away from to go check the progress of his stocks at the telegraph office. He got the usual letters from his sister Caddy (threatening), his girlfriend Lorraine (admiring), and his Uncle Maury (panhandling). He disregarded all, save for the check in Caddy's which as usual he would make Quentin sign the back of without seeing the front of, and for which he paid her $10 (instead of the $50 for which it was made out). Later in the afternoon Jason was again reprimanded by his boss, Earl, for the sloppy way he did his job and was told that the only reason he was still employed at the store was for his mother's sake—she had no other means of support. Then, at 2:30, Jason felt terminally threatened when he spotted Quentin in the alley outside with a pitchman in a red tie; since school was not due to be out until 3:15, Jason leapt in his car and pursued them out of town, all the while trying to restrain his retching from the gas fumes his car threw off. Seeing their car parked on a roadside, he chased them into the woods where, though he didn't find them, he did find poison oak and thistles and, shortly thereafter, his car with flat tires. After borrowing a pump at Russell's farm, he returned to town, only to discover—on top of everything else—that his stocks had dropped forty points during his afternoon's chase.

Earl gave Jason two free passes for the circus show that night, passes he spitefully burnt in front of Luster at supper time when Luster could not come up with any money to buy them from him. At dinner he loudly protested to Mrs. Compson that he was *not* driving his car that afternoon but rather had lent it to the brother of one of the showgirls whose husband, he said, had been seen running around with a town slut. Quentin listened carefully. After dinner, Jason routinely checked his cash box, listened to Benjy snore, and went to bed as secure as he ever did, which wasn't very.

On Holy Saturday, the 7th, his thirty-third birthday, Benjy spent most of the day, as he normally did now, hanging on the golf course fence listening to the golfers call out the word "caddie." Luster was in a frenzy of his own, having lost the quarter Frony had given him to go to the show that night, and thus was ignoring Benjy's activities. So Benjy shambled upon Quentin and the pitchman, who stopped necking as Benjy sat down to toy with a shiny contraceptive box. The showman inquired of Luster who it was Quentin had seen the previous night, but the black boy merely replied that he did not know because Quentin climbed out the window of her room and down the tree outside her window nearly every night [1898]. In the midst of this, poor Luster lost his chance to recoup his quarter when a golfer just pocketed the ball Luster was trying to sell him. That night, amidst Mrs. Compson's and Jason's complaining about Benjy's racket, Dilsey presented the unfortunate idiot with his birthday cake. During the "party" an argument broke out in which Jason roared at Quentin that he would not tolerate her hanging around with the showman, whereupon she threatened to run away. When Jason responded cynically to this, she flung a water glass at him, but Dilsey knocked her aim off. Later that night, as Luster undressed Benjy in his room, they saw Quentin climb down the tree as usual, neither of them able to know that this would be the last time she would ever do so, simply because she would never climb back up it again either.

On the 8th, Easter Sunday, Dilsey was dressing to go to church to hear the Reverend Shegog, a well-known Negro preacher from St. Louis. It was a bleak, cold day, and Jason was irritated that the servants were being allowed to go to church at all. His lunch would be served late as a result. Luster, who had gotten to go to the show after all the night before, overslept and awakened the whole household by dropping the armful of logs he was rushing in for the fire. It was amidst this unexceptional tension that Mrs. Compson spotted the broken window in Jason's room. Knowing exactly what must have happened, Jason raced upstairs and discovered that Quentin had stolen the $7000 he kept in his money box (at least half of which was really Quentin's anyway). Jason called the sheriff, Watt Kennedy, and he was frankly reluctant to help Jason out because of lack of proof and because he must have had some vague notion of how much Jason had stolen from the girl over the years. Kennedy did tell him, though, that the show had moved to Mottstown, and Jason drove there after filling his flattened tires once again.

Once he got there he began making all sorts of accusations around the show train and finally got himself attacked by a man wielding a rusty hatchet and chased home. Back in Jefferson, Dilsey, Luster, and Benjy had already returned from the Easter sermon; Luster had set himself to thinking up this day's ways to devil Benjy. To stop Benjy's howling, Dilsey allowed Luster to take him for a ride, on the promise, which Luster immediately broke, not to drive the horses fast nor scare Benjy. As Jason drove into town, from the other direction, he saw Luster driving the cart around the Confederate Monument the wrong way (not the way Benjy was used to going around it); as a result Benjy was howling more vociferously than ever. Jason ran up, hit both of them, and sent them home. His money was never recovered; and, since Quentin was gone for good, Jason now had to seek another scapegoat for his wrath—this, of course, would be his brother Benjy in the years to come [1933]. But for the next five years, Jason would awaken in the night with horrible visions of Quentin and his lost money.

Not far away, on Joanna Burden's property, Joe Christmas had, earlier this year, entered into a bootlegging business on the side while keeping his planing mill job as a legitimate front {L}. Meanwhile, whether he wanted to or not, he was becoming enmeshed in this spinster's life as well. He began to notice that she got a lot of mail and was presumably supporting twelve Negro colleges in the south, one of which she frequently spoke of having him attend. Perhaps this was the woman's way of trying to relieve the curse her racially obsessed father placed upon her in her girlhood [1891]. And then one night Christmas sexually assaulted her and was amazed to discover that, instead of resisting him, she helped him; instead of retreating into her years of virginal self-denial, she became almost nymphomaniacal and would not even wait for him to come to her but would go to his cabin for him, hiding in

[216]

the bushes and luring him with notes. She even spoke of having his child. All the while, Joe put this aside in his mind, peddling his liquor and planing his wood and waiting as he always waited for something he could neither define nor identify [1930].

Some of the town's other eccentric women were active this year. Minnie Cooper, her cashier boyfriend long gone by now [1921], reported to Watt Kennedy one day that a man was watching her undress, peering through her window from a neighboring kitchen roof {"Dry September"}. No trace of one was found, there surely being better women in Jefferson to watch take their clothes off. Emily Grierson was confronted this year by a town deposition which firmly demanded that she start paying taxes like everyone else; to which Miss Emily just as firmly replied that Bayard Sartoris had forgiven her taxes *ad infinitum* just thirty-four years ago [1894] {"A Rose for Emily"}.

And there was a murder in town this year, just as there would be for the next several, unfortunately. A week after Quentin Compson left town, feeble-minded Monk Odlethrop, who still worked at the filling station, was discovered out behind it standing over the body of a dead man with a smoking pistol in his hand with two witnesses conveniently nearby to notice it {K}. Monk had no conception of death that anyone knew of, so I did not know what to make of this. But Eustace Graham, our City Attorney who was always on the way upward (he thought) [1910], had Monk swiftly brought to trial and, because of a weak defense, convicted. He was conveyed to prison on June 1, although I was not sure, personally, that the case should have been closed so quickly. Some years hence, I was to be proven correct [1936].

Out on the Harriss, no longer the Backus, property, its owner had now hired a butler to run the house for him while he was gone. This man carried a pistol with him at all times, not to mention a stack of signed blank checks to pay off the tenant farmers when they brought in their crops. And finally, down at the Bend, Lonnie Grinnup took in an orphaned idiot boy to raise him for the next ten years [1938].

An air show came to town this summer featuring Demon Duncan Ginsfarb and his supposedly famous death drag {"Death Drag"}. It turned out that Ginsfarb had been a companion of Jefferson's own Captain Warren during the war [1917], so some of us took a mild interest in his stunt—which was jumping out of a plane and landing on a moving car. When he did the trick here, however, he jumped through the roof of a barn rather than onto the car. We later discovered that this was intentional, for his pilot had informed him in the air that he had not been able to collect sufficient money in advance to make the effort worth his while financially. I got entangled in this a bit myself when a man named Harris, who had rented Ginsfarb the car to jump onto, told me that he was never paid, on Ginsfarb's contention that the car—though it had raced down the road under the plane—had not been used to catch anybody. I tried to collect, but I couldn't. Some years later I would

[217]

have advised Harris not to press it [1929]. I probably had by then come to feel that, if you couldn't put Percy Grimm [1930] or Jackson McLendon away for lynchings [1929] or if you couldn't get Popeye Vitelli convicted of the right crime instead of the wrong one [1930], you weren't likely to get a few bucks out of a barnstormer who was already storming barns (or maybe dropping through their roofs) elsewhere by the time the collection could be ordered.

Elsewhere, but still connected to our collective fates, these events took place. Temple Drake, daughter of a Jackson judge, entered the University of Mississippi in the same class as a former citizen of Jefferson who now lived in Kinston—Little Belle Mitchell [1919] {Y}. And the Sartorises' war friend, Buck Monaghan, had still found no roots and quit his job as a car salesman {"Honor"}.

I was thirty-nine this year, long ago gray, but not about to be disillusioned or bitter as long as I could try to keep on being otherwise.

THE PRESIDENCY OF HERBERT HOOVER, 1929–1933

1929

Died: Judge Dunkinfield (b. 1866)

Died: Emily Grierson (b. 1855)

Died: Anse Holland, "Old Anse"

Died: Will Mayes

Died: Lee Goodwin

Died: Tommy (b. 1891)

Died: Alabama Red

Died: Paul de Montigny

Died: Grandmother of a local girl named Elly

Though there would be some dreary and uneventful years to follow, 1929 and 1930 were just about two of the most hectic ones I can remember, and not only because we all became financially poorer during them due to the manipulations of men in New York we did not even know, ever hear of, or even want to know either. But these men affected our lives, and we could not have retaliated even if we had wanted to. More important though, equally uncontrollable things were happening here.

For a while this year we thought we were in a Snopes doldrum for the first time in the last twenty—and in retrospect it was a good thing because I spent more clock time in court this year than any other I can recall {M}. Only two folk named Snopes were even *in* Jefferson this year—Flem and Ab. All the others had either moved, been thrown out, driven out, or thrown in prison. Linda Snopes had taken up living with a Village artist named Bart Kohl, and I went to New York for ten days, mainly to attend their housewarming. V. K. Ratliff was invited, too, but would not go because his moral sensibilities were offended by the unofficiality of the "marriage." He *would* go another time, though [1936]. But by July we had four new Snopeses in town, though they would not stay long. At Clarence Snopes' instigation, Byron had mailed his four half-Indian children to Flem from El Paso [1928]; and, even before Flem could figure out what to do with them, they had taken up residence in a cave outside of town {T}. Each carrying his own personal knife, the little savages—none older than nine, two boys, a girl, and one whose sex no one ever got close enough to determine—would wander into town each day and, later, out of it. One day they actually captured Mrs. Widrington's $500 Pekingese dog, took it to their cave, and (probably) ate it. The dog's whereabouts remained a mystery to the town until Hub Hampton saw one of the children emerging from a store with the dog's collar around its neck; so Hub went out to inspect the cave—where he found a pile of bones which looked curiously like those of a small animal of the canine family. Flem, of course, showed up quickly to pay Mrs. Widrington for the dog and just as quickly to send them down to the Bend to live with his sister Net and her husband, DeWitt Binford. He also sent some meager amount of money along for their support. On the first night they were there, though, they disassembled a bed in DeWitt's house; and when he heard the strange noises that went along with this usually daytime activity, he borrowed Vernon Tull's flashlight to sneak in and check on it. Before he could even turn the light on, however, one of them slashed DeWitt's throat and laid him up for the next six months. They were missing for days thereafter, and in the interim they managed to break into the Coca Cola Bottling Plant outside the Bend without even setting off the alarm. Doris Snopes, I. O.'s seventeen-year-old son, then took them over and tried to teach them a modicum of civilized behavior by employing Pavlovian methods. But the feeling of power Doris now began to have suddenly took hold of him, and he began to treat the four as trained seals. One day, while Doris was tantalizing them, they turned on him, tied him to a tree, stacked a cord of wood around his feet, and set him ablaze. Only his furious screaming saved him. So Jody Varner phoned Flem

[219]

and told him the children had to go back to either Jefferson or El Paso. On the morning they were brought to the Jefferson station, Miss Habersham notified the traveler's Aid in New Orleans; and my nephew, Chick Mallison, and V. K. Ratliff brought them four boxes of food which V. K. dispensed like you would dispense the carcass of a fawn to a grizzly bear just out of hibernation. So the children departed and, Flem perhaps too easily presumed, got back to El Paso.

The most sensational episode this year (a year of sensational episodes to begin with) also took place down at the Bend but about two months before Byron's wild kids got there. On Thursday, May 2nd, Horace Benbow finally left Belle after nine wretched years [1919] {Y}. The following Tuesday, the 7th, he was thumbing a ride in the vicinity of the Old Frenchman Place, stopped to drink from a stream, and wound up eating dinner with Lee Goodwin (whom my cousin Gowan already knew well) and a sleazy gangster type named Popeye Vitelli (who at twenty-nine had finally made his way here from Pensacola and a number of other points south). Popeye and Goodwin were running what was at the time probably the biggest bootlegging operation in the whole history of Prohibition in this County. After supper another man named Tommy took Horace to catch the liquor truck for a ride to Jefferson. Once he got here, Horace lived for several days in the home of his widowed sister, Narcissa, and her son, Bory. While Horace was there, Gowan happened along one night and proposed marriage to her; but she declined, perhaps because no man ever surpassed Horace in her eyes and certainly the ne'er-do-well Gowan could not.

On Friday, May 10th, at the University in Oxford, Gowan had a date with the daughter of a Jackson judge, Temple Drake. After taking her home, he drank heavily with some strangers and passed out. These events were but preliminaries for the horror which now followed.

Saturday, May 11th: As a result of his previous night's activities, Gowan missed the train which was to take him and Temple to the college baseball game at Starkville; so he drove as fast as his auto could take him to Taylor, where he overtook the train and where the reckless Temple jumped off it and into his car while the train was still moving. They decided to take a sidetrip to Frenchman's Bend to buy some liquor from Lee Goodwin for the day's festivities. As they approached too quickly, however, they skidded around a bend and crashed the car into a tree which was lying across the road, disabling it entirely and knocking them cold as well. They were revived at the Old Frenchman Place, and Gowan spent the rest of the day getting drunk while Temple became progressively more frightened by the ominous Popeye. Unable to get back to Oxford that night, Temple was given a room and forced to sleep there, despite the fact that she had endured an uneasy day in which Lee Goodwin and another man, named Van, fought for her attentions

[220]

and Popeye continually cursed her. Only Tommy tried to help her out, but he was unable to stop Popeye from entering her room in the middle of the night and peeking under her nightgown. Gowan was too drunk to do anything. Meanwhile, back in Jefferson, Horace had moved back into his old house, which had been boarded up for nine years now [1919]. On this same day, in Memphis, Virgil Snopes and Fonzo Winbush had arrived at Miss Reba's for one of their (now) yearly visits [1922]. Three apparently unrelated events which really weren't.

SUNDAY, MAY 12TH: Gowan awakened early and went to Vernon Tull's to borrow a car, directed there by Goodwin's common-law wife, Ruby LaMarr, who feared for Temple's safety [1919]. Guilt-ridden, Gowan ran away instead. Meanwhile, Temple was hiding in the barn and had to stave off a rat. In terror she asked the kind-hearted but simple-minded Tommy to protect her, a request he tried to honor, but he was shot dead by Popeye when he tried to protect her from him. Popeye, syphlitic and impotent, then raped Temple with a corncob and hauled her away, bleeding, in his car. After stopping en route at Dumphries to buy candy bars and to clean the blood off her, they reached Miss Reba's in Memphis by midafternoon, where Reba had Temple attended to by a doctor. Meanwhile, back in Yoknapatawpha, Gowan had relieved his mind of Temple's fate by swearing off drinking forever and, probably, resolving that he would not let any other girls get into the mess (whatever it might be) that Temple must be in.

MONDAY-FRIDAY, MAY 13TH–17TH: On Monday Tommy's body was brought to Jefferson and became an object of curiosity to the town loiterers. On Wednesday Lee Goodwin was brought in by the Sheriff, and I had him charged with Tommy's murder. Horace Benbow, an attorney even though he had not practiced in some years, remembered him and came to counsel him in his cell and also to put Ruby and their year-old baby up in his own house. When Narcissa objected to this, Horace and Isom transferred her to the Holston House. By Friday Lee Goodwin's suddenly self-righteous clients had turned on him and overturned his still. During this entire week, Temple was still being held in Memphis to keep her from going to the Jefferson authorities about Tommy's murder; she was treated quite well and quickly formed an attachment to a frequenter of Reba's establishment known only as Alabama Red.

THE WEEK OF MAY 19TH: On Sunday, Horace confided to Narcissa that Goodwin would appear guilty of Tommy's murder because he was too scared of Popeye to tell the truth about the crime. Narcissa thought him guilty anyway. She mentioned to Horace a letter she had received from Gowan the previous afternoon which announced that he would never see her again because he was too ashamed of something he had done; but it would be a while before Horace would connect this with the crime. In the next couple of days he discovered, via Ruby, that Temple had been at the murder scene, so he went on a wild goose chase to Oxford to see her, where, of course, she had not been since Saturday morning, the 11th. So he rode the evening train back to Jefferson and had the ill luck to sit with none other than Senator Clarence Snopes; and when he got here he found that Ruby and her baby had been run out of the hotel by a delegation of Christian women, though Horace secretly believed that Eustace Graham, the district attorney, had put them up to this [1928]. By week's end he had found a home for her with a half-crazy white woman on the edge of town (Narcissa having once again refused to house her) and had a phone installed at his own long-out-of-use home. Horace seemed suddenly to have a purpose in life again after many years of wasting it on Belle Mitchell.

THE WEEK OF JUNE 6TH TO THE 15TH: Relations with his sister had deteriorated so badly by this time that Horace stopped visiting her entirely. On Thursday the 13th, Clarence Snopes called him at home and *sold* him information about Temple Drake's whereabouts. So on Friday the 14th, Horace confronted her at Miss Reba's; and, in her crazed ranting, she assured him that it was Popeye, whom he had met a month earlier at the Old Frenchman Place, who had killed Tommy.

MONDAY, JUNE 17TH: In Jefferson, Horace wrote Belle and asked for a divorce, vowing to go to Europe after Lee Goodwin's trial. Meanwhile, Eustace Graham, who was known to be seeking election to Congress based solely on his conviction record, assured Narcissa that Horace could not win this case; whereupon she went home and wrote Belle that Horace would, in fact, be back in Kinston on the 24th, no matter what his own correspondence implied. In Memphis, however, things were coming to a head. Anxious to run away from Miss Reba's with Alabama Red, Temple made plans to escape with him. As she was bolting the door, however, Popeye caught her and took her to an infamous booze-and-gambling house known as The Grotto where she got drunk and escorted out. Popeye, however, stayed behind and murdered Red in an alley. At almost the very moment he was doing this, in an unrelated incident in a small Alabama town, the deputy sheriff was killed as well. *This* crime, and none of his own, was the one for which Popeye would, in the long run, pay [1930].

TUESDAY, JUNE 18TH: At The Grotto, the patrons held a funeral for Red, though in the process of a tangentially related fight his coffin was knocked over and his body rolled out on the floor. At Miss Reba's there was upheaval and general fury over the week's events, the girls all feeling that Popeye had given their place a bad name by turning it into what they referred to as a "French joint" when he contracted to pay Alabama Red to make love to Temple while he, Popeye, looked on and whined. In Jefferson, Clarence Snopes visited a dentist this day to get his teeth fixed after getting hit in them by an angry Memphis lawyer who needed Goodwin convicted to have

Popeye exonerated of Tommy's murder. With Temple's information this ought to have been impossible, but it wasn't.

THURSDAY, JUNE 20TH: As Lee Goodwin's trial opened, Horace was again in the dark as to Temple's whereabouts. Graham was quickly on the offensive, with the string of cheap tricks that the county Bar Association knew him to use. By nightfall he was in command, so Horace visited Lee in his cell to go over the second day's strategy. After their talk, Lee would not let Ruby leave with Horace, for Ruby had already paid twice before for legal services with her own body [1916] [1919]. While Horace understood this, he told me later that the pressure of the whole case and the events surrounding it broke right there. He spun and shouted at Goodwin: "Can't you see that perhaps a man might do something just because he knew it was right, necessary to the harmony of things that it be done?" I guess I once believed this myself, probably still do, but I have quit trying to convince anybody else of it.

FRIDAY, JUNE 21ST: Temple Drake and the Memphis Jew lawyer appeared in court this morning. To create animosity against Lee among the jury members, Graham displayed the corncob with which Popeye had raped Temple but suggested that it was Goodwin himself who had done it. Then Horace did what I would have done, though I probably would have checked on things a little better beforehand. He put Temple on the stand, only to have her perjure herself by inserting Lee's name in place of Popeye's at every step of the recounting. The jury deliberated for only eight minutes and convicted Lee of Tommy's murder. So Horace, a man now fully resigned to the futility of pursuing truth, packed his bags and slept at the railroad station that night until the train passed through that would take him back to Kinston and back to Belle.

SATURDAY, JUNE 22ND: Lee Goodwin fell into the hands of a lynch mob just after midnight and was burnt alive in a vacant lot. Had Horace still been in town, he probably would have been thrown in, too. Later in the day he and Belle reunited for a loveless infinity. None of us ever saw or heard of Horace again. And so ended the old name of Benbow in the County. Popeye Vitelli was found "not guilty" in a trial he didn't even stand. But the fate which brought him here and substituted Lee Goodwin for him in court, and also in the vacant lot, did one thing to redeem itself in some minuscule way. In August, Popeye was arrested for the murder—on June 17th, the same night he killed Red—of the deputy sheriff in that small Alabama town. Popeye had probably never been there and certainly had not been on that night. In September, a jury convicted him, again in eight minutes, and sentenced him to be executed the following year. In October Temple and her father went to Paris, where she got bored enough to solicit Gowan to visit her, which, late in the year, he did.

Nor was Lee Goodwin's the only "lynching" we had here that year. Will

Mayes, a quite respectable and hard-working young black man, was run down—solely on Minnie Cooper's word that he had raped her—by a mob organized by our local war hero, Jackson McLendon [1917] {"Dry September"}. I recall Hawkshaw Stribling, the barber, doing everything he could to prevent it; but, when emotions get fired up, common sense is like an eyedropperful of water. McLendon, a sensation a dozen years ago, had degenerated to nothing much as middle age took hold of him. And Minnie Cooper, once (also back twelve years) with a torrid love affair underway [1917], was drying up with nary another man bothering to notice her once her cashier left town [1912]. So Mayes became, in her deluded mind, the latest male to covet her body, and, in McLendon's, a way to revive the image of himself the town had long since forgotten. Shortly after the lynching, Minnie went stark raving mad, but McLendon went scot-free since no one at the scene of the murder would testify against him.

And we uncovered yet another murder this year, but not until after the murderess was dead and the crime was forty-two years old [1887] {"A Rose for Emily"}. When Miss Emily Grierson died at seventy-four, a locked room in the upper portion of her house had to be broken into shortly after her funeral. In the bedroom was the barely preserved body of Homer Barron, the northerner who had come to Jefferson in the 1880s to lay the town's sidewalks. Perhaps it is fortunate that Miss Emily passed on before this could come to court, though probably it would have been impossible by now to prove she had killed him.

As I said, 1929 was a heavy year in court. In the early months of the year, Old Anse Holland was discovered in a graveyard digging up the bodies of his wife's people {K}. The county health office put a stop to this; and, two days later, Anse himself turned up dead, caught in the stirrup of a whipped horse. Though Judge Dunkinfield, executor of Anse's will, surely would not have given all Anse's property to Virginius, one of his two sons, as the will ordered, Dunkinfield himself was then found shot dead between the eyes in his own courtroom. Young Anse, the disinherited son, was the immediate suspect, of course, so he was rousted out of the dirt-floor cabin he had lived in for the last fourteen years and jailed [1915]. Despite his admission in open court, I was not convinced he was guilty; I said candidly I thought the son had beaten his father up but not killed him. Furthermore, I pointedly accused Granby Dodge of killing Old Anse and then hiring a Memphis hit man to do in the judge. This was because I recalled that Granby and Virginius had made each other their sole heirs, and Granby would probably not want to see the judge split what he expected Virginius to get—a large parcel of land—in half. I also could prove that Granby had bought some rat poison which I presumed to be headed for Virginius' insides once the property was legally his. Granby chided the story, naturally; so I constructed a ruse in which I contended that a silver box in Dunkinfield's office (the one his daughter brought him from Europe at the outbreak of the war [1917]) contained smoke from the hit man's cigarettes, a brand which was so foul-smelling that no one in the county smoked it but which, I could prove, the hit man had bought two packs of the day of the crime. I also said that that hit man had been picked up in Battenburg for running down a child; and, in the process, he ratted on Granby—none of which was true. But Granby, probably to gain the court's mercy, jumped up and admitted both crimes.

And there was a girl in town named Elly who was in love with a part-black man named Paul de Montigny. She was, however, engaged to a bank cashier because of her grandmother's refusal to let her marry Paul {"Elly"}. Evidently the situation crested this year, for she got Paul to drive her to pick up the grandmother in Mills City and, while they were driving, presented a plan to have him murder her. When he refused, she caused him, on the return trip with her grandmother in the car, to drive his car off the road, an accident which killed the other two but which left Elly alive to bleed along the roadside until someone bothered to stop and give her aid. No evidence here either, though Elly's intentions and motives were widely known. Save for the Granby Dodge conviction, which I had to lie through my teeth to effect, I was beginning to think as Horace Benbow did.

Some events this year were of a tamer nature. A new golf course was built outside of town, so Jason Compson rebought the land adjoining the Compson property when the old course was abandoned after less than twenty years of use [1908] {M}. I suppose he was planning to grow cotton on it, for the next thing I knew he was in Memphis to learn cotton trading {F}. Harriss built a polo field on the Backus plantation this year, and he and his friends were often seen knocking around on it {K}. This was also the year that Uncle Willy Christian, who operated the town drugstore and also had a terrific drug habit that most people knew about, was "captured" by the ladies of the local church and sent to Memphis for "rehabilitation" {"Uncle Willy"}. Their reasoning was that he was having too much influence on the local boys—and he was, but not because he took dope. It was because he supported their baseball teams, gave them ice cream sodas without shaking them down for their last bit of cash, and listened to their individual problems and helped them solve them. When he was sent away, he was ruined and so were many of them [1934].

If there was one thing that Jefferson was not short on at this time, it was the good intentions of people who considered themselves religious and patriotic—I suppose the ruinations of Lee Goodwin, Ruby LaMarr, Will Mayes, and Willy Christian all attest to that. But we had a different sort of person headed our way, one which would make Jefferson respond somewhat differently: at Doane's Mill, which next year would send us Lena Grove, the timber supply was exhausted years earlier than anyone had expected it to be. And so, apparently, was American prosperity. 1929, as everyone knows, was, finally, the year of The Crash.

1930

Born: Son of Lena Grove and Lucas Burch

Married: Temple Drake and Gowan Stevens

Married: Byron Bunch and Lena Grove (probably)

Married: Henry "Hawkshaw" Stribling and Susan Reed

Married: Anse Bundren and his second wife

Died: Virginia Sartoris "Aunt Jenny" DuPre (b. 1840)

Died: Joanna Burden (b. 1887)

Died: Joe Christmas (b. 1893)

Died: Addie Bundren (b. 1875)

Died: Howard Boyd (b. 1903)

Died: Popeye Vitelli (b. 1900)

This was to be the second seething year in a row for the county, with the Depression now a reality to intensify it. Uncle Ike McCaslin, perhaps in need of ready cash, sold his hardware store to a man named Triplett who would later sell it to another man with long hardware experience, Jason Compson [1945] {M}. For now, with the stock market shot, Jason had established himself as a buyer and dealer in cotton in Jefferson {F}. Crawford Gowrie left the bootlegging business to the bigger syndicates and returned to the county [1921] to enter into a timber and cattle business and also work some small portions of the land on the side {I}. Late in the year Hub Hampton began his second term as sheriff, replacing Watt Kennedy because no man was allowed by law to serve two successive terms—Hampton and Kennedy alternated for years, each more or less serving as the other's right-hand man during the years he was out of office. Also seeking a better job in these tough times was

Clarence Egglestone Snopes who announced that he had designs on the state governorship on a soak-the-rich platform {M}. Back at his old job was Uncle Willy Christian, released from the Memphis hospital where he was receiving psychiatric treatment for his dope addiction; he still had to go there every week for "boosters," though {"Uncle Willy"}. Harriss was spending more time on his property each year now and less in New Orleans—this year he built a steeplechase out there, made entirely out of phony cardboard materials so that the whole thing, whether by design or accident, looked like a Hollywood set {K}. Melisandre remained in Paris. Other countians in Paris were Temple Drake and Gowan Stevens, in my opinion with not a single complementing quality between them. They were married in the American embassy anyway. And in the summer, at almost the same time we were at the height of our Joe Christmas–Joanna Burden–Percy Grimm problems, Popeye was hanged in Alabama for a murder he did not commit, this despite the fact that he could have gained time by appealing his conviction. To the incredulity of the same Memphis lawyer who suborned Temple Drake's perjury here last year, he refused to [1929] {Y}. So much for the year's random gossip.

Aunt Jenny DuPre died in a wheelchair at ninety; and indirectly this might be tied to Snopesism, now so rampant in the county as to be unnoticed {"There Was a Queen"}. Her relative by marriage, Narcissa Benbow Sartoris, took an undisguised trip to Memphis one weekend with a Jewish man from the North. Aunt Jenny and the Sartoris Negroes still around bemoaned her lack of class and sexual ethics, except that the reason for her behavior was at least partially explained for them later. The man was in fact a federal agent who had, years before, successfully investigated the Byron Snopes bank robbery of 1919. In the process he ran across the stack of obscene letters that Byron had written Narcissa and then stolen from her. In the intervening years, this agent had snooped into who Narcissa was, been impressed by her, and offered to exchange the letters for this weekend in Memphis. To protect her image before her ten-year-old son, Bory, and to save the Sartoris name from further blemish, she accepted—but in accepting she brought death to Aunt Jenny, the last real Sartoris around and the queen of the family. This last blow was simply too much for her to accept.

Another, though less queenly, woman caused death in the county in 1930 as well. We had long known of the unnatural relationship between Howard Boyd and his mother, but this year it became apparent just how strong her hold on him was when his wife, out of sheer frustration, began to "run around" with some of the looser men in the district [1921] {"The Brooch"}. When Mrs. Boyd found out what she was up to and that she had lost an heirloom brooch, she ordered Amy Boyd from the house. Howard, who had—even through his wife's period of indiscretion—tried to keep the two women apart, realized finally how trapped he was and chose the only way possible to break loose from his tyrannical mother. He retired to the bathroom and shot himself.

Perhaps these two tales of death require one of regeneration to offset them. Hawkshaw Stribling married seventeen-year-old Susan Reed after twenty-five years of total devotion to the Starnes family in Division, the kin of his first intended who died in 1905 {"Hair"}. Susan was a five-year-old orphan when Hawkshaw came to Jefferson to cut hair in 1918. He had watched her grow up, trimmed her hair, and given her candy at his shop ever since then— and then watched in dismay when—three or four years earlier—Susan began to paint herself and act like (and probably be) a harlot [1926]. Hawkshaw must quietly have decided to save her then, but knew he had an obligation, entirely self-imposed, to pay off the Starnes mortgage until 1930 [1917]. When he made the last payment on April 16th of this year, he proposed to Susan Reed; and she accepted. Somehow good men like Hawkshaw sneak through the web without being eaten by the spider.

This same month, down at the Bend, Addie Bundren died, and Anse was forced to honor his long-ago-made promise to bury her in Jefferson [1899] {D}. The seven-day odyssey it took to get her here is a great demonstration of the insignificance of man on this earth, of the foolishness of his petty hopes, and of the essential uselessness of his life *if* he ever dared to admit such foolishness and insignificance to himself. On the day Addie died, Anse was lamenting his lot in life more loudly than ever: four lazy sons and a loose-loined daughter. When Doc Peabody came to examine Addie for the last time, he predicted imminent death, saying she was simply too tired to live any longer. And before nightfall, amidst a terrific downpour, Addie passed away to the music of Cash's saw building her coffin. Meanwhile everyone else-- with the exception of the youngest child, Vardaman—barely acknowledged their wife-mother's end. Dewey Dell was trying to get Peabody to abort her illegitimate foetus, and Jewel and Darl were out stuck in the mud during their daily pursuit of money. But Vardaman, who had concluded in his child's mind that Doc Peabody had killed his mother, whipped Doc's team out into the woods on him.

On the second day, they loaded Addie into the coffin in reverse so that her wedding dress, in which she had insisted upon being buried, could be spread out at the wide end. Then they held the funeral in their home, with the Reverend Whitfield officiating [1904] and the parlor packed with all the Tulls, Bookwrights, Armstids, and such. But as they started toward Jefferson, the Bundrens learned that the bridge at Tull's, for many years an essential link between the folks south of the Bend and Jefferson [1888], had washed out during the recent heavy rainfall. So, already pursued by buzzards, they proceeded farther downstream to the one at Sampson's, only to find it gone too. They spent the night there, and it was at this point that Vardamen drilled holes in the coffin so his mother could breathe, two of which went into her skull.

The third day they doubled back to Tull's, and Tull advised them to postpone the trip until the water receded. Anse refused; whereupon Tull refused to lend him his best mule for the fording of the Yoknapatawpha River. So the Bundrens simply pushed their rickety wagon and tired mules into the river; but the wagon overturned, spilling the coffin, drowning the mules, and breaking Cash's leg in the process. Tull jumped into the river to help them save what they could, which amounted to Cash, the coffin, and Cash's beloved box of tools. They put up at Armstid's for the night, resolving to get to the Mottstown bridge the next day. Although they sent to Loosh Peabody to fix Cash's leg, it had to be the inevitable Will Varner who came along to do the job [1907].

They stayed the entire fourth day at Armstid's while Anse bargained with I. O. Snopes for a new team [1926]—which it took Jewel's horse and Cash's record-player money (he had placed an order with V. K. Ratliff a while back) to get [1920]. Jewel was infuriated when he heard this, and for a time deserted the cortege. Meanwhile, buzzards were thick over the Armstid property, though Mrs. Armstid—consistent with the treatment she always afforded her meek-headed husband [1908] and would afford, four months from now, Lena Grove—was more concerned about the mistreatment of Addie's body than the swirling-swarming birds.

On the fifth day, Eustace Grimm arrived with a mule team, Cash was strapped to the top of the coffin, and the party made its way to Mottstown, where they attracted immediate attention because of the stench which accompanied them, not to mention those birds. While Dewey Dell tried to get the clerk in the drugstore to sell her some medicine to abort her baby, the marshal rode up and straightforwardly asked all of them to leave town. After making a crude cement cast for Cash's deteriorating and painful leg, they crossed the bridge north of town and stopped at the Gillespie farm for the evening. The Gillespie boy secretly pushed the wagon and coffin into the barn to control the stink; but later that same evening Darl, the only one rational enough to see this fiasco for what it was, rushed out to the barn and set it afire in an attempt to end the entire travesty. They got the animals, the coffin, and the wagon out in time; but the barn burned to the ground. Gillespie threatened to sue them, for what return I can't imagine, if Darl were not locked up in an asylum where many people (especially Jewel) had long felt he belonged.

On the sixth day they arrived in Jefferson, Dewey Dell donning her Sunday clothes behind a bush a mile before they got here. When they entered the town we knew it immediately—and Jewel almost got in a knife fight with a man who commented on the smell. Anse borrowed a shovel and they dug Addie's grave and they buried her. Then, at the gates of the cemetery, two

[229]

lawmen pounced on Darl. After disposing of Jewel and Dewey Dell, who had jumped on their brother, too, they took him away to have him sent to the asylum at Jackson, where Benjy Compson before many more years would join him [1933] and where Henry Armstid had already spent a good deal of his life trying not to remember Flem Snopes [1908]. We later found out that Jewel's special hate for Darl stemmed from the fact that it was only he who knew, or at least suspected, that Jewel was Reverend Whitfield's son and not Anse's. That night, while Vardaman sat on a curb, Dewey Dell entered Willy Christian's drugstore and submitted herself to the night clerk, the no-good named Skeets McGowan [1919], in return for a box of worthless pills he convinced her would abort the baby. Loosh Peabody treated Cash's badly ruined leg, advising him that the cement cast he had just removed would probably cause it to be shorter than the other for the rest of his life.

On the seventh day they rested and prepared to return to the Bend. Darl watched them from the window of the train to Jackson, while Dewey Dell, Vardaman, and Cash sat in the wagon eating bananas. Then Anse strolled up, sporting a new set of teeth purchased with the $10 his daughter had been given by her seducer, Lafe, to get medical treatment. During the time he was absent, he purchased a gramophone for himself and also married the bug-eyed, duck-shaped woman who lent him the shovel to dig Addie's grave.

Perhaps the biggest story of this year, however, was the two murders, within ten days of each other in August, of Joanna Burden and Joe Christmas {L}. Like any other such crimes, much precedes them to cause them to happen, most of it uncontrollable by the parties who either commit them or are their victims. So when Christmas killed Miss Burden and Percy Grimm killed Christmas, what the County saw was only the results, not the causes.

In either December of last year or January of this, the loveless affair between Christmas and Miss Burden reached its climax when Joanna said she was pregnant. For the next two months, into late February, Joe never appeared at her house; so finally she sent him a note requesting he visit her. He did so, on which occasion she announced that she would like to send him to a Negro college and then have him study law with her black lawyer, E. E. Peebles, in Memphis. After that they could go on a lecture tour together. Joe categorically refused, and in the process he raised the possibility that he had no Negro blood in his veins at all—his father was known only to be a dark-skinned man [1892]. Joanna was thunderstruck: she had given herself to him to "raise up a Negro" [1891] and so lift the curse her father told her God had put on the white man. Now, if he were white, she had, in the terms of her Calvinistic upbringing, damned herself to hell. In a panic, she considered what to do next.

Also in February a man named Joe Brown, but whose real name later turned out to be Lucas Burch, arrived in Jefferson from Alabama and began working at the planing mill with Christmas. He lost his first week's paycheck in Birdsong's crap game, but he moved with unexplainable celerity into Joe's bootlegging operation. With Lee Goodwin's business now defunct, Christmas probably required a partner to keep up with the trade, though Brown-Burch did not seem to me a likely selection. In March they apparently hijacked a liquor truck outside Memphis and made a lot of money, for Christmas immediately quit his job at the mill and in April began riding around town in a brand new car and dealing the booze straight out of Brown's shirtfront. The reason I know this is that Brown started bragging about it while he was in the chair next to me at Maxey's barbershop one Saturday; but I didn't find out too much, for Christmas himself burst in just then and literally yanked him out of the chair while Hawkshaw's razor was still on his cheek. Joe made a vague threat against Brown's life and apparently made another one the next month when Brown laughed at him for hanging around in Joanna's bedroom.

Things in their affair were worsening. Joe accused Joanna of being too old to get pregnant, at which they wound up hitting each other. Joanna remarked wearily that perhaps it would be better if they both were dead. But if Joe was having his woman problems, it would not be long before Brown-Burch would have his as well. A girl named Lena Grove had discovered, down at Doane's Mill in January, that she was pregnant and decided that she and her seducer—none other than Brown-Burch—ought to get married. Having told her that he would be back for her after he got a job, he got himself to Jefferson and promptly forgot about her, not to mention about the name he used to go by as well. But in mid-July she left Doane's Mill and got as far as Frenchman's Bend in a couple of weeks, not really knowing where she was going but presuming that something or someone would lead her to the right place. So she was told at Varner's Store that there was a man in Jefferson with a name like Burch (but it was really Byron Bunch they were thinking of), and she got herself here on Saturday, the 16th of August. At this point the divergent destinies of Joe Christmas, Joanna Burden, Byron Bunch, Lena Grove, Lucas Burch, Percy Grimm, and Gail Hightower—a ragtag group of motleys with little in common among them except that fate had put them all in the same place at the same time, a place, Jefferson where none of them belonged or were wanted in the first place—wove themselves together.

On the night of Wednesday the 13th, Joanna had ordered Christmas to kneel with her to pray for their mutually damned souls, but Christmas had refused. On the night of Friday, the 15th, Joe had decided, though probably only subconsciously, that the confrontation with this woman who had come to symbolize the things in the world he most detested—sex, religion, womanhood, race—could no longer be avoided. After a day of near-hysteria in which he groped for the identity he had never been able to find for himself [1897], and after (according to one report the sheriff got) he had exposed himself in the headlights of a car, he went late that night to Joanna's room for

[231]

the last time. She again ordered him, this time at gunpoint, to kneel and pray; and when he again refused she fired the first barrel of an old Civil War cap-and-ball pistol directly into his face. It misfired, and Joe then slashed her throat before she could fire the second one. Then, without realizing that he had Joanna's gun in his hand, he ran outside and flagged down a young couple in a car and, without meaning to, terrified them into driving him away from the scene.

By the time Lena Grove reached town around noon the following day, the Burden house had been discovered afire, Joanna's body had been pulled out by Hamp Waller, and Joe Brown had been seen there drunk. It was he apparently who set the fire to cover the murder. Later in the day, while Lena was discovering that Byron Bunch wasn't Lucas Burch, Miss Burden's New Hampshire relatives wired a $1000 reward for the capture of the murderer, which of course provoked Brown to come forward and assist (though accidentally hamper) the pursuit. Up until this moment Watt Kennedy had been trying to pin the crime on a number of people, but now the pursuit was on of the surly man that no one had liked anyway and now liked even less since Brown had told them all that Christmas had nigger blood in him and was sleeping with a white woman he had seen fit to kill once he was done with her.

Sunday, the 17th, was a day of pursuit which turned up nothing but the gun and a lot of reward-seekers who claimed to have information. Joe Brown was still in front of the search party, often confusing the bloodhounds which had arrived by train from Jackson that very morning. Meanwhile, Bunch had put Brown's "wife" up in Mrs. Beard's boarding house to care for her until Brown-Burch got back from the chase. On the next day, Byron and his confidant, the Reverend Hightower, had a discussion of the weekend's events which wound up with Hightower's caution, spoken as a man who had ruined himself with a woman, that Byron not become involved any further with the pregnant and obviously sinful Lena. Byron waved this off and returned to her with food.

TUESDAY, AUGUST 19TH: Still on the loose, Christmas was reported to have broken up a Negro revival meeting at a country church, ripping Brother Bedenberry literally from the pulpit and knocking down Pappy Thompson on the way up the aisle. Roz Thompson, his son, pulled a knife on Christmas, for which Christmas broke his skull. While all the Negroes hid in the bushes surrounding the church, Joe casually smoked a cigarette on the front porch and then departed. I began to suspect he wanted to be caught but could not stop running long enough to realize it.

WEDNESDAY, AUGUST 20TH: Byron Bunch asked Lena to marry him this day and was refused. But back on the chase, Kennedy thought he had Christmas cornered when he followed his footprints to a Negro cabin—whereupon he discovered that Joe had traded his shoes to a black woman and now was wearing her brogans instead. Joe, though, must have been getting very weary, perhaps falling asleep on his feet. This is what Kennedy was counting on, at least.

THURSDAY, AUGUST 21ST: Joe was reported to have scared a Negro family out of its cabin and eaten its dinner; later he threatened a number of people along the road.

FRIDAY, AUGUST 22ND: Joe hitched a ride to Mottstown in the wagon of a Negro boy who had not heard of him as yet; and, for the first time, he had a moment to think about how trapped he was, both by the present circumstances and by the long road which to this point was the totality of his life.

SATURDAY, AUGUST 23RD: Now it was clear that Joe wanted to be caught; he finally was—by a man named Halliday—outside a barbershop in Mottstown. To the surprise of both capturer and captured, Uncle Doc Hines pounced upon both of them in the process, screaming "Kill him, kill him!" No one of course yet knew that Doc was Christmas' grandfather [1898] who had intended to kill him over thirty years ago but had missed his chance. While Joe languished in jail waiting for the Jefferson deputies to come for him, a lynch mob gathered but was dispersed by the sheriff, who warned that Halliday would not get his reward (and spend it in Mottstown) if Joe were killed. So, as Joe was travelling in chains to Jefferson, Uncle Doc Hines and his wife were headed there as well on the train. All this while Percy Grimm was busily gathering together the local militia in Jefferson, of which he was captain, to protect civic order and prevent a lynching which would disrupt it [1929].

SUNDAY, AUGUST 24TH: Watt Kennedy publicly warned Grimm to stop waving his pistol around town. The Hineses were led to Reverend Hightower's by Byron Bunch, and Mrs. Hines made the blatant request that Hightower say that he and Christmas had "been together" on the night of the murder to provide him with an alibi [1907]. Mrs. Hines was undoubtedly trying to relieve some of the familial guilt she felt for her husband's role in making Joe what he was; but, understandably, Hightower kicked them out.

MONDAY, AUGUST 25TH: Lena Grove's baby was born this morning, with none other than poor Hightower having to serve as midwife [1926]. Later in the day, Byron quit at the sawmill and then asked Sheriff Kennedy to let Lucas Burch (or Brown) go to his cabin to see his wife and child. Lucas was so allowed, but he fled through the rear window of the cabin without being noticed by the deputy who was guarding the front door. Byron tried to stop him to bring him back, but all he got was his face bloodied. Burch hopped a northbound freight and left the county forever. Meanwhile, Joe Christmas had just been indicted for Joanna Burden's murder and was being led away from the courthouse when he, too, broke loose and fled. In hot pursuit was Percy Grimm, in his conscious mind wanting only to recapture the prisoner. However, when he finally chased him into Hightower's house and Hightower screamed out that Grimm should hold up because Joe had, he said, spent the night with him when Joanna Burden was killed, Grimm's southern heritage and martial instinct erupted from his subconscious and overcame him—he fired five shots through the table Joe was hiding behind and then ran forward and hacked off his testicles with a butcher knife. While those around him vomited, he yelled at Christmas' lifeless body: "That will teach you to leave white women alone, even in hell."

I recall that the events of this day particularly unnerved me, and I made a series of foolish statements around town about how Joe did what he did because of the mixture of white blood and black blood in his veins. But I knew then, and now realize, that in saying such a thing, I was—like Grimm— a victim of my heritage. What ruined Joe was, among countless other things, a psychological mixture of abstractions of whiteness and blackness which rendered him unable to know who or what he was or be accepted by anybody who knew he was in doubt.

In September, Lena and Byron left town and probably got married, though the last we heard of them was from an itinerant furniture salesman who passed through town occasionally and had given them a ride along the road. She claimed still to be looking for Lucas Burch, he said, and was kicking Byron out every time he tried to crawl into bed with her in his truck. Byron ran off and left her for a while, but his resolve to keep trying was by this time too great. They met him again farther along the highway, and he was with her once again, as she fully expected he would be.

1931

Born: Bucky Stevens, first child of Gowan and Temple Drake Stevens

Born: Child of Dewey Dell Bundren and "Lafe"

Died: Judge Allison (b. 1866)

A very quiet year for the most part in terms of external events, so marriages started to come apart instead. In my family, my cousin Gowan and his wife were back from Paris and known about town as the popular young couple in the country club set; yet internally their marriage was already the hodgepodge I could have predicted {N}. Temple was not sleeping well at night, tormented by something she could not identify. She gave birth to their first child this year; but Gowan, trying to understand the frenzy which began when she first became pregnant, assumed the child was not his and told her so. I thought instead that she might have been feeling some remorse over what she had done to Lee Goodwin [1929]; but it is more likely that she was still haunted by the spectre of Popeye or pining over the loss of Alabama Red, whom she must truly have loved. At any rate, it was not a happy marriage, and the family prepared for trouble [1936]. In my sister Margaret's family there was mild panic over the fact that my seven-year-old nephew, Chick, was learning to play every card game, deadpanned, from a local spinster {I}.

Harriss, still without Melisandre and apparently not caring, had foxhounds on the Backus property now to chase around his cardboard-covered estate {K}. Molly Beauchamp made one of her rare visits to her brother Hamp in Jefferson in the summer, the last in fact until her own marital problems some years later [1941] {G}.

And Judge Allison died, though in some ways he had died in 1913 when his young son was dragged to death by his pony. According to the town atheist, who had been the judge's best friend for the past fifteen years [1916], the judge was awaiting death in the form of some sort of mystic transition into a nebulous state in which universal justice would be done and he would be united with his dead son {"Beyond"}. One can only hope he knew something most of the rest of us don't.

1932

Died: Wife of Will Varner

The Depression thickened, but 1932—perhaps because of that—was another year in which little happened in the county. Willy Christian was still going for his psychiatric treatments in Memphis every week, but by year's end he had finished them [1930] {"Uncle Willy"}. He was declared "cured" of his dope habit. The ill-fated Spoot Rider went to work at the sawmill and, probably, to shoot craps in Birdsong's crooked dice game as well [1941] {G}. Elsewhere, Signor Canova, really Joe Flint, performed his last act as "The Master of Illusion" this year and began to take lesser jobs in circuses and carnivals {K}. He would be Jefferson's problem soon, however; he was earmarked to come here [1940].

It did not seem as if we were out of Germany very long, but now we began to recognize the seeds of something that would have to make us go back. A man named Hitler, thriving on a people looking to place blame for the Depression upon some suitable scapegoat, ran against Hindenburg in the presidential elections this year—and lost. But his party itself became the largest in the Reichstag; and, by January of the next year, Hitler would have to be appointed Chancellor and, by March, absolute dictator. On the other side of the Atlantic, Dwight D. Eisenhower was forty-two and working for the Assistant Secretary of War in 1932. He did not now know of, nor would he ever, Chick Mallison, DeSpain, Pete Grier, Bory Sartoris, Sebastian

Gauldres, Luther Biglin, Devries, Linda Snopes, Turpin, McKinley Smith or any of the others we would send to fight for him. He never realized that Grier and DeSpain would never make it back alive, that Chick Mallison would have to spend over a year of his life in a German concentration camp, and that Devries would return a hero without a leg. Nor would he know of Flem Snopes nor Jason Compson who, though too old to fight, were prepared to make a buck out of the fact that others weren't.

So, in 1932, this was what fate had in store for some Yoknapatawphans, most of whom had not, in this year, advanced beyond squabbles in vacant lots and tattletaling to their moms after they managed to get on the losing ends of them.

THE PRESIDENCY OF FRANKLIN DELANO ROOSEVELT, 1933–1945

1933

Born: Son of Res and Maw Grier

Married: Willy Christian and a Memphis prostitute

Died: Caroline Bascomb Compson

Died: Stonewall Jackson "Monk" Odlethrop (b. 1903)

Died: Warden Gambrell, in Parchman

There were some tragic new developments in the five-year-old case of Monk Odlethrop this year [1928]; but the case would not yet lay itself to rest, though by year's end it had so laid poor Monk {K}. We had a new state's attorney in Jefferson this year {G}, and together he and I managed to obtain a pardon for Monk when a dying man here—one of the two witnesses to the 1928 murder of Fraser for which Monk was convicted and imprisoned—admitted that he had committed the crime and then jammed the pistol in the simple-minded young man's hand {K}. But Monk now refused to leave the penitentiary, for he had become so devoted to Warden Gambrell that he wanted to remain with him forever. I was in consternation as to what to do next, but the problem was solved a week later when Monk supposedly shot Gambrell during an escape attempt. He was once again quickly tried, convicted, and (this time) sentenced for execution by hanging. On the gallows, still with no more conception of death than he had when he was falsely accused of the first murder, Monk waited benignly, uttering only the follow-

[236]

ing mixture of pulpit rhetoric and agrarian poetry: "I have sinned against God and man and I have now paid it out with my suffering. And now I am going out into the free world and farm." That did not ring true to say the least; but Monk went to his death before I could figure out why it didn't [1936].

Still in a fury over the money that Miss Quentin had stolen from him on Easter Sunday, 1928, Jason Compson committed his brother, Benjy, to the state asylum this year. Thereupon, he also "freed the Compsons from the niggers" when he packed off Dilsey and all her relatives to live in Memphis and, later, a number of scattered other places {F}. He soon discovered, however, that he had traded Benjy's howling and the Negroes' moaning for Mrs. Compson's whining—whining that she wanted Benjy back {M}! So Jason relented and got Benjy out, only to have his mother die before the year was out. Though he probably did try to recommit Benjy, the asylum would not have taken him, since Jason seemed to be treating the whole institution as some sort of dog pound by this point. And poor Jason with nary a Negro at home any longer to watch over and clean up after Benjy. Fate does good at times.

My cousin Gowan Stevens allowed his unstable wife, Temple, to hire a black woman named Nancy Mannigoe (Mannigault) as a maid this year [1936], though he understood she was more someone who could talk with Temple and console her because of their similar "loose" backgrounds {N}. Another woman of loose background arrived in Jefferson as well: a Memphis whore to whom poor, rehabilitated Willy Christian, the drugstore owner, had gotten himself married {"Uncle Willy"}. They were separated within six months, however, most of us thought to Willy's distinct benefit. And into town also, from the McCaslin land seventeen miles out, came Samuel "Butch" Beauchamp, nineteen-year-old roughhouse grandson of Lucas and Molly, and son of their elder daughter {G}. He would raise riot here for a bit and then move on to do the same in various northern cities [1940].

Boon Hogganbeck, in his seventies now but still a big strapping man, heard from some of his old friends in Parsham, Tennessee [1905], that the town in which they had staged the legendary race between Coppermine and Acheron had become the bird-hunting capital of the South for businessmen from the North who had either purchased land there or lived in the hotel during the season {R}. One of these capitalists, Horace Lytle, whose business was in a terrible state due to the Depression, was so devoted to the sport that one night he refused an offer of $5000 cold cash for one of his hunting dogs. Tales like these, especially when told by old Boon—the conqueror of Old Ben and charter member of the original DeSpain hunting parties—rekindled the ardor for hunting which ran in our blood. We deeply regretted that we had no place left in the county to hunt anything bigger than a squirrel. But in 1933, there was no money to do it with either.

1934

Born: Orphan boy later adopted by Mister Ernest

Died: Willy Christian (b. 1869)

Died: Ned McCaslin (b. 1860)

Airplane barnstorming was big in the district this year, but we lost one of our own in a crash—Uncle Willy Christian {"Uncle Willy"}. Perhaps more beloved by the boys in town than any other man I can think of [1929], Uncle Willy had in his later years been badgered by church groups to cure himself of his notorious dope habit, one it was easy for him to maintain through his own prescription stock in his drugstore. Since he had completed his psychiatric treatments in Memphis, he had developed a drinking problem and married a whore who quickly left him [1933]. So Mrs. Merridew, ever the leader in trying to reform him, threatened to have him tossed back in the hospital again. Willy, in panic over this possibility, took all the money his sister had been sending for his support and hospitalization and bought himself an airplane in which he planned to make an escape. The scheme was that he and three others—the boy who followed him around in these last years, Old Job Wylie, and Willy's Negro chauffeur named Secretary—were to go to California, with Secretary piloting the plane. But Secretary couldn't handle it and Willy wasn't allowed to fly a plane without medical approval which he had no way in the world of getting; so Willy tried to take the plane up himself without bothering about medical approvals, licenses, or even flying lessons. As he sat at the end of the runway for his first solo flight, Mrs. Merridew, the young boy's father, and several local authorities rushed up to have them stopped. But the boy detained them until Uncle Willy could take off, even though Job and Secretary were also trying to stop him for what they perceived to be his own good. The boy knew better, however, and still believed he was right even after Uncle Willy crashed the thing and killed himself. Perhaps the child was correct. Willy would rather be dead than living under the constant pressure from Mrs. Merridew and the local church group; and he would rather die trying to get away from them than live knowing he hadn't tried.

My own "problem," my ten-year-old nephew Chick, had become greatly intrigued this year by Cecilia Farmer's scratch in the jailhouse window [1861] and went about three times a year for roughly the next six to look at it and try to figure out what it meant [1940] {I}. I was not sure I could myself articulate what it meant, but it meant the diametric opposite of the other memorable events in Jefferson in 1934. Flem Snopes, for instance, was now totally disinterested in the hotel business and leased his building to a brassy-haired woman who turned it into something no one could define either; but, because it became known as Little Chicago, we felt but couldn't prove that it was a boozing, gambling, whoring place on the order of Ballenbaugh's in the second half of the last century [1886] {R}. As Prohibition wore down to its conclusion and general lawlessness became less a headline activity, we seemed to have more of it than ever in Jefferson. Butch Beauchamp, for instance, was a predictable local rowdy who got into fights over anything and everything with anybody and everybody. But he was finally nabbed in Rouncewell's Flower Store one night by Hub Hampton after he had broken and entered, and Hub had to jail him {G}. Even Butch probably knew he was better off locked up.

Not so lawless, but not so respectable either, were some of the other marginal citizens of the county. Jason Compson, a cotton trader now, had an office above the hardware store he was eventually to own [1945]; there Lorraine, his "honest whore," visited him every weekend and departed each Sunday {F}. A man named Meadowfill transferred all his property to his nine-year-old daughter, Essie, this year, which none of us understood then but we would a number of years later when he got into a squabble with Res Snopes over it [1944] {M}. And there was an altercation at the Priest bank this year when Nancy Mannigoe broke into a line and demanded the two dollars she had on deposit there, except she didn't have it on deposit since she had already withdrawn it {N}. When she persisted, the bank president, no longer anyone named Priest, struck her and was later fined.

In another tale of lawlessness in the county, a seven-year-old boy named Georgie had spent most of the year covering (without knowing it) for his Uncle Rodney who was busy robbing cash and wives from various men in Jefferson and Mottstown both {"That Will Be Fine"}. Rodney was finally picked up on Christmas Eve but allowed by the Mottstown sheriff to stay out of jail until after the holidays. But Rodney used the reprieve to set up a jewel heist in town, again promising Georgie twenty quarters to cover for him. Georgie did so, mainly to buy his grandpa a Christmas present [1917]; but Rodney was shot dead as a prowler by Rufus Pruitt, though it was clear that Rufus took some pleasure in delivering him home as a "side of beef." Rufus was one of the husbands in Mottstown whom Rodney had most consistently wronged; and the court down there was quick to call it both self-defense and justifiable homicide.

1935

Died: Benjy Compson (b. 1895)

There was an air show in New Valois this year that some countians attended, but otherwise 1935 was not particularly a memorable year. Still, though, you had a sense of decay setting in.

Jason Compson, now motherless and niggerless but not Benjy-less [1933], converted the old Compson place into apartments and sold it to a local man as a boarding house, renting one apartment back in which to house Benjy and hiring whomever he could for whatever period of time they would stick it out to tend him {F}. But one night Benjy's deranged mind passed the level of commotion and dissolution it could tolerate; so he burnt the house down from within {M}. Everyone got himself out, if not his or her possessions, except for Benjy who, surely, knew enough at least not to bother.

In my family things deteriorated as well, especially for Gowan and his wife. Temple conceived her second child this year and awaited it with a doomed expression on her face that none of us could fully comprehend yet {N}. Perhaps I never really did, but I learned something later that helped me, partially at least, to do so. A man named Pete, the brother of Alabama Red with whom Temple had had the affair at Miss Reba's [1929], discovered a packet of letters she had written to Red and was using them to blackmail her and mire her in the past she could neither escape nor do anything to absorb. Blackmail was not the full scope of the problem, for Pete looked enough like Red to draw her away from Gowan nonetheless. I was not sure whose child this second one was, just as Gowan was not sure about the first. But it was not to live long enough to make it more than a moot question anyway [1936].

Meanwhile, my eleven-year-old nephew Chick was reaching the age when some of the local Negroes could suck him into believing just about anything they had a mind to {I}. When Margaret, his mother, lost her ring this year, Chick paid old Ephraim fifty cents to find it while he himself went off to Boy Scout camp. When he returned Ephraim told him to look under the hog trough on his father's farm—which Chick did and found the ring. Ephraim probably just guessed his way intuitively to this, or else he knew where the ring was all along and planted it there—but he managed to make Chick believe that he had paid the whole fifty cents to a fortune teller to get the information. But out of this piece of hocus-pocus came an attitude on Chick's part which I believe to be essentially correct and which was to save Lucas Beauchamp's life for him a few years hence [1940]. To quote Ephraim, "if you ever need to have anything done out of the common run, don't waste your time with menfolks but turn to women and children instead." This is just what Lucas knew to do, and it paid off for him.

Butch Beauchamp got out of jail after the year he got for breaking into Rouncewell's and disappeared from the county [1934] {G}. To the best of my knowledge, he never returned here again, alive anyway [1940]. Also gone from the county forever was passenger train service; the last one passed along the Sartoris railroad tracks (now the Illinois Central) during the summer [1872] {M}.

But if the county lost some of its people and identity this year, it also

[240]

gained some, though not many we wanted. A group of men and two women set up a camp in the northern part of the county to dig for artifacts in the ancient Indian mound {G}. Boyd Ballenbaugh returned to the area to live with his brother Tyler and, it seemed, to hide from the Memphis employers for whom he had been working as a guard [1938] {K}. But if Boyd did not give the trouble we expected, Spoot Rider had taken over in Butch Beauchamp's place, though not so thoroughly, as fighter, dicer, whisky drinker, and general wild liver {G}. And Clarence Snopes was in town quite a bit on one of his frequent pursuits of the gubernatorial nomination on his rudimentary soak-the-rich platform [1930] {M}. Since one of the few rich men in Jefferson to be so soaked would be Flem, he would be just as glad when, a few years later, Clarence's political career would be brought to an ignominious halt by a pack of stray dogs [1945].

1936

Born: Daughter of Gowan and Temple Drake Stevens

Married: Linda Snopes and Bart Kohl

Died: Daughter of Gowan and Temple Drake Stevens

After seven years of living in a common-law marriage in Greenwich Village [1929], Linda Snopes and Bart Kohl decided to make it official this year; so V. K. Ratliff agreed to accompany me to New York for the ceremony {M}. Before leaving town, though, I managed to make contact with Hoake McCarron, Linda's true father even though he had never seen her, and convinced him to come to New York [1907]. V. K. and I met him in a bar and brought him to meet Linda; we introduced him merely as "an old friend of the family." After he made her acquaintance at City Hall, they went for a ride in Central Park; and, by the time they returned (though he probably said nothing about it), Linda had intuited that Hoake, and not Flem, was her true father. Two days later, after a Russian woman had presented V. K. with a $75 tie to commemorate his Slavic heritage, we returned to Jefferson to see what the Snopeses who were left were up to. But the trouble was more in my own family and in the governor's office this year.

On the occasion of the state jubilee, Governor Bilbo announced that he was going to issue pardons to various and sundry Parchman prisoners (where Mink Snopes and the Tall Convict were still incarcerated, though they were not among those chosen for grace [1908] [1921] [1927]), this to gain votes in the upcoming election from the convicts' relatives {K}. A number of other lawyers in the state and I went to Parchman on the day of the mass liberation to implore Bilbo not to do it, though all I got for my efforts was a scornful remark from the governor that I was a fool if I thought I could change twentieth-century politics. But what I did solve was the murder of Warden Gambrell [1933], which three years earlier had been pinned on Monk Odlethrop and had sent him to execution. At a hearing in the prison dining room, I heard a prisoner named Terrel utter the very words Monk had let fly at the instant of his execution, something about paying his debt and farming, and suddenly I felt I had the person who must have put Monk up to murdering the warden, a man Monk had loved. After some checking I learned that Gambrell had twice received and twice denied requests for parole from Terrel. I also noted that Terrel was in on a manslaughter rap that looked very much like first-degree murder to me. I thought I had the symbolic case I needed, so I sought Bilbo and explained it to him, only to discover that Bilbo was much more interested in his citizens' votes than in their safety. Even after Terrel admitted, under pressure, saying these words to Monk when the feeble-minded young man admitted that he knew where Gambrell kept his pistol, Bilbo still showed no concern—and Terrel was pardoned with the rest of the derelicts who were set loose on society once again. The only recourse I had was to tell Terrel that I would be watching his every move once he was out—but I never heard any more about him, perhaps because there was nothing to hear or perhaps because the Snopes problem would heat up again over the next few years.

In the summer of 1936, certain problems which had been incipient in my cousin Gowan's marriage began to actualize. As I later learned, Temple had apparently made plans to run away with Pete, brother of Alabama Red, the man Temple had loved in 1929 and who had been killed in Memphis by Popeye [1935] {N}. They were busy gathering up all the cash and jewelry when they fell under the suspicion of Nancy Mannigoe, Temple's black maid. The escape was to be made on Sunday, September 13th, a day when Gowan left town with Bucky at 6 A.M., headed for New Orleans (to drop Bucky off with Judge Drake) and then on to Texas for a fishing trip. Later that night, around 9:30, Pete and Temple began ransacking Temple's dressing room to find the jewels and money the scheming Nancy had hidden from them. Apparently their plan was to leave Temple's and Gowan's (or was it Temple's and Pete's?) newborn daughter in the nursery to die. So they cornered Nancy and threatened to burn her foot with a cigarette unless she told them where to find the loot. At one point, Temple struck Nancy; and Nancy, when she saw they would not be stopped, turned and went into the nursery and murdered the young child in order to get it over with more quickly than Temple's way of doing it would have. Nonetheless, Temple's shriek was Dido-like when she discovered the child's corpse.

On the next day, Monday the 14th, Gowan chartered a plane in New Orleans and flew back for the baby's funeral. Nancy, meanwhile, had been apprehended easily and placed in the Jefferson jailhouse to await trial, which was set for mid-November. When the day of the verdict came—Friday, November 13th—I waited to see if a jury could make so fine a distinction as the one I had asked for. (Even though I was County Attorney, I could not in conscience prosecute the case and took up Nancy's defense instead.) But the jury could not understand that Nancy, though clearly in the wrong, had more committed euthanasia than first-degree murder, that she had tried to end before it got started the miserable life the child would have had to endure (she thought) if it managed to survive the slow starvation Temple and Pete had planned for it. So, at 5:30, Nancy was found guilty and condemned to be hanged on the following March 13th.

That night I pleaded with Temple, who had already perjured herself in the Lee Goodwin case seven years ago [1929], to go to the judge and tell him all the facts surrounding her daughter's death and so rescue Nancy from execution. Temple called her a "dope fiend nigger whore," though she seemed to imply that she had four long months to decide whether she would help Nancy or not—that she would think the problem over while she and Gowan vacationed in California and, perhaps, Hawaii until the following June. My appeal to Gowan fared no better, for he had acquired an image of himself at the University of Virginia which had him the member of some master race which did not have to concern itself with the likes of nigger whores such as Nancy Mannigoe. So off they went, and all I could do was hope that Temple's conscience would get the better of her—yet, if it hadn't for seven years, it probably couldn't in just four more months [1937].

My nephew Chick reached twelve this year, so I gave him a shotgun for his birthday, complete with all the warnings of where to shoot it and what not to shoot at. If Chick abided by all this, that did not mean that anyone else had to, I guess {T}. On one particular occasion, Aleck Sander, a black boy his age, bet four white boys that he could, and would, jump into an icy pond with all his clothes on. Aleck did it, and each of the boys demanded an opportunity to win back the dollar they had each lost to him. So Aleck thought up variations on this stunt for the first three boys, all of whom rescued their dollars by doing his bidding. John Wesley Roebuck, the boy Ab Snopes had gunned out of his watermelon patch [1924], had the ill luck to be last; and you can bet that Aleck wanted real recompense for this last of his four hard-earned dollars. At Aleck's bidding, John Wesley, it seems, put on every boy's hunting coat, one on top of the other, including the brand new one Chick had just gotten for his birthday. Then Aleck demanded, and got, the opportunity to fire number six buckshot out of Chick's new gun into John Wesley's back. He survived, miraculously unmaimed, so Aleck had to return the dollar and Chick had to burn his new coat, which was riddled beyond repair. I was beginning to worry that the Stevenses would be the next family to have to be cleared out of the county after the Snopeses.

[243]

Chick, as a tenderfoot scout, had suddenly developed a very great interest in the Civil War and the relationship between whites and blacks—both now and in ante-bellum times {I}. So he and I began having the sorts of talks we would come to have over the next five or six years, talks which tried to preserve both the dignity of the black man and the viability of the southern cause in the same tension-packed statements. Then an incident occurred which began to allow Chick to grasp the difficulties and contradictions of this more clearly.

In February, Chick, Aleck Sander, and another boy were rabbit hunting on Roth Edmonds' land when Chick fell through some thin ice into a pond. Just then Lucas Beauchamp happened along and pulled him out, took him home, and had him take his clothes off. He wrapped him in a blanket and fed him, all of this—of course—in that firm, proud manner which had him known among many as the county's most uppity nigger. After his clothes had dried, Chick tried to pay Lucas seventy cents—all he had on him—but Lucas knocked it to the floor and ordered him to pick it up. Soon they all returned to their rabbit hunt, but Chick was no longer up to it. He felt he had sacrificed his own manhood and the dignity of his race. For some years thereafter, Chick would be quietly preoccupied with the question of how to get both back [1940].

Lucas had a setback of his own this year—because of some unidentified "crisis" (perhaps he had gotten in the way of Uncle Pete Gombault's enter-prises [1921]) he was forced to abandon his fifteen-year-old distillery busi-ness, though he would pick it up again in the future [1941] {G}. It was well known that his wife, Molly, was becoming fed up with this and various other of Lucas' schemes for quick money, schemes that she felt were making him more like a white man and less like a black one every day.

Jason Compson built himself a new bungalow this summer, for which he took out an ill-conceived mortgage with Flem Snopes's bank [1942] {M}. Jason was forty-three now; and, though he continued to hang around with her, he still showed no inclination toward marrying Lorraine.

Finally, I think it was in 1936 that I began to notice that, if national morality and honor were in evident decline for the last countless number of years, personal systems of honor—such as Chick's or Lucas'—had become more noticeable. Perhaps, however, this sets in thoroughgoing relief the conduct of my cousin Gowan and his thoroughly honorless wife, Temple.

1937

Died: Bart Kohl

Died: Nancy Mannigoe (b. 1906)

[244]

Through the late winter months I waited anxiously to see if Temple would make her move to save Nancy Mannigoe, but it looked ever less likely that she would bother to return from California to do it [1936] {N}. I recollect several occasions in January when I stood on the street outside the jailhouse and sang hymns with Nancy, who joined me through the jail window. But if this kept Nancy's spirits up, it did little to stay her execution; so, on March 6th, I wired Temple and Gowan to come home. They did so, led I think by Gowan, who was beginning to feel some remorse over the way their lives had infringed so directly and so blatantly on those of so many others [1929].

So they got back on Thursday, March 11th, and I wasted little time in sitting Temple down and asking her to aid me in having Nancy's charges reduced by saying that Nancy was out of her mind at the time of the crime. With her own mind in total chaos by now, Temple was reluctant to do this; so Gowan and I devised a plan for getting her to the governor's office to speak to him personally. Temple and I set out for Jackson late that night, though Temple was still balking at doing anything which would redirect the case. Around 11:30 we pulled off the road to change a tire I claimed was bad; but this was merely to let Gowan, in another car, get ahead of us and reach Jackson first.

By 2 A.M. Temple and I were sitting in the governor's office while I recounted Nancy's story. In the midst of this, though Temple at first thought she was being made to suffer unfairly, she began to admit that she had killed her own daughter, or at least set Nancy up to do it, when she jumped off the train on the way to the baseball game eight years go [1929]. By 3 A.M. Temple had her head down on the desk, so the Governor stood up and allowed Gowan to slip into his chair. There her husband listened to, and found true, the entire story of how Nancy came to kill their daughter when Temple was about to run away with Pete. In the process, Temple vowed to save her soul if, in fact, (as she said) she was even born with one in the first place.

But as in the trial itself, the distinctions were too fine for the Governor, and I had no luck. By 10:30 that same morning we were back in the Jefferson jailhouse. Tubbs allowed us a half-hour with Nancy, a tiny spot of time in which we had to tell this cruelly predestined black woman that she had not much more time than that left. But, and I should not have been amazed at this, Nancy did not really appear surprised. Instead, she took Temple under her wing and began to teach her about faith. Temple frankly considered herself doomed, but Nancy told her touchingly to have faith in God. Even I had to retort that it was an odd world that made man's suffering a necessity for his salvation, but Nancy calmly replied that it was necessary. Man's suffering, she said, "keeps him out of devilment." Then Tubbs asked us to leave; and Nancy remained in jail until the next day, when she was executed.

[245]

Gowan and Temple went home with no such luck, trapped in the jail of their lives to live much longer than they wanted to.

Linda Snopes and Bart Kohl went to Spain this year to fight in the Spanish Civil War. But Bart was killed early in a plane crash, and Linda lost most of her hearing when her eardrums were shattered in an explosion {M}. So when Chick, V. K., and I picked her up at the Memphis airport in August, everything we wanted to say to her had to be written down on a pad of paper; and all her replies came in a strange duckquack voice which quickly warned anyone who listened that the speaker *must* be deaf because she would not allow herself to sound like that if she weren't. So she spent the rest of the year back in Flem's house, where her deafness didn't matter because Flem had so little to say anyway. She gave Ratliff the Italian sculpture that Bart had bought some years back in the Village [1928]. Pretty soon, though, most of the town assumed that she and I would marry, and one part of it assumed that we were going to be too late if we didn't. But this was not right either. We were the same sort of friends, who loved each other but were not lovers, that we used to be. We had Thanksgiving and Christmas dinners together, two occasions which Flem surely did not make much of; and after that I got Linda to take voice lessons to try to eliminate the duckquack. She took them but never quite succeeded.

So the year ended this way, save that Chick had found a new hunting companion in Benbow Sartoris and hung around Ratliff and me less and less, which was something that V. K. was sorry to see happen. He was sixty-three and I was forty-eight; he probably thought it was time to cultivate an apostle.

Chick, though, was also still trying to pay his debt to Lucas Beauchamp for pulling him out of the lake and feeding him the year before [1936] {I}. He bought Molly a dress with some of his summer earnings; but the frock had not been at Lucas' house for two days before Lucas sent a white boy on a mule (only Lucas would arrange it this way) with a jar of molasses for Chick. He was one down again, but he would try again next year. Honor. But he almost did not have to try, because Lucas came very close to having his skull bashed in by a sawmill worker at Fraser's store. It was over the way Lucas idled around the place eating gingersnaps—which might seem trivial, but you'd have to see the way Lucas ate gingersnaps to know how provoking some people could find it. But he was saved by a last minute effort on the part of the proprietor's son who, whether or not he cared two hoots about Lucas, didn't want his black and white McCaslin blood smeared all over his father's inventory. Meanwhile, in Tennessee, a man who never met Lucas and never would, yet whose fate would become entwined with his—Jake Montgomery—was victimized by a killing which happened in a restaurant he owned and was, as a consequence, forced to flee to Mississippi and, later, forced into Yoknapatawpha just in time to get himself killed here. But that was to happen in another year [1940].

1938

Married: Ellie Pritchel and Joel Flint

Died: Louis Grenier (Lonnie Grinnup) (b. 1902)

Died: Boyd Ballenbaugh

Died: Harriss

Died: Father of Roth Edmonds' woman

I probably must take all the credit for making Linda Snopes Kohl whatever sort of idealist she became, but her beliefs were becoming an annoying thorn in the town's collective side {M}. Early this year she teamed up with the two Finns, the cobbler and the tinsmith [1917] [1919], to form a Communist party enclave in Jefferson—meetings, incredibly, were held in Flem's house! When this failed to attract much of a following, she began in the spring to visit the Negro school and established a test whereby the best students could be tutored at a private academy to be held, again incredibly, in Flem's living room. I don't know how strongly Flem objected to this, because Linda could not have heard him if he had. But someone who did object was the principal of the Negro school, who pleaded with me to call her off. I managed to do this, but only after hours of scrawling arguments and threats on her pad. The townspeople themselves started scrawling "niggerlover" on Flem's sidewalks; but this did not deter her nearly as much as it angered Flem. She started trying to reform the county by attending every meeting of the Board of Supervisors and then buttonholing members outside to give them a good quacking. But soon the Board took to ordering its lunches through the window of the Courthouse from a prehired intermediary with the Dixie Cafe. During the summer somebody burned a cross on Flem's lawn; and in September, when the Munich Pact was signed, the beleaguered bank president found the words "Kohl—Communist—Jew" engraved in the new cement sidewalk in front of his house. So all I could do, before she got herself lynched, was to try to return her to some form of southern fundamentalism. I gave her a gold-cornered ivory tablet for her messages, I drove around town with her in Flem's big car (and Flem did when I didn't because she had to have somebody with her to listen to horns at all times), and I drove her out to Jakeleg Wattman's fishing camp at Wyott's Crossing to teach her how to buy bootleg whiskey. (Though Prohibition officially ended in 1933, Mississippi remained a "dry" state as it had always supposedly been.) After this Flem had to accompany her. So we calmed her down; but this would not ultimately be to Flem's benefit, for she would later catch sight of another cause which would prove his undoing [1946].

In mid-July I was particularly distressed to learn of the death of Lonnie Grinnup (real name, Louis Grenier), the last of the Greniers in the county. The Greniers were a family which helped found it and which established the Old Frenchman Place [1827] as the first and perhaps finest plantation house the county ever knew (but which for years had been being torn down for firewood or inhabited by the likes of Popeye Vitelli and his gang of liquor smugglers) [1880] [1929] {K}. When Grinnup's body was found in the river near the house he lived in with the idiot boy named Joe for the last ten years, I immediately suspected Tyler Ballenbaugh, who had taken out a $5000 insurance policy on Grinnup not so long ago [1927]. A Mottstown insurance investigator and I devised a plan to pin the murder on Tyler; but, when I confronted Tyler and his brother Boyd nine days later when they were in the process of ransacking Grinnup's cabin, I learned (as did Tyler) that Boyd was really the killer. It seemed incredible, but Boyd had killed Lonnie so he could borrow $10 from Tyler, and the only way he could borrow any such money was to assure Tyler that he was worth $5000. At that point a fight broke out, and Boyd shot Tyler, wounding him, and winged me. He probably would have killed both of us, but suddenly the half-wit Joe jumped out of a tree on top of Boyd and killed him by dragging him down to the river and throwing him in, the same way Boyd had killed Lonnie. Once again, no conviction, but this time none was sought either.

If there was another major development in the county this year, it had to do with the Backus-Harriss family. As the year began, Melisandre and her two children were still in Europe and postcards were still coming in, usually around holidays, to my sister Margaret and various other school chums [1915]. But one day Harriss turned up dead in New Orleans—one account had it that he was gunned down at his desk by a gangland rival, another that it happened in a barber chair {M}. In any event, he was dead in June, and by August Melisandre and the children were back in the States for the first time in many years [1924] {K}. They moved briefly into the now-completely-renovated house, though the house seemed like a tomb in contrast to the ever-present vitality which still typified Melisandre (whom I hadn't seen in fourteen years) and to the spirited activities of the teenagers. The boy, Max, was, for example, particularly adept at horseback riding and fencing. But few in the vicinity got to know them before they departed, again, in October, this time for South America.

The rest of the news this year is incidental, though, like all incidental events, a few were not so in retrospect a few years later. Chick Mallison, now fourteen, was on the high school football team despite his mother's protestations {I}. In the first game of the season, in Mottstown, Margaret actually left the stands in the first quarter, however, and came down on the sidelines where she ran up and down shouting instructions to Chick at the beginning of every play. When he wasn't playing football, he and I hunted together a lot, especially for quail with the MacCallum twins, Stuart and Rafe {K}. This would be one of their favorite activities until both MacCallums enlisted in the army in 1940. Hitler was already stampeding across Europe this year; and they, and even Chick, knew that they would have to fight in his war before long. As my fiftieth birthday approached, I really did not think I would be going this time, not even to run a YMCA canteen for the latest unoccupied Snopes to disgrace [1917].

Hub Hampton was elected for his third term as sheriff. His opponent had argued that, in the eight years Hub had been sheriff already, he had worn out a car a year (and he *had,* not by speed but by sheer friction) and that the town coffers could not afford this {I}. But Hub merely promised to wear out more cars cleaning out corruption, especially Little Chicago over at the Snopes Hotel [1934]. He had done it by year's end, too, as Hub usually did things he had promised to; and now the Snopes Hotel, which Flem had wanted no part of for years, became Mrs. Rouncewell's boarding house {R}. The other Snopes in the news this year was Montgomery Ward again {M}. Out of prison many years now, though poor Mink was still paying for the escape attempt that Montgomery Ward had rigged for him and coaxed him into [1925], he had gotten a lucrative job in the movie industry. Jefferson never saw or heard of him again, but I saw *Gone with the Wind* a year later [1939] and felt sure that Montgomery Ward must have had something to do with the production.

Strangers in the county caused a bit of consternation, too. Two white men were reported to have dug up $22,000 worth of gold in an old churn and gotten out of the area unnoticed. Lucas Beauchamp, though, was convinced that they had reburied it {G}. Money, I have come to feel, is of little use to Lucas unless it is concealed enough to encourage wasting time looking for it. He would, indeed, shortly be in search of it [1941]. And Joel Flint, a carnival pitch man from the north, left his employment when he passed through Jefferson and married the dimwitted spinster Ellie Pritchel. His motives would not be clear for a while {K} [1940]. And the woman destined to become Roth Edmonds' part-black mistress, actually the granddaughter of Tennie's Jim and great-granddaughter of Tomey's Turl and great-great-granddaughter of none other than old Lucius Quintus Carothers McCaslin himself, moved to Mississippi from Indianapolis after living first in Memphis where she was a schoolteacher and also washerwoman on the side {G}. She did not know Roth yet, but she would [1940]. There is no design behind the way fate works?

And Eunice Habersham purchased her now-notorious second-hand pick-up truck to deliver her produce in {I}. In a couple of years she would be carrying more than vegetables in it [1940].

Melisandre Backus Harriss and her children returned from South America in the spring [1938], accompanied by an Argentinian military man named Captain Gauldres {K}. He was first looked upon by the county as a curiosity, but soon he had made a number of friends. Though his sexual morality was rumored to be a bit loose, this seemed to be more or less expected of a South American. For a time I thought he was engaged to marry Melisandre; but when I congratulated her on the town square one day, she just looked at me blankly, making me feel stupid for reasons I could not identify. But then I heard there was a rift between Gauldres and Melisandre's son, Max, this apparently because the former was a better horseman, fencer, and—perhaps—lover [1941]. Gauldres had, it seems, walked off with the heart of the Cayley girl, in whom Max himself appeared quite interested.

But the degradation and degeneration which had long stalked the ancient nobles of the county were never more apparent than in what happened to Roth Edmonds this year {G}. Off on one of the renewed hunting expeditions, which took place many miles farther away now, the group—which included among others Henry Wyatt, Uncle Ike McCaslin, young Will Legate, and Roth himself—lost a box of food overboard while they paddled downstream to their campsite. Roth went to a nearby town to replace it and there seduced the woman (who turned out not only to be part-black but also part-cousin [1938]) who would next year provide him with a son he would have to deny. When he returned to the camp, everyone noticed a difference in him, but no one would know why until the next year's trip [1940].

Linda Snopes continued to be active in the Jefferson Communist Party [1938], or what there was of it, though at some time during the year Flem stole her membership card, which even Chick said she should have burnt long ago because all humans were essentially worthless {M}. But I wasn't in on that year's Snopes-watching very much, first because of some drainage district business which kept me out of town a lot, and second because in September Hitler invaded Poland. We knew war would come again, and Chick (though not even sixteen yet) was anxious to enlist and get to it, even though our country had not bothered to join in yet. Ratliff calmed him down for the time being by inviting him for a friendly Christmas drink in what V. K. liked to refer to as the Eula Varner Room of his house. Before this, though, Chick had gone so far as to visit Captain Warren to ask about the advisability of joining the Royal Air Force [1917]; Warren told him he would have to be eighteen at least, even for that. So, by year's end, Chick was back to more mundane concerns, like trying to figure out how to square his debt with Lucas Beauchamp [1936]—whom he had seen (and been recognized by) in January when Lucas was in town paying his taxes—without, that is, having it unsquared on him before he could even draw two easy breaths {I}.

There was a scattering of other interesting events this year, some of which would materialize into bigger things later. An architect from a big city was in town one weekend and, while he was drunk, ran his car through a wall and a plate glass window {I}. We had to have him jailed, if only long enough to keep him away from his bottle and get sober enough to write a check for the damage he had done. But when he dried out, he became enamored of the thick oak door on the interior of the jailhouse and wanted to pay for that too, so he could take it home with him. We felt compelled to refuse, for too much of our county's history had gone on behind it.

Joel Flint took out a substantial life insurance policy on his wife of a year, Ellie Pritchel [1938], something we would soon understand more fully than we did when the rumor went around that he had bought it {K} [1940]. And *Gone with the Wind* showed up here and lasted two days at the local theater— the audience walked out on both showings. {N}.

1940

Born: Grandchild of Hub Hampton

Born: Illegitimate son of Roth Edmonds and the part-black granddaughter of Tennie's Jim

Died: Hub Hampton

Died: Vinson Gowrie (b. 1912)

Died: Crawford Gowrie (b. 1900)

Died: Jake Montgomery

Died: Ellie Pritchel Flint

Died: Wesley Pritchel (b. 1869)

Died: Samuel "Butch" Beauchamp (b. 1914)

The war was coming but it continued to refuse to show up. I was made chairman of the county draftboard, though, and I got ready to ship young Yoknapatawphans north and west for deportation against whichever menace became the first to strike us.

Early in the year a federal agent named Gihon showed up in the county and sought me out to tell me that he planned to take Linda Snopes Kohl into custody unless she bought immunity by swapping him her Party card and a list of her associates {M}. I threw him out of my office and then learned from Linda that she no longer had the card [1939], that Flem had stolen it from her the year before. It occurred to me that I ought to write J. Edgar Hoover a letter to tell him to have his heavies search Flem for it, but I was diverted from such folderol by more pressing events. Abroad, for instance, the Battle of Britain was fought through the summer and fall; and at home—because of it—Linda announced that she was going to California to work in an aircraft factory. An ideal place, I suppose, for a woman who would not be allowed to fight in this war (though she had already fought in another [1937]) and who was hard of hearing against the rat-a-tat of rivet guns aimed at airplane wings. I managed to convince her to go to work in the shipyards at Pascagoula instead, so she could come home on weekends. We almost landed in bed together this year but didn't.

Lucas Beauchamp, sixty-six now, became the focus of much consternation and controversy in 1940, as did various other Edmondses and McCaslins whose bloodlines were so inextricably mixed {I}. In January Chick saw Lucas in town on his annual trip to pay his taxes, but for the first time in four years Lucas ignored him. Chick considered himself a free man for the first time since the day he had fallen in the pond and been pulled out and then dried out by this old part-Negro man [1936]. Lucas was apparently too preoccupied by sudden competition from George Wilkins, a beau of his daughter's, in the distilling of corn liquor {G}. But then he got involved in something that didn't concern him—for which Lucas had a real talent—and nearly got himself hanged on the state gallows.

It seems that Crawford Gowrie and Jake Montgomery, partners now, had contracted to buy lumber from Crawford's brother Vinson and Uncle Sudley Workitt {I} [1918] [1920] [1937]. Since the order was quite large, it took Vinson and Workitt several days to cut and plane it all. Each night, Crawford and Jake would sneak up to the cut pile, steal just enough not to get caught, and sell it off to a man from Memphis. But pretty soon Vinson got wise, and Crawford had to kill him. Fratricide was no special problem to the current generation of Gowries, nor perhaps to the previous ones either. Now, where Lucas got into it is that he was the first one who knew Crawford was pilfering the wood and threatened to turn him in to the sheriff unless he could produce a receipt signed by Uncle Sudley, which, of course, Crawford couldn't. So it was on Saturday, the 11th of May, that he lured Lucas to Fraser's store, in Beat Four no less, supposedly to produce the receipt. Before doing so, he apparently bet Lucas fifty cents that his old pistol, which was bequeathed to him by old Lucas Quintus Carothers McCaslin himself [1836], would no longer shoot. Lucas fired the gun, won the half dollar, and waited patiently for Crawford to return with the receipt; but Crawford never came back—he sent the authorities instead, for in the weeds near where Lucas had shot his gun lay the body of Vinson Gowrie. In Beat Four

[252]

conclusions about Negroes with fired pistols standing near bodies of dead white men are drawn quickly, so Constable Skipworth apprehended Lucas just as quickly and took him home to chain him to his bedpost until Hub Hampton could get out from Jefferson to pick him up. Only two people knew that Lucas didn't do it: one was Crawford, and he wasn't talking; the other was Jake Montgomery, who must have seen it happen, and he was more interested in blackmailing Crawford than in freeing Lucas. Meanwhile, the rest of the Gowries and Workitts, I and others presumed, were getting ready to get Lucas out of jail and string him up. The Negroes cleared off the town square, all too happy to let Lucas be the only one of their kind to cross over it this weekend.

So on Sunday, May 12th, Hampton brought Lucas in to jail and waited for midnight, since even the Gowries wouldn't lynch a man, a black one not withstanding, on a Sunday [1920]. Word was about that Forrest Gowrie was in from Vicksburg for Vinson's funeral and probably for his revenge as well. It was during this afternoon, though, that Lucas decided it was time that Chick repaid his debt for the pond incident, and maybe Chick decided the same thing. Anyway, Lucas ordered him to bring me to his cell. I went, privately feeling that Lucas knew better than to kill anybody, especially a Gowrie, but I also felt that the evidence against him was pretty tight. So, as the Gowries circled the town square once as a warning, I took the case and tried to figure out how it tied in with the lumber deal. Lucas, of course, did not know how Vinson got killed; but he did know that, if the body were to be exhumed from the Caledonia cemetery out in Beat Four, no bullet that fit his old pistol would be found inside it. So, without my knowledge, Lucas sent Chick out to dig it up. Chick, ready to do anything to clear the books with Lucas, got Aleck Sander and Miss Eunice Habersham, seventy now, to go with him. They rode in Miss Habersham's produce truck, while Chick rode Highboy, the horse they planned to use to do the packwork that the truck couldn't get in close enough to accomplish. As they approached the graveyard, a rider passed them in the dark; he was riding a mule with something else of great size over its neck. What they didn't know was that the rider was Crawford Gowrie, the something else was Vinson's body, and what they would (and did) find when they opened the grave was the body of Jake Montgomery instead, whom Crawford had already killed to end the black-mailing and potential information leakage. So Chick, Miss Habersham, and Aleck Sander returned to Jefferson after midnight with the news that Vinson's grave was now Jake Montgomery's.

At 3:30 on the morning of Monday, the 13th, probably the very moment that Crawford was back at the cemetery digging up Montgomery's body as well, the threesome told Hampton the story over a pot of coffee in the sheriff's kitchen. So later on, while Lucas was incarcerated in Hampton's house, even though Miss Habersham and my sister Margaret were down at the jailhouse where they thought they were guarding him, we all (Chick, Hampton, I, and two Negroes from the state pen) left town amidst the taunts of potential lynchers to drive to Caledonia cemetery to dig up the grave for what was now to be at least the fourth time. I recall, as we were driving out there in my car, trying to explain to Chick why Lucas had become the innocent victim in all of this, why the crowd was anxious to pin this on a black man even though the black man was and always had been an essential part of our way of life and without him it would not be what it was; but I was not sure that Chick understood and I was not so sure that I did either. When we got to the cemetery, the digging had not gone far before Nub Gowrie, the father-figure to this lot, appeared and, with his twin sons—Vardaman and Bilbo—to back him up, asked what the devil was going on. When Hampton told him about the body switch, the Gowrie twins finished the digging, except now that there was no body at all in the grave much less Montgomery's, which should not have been there anyway. So, with the two blood-hounds that Hub had been insightful enough to bring with him, they went down to the river bed where Chick and his two helpmates had seen the mysterious rider the night before and there found Montgomery's body in the sand and, eventually, Vinson's in the quicksand farther on. Poor Nub sank waist deep looking for him and finally wound up standing on his dead son's head.

Vinson was pulled out. When the bullet hole in his body proved to be the result of Crawford's notorious luger [1918] and not Lucas' equally notorious heirloom, the lynching was off. When word reached Jefferson, the mob dispersed, and we devised a plan to capture Crawford. I told Willy Ingrum, the town marshal, that Hub and Lucas were going to testify at Montgomery's inquest. Since Willy had never kept a secret in his life, we knew it would not be long before this confidential information filtered back to Crawford; and we figured he'd be digging up Vinson's body as quickly as the quicksand would allow him to do it. But we were wrong. Crawford committed suicide before we had time to catch him and have the state do the job for him.

Throughout all this, Lucas remained Lucas. Chick owed him a favor, and he had collected on it. But as Lucas always could, he made you believe that the white race owed him a favor, too; and he more than collected on that. Perhaps we believed we did. On Tuesday I wrote up Lucas' version of the episode to get him out of jail; and on Saturday I charged him only two dollars, the price of a pen I had ruined jamming it in frustration into my desktop for all the trouble. Lest I thought I was too big a deal for charging so small a fee, Lucas paid me in a pile of small change and then demanded a receipt. And, lest Lucas think that everything we had done for him was his due, I compelled him to carry a bouquet of flowers to Miss Habersham— which he did. Lucas would be back in trouble in less than a year, though [1941].

Elsewhere in the McCaslin lineage this year, Roth Edmonds was having

[254]

his own troubles. One of his Negroes, Oscar, had brought a black slut home from Memphis as what he called his wife, but Roth bought her a train ticket back home when the woman was discovered not only to be carrying a razor but to be flashing it around regularly as well {G}. And Roth had a black woman of his own now, though she was only fifteen percent or so. In January, when she revealed to him that she was pregnant as a result of the previous November's hunting trip [1939], Roth sent for her and they went off to New Mexico for six weeks. Then, in February, Roth came home to the county and promised to send for her—but all he apparently ever did was send money to her Vicksburg bank account. In August, when their child was born, she wrote Roth from her hospital bed but probably received no response. So, between then and October, the opening of deer season, she rented a room in Memphis and waited for the annual hunting party to arrive at its present camp two hundred miles north of Jefferson {R}.

But it was seventy-three-year-old Ike McCaslin who was left to do Roth's dirty work for him that November {G}. When Roth, Wyatt, Legate, Ike, Isham, and two other Negroes arrived at the camp, they went through all the normal rituals of disposing of their store-bought meat the first night in order to force survival on game for the rest of the trip. Then, the next morning, Roth told Ike, who was now too old to go out on the hunt but more or less supervised the camp until the others returned, that a woman would be coming to see him but that Ike should just tell her "No" and give her an envelope he had brought with him from Jefferson. When the woman showed up, Ike, though confused, did what he was told and was initially startled when the woman snarled that what he gave her was "just money." She then turned on Ike himself, blaming him for making Roth the way he was by bequeathing Roth's grandfather the McCaslin land [1888]. Through it all, Ike detected that Roth's problem in marrying this woman was the same one which his own grandfather and Thomas Sutpen and John Sartoris all had had before him—the woman was "marred" by a slight trace of Negro blood and was, in fact, a cousin of Roth's several times removed. Full of compassion and an intensified sense of doom, Ike gave her the hunting horn that General Compson had given him many years ago, and told her to go north, to marry a black man and forget Roth. Ike stopped himself, but it was too late—his southern heritage, which he had tried so hard to defeat, had oozed out at the wrong time in the wrong way. The woman stood over his bent figure, glowering at him, and said: "Old man, have you lived so long and forgotten so much that you don't remember anything you ever knew or felt or even heard about love?" Then she left without another word; and, as Ike confided to me later, he had the sensation that they all were lost. That afternoon the hunting party arrived back at the camp. Roth had bagged a doe.

One who was lost this year was Butch Beauchamp, Lucas and Molly's grandson. He was executed in Joliet, Illinois, for murder; and Molly, too, blamed the whole thing on Roth, who several years before had forced the boy to leave the McCaslin land and come into Jefferson {G} [1933]. Everyone but Molly, of course, knew that Butch was too wild for Roth to contain; but she kept wailing that Roth sold Samuel into Egypt. Luckily Molly never found out how Butch had died, only that he had; and it was Belle Worsham who came to me and recommended that we keep Molly in the dark as to the circumstances. Wilmoth, editor of the Jefferson newspaper, agreed not to print the execution story and helped me raise $225 for the fancy funeral Molly wanted her grandson to have. I passed the hat around the town square, and just about everybody gave something. Perhaps we were not all as lost as Uncle Ike had thought. I took the money to Miss Worsham's and accidentally interrupted a mourning service that she, Molly, and several Negro women were conducting. I apologized and left, feeling the constrictions of our common past, and the white man's guilt, with the Negroes all around me. On the day of the burial, Molly told Wilmoth that she wanted to see the details of Butch's funeral printed up in the paper, even though she could not read it; and, at this point, I probably understood, finally, that Molly didn't care what Butch had done. She just wanted him to come home right and have a fancy funeral, which the white man had taught her was the correct way to commemorate each man's futile try to make a difference in this life.

Two other Jefferson citizens were killed this year, though it took Hub Hampton and I much longer to determine the circumstances {K}. Joel Flint, married for two years now to the dimwitted Ellie Pritchel [1938], was out on a squirrel hunt one day and, upon his return, tripped on the front step of their cabin and accidentally shot Ellie in the face. He called up Hub, told him what he had done, and recommended that Hub take him in until the circumstances of the death could be determined. Hub thought this a noble, if unnecessary, gesture and did so, only to have Flint inexplicably break out of jail a short time later. Meanwhile, Ellie's father had locked himself and his grief inside his cabin, or at least we thought he had. Some time later he was around again and did the very thing he had refused to do for so long a time— he sold his land, which had valuable clay on it for road construction materials, to three men who had been trying to buy it for years. Hub and I could not understand the sudden change of heart, so we went out to question him about it and also to inquire if he had heard anything more of his son-in-law, Flint. While we spoke to him I noticed that he was mixing a cold toddy, known to be his favorite drink, but was doing it incorrectly. At this moment, the fact that Flint had once been a master of disguises [1932] and that this was not Old Man Pritchel but somebody imitating him became very clear to me. Hub grabbed him, and it was Flint sure enough—out to fool us one more time before skipping the county with the money he had gotten for Pritchel's land. He had, of course, murdered Pritchell shortly after breaking out of jail; and Ellie's death was probably no accident either, for he had insured her life fairly heavily just seventeen months ago [1939].

So, as we waited for war in 1940, things were not quiet at home. We learned that the long-missing Caddy Compson had vanished in Paris around the time of the German occupation [1912] {F}. Spoot Rider was still dicing and drinking ostentatiously around town {G}. Captain Gauldres was busy out at the Backus-Harriss property replacing the gangster's fake steeplechase with a real one of his own, built from rocks shipped from Tennessee and Virginia {K} [1930]. Rafe MacCallum particularly admired this Argentinian's horsemanship and even bought a wild stallion to use in competition with him. But the horse proved unbreakable, though this was the only bad horse trade Rafe had ever made. Chick was still visiting the jailhouse and studying the names scratched on the window {I}. (There were others there now beside Cecilia Farmer's.) Wall Snopes, who had moved out of the County by now, was reported to own a chain of grocery stores all over Tennessee, Arkansas, and northern Mississippi {M}. Hub Hampton's wife went to Memphis in May to be with her expectant daughter, and by June Hub was a grandpa {I}. By the end of the year, though, Hub was dead.

But war was coming, and we all knew it. A man named Devries, whom Yoknapatawpha didn't know yet but soon would, was number one in his ROTC class at the University of Mississippi and was on his way to being a war hero {M}. Locally I had a peculiar problem in that, as head of the local draft board, I was expected to run down both those who evaded it and those who had failed to register for it. Among the latter were the MacCallum twins, Anse and Lucius; and, being a great admirer of the natural virtues, courage, and heroism for which the MacCallums stood, I was reluctant to go after them. I claimed I would have eventually; but a federal investigator named Pearson arrived in the county and beat me to it {"The Tall Men"}. Pearson got Marshal Gombault to lead him to the MacCallum land and arrived there in the midst of Doc Schofield's amputation of Buddy's leg, the result of a hammermill accident [1917]. Forced to wait through the amputatory trauma, Pearson realized he was alone, that even Gombault was so derisive with regard to federal laws, agencies, and agents that he was going to do no more than drive the car back to town after Pearson had made the arrest on his own. He finally took them, but not until after he himself had been involved in the ceremonial burying of Buddy's leg in the family graveyard. Nor did he press charges—he just made them sign up which, because of some tacit understanding which their father's suffering had created among the family, they did.

1941

Married: Sebastian Gauldres and the Harriss girl

Married: George Wilkins and Nat Beauchamp

Married: Spoot Rider and Mannie

Died: Mannie Rider

Died: Spoot Rider (b. 1917)

Died: Birdsong

Died: Wife of Mr. Ernest

1941 marked the twentieth anniversary of my Old Testament translation project [1921]. Though I had worked two or three nights a week on it, it was still nowhere near completion and (I now had to admit) probably never would be {K}.

Having had a taste of jail the year before, Lucas Beauchamp resolved to stay out of it at all cost this year, though this resolution almost cost him his life {G}. With the less-than-bright George Wilkins in the distillery business on the McCaslin land now as well, Lucas decided to dismantle his own still before the Feds inevitably arrived [1940]. While he was burying its components in the old Indian Mound, the Mound collapsed and a gold coin turned up. Lucas dug furiously for more but soon ran out of steam. As he sat down to think how to aid his aged body in the uprooting of a presumed fabulous treasure, he realized that George and his own daughter, Nat, had been watching him and, probably, gotten a peek of their own at the coin. Not wishing to use George to assist him—both because he considered him too stupid and because George possessed none of the McCaslin blood which Lucas considered requisite for any important undertaking—Lucas journeyed into town and notified the sheriff about George's still. The sheriff passed the word on to the D.A., who had George arraigned, and to Roth Edmonds, who flew into a rage because, if there was anything he had continually warned his Negroes against, it was moonshining. At the trial, however, the D.A. dismissed the case because, as he suspected, George had broken all the jugs before the evidence could be gathered. A considerable amount of liquor, the judge went on, *was* discovered on Lucas' back porch, though, leading him and (he implied) the sheriff to conclude that there were two stills on the Edmonds land and not just one. Having already given up farming for gold-digging in the most literal sense, Lucas feared another bout with the jail cell. So he married Nat off to George, even thought he had been preventing such a union for a long time and even though Nat did not want to marry George until he fixed his back porch and dug a well on his property. In any event, George could now no longer testify against Lucas, and so the case was dropped.

In May, realizing that they were now up to their mutual necks in conspiracies, which included forging a marriage certificate to read about seven months earlier than it should have, Lucas and George chopped up their stills, buried the hatchet, and began digging for gold together. George had not dug his well nor rebuilt his porch; and Nat was ready, had the law permitted it, to testify against *both* her husband and her father. Meanwhile Lucas was on the road to trouble in his own marriage, but not before he had long since arrived at trouble with Roth. Having had a gold-divining machine delivered from St. Louis, complete with a salesman to demonstrate its operation, Lucas needed money to buy it, which he was annoyed to find Roth would not lend him. So he stole Roth's best mule, Alice Ben Bolt, and offered to trade it to the salesman on the condition that he, Lucas, would buy it back for $300 as soon as the gold was discovered. But before this could even happen, though probably it would not have anyway, the sheriff was on Alice's trail and Lucas, therefore, was being trailed by jail again. So he arranged to rent the machine for $25 for the first night of digging. Then, having already sent George into town for fifty silver dollars, Lucas buried them some two hours away in another location from the Indian Mound. Then he led the salesman there with the gold divining machine and proceeded to uncover the coins with it. In a complicated series of manipulations of which only Lucas or a Snopes was capable, Lucas got the newly enthused salesman not only to accept the mule as a payment but also to rent the machine back from Lucas for $25 a night, at the end of which time Lucas traded the money for the mule, returned the mule to Roth, and now owned the gold-divining machine free and clear. Nor did he have any further competition for its use from the salesman, for after twelve fruitless nights he simply went back to St. Louis short $300 of his own money.

Roth, of course, was furious and finally told Lucas to go away and never come back. Lucas might as well have, for he now slept all day and stayed up all night searching the Indian Mound for gold. Molly Beauchamp had finally had enough of this and confronted Roth, whom she still considered something of her boss, owner, and legal advisor, with a demand for a divorce (at the age of sixty-seven no less from a sixty-seven-year-old husband). Roth's better instincts now took over, and he tried to prevent the divorce by having Molly refuse to prepare meals and spend the day instead searching for gold with Lucas' contraption. She refused to do this, and even Lucas said she could have the divorce if she wanted it, telling Roth just to end their marriage like he had the one the previous year [1940] between Oscar and the razor-packing slut from Memphis. Roth tried to work out an agreement whereby Lucas could have two nights a week on the machine; but, when he went to present it to Molly, he was chastened to find her lying collapsed in a creekbed where she had been trying to ditch the machine once and for all.

So divorce proceedings opened at the courthouse, and the judge ordered Lucas to give Molly one half of his annual crop as alimony each year. But then, without notice, Lucas suddenly called the whole thing off and promised not to do any more digging. Since the Bible told him he had only threescore and ten years on earth, he said, he simply figured he had better things to do with his last three than monkey with his infernal machine. He bought Molly a nickel's worth of candy to patch things up and even refused Roth's secret offer to let him use the machine one night a month on the sly. Lucas merely told, not asked, him to get it out of the county as fast as he could. The whole series of events seemed to have sobered George Wilkins as well, for he got down to well-digging and porch-building; and Nat got down to being happy with him.

In a somewhat similar case that turned out much more tragically, the rowdy black man named Spoot Rider got married in February, did an about-face, and settled down to hard-working happiness with his new wife, Mannie [1935] {G}. He had become head of a timber gang now and, the antithesis of George Wilkins, invested some of his higher pay in reflooring his porch and rebuilding the kitchen in the house he rented from Roth Edmonds. He even managed to save some of his money, which he kept in Roth's safe. But in August Mannie became ill and died, and Rider went mad with grief. Shortly after the funeral, he went to a local white still-operator and demanded that he be allowed to *buy* a gallon of whiskey, even though the white man wanted to *give* him a pint instead. Rider got the gallon and by midnight had drained it. He went to the mill where he worked, mumbling that he was snake-bit and doomed to die. He then lost his last six dollars in Birdsong's crooked dice game [1926], a game which closed forever this night because Rider slit Birdsong's throat when he saw him switch the dice. He then returned to his house and waited to be captured, which he soon was by Sheriff Maydew and imprisoned in a cell with his aunt to prevent the lynching the sheriff supposed the other Birdsongs were planning to have happen. But, before the aunt could call for help, Rider had torn the metal door from his cell and gone directly to the Birdsong clan to give himself up. That night they hanged him from the bellrope in the Negro schoolhouse.

Down in Frenchman's Bend, the Reverend Whitfield, still around this summer [1930], decided that he needed his church roof reshingled and wound up losing his entire church to a spectacular fire {"Shingles for the Lord"}. It seems he enlisted all the local men to do the work *gratis;* so various Armstids, Tulls, Bookwrights, Quicks, and even one Snopes showed up to go at it one weekend. Pap Grier, though, had to turn the occasion into a contest to beat Vernon Tull out of his half of a mutually owned dog that was given to both of them some years before by none other than Will Varner. The first day's work progressed well enough, though Pap and Vernon got into a number of arguments about who was doing the most work, Pap always making sure that he wasn't while all the while seeming like he might be. At night, though, in order to win the bet with Tull, he and his grandson took a lantern up on the church roof and started ripping off the shingles. In the process, one of them—probably Pap—knocked the lantern down inside the church and burnt it to the ground. The next day Whitfield regathered his work force, this time to rebuild rather than just reshingle the church. But this time Pap was exempted from both it and, tacitly, from the human race.

The Grier grandson was the same one who, the following December, tried to trail his eighteen-year-old brother to Pearl Harbor {"Two Soldiers"}. Peter Grier left the county for the fighting the day after the Japanese attack, and the boy was unable to sleep the next night. Whether this was for patriotic or brotherly reasons, I cannot say. However, he got himself up to Jefferson and managed to get himself a ticket to Memphis, where he overtook Pete at the induction center. The trouble was that he was pulling a knife on various people in order to keep from being kicked out of a bus station and various military operations until he found his brother. Finally, Pete convinced him that, at less than nine-years-old, he was too young to fight. But a Colonel named McKellogg admired his spunk so much that he had his own driver bring the boy all the way back to the Bend.

I guess Flem Snopes knew, even though he wasn't a bank president yet during the last one, that wars meant money for anyone who had a little of it to lend around; so he hired himself a professional cashier and working vice president from Memphis to await the fighting {M}. Linda was already riveting ships in the Pascagoula yard and trying to buy a car with some of her earnings. I managed to stop this by convincing her that her deafness would make her a menace on the road to herself and others. During the summer, before any of us even knew that Pearl Harbor was going to happen, I had made a trip to Pascagoula to see her. We walked on the beaches, ate a dinner at a restaurant that turned out to be a strip joint, and then spent the night in two separate hotel rooms. I had gotten the feeling during my last few encounters with Linda that she was trying to seduce me—and this time I was sure she was—but there was something in my head about my relationship with her and her mother that would prevent me from ever landing in the same bed with her, no matter how many people, Chick and Ratliff included, presumed we had already been there [1937]. After this attempt, though, she made me promise to marry someone, anyone, within the next two years. I so promised after telling her that I loved her; but I would later be surprised when I lived up to it [1942]. I left for Jefferson the next morning.

In September Captain Gauldres was back in the public eye [1939] {K}. He took a trip to St. Louis and returned with a thoroughbred mare that, the county quickly knew, was going blind. For a horseman such as Gauldres, this could be no mistake; so most of us were only partially surprised when we knew as well that he was teaching it to run around the Harriss paddock without bumping into the fence it could barely even see. His purpose, we later discovered, was to use the horse as his alibi while he went on his nightly

[261]

visits to the young Cayley girl—the mare was left to gallop around the paddock unridden and, not knowing night from day, create the impression that Gauldres, rather than off courting, was involved in some sort of insomniacal midnight riding. For a while, he fooled everyone.

It was on the evening of Thursday, December 4th, that this activity became somewhat dangerous for the Argentinian. As Chick and I sat playing chess at my home, Melisandre Backus Harriss' two children—Max and his sister—came to the door. After I had let them in (or after they had forced their own way in—it was a combination of both), Max warned me that he was prepared to harm Gauldres unless he ceased his pursuit of his mother. He went on to explain that the captain had been interested in his sister until he discovered that the Harriss bootleg fortune had been willed to her mother, at which point he quickly shifted his affections. The boy was hysterical and overwrought, so I told him to go home and cool off, that this was none of my business (and I surely did not want it to be because of my own love for Melisandre two decades earlier [1919]). So I got rid of them, but the girl was soon back, insisting that she did, in fact, love Gauldres and that Max would, in fact, do him in. She wanted me to use my official capacity to have Max locked up or Gauldres deported. But there were no grounds for either, as I told her; yet I *did* learn that Max's real dislike for the man stemmed from the fact that he could do everything better than Max could—horseback ride, fence, and (most important of all) seduce the Cayley girl, in whom Max was interested as well. Then the Harriss girl revealed that she had brought the Cayley girl back with her to explain herself, though the Harriss girl started kicking and scratching her when she revealed that she loved Max and was already engaged to him. The Harriss girl apparently wanted her brother for herself and would rather have had Gauldres woo her mother instead. I finally broke this up with Chick's help and sent them on their way; but I was convinced that there was real trouble brewing and called Robert Markey in Memphis to have him watch out for Max who, word had it, was headed there.

On the next night, December 5th, I became even more concerned to discover that Max had purchased the wild stallion that Rafe MacCallum had mistakenly bought the year before. I suspected immediately what was up, connecting this information with the recent purchase of another (Gauldres') less-than-desirable horse. So I went down to the all-night inn, fetched Rafe from his customary evening beer, and we ran on out to the Harriss property, where Gauldres was about to release his blind mare from the stable for her nightly futile run around the perimeter of the corral. But Rafe beat him to the door because we knew (or thought we did) that Max had substituted Rafe's killer stallion in her place. In a wild commotion of neighing and squealing, mixed with Gauldres' English and Spanish epithets, Rafe's substitute horse blasted its way out of the stable, circled the corral twice, jumped the fence, and disappeared into the distance, forever.

On Saturday, December 6th, the vigilant Markey caught up with Max and sent him home from Memphis; the boy arrived here in the afternoon, fully expecting to be locked up for attempted murder. But Gauldres refused to press charges; so I advised Max, who hadn't yet gotten around to registering for the draft, to enlist in the army before I got him put in the federal pen for that omission. Max grudgingly, though not ungratefully, did so. Gauldres had married Max's sister earlier in the day, and they departed as well on what was to have been an extended honeymoon but was destined to be cut short.

On Sunday, December 7th, Pearl Harbor was bombed and the long-awaited war had finally come. As I mentioned, Pete Grier was the first countian to leave for it {"Two Soldiers"}, though Chick was already getting ready to be not far behind him. He had, he revealed, been taking flying lessons from a cropduster and had fifteen hours, three of them solo, under his belt already {M}. So, for the next four years, soldiers from Jefferson went off to barracks on various college campuses to train there and then, for some, off to Europe and the South Pacific to fight and die there.

I have often wondered why southern boys, whose homeland was ravaged by the United States Army three quarters of a century before and who hated that fact in their veins from birth, were always the first to volunteer to fight in that very same army which stood for principles they despised and, while fighting, to fight the hardest. Honor?

1942

Born: First child of George Wilkins and Nat Beauchamp

Married: Gavin Stevens and Melisandre Backus Harriss

Died: Son of Young Major DeSpain (b. 1919), at war

Died: Pete Grier (b. 1923), at war

Died: Son of Young Anse Holland, at war

A number of theories have been ventured as to why I, at fifty-four, married in 1942. Perhaps it was the renewed sense of doom that the latest war had brought on all of us, especially those whose roots in the South were so deep that we knew that doom had stalked it since 1861 and probably from before that. We wanted someone to run from it with. Perhaps it was because I promised Linda Snopes that I would marry someone within two years and my time was running out [1941]. Or perhaps it was that Melisandre Backus Harriss, my wife, was free of husband [1938] or lover [1941] or child [1941] for the first time in a quarter-century and that fate had always predestined that she was the only woman I would be allowed to marry anyway. But we were finally together when Chick left this spring for the war {L}. On the occasion that we saw him off at the station, he also told us that he had found out that Captain Gauldres, technically my son-in-law now, had renounced his Argentinian citizenship and had joined a U.S. Cavalry regiment. So Chick departed, and Melisandre and I drove home to the Harriss monstrosity in the cadillac roadster she had given me as a wedding present and which, for lack of the necessary gasoline ration stamps, I would now have to store at $10 a month in a local garage. Over the next few years, I disassembled most of it and mortgaged the remainder with Flem Snopes's bank {M}.

The news of the war was generally scarifying, as it always is in the first year of any war before one gets conditioned to a perpetual, and muted, sense of fright. At eighteen Chick was a bombadier in France {M}. Benbow Sartoris was a commissioned officer in England doing some sort of intelligence work {K}. Devries, the outstanding ROTC cadet at the university [1940], had been given command of a Negro battalion in Europe {M}. Luther Biglin volunteered to go to the Pacific with the Marines but was rejected when they discovered that he had almost no sight at all in his right eye. So he came home. But Pete Grier did not—he was torpedoed by a Japanese submarine in April. Nor did Young Major DeSpain's boy, who died when he crashed his crippled plane into a Japanese battleship, probably to give them a foretaste of their own medicine, in late July {"Shall Not Perish"}.

The reactions of the Grier and DeSpain families to their similar tragedies were in marked contrast to each other. The Griers mourned for one day, then returned to the business of living and working their land. When they heard of the paralyzing grief the DeSpains were enduring, however, they went to counsel "Young" Major and his family, who did not even know them. Maw Grier all but accused DeSpain of rank self-pity and reminded him that the dead should be remembered with honor but not allowed to stifle the lives of the living. As an example she used old Grandpap Grier who was now nearly a hundred and had fought in the Civil War. On Saturday afternoons he would go to the local movie house to see cowboy serials, there fall asleep, and later wake up shouting the names of cavalry leaders and rebel heroes amidst the guns of Johnny Mack Brown and Kermit Maynard. Evidently she did De-Spain some good, because he was seen around town again and soon was speaking of his son in terms of enduring immortality instead of tragic loss.

During the spring and summer, a rumor started in Jefferson that the government planned to build an air training field on the old Compson golf course {M}. Two of the town's most aggressive capitalists—the shrewd Flem

Snopes and the fumbling Jason Compson—soon got to dickering over it [1936]. Flem threatened to foreclose on Jason's house in order to get the land, while Jason promised to sell Flem the land for him in turn to sell to the government if Flem would cancel the mortgage on his house. Flem seemed to close the deal by promising all this and by agreeing to name the installation "Compson Field," after General Compson and Governor Compson as well. But time would prove that it would not all be this easy [1943].

And it was in 1942 that Jefferson first took notice of Essie Meadowfill {M}. Having achieved the highest grades ever earned at Jefferson High School, surpassing even my own and Quentin Compson's, she was awarded a $500 college scholarship by Mr. Holland, now president of the Priest bank. She declined it with gratitude, so Holland gave her a job for life in his bank and even paid to have a bathroom built inside the Meadowfill house. All of this was probably because the town felt sorry for her having to endure the considerable burden of her lazy father [1934], who within a few years would use his spare time to get himself entangled in a blood-and-guts struggle with another new Snopes, a tangle she and Chick and I would all have to combine to get him out of [1946].

Lastly, a potent faction in Mississippi state politics offered to run Clarence Snopes, erstwhile state senator, for the governorship this year; but he respectfully declined and ended his political career for the time being, until a pack of dogs could ruin it for him for good after the war {M} [1945].

1943

Died: Paralytic woman whose wheelchair Meadowfill bought so he would no longer have to bother with walking

Melissa Meek, the town librarian, spotted a picture of a woman who, though older, greatly resembled the Caddy Compson she had gone to school with at the turn of the century [1899] {F}. It was in a news magazine and showed her in the company of a Nazi staff officer in Europe. Melissa ran over to Jason's store and showed it to him; but, though he was quick to admit it was his sister (whom he had not seen in thirty years [1912]), he admitted as well that he had no interest in helping her. So the timid booklady bought a train ticket to Memphis, where she knew that Dilsey, if she were still alive, lived with her daughter Frony and her railroader husband. But Dilsey, though living, was either blind or pretending to be and thus could not identify Caddy's picture; and, on the train back to Jefferson, Melissa understood the point that Dilsey was tacitly trying to make—that Caddy, at fifty-one, had endured enough from Jeffersonians and ought to be left to construct whatever portion of her own fate events would still allow her to.

Jason, meanwhile, was outdone by Flem Snopes when the latter changed the name of the imminent airport, against his promise, to Snopes Field instead of Compson Field, except that the U.S. government outdid both of them by building two airfields in northern Mississippi instead of just one and locating neither of them at Jefferson {M}. So Jason had the last laugh and spent a lot of his idle time around town summarizing what he called the "Snopes Airport Plan."

The war went on in Europe and the Pacific, but after the heavy casualties of 1942, no countian that I knew of was killed this year. Devries, the ROTC leader who commanded the black division, was badly wounded and returned to the States to sell Savings Bonds [1942] {M}. But he did poorly at this—his heart wasn't in such a tame corner of the war effort; so he got himself shipped back to his battalion in Europe even though he would not have had to fight again. McKinley Smith, the man who was to show up in the county after the war to marry Essie Meadowfill [1946], was a Marine corporal in Europe and was amassing a considerable combat record. And we shipped another of our own over this year, a draft dodger from Frenchman's Bend named Turpin; but I had to run him down there myself and literally force him into uniform.

After a goodly number of years in which we had not been bothered by Snopesism, if only because we had by now accepted it as normality, events for the next three or four seemed to be building toward some kind of Snopes crescendo [1946]. Down at Parchman, for example, where Mink Snopes was in his 35th year as an inmate [1908] and anticipating his release (he hoped) in 1948 (after his second twenty years of good behavior [1923]), the chain gang on which he was working one day began plotting an escape attempt {M}. Mink, of course, whose sentence had already been doubled by one abortive attempt, went into a panic and spoiled the escape. Several prisoners were killed in the try, and only a man named Stillwell—who nearly killed Mink with a knife during the commotion—got away. As he fled from the prison grounds he shouted back to Mink that he would kill him the minute he got out of prison and even sent him a Christmas card from Texarkana reminding him of this at the end of the year [1945].

Back in Jefferson, a new Snopes—one of the old breed, named Orestes—arrived in the County {M}. None of us knew what his particular relation to Flem was, and Flem probably didn't either. But he was soon to make trouble for old Meadowfill [1944] who, with his daughter now working and supporting him fully, this year purchased an old wheelchair from the family of a paralyzed woman who had recently passed on. He retired on it to his back porch and spent his entire days flinging rocks at boys and dogs who wandered onto his property. My office got lots of complaints about this, but what could I do but warn the parents to have their mongrels and sons respect abstract boundary lines they couldn't even see?

[266]

1944

Married: Will Varner and his second wife

In February, Mink got a Valentine from Stillwell that renewed the threat on his life [1943]; and at Christmas—while the rest of us were awaiting liberation from the war, Mink dreaded his own from prison because a Christmas card, more emphatic than ever, threatened him again {M}.

The war had been hard on the Stevens family this year. In June, Chick, flying copilot for a comrade named Harold Badrington, was shot down over Germany. Badrington flew the plane safely to the ground, but both were taken prisoner by the German patrols. My wife and I received an occasional communication from him until his release the following April [1945], and he assured us that the only real danger he faced was on Wednesday nights when the RAF bombed only thirty or forty feet from his stalag.

Back in Jefferson, old Meadowfill was creating himself a situation which was potentially more lethal than Chick's five thousand miles away in a war zone {M}. Orestes "Res" Snopes had moved into the Compson carriagehouse, which had been refurbished by Watkins Products Snopes (his cousin, I suppose), and set up in the business of buying and selling hogs. His property bordered on Meadowfill's, however; and Meadowfill, with nothing better to think about, worried about Res's hogs wandering onto his land. Res promised to pay a pound fee if Meadowfill could ever catch a hog on his land; so now Meadowfill had a greater, more meaningful purpose to life. He watched vigilantly every day; then, sometime during the summer, he finally spotted one. However, before he could leap out of his wheelchair to nab it, Res tackled it and dragged it home. Next the hog started showing up virtually every day, and every day Meadowfill peppered it with buckshot. He did not know yet that this was part of a money-making scheme of Res's own. Nor did those of us who enforced the law either.

Devries was decorated for more heroism this year and returned to the United States to be honored as an officer—a colonel now—who had served more than enough {M}. As was his custom, he tossed his decorations in a footlocker and asked to go back to war a third time. He was allowed to, and this time he personally saved an entire company of captured Negro soldiers and, in the process, was even dragged to safety by one of them himself. Devries lost a leg in the encounter; but when he was up and around again he got his latest ribbon out of his footlocker and pinned it on the black man who had saved him.

And this year a local ten-year-old boy whose name I never knew was abandoned by his mother (who ran off with a fellow from a Vicksburg roadhouse) and, the very next day, by his father as well {"Race at Morning"}.

On the next day after this, Mr. Ernest—one of the best of our countians in that he did good and did it quietly—rode up to the boy's house and adopted him. Soon he would take him on the yearly hunts [1946], of which party Ernest himself was now a member (as was, still, Uncle Ike McCaslin who, at seventy-seven, had only a few more left [1947]).

Down in Frenchman's Bend, Will Varner, a widower for a dozen years now and a living human being for an incredible ninety-two, took a second wife to see him through his remaining, but still active, years. Endurance.

THE PRESIDENCY OF HARRY S. TRUMAN, 1945–

1945

Died: Stillwell, in San Diego

So the war ended in Europe in May, and at virtually the same moment President Roosevelt died; and then the war ended in the Pacific in August and we were back to whatever it is we call normal once again.

But this same April the Meadowfill–Res Snopes war was getting hotter than ever [1944] {M}. The Snopes hog was still wandering into Meadowfill's orchard, and the old man was still spraying it with buckshot. Res, for some reasons of his own, was simply waiting until he used a solid bullet so he could have Meadowfill locked up on the firearms act. Meadowfill, meanwhile, was littering his yard with garbage so he could lure the animal in for the kill.

In May, Devries, the one-legged war hero [1944], returned to America and showed up in Yoknapatawpha where he entered the primary campaign for U.S. senator against none other than Clarence Snopes {M}. Now Clarence, whose career was checkered already, had to admit that he stood little chance of winning against a heavily decorated military officer in 1945. So he withdrew from the race on the pretense that Devries would be better for Mississippi since, having commanded a nigger battalion and having saved the nigger lives of most of it, he knew more about niggers; and niggers, after all, were taking over the state anyway. And perhaps the country was going to the niggers, too. This, of course, created a great groundswell for Clarence; and he "reluctantly" re-entered the race. In June Snopes campaigned from a car, shaking hands out the window, while the one-legged Devries hobbled up on platforms and stood while he made his speeches. One of the most alarmed about what was going to happen was V. K. Ratliff, who had devoted too much time to ridding the county of Snopeses to let one of them wind up representing us in Washington. So in July, at Will Varner's regular election-year picnic down at Frenchman's Bend, V. K. paid some boys to go down to a dog thicket, pick some branches with leaves on them, and come behind Clarence and wipe them on his pant legs. Clarence did not know what they were up to, but he was savvy enough to know that a candidate patted childrens' heads and did not merely tell them to get the hell away from him. But then dogs ran up and started urinating on his legs as he stood among his loyal supporters and their picnic baskets. He ran for his car and managed to outdistance the last dog two miles later. He changed his pants at home and returned to the picnic, only to find out that Will Varner had already removed him from the race, the one he was *supposed* to be running that day. Varner simply said that he refused to support a man that dogs couldn't tell from a fence post. It wasn't until September that Ratliff told me how this had happened; but by then Devries had already won the primary.

In July Chick got back from his German captivity, at twenty-one already a major. In August Jason Compson tried to get me to void his property deal with Flem Snopes; but it was too legal and, furthermore, I didn't want to be involved with either of them anyway {M}. In September, Flem began to build a veterans' housing development on the Compson land (which was to have been an airfield and had already been a pasture and a golf course). He named his subdivision "Eula Acres." In October, Linda Snopes returned—still as deaf as ever but now with a shock of white hair on her head—from the Pascagoula shipyards. Her Finnish friends were not only no longer communists, they were now thoroughgoing capitalists. Besides, it was about to be very dangerous to be a communist, and I felt Linda had already lost interest anyway. She seemed to have no cause to work for now, though next year we would discover that she did indeed have at least one left [1946]. Chick still thought her beautiful, as did I, and asked my permission to go to bed with her. I don't remember whether I gave it or not, but I know Chick never did. Linda, though, quickly developed a drinking habit when she got home and made frequent trips with Flem out to Jakeleg Wattman's to buy liquor. At first I could not figure out why Flem allowed this; but later I found out that, while Linda was bringing home jugs, Flem was bringing back Jakeleg's money for safekeeping in his bank vault. Flem!

I was living at the old Harriss house now, from which we had finally removed enough trappings to make it a fitting abode {K}; and Linda visited—as did Chick and Ratliff—quite often. Melisandre did not mind their coming, but she did not associate with them much either.

Ike McCaslin sold off his last share in what had one time been his hardware store, as did Triplett, so Jason Compson became its sole owner and proprietor now [1886] [1930] [1943]. McKinley Smith returned from war to live here and was one of the first to buy a home in Eula Acres.

During the fall, the warden at Parchman received a telegram from the San Diego police chief which said that one of his escapees—Stillwell—had been killed there when an old church collapsed on him {M} [1943]. The warden went directly to Mink Snopes and told him that, because of his role in foiling the escape attempt in which Stillwell was the only one to get loose, he could obtain an early release if he could get someone to petition for it. Mink could think of no one to do it; but, by early next year, someone would [1946].

1946

Married: Essie Meadowfill and McKinley Smith

Died: Flem Snopes (b. 1882)

This was a year of justice, finally, though in at least one case justice had reverted to the type practiced in *Agamemnon,* eye for an eye. But, on the other hand, Devries was elected to Congress {M}; the Tall Convict [1921] (who had saved a pregnant woman from drowning in the Mississippi River during the Great Flood of 1927) was finally released from jail after serving an unwarranted additional ten years to protect the warden's image {W}; and I finally admitted that my Old Testament translation was wasting valuable time—at fifty-seven I was too old now to do anything but pay attention to the welfare of the county, which I still represented as its elected attorney.

The greatest justices were done, however, in and around the Snopes family, many members of which had terrorized the county for over eighty years now but particularly the last forty {M}.

First of all, Res Snopes got what was coming to him—which by this time was plenty. By New Year's Day, a new arterial highway had been completed near Eula Acres, and various oil companies began to express an interest in the land which he and old Meadowfill each owned part of in order that the chosen among these firms might erect a service station to handle the too-fast-moving cars which no longer had to confront the center of things but now could skirt around it. Res was all set to sell his, but Meadowfill refused, probably only so Res (whom along with his hog Meadowfill bitterly hated) could not get the money [1945]. At about the same time, Essie Meadowfill and the war veteran McKinley Smith began dating and before long announced an upcoming wedding, this despite the fact that old Meadowfill hated his daughter's beau as much as he did Res. Smith purchased two properties on various G.I. bills, one to farm and another in Eula Acres on which to build a house. Res saw an opportunity to wrest Meadowfill's property from him and initiated his plan by presenting his buckshot-splattered hog to Smith as a wedding gift. But Chick and I had been watching these developments and, knowing Res to be a Snopes and so unlikely to give anything at all away, decided to watch old Meadowfill's house for a few days to see what was about to happen. After rising two days early without success, we realized what was up on the third. The hog once again, but for the first time in a long time, came trotting up the old man's garbage-strewn driveway. But Chick spotted something else at the same moment; and we charged into Meadowfill's house, without knocking, just as the old man raised his window sash to get a better-than-average shot at the wandering animal. Chick knocked Meadowfill aside just in time to have him be only slightly wounded by a gun Res had wedged in a tree just opposite the window. It had its trigger tied to the sash. Meadowfill, knowing that Smith now owned the hog, concluded that his future son-in-law and not Res was the foiled assassin; but I knew better and immediately approached Res with an offer to trade his booby trap to him in return for the deed to his half of the land that the oil companies wanted. With jail as the alternative, Res made the trade and left the county forever. Essie could now sell both properties for an exceptional amount of money. So much for that Snopes, gone by August.

In April justice began to grind its wheels for Linda, Flem, and the long-imprisoned Mink Snopes as well. Linda had been looking for a cause ever since her return from Pascagoula [1945], but postwar periods are notoriously causeless for the average citizen {M}. In April Linda requested a late-night meeting with me and revealed that Mink could be released from Parchman if someone petitioned for it; this was to be her cause now apparently. She had already given the details of this to Jody Varner, sixty-six now and Justice of the Peace in the district—the Bend—in which Mink had long ago murdered Jack Houston [1907]. So Little Hub (Hampton's son, who now alternated terms with Sheriff Bishop), V. K. Ratliff, Linda, and Bishop himself signed the petition; and I had it conveyed to the warden. With Linda abjuring for some odd reason, the rest of us decided that we would ask that Mink not be let go until September when there would be harvest work for him to fall back on. Also, we established a scheme whereby Mink would promise to leave Mississippi forever; we would pay him $250 upon his release and the same amount every three months for the rest of his life. What we didn't want, of course, was Mink and Flem in the same state [1908].

So, with the warden agreeing and (we thought) Mink, my cronies and I waited through the summer to activate our plan. In July Linda ordered and paid for a Jaguar from a Memphis auto dealership, even though they could not deliver it until October. None of us knew what this was about either.

On Thursday, September 26th, Mink was released from Parchman to set foot outside for the first time in thirty-eight years [1908]. The warden gave him his $250; but what neither he nor we knew at the time, but were to find out later, was that Mink had taken the cash into the prison washroom and given it to a trustee to return to the warden. The trustee, a lifer, was not so sure that he really *was* in here for life to begin with and so decided to stash the cash for his own future use.

So Mink was out without having made the promise we had thought he made. It took him several days to even comprehend the world and the changes it had undergone since 1908. Stop lights, high prices, paved roads—these were all things we all took for granted by now; but Mink had never seen any of them. So he hitched a ride on a truck bound for Memphis and managed to get himself gypped at every turn by the store owners who had the distinct advantage of not having spent the formative years of the twentieth century in Parchman. When he got to Memphis, he realized that he had too little money to buy a gun, which is what he went there for, at postwar inflationary prices; so he began to do odd jobs for meals until he could figure out where to get one. Finally he was directed to J. C. Goodyhay's camp for war veterans where this erstwhile preacher—who delivered sermons riddled with profanities and war stories and whose wife had deserted him while he was still at war—managed to feed the unemployable and unwanted war-hero patriots by having them perform cheap, nonunion labor. Mink sat through it while Goodyhay spoke of having been killed by the war but restored to life by Christ—he sat through it for four days, which was long enough to earn the gun money he needed but which was also long enough to get his other money stolen from him by another veteran named Dad. But on Sunday Goodyhay's men took up a collection to set Mink on his way (they knew not where and neither did we, yet) which netted another $10. It is interesting that Mink, by his own admission, had the opportunity while there to steal Goodyhay's pistol but was too honorable to do it. Mink never stole anything in his life, that any of us knows of, unless it was the grass on Houston's pasture land that his heifer ate without Mink telling her not to [1906].

So, on Sunday, September 29th, Mink went back to Memphis, went to sleep on a park bench and then went to "sleep at the depot for fifty cents" when a policeman ran him off. The stationmaster was flabbergasted the next morning when Mink tried to collect the fifty cents his newly-acquired economic sense convinced him he was entitled to; and, on his way out of town, he passed a brothel he used to patronize [1902] and which, Mink did not know, his younger daughter was now the madam of. By late afternoon he had hitched to within eight miles of Jefferson and spent the remainder of the day helping Negroes pick cotton beside the Sartoris railroad tracks north of town.

When I later learned what Mink had been up to between Thursday the 26th and Monday the 30th, I felt rather stupid about what V. K. and I had been doing in the same period. We had learned late Thursday afternoon that Mink had not accepted the bribe to leave the state, so I felt I had better get down to Flem's office to warn him—to which Flem merely remarked "Much obliged." I recall having a very vague sense that Flem, who two dozen years ago had cleverly succeeded in having Mink's sentence doubled, had no desire left to live and this time did not care if Mink was on his way. Had he acquired all that was worth getting and did he now want to die with it to see if his

Baptist church was wrong when it said that he couldn't take it with him? So Sheriff Bishop used Ratliff as a lookout, for V. K. was the only one in Jefferson who had ever met Mink [1906], though that was a good forty years ago. I phoned Robert Markey in Memphis and, as he had successfully done with Max Harriss, asked him to be on the watch for Mink [1941]. On Friday the 27th, Bishop deputized two men from Frenchman's Bend who claimed to remember Mink. The jailer, Luther Biglin, established a watch outside Flem's house every night from 9:30 till dawn, not so much to protect Flem (whom he despised as much as the rest of us did) but to keep Bishop's tenure in office pure. No one knew Biglin was doing this except his wife, who had the duty of waking him up every night when she returned from the picture show at 9:30. On Saturday, the Memphis police hunted Mink all over the city. On Sunday Sheriff Bishop and I agreed on one theory—that Mink had to be dead by now or he would already have gotten to Jefferson. We did not know how; we just assumed that modernity must have run him over. What neither we nor the Memphis police knew, of course, was that Mink was working for gun money at Goodyhay's on these two days.

Some of us later described Tuesday, October 1st, 1946, as "the day Jefferson had waited for since September of 1908," or—maybe—even since Jody Varner bought fire insurance in April of 1904. Mink picked cotton with the Negroes until noon, and then one of them drove him to within four miles of Jefferson. There he walked into a field to test-fire his gun. The first one misfired, but the second roared—now Mink had only one shell left, which he truly believed would not fail him because "Old Moster just punishes, He don't play jokes." So he walked along the Sartoris tracks, which now carried only two freights daily [1935], until he met a Negro boy who told him how to find Flem's house. Waiting till dark, Mink then gained access to the house through an unlocked back door (who unlocked it?), walked down the hall and past the room where Linda was reading, entered Flem's study, and confronted him. Flem sat five feet away, staring at him, chewing continually after only a momentary pause. Mink pointed the gun, held it with two hands, and pulled the trigger. It misfired. Except for his jaws going rhythmically up and down, Flem did not move. Mink backed up the shell chamber, pointed the gun, fired, and this time blew away half of Flem's face. Mink then ran for the first door he could find, only to notice Linda staring at him, very calmly. He flung the gun at her but missed. In her duckquack she said only "Here come take it. That door is a closet. You'll have to come back this way to get out." She *must* have *seen* him enter the house in the first place; she could not have heard the shot. She apparently had had time to warn Flem, but definitely she didn't. Mink took the gun, ran outside, flung it in the bushes, and disappeared. All this happened around 9 P.M., one half-hour before Biglin showed up to assume his nightly vigil and one full hour before V. K. Ratliff phoned me to tell me that Flem Snopes had been murdered.

On Wednesday, October 2nd, Linda's Jaguar arrived at the height of the commotion caused by Flem's assassination. She told me she was going to New York and never coming back, though before she left she made arrangements to have DeSpain's mansion—where Flem's father once had tracked horse manure across the living room rug [1894] and where Flem had replaced that rug with a more expensive one [1927] and then been shot in an upstairs room—given back to the DeSpain family. Only two DeSpains remained now: the eighty-year-old sister of Old Major DeSpain and her sixty-year-old spinster daughter. Both lived in Los Angeles where the daughter taught school. On Thursday the 3rd Flem's funeral was attended by various town dignitaries, Jody Varner, Linda, and me. Only one other Snopes showed up—Wall, in a business suit, from the home office of his chain of grocery stores. Shortly after it was over, Linda and I kissed one last time, admitted to each other that we were still in love (even though I was married and she was leaving), and then she gave me $1000 to give to Mink. As she roared out of town in her new Jaguar, with her cutout symbolically open as had various DeSpains [1904], Hogganbecks [1905], and Levitts [1925], I realized that she had been an accessory to Flem's murder and now I was about to be as well.

If the police did not know where to find Mink, Ratliff thought he did. So after dark he and I rode to the Bend and then beyond it to the broken-down house where Mink used to live [1907]. This was before he had to kill Jack Houston over an unfair pound fee levied on him after he had worked 38½ consecutive nights stringing Houston's fence wire at fifty cents a night, money he never saw in cash but only in the elimination of debt incurred by legal penalty. Mink was there, as V. K. had predicted, sleeping in what was left of it as if it were a cave. We gave him $250 of Linda's money and promised to mail him the rest in three months to wherever he was living at the time. He thanked us, laid down on the bare ground, and went back to sleep. When he vanished from Yoknapatawpha County the next day, there were no Snopeses left. But it had been my public duty to keep this one here, to lock him up once again—but I had not done it.

I lived in moral confusion for the next five or six weeks. The Snopeses were gone, a fact that no thinking Yoknapatawphan could have seen as anything but a boon, a start on the road back from where the Civil War had landed us. Yet the County Attorney had willingly allowed a cold-blooded murderer to walk away scot free with cash in his pocket this same County Attorney had put there to boot. I fell very ill this fall. But not too ill to take note of one more event which, if insignificant in itself, was a symbol of hope.

Ike McCaslin, Will Legate, Roth Edmonds, Walter Ewell, Mr. Ernest, and the latter's adopted son [1944] went on the November hunt once again this year, a hunt not so well organized or as skillful as it used to be, but equally meaningful {"Race at Morning"}. Ernest and his boy, for instance, got ripped

[274]

off their horse by a grapevine and landed in a heap, something Chick thought was a riot when he heard about it. But the hunt transcended this or even how many deer they killed. Since Ernest was deaf, the boy had to serve as his ears to direct him after the barking dogs in pursuit of the deer. But there was one special deer they had pursued for a few years now, an animal who was the symbol to this party that Old Ben, the bear, used to be to its forebears some sixty years ago. This deer showed up in the woods for the two-week hunting season each year and spent the remaining fifty eating freely from the hunters' fields. As Ernest and his boy approached him one day on this year's hunt, Ernest unloaded his gun so he would not, could not, kill it—like Sam Fathers, he needed to have him to hunt a year from now or, like Sam, Ernest would die [1883]. So they saw him and let him go—there was a code of honor between man and beast that made no other alternative possible. Perhaps that was why I let Mink go: in his own way he was a man of great honor, as I was in my own. Yet Mink, on the other hand, was a murderer, twice.

Around Christmastime, Ernest told the boy, who was twelve now, that he would have to start school right after the new year. Man, he said, could no longer know right from wrong nor even survive with just a knowledge of hunting or farming. It was still the basis for knowing it, but its distinctions were no longer sharp enough. Perhaps school *was* the difference—perhaps I had learned something there that allowed me to let Mink go free. If I had, no professor or textbook had taught it to me. Maybe it was there in school in the same way that things are there in a poem that the poet did not tell you but tried, in his own peculiar way, to make you feel nonetheless. Objective correlative T. S. Eliot had called it. Maybe Mr. Ernest's boy would learn it in school, too; but maybe he already knew it, for he was a hunter and knew the code of life. Ernest would have let Mink go, and he would have told his boy to also. And Ike McCaslin, for most of us the symbol, at seventy-nine, of the code—Ike would have let Mink go. Uncle Ike would have approved of what I had done. Probably.

1947

Born: Child of Essie Meadowfill and McKinley Smith

Died: Isaac McCaslin (b. 1867), in January

[Here the Yoknapatawpha Chronicle ceases.]

[Note in the hand of Charles "Chick" Mallison, Jr., nephew of the late Gavin Stevens: "This chronicle was found in my uncle's papers shortly after his death in February, 1947, from complications surrounding what a Memphis specialist termed a 'mild heart seizure' in January. It was found in a ragged manila folder containing some 500 handwritten pages underneath another ragged folder which contained the abandoned Old Testament translation upon which Uncle Gavin had worked for a quarter of a century. Unlike the translation, none of us knew he was keeping it; and also unlike the translation, this chronicle is important. Therefore, as appointed executor of his last will and testament, I have ordered it preserved in the Records Hall of the Courthouse, located (as young Stephen Dedalus would have said it) in the City of Jefferson, County of Yoknapatawpha, State of Mississippi, Country of the United States, Continent of North America, The World, The Universe."]

Afterword

Having read, reread, and edited Gavin Stevens' chronicle of this county, I can only conclude with one statement which, for me, is a meaningful one. If you were to thumb the pages of the 1947–48 telephone book for Yoknapatawpha County, you would find no one listed with the last names of Sartoris, McCaslin, Sutpen, Benbow, Grenier, or Weddel. There is not even a Snopes. There is one Stevens (Gavin, destined to die without an heir of that name), one Edmonds (Roth, destined to die with one heir to whom he refused to give his name), one Compson (Jason, who has no time for one), two DeSpains (both spinsters long beyond the time for child-bearing), and one Beauchamp (Lucas, now seventy-three). There are two Varners (Will, ninety-five, and Jody, sixty-seven). There are two Hogganbecks (Boon, eighty-six, and his son Luke, forty-one). There are five Gowries (Nub and his four remaining sons, all in their mid-thirties to mid-forties), but they are offset by eight MacCallums of three different generations. Down around the Bend there is the expected number of Tulls, Armstids, Bookwrights, Bundrens, Binfords, Griers, and Littlejohns. There is one unmarried seventy-three-year-old Ratliff. But still, there are no Sartorises, no McCaslins, no future Stevenses. There are still four Priests and two Mallisons. They? Can it all begin again with them?

Melissa Meek

Genealogical Tables

Complete genealogical charts are provided for the following families:

BACKUS
BALLENBAUGH
BEAUCHAMP (NEGROES)
BENBOW
BUNDREN
BURDEN
CHICKASAW INDIANS
COLDFIELD
COMPSON
DESPAIN
DRAKE
EDMONDS
GIBSON (NEGROES)
GOWRIE
GRIER
HOGGANBECK
HOLLAND
MACCALLUM
MCCASLIN
PEABODY
PRIEST
SARTORIS
SNOPES
STEVENS
STROTHER (NEGROES)
SUTPEN
VARNER
WEDDEL

FAMILY	CHART
Backhouse	Backus
Bascomb	Compson
Beauchamp (White)	McCaslin
Binford	Snopes
Bon	Sutpen
Bond	Sutpen
Burrington	Burden
Carpenter	Benbow
Carter	MacCallum
Cranston	Sartoris
Dandridge	Stevens
Doshey	Snopes
DuPre	Sartoris
Grimm	Snopes
Habersham	Chickasaw Indians
Harriss	Backus, Stevens
Hawk	Sartoris
Head	Compson
Jones	Sutpen
Kohl	Varner
Lessep	Priest
McCarron	Varner
Mallison	Stevens
Mardis	Holland
Millard	Sartoris
Mitchell	Benbow
Vidal	Weddel
White	Sartoris
Whitfield	Bundren
Wilkens	Beauchamp
Workitt (Urquhart)	Gowrie

BACKUS

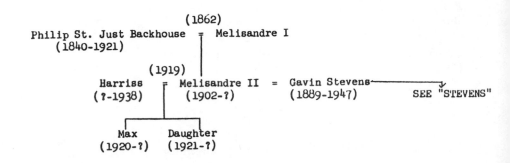

(1862)

Philip St. Just Backhouse   =   Melisandre I
    (1840-1921)

                    (1919)

        Harriss   =   Melisandre II   =   Gavin Stevens
        (?-1938)   (1902-?)   (1889-1947)   SEE "STEVENS"

            Max   Daughter
        (1920-?)   (1921-?)

BALLENBAUGH

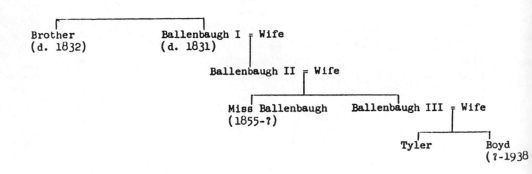

Brother   Ballenbaugh I = Wife
(d. 1832)   (d. 1831)

                      Ballenbaugh II = Wife

                Miss Ballenbaugh   Ballenbaugh III = Wife
                (1855-?)

                                        Tyler   Boyd
                                               (?-1938

[280]

BEAUCHAMP

(A genealogy of varying shades of Negro blood. Last name comes from that of their pre-Civil War owner, Hubert Beauchamp. He pronounced it "Bow-shomp," but the Blacks came to use and prefer "Beecham.")

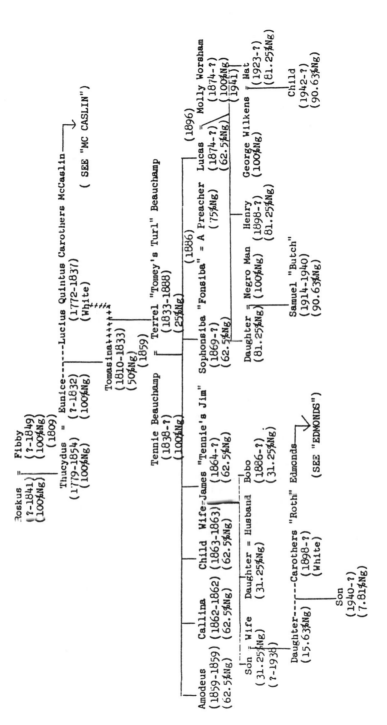

BENBOW

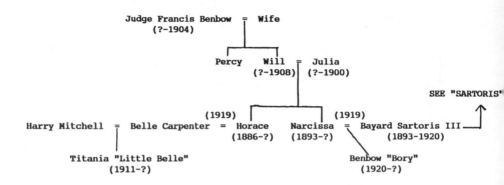

Judge Francis Benbow = Wife
(?-1904)

Percy   Will = Julia
(?-1908) (?-1900)

SEE "SARTORIS"

(1919)   (1919)
Harry Mitchell = Belle Carpenter = Horace   Narcissa = Bayard Sartoris III
                                      (1886-?)   (1893-?)   (1893-1920)

Titania "Little Belle"   Benbow "Bory"
(1911-?)   (1920-?)

BUNDREN

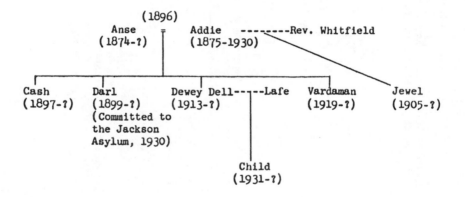

(1896)
Anse = Addie --------Rev. Whitfield
(1874-?)   (1875-1930)

Cash   Darl   Dewey Dell----Lafe   Vardaman   Jewel
(1897-?) (1899-?)   (1913-?)   (1919-?)   (1905-?)
          (Committed to
          the Jackson
          Asylum, 1930)

Child
(1931-?)

[282]

BURDEN

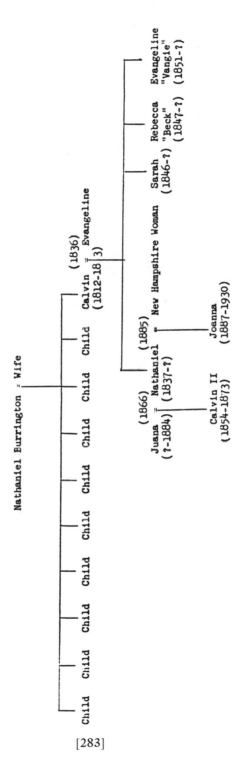

[283]

CHICKASAW INDIANS

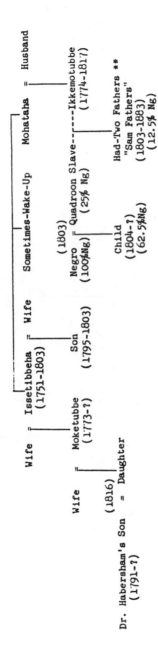

Wife = Issetibbeha   Wife   Sometimes-Wake-Up   Mohataha = Husband
       (1751-1803)

                           (1803)
Wife = Moketubbe   Son   Negro = Quadroon Slave----Ikkemotubbe
       (1773-?)   (1795-1803) (100%Ng) (25% Ng)   (1774-1817?)

                                  Child   Had-Two Fathers **
                                  (1804-?)   "Sam Fathers"
Dr. Habersham's Son = Daughter   (62.5%Ng)   (1803-1883)
(1791-?)   (1816)   (12.5% Ng)

** Alternative Genealogy for Sam Fathers

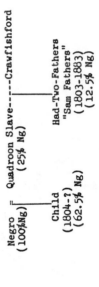

Negro = Quadroon Slave----Crawfishford
(100%Ng) (25% Ng)

         Child   Had-Two-Fathers
         (1804-?)   "Sam Fathers"
         (62.5% Ng)   (1803-1883)
                          (12.5% Ng)

[284]

COLDFIELD

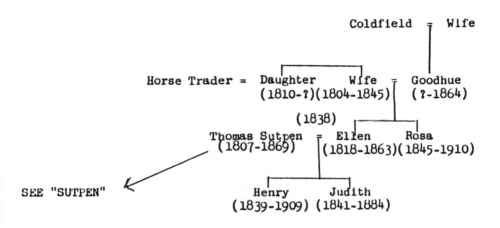

SEE "SUTPEN"

COMPSON

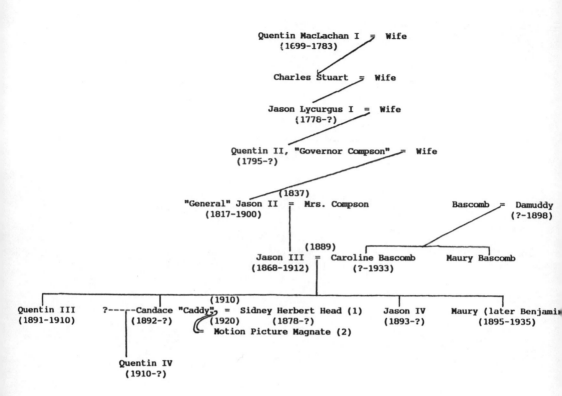

Quentin MacLachan I = Wife
(1699-1783)

Charles Stuart = Wife

Jason Lycurgus I = Wife
(1778-?)

Quentin II, "Governor Compson" = Wife
(1795-?)

(1837)
"General" Jason II = Mrs. Compson   Bascomb = Damuddy
(1817-1900)   (?-1898)

(1889)
Jason III = Caroline Bascomb   Maury Bascomb
(1868-1912)   (?-1933)

Quentin III   ?----Candace "Caddy" = Sidney Herbert Head (1)   Jason IV   Maury (later Benjamin
(1891-1910)   (1892-?)   (1920)   (1878-?)   (1893-?)   (1895-1935)
                           (1910)   Motion Picture Magnate (2)

Quentin IV
(1910-?)

DE SPAIN

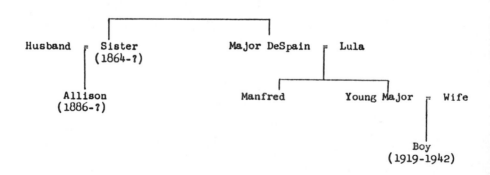

Husband = Sister   Major DeSpain = Lula
          (1864-?)

Allison   Manfred   Young Major = Wife
(1886-?)

                                                    Boy
                                                    (1919-1942)

[286]

DRAKE

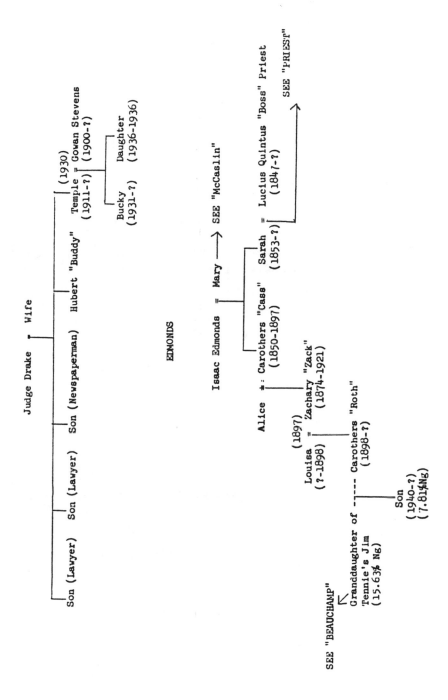

Judge Drake ┬ Wife

Son (Lawyer)   Son (Lawyer)   Son (Newspaperman)   Hubert "Buddy"   "Temple" ╤ Gowan Stevens (1930)
                                                                        (1911-?)   (1900-?)

                                                                        Bucky   Daughter
                                                                        (1931-?)   (1936-1936)

SEE "BEAUCHAMP"

EDMONDS

Isaac Edmonds ╪ Mary ⟶ SEE "McCaslin"

Alice ╪ Carothers "Cass"   Sarah ╪ Lucius Quintus "Boss" Priest
        (1850-1897)   (1853-?)   (1847-?)

        Zachary "Zack"   SEE "PRIEST"
        (1874-1921)

Louisa ╪ ---- Carothers "Roth"
(?-1898)   (1898-?)   (1897)

Granddaughter of ----┐
Tennie's Jim   │
(15.63% Ng)   Son
                  (1940-?)
                  (7.81% Ng)

[287]

GIBSON
(All members 100% Negro)

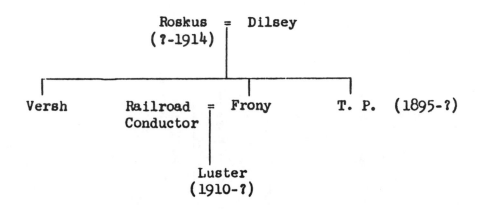

```
                 Roskus  =  Dilsey
                 (?-1914)
        ┌───────────────────┴───────────────────────┐
      Versh         Railroad  =  Frony          T. P.  (1895-?)
                     Conductor
                        │
                     Luster
                     (1910-?)
```

GOWRIE

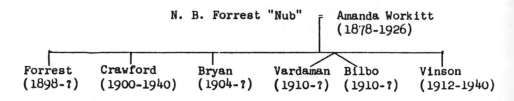

```
              N. B. Forrest "Nub"  =  Amanda Workitt
                                       (1878-1926)
     ┌──────────┬──────────┬─────────┴──┬────────┬──────────┐
  Forrest   Crawford    Bryan      Vardaman  Bilbo       Vinson
 (1898-?)  (1900-1940) (1904-?)   (1910-?) (1910-?)   (1912-1940)
```

GRIER

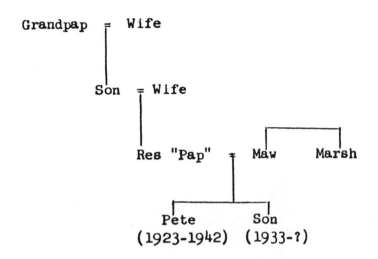

```
Grandpap  =  Wife
          |
          |
       Son  =  Wife
            |
            |
      Res "Pap"  =  Maw        Marsh
               |
          Pete         Son
       (1923-1942)  (1933-?)
```

HOGGANBECK

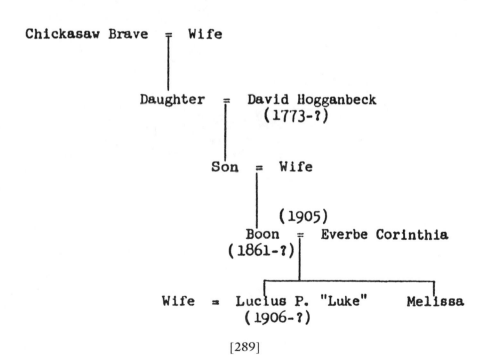

```
Chickasaw Brave  =  Wife
                 |
                 |
        Daughter  =  David Hogganbeck
                  |      (1773-?)
                  |
               Son  =  Wife
                    |
                    |      (1905)
                  Boon  =  Everbe Corinthia
               (1861-?)|
                       |
        Wife  =  Lucius P. "Luke"        Melissa
                   (1906-?)
```

[289]

HOLLAND

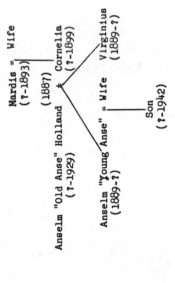

Mardis = Wife
(?-1893)
(1887)
Anselm "Old Anse" Holland
(?-1929)
Cornelia
(?-1899)
Virginius
(1889-?)
Anselm "Young Anse" = Wife
(1889-?)
Son
(?-1942)

MAC CALLUM

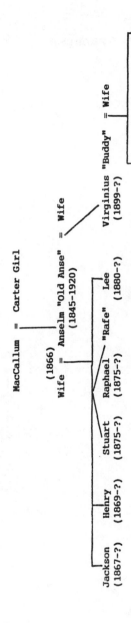

MacCallum = Carter Girl
(1866)
Wife = Anselm "Old Anse" = Wife
(1845-1920)
Jackson   Henry   Stuart   Raphael "Rafe"   Lee   Virginius "Buddy" = Wife
(1867-?) (1869-?) (1875-?)   (1875-?)   (1880-?) (1899-?)
Anselm "Young Anse"   Lucius

[290]

MC CASLIN

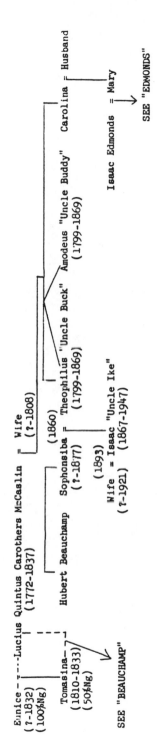

Eunice - - - -Lucius Quintus Carothers McCaslin = Wife
(?-1832)   (1772-1837)   (?-1808)
(100%Ng)

Tomasina--
(1810-1833)
(50%Ng)

SEE "BEAUCHAMP"

Hubert Beauchamp   Sophonsiba = Theophilus "Uncle Buck"   Amodeus "Uncle Buddy"   Carolina = Husband
                   (?-1877)   (1799-1869)   (1799-1869)
                   (1860)

Wife = Isaac "Uncle Ike"   Isaac Edmonds = Mary
(?-1921) (1867-1947)
       (1893)   SEE "EDMONDS"

PEABODY

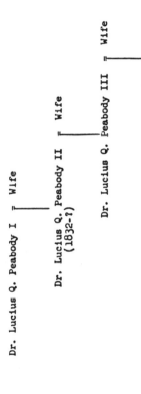

Dr. Lucius Q. Peabody I = Wife

Dr. Lucius Q. Peabody II = Wife
(1832-?)

Dr. Lucius Q. Peabody III = Wife

Dr. Lucius Q. Peabody IV

[291]

PRIEST

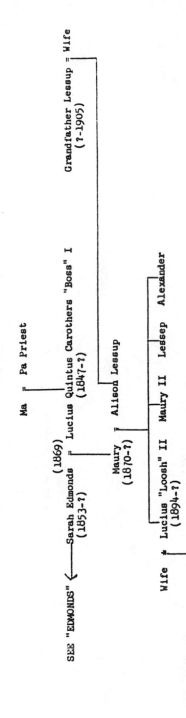

Grandfather Lessup = Wife
(?-1905)

Pa Priest
Ma =

Lucius Quintus Carothers "Boss" I
(1847-?)

Alison Lessup =

SEE "EDMONDS"
← Sarah Edmonds
(1853-?)
(1869) =

Maury
(1870-?) =

Lucius "Loosh" II   Maury II   Lessep   Alexander
(1894-?)

Wife =

Son = Wife

Lucius III

[292]

SARTORIS

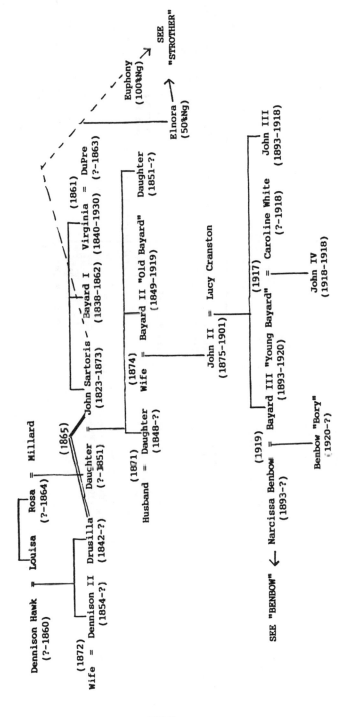

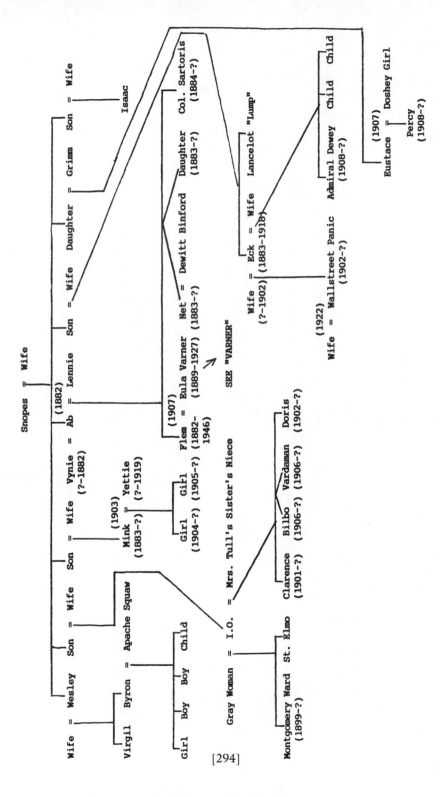

SNOPES

(The relationship of both Orestes "Res" Snopes and Watkins Products "Wat" Snopes to the rest of the Snopeses is unclear.)

[294]

STEVENS

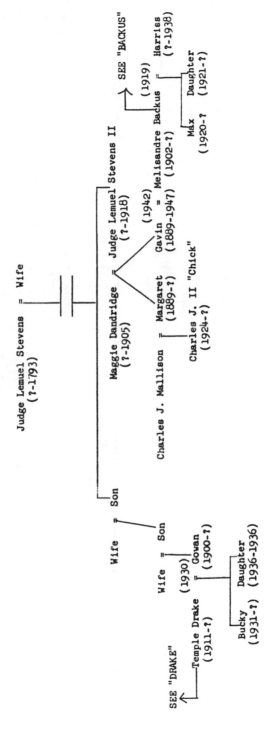

STROTHER

(Blacks in the Sartoris household)

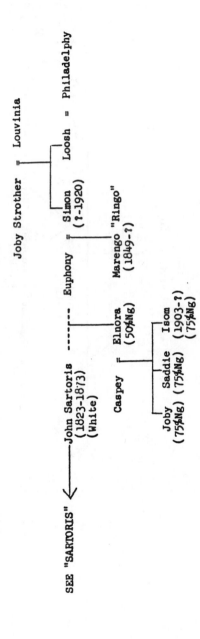

Joby Strother = Louvinia

Simon
(?-1920)

Loosh = Philadelphy

Euphony =

Marengo "Ringo"
(1849-?)

John Sartoris ------ Euphony
(1823-1873)
(White)

SEE "SARTORIS"

Elnora
(50%Ng)

Caspey =

Joby   Saddie   Isom
(75%Ng)   (75%Ng)   (1903-?)
                          (75%Ng)

[296]

SUTPEN

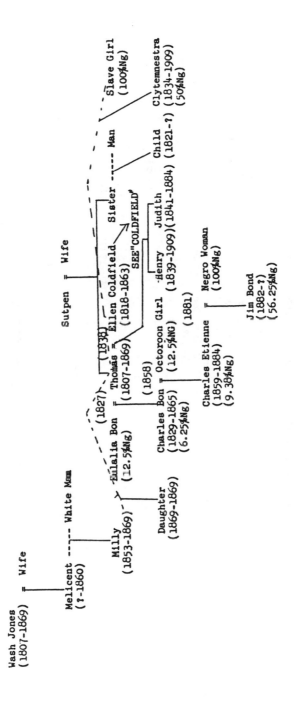

VARNER

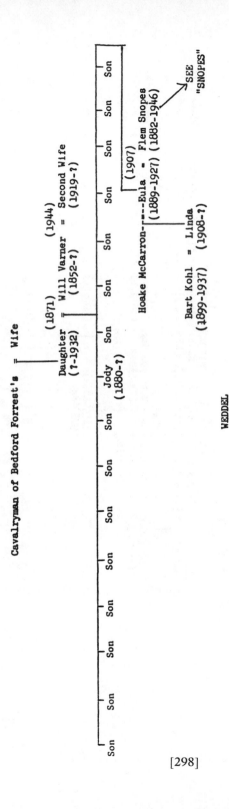

Cavalryman of Bedford Forrest's = Wife

Daughter   (1871)   Will Varner = Second Wife
(?-1932)   (1852-?)   (1919-?)
                        (1944)

Jody
(1880-?)
Son Son Son Son Son Son Son Son Son Son Son Son Son

Hoake McCarron----Eula = Flem Snopes
                  (1889-1927) (1882-1946)
                        (1907)

Bart Kohl = Linda
(1899-1937) (1908-?)

SEE
"SNOPES"

WEDDEL

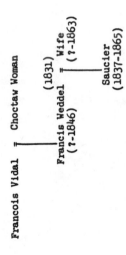

Francois Vidal = Choctaw Woman

Francis Weddel = Wife
(?-1846)   (?-1863)
        (1831)

Saucier
(1837-1865)

[298]

Index of Names and Characters

Beauchamp, Samuel Worsham "Butch," 177, 237, 239, 240, 241, 251, 255, 256
Beauchamp, Sophonsiba (Ike McCaslin's mother), 70, 71, 72, 99, 110
Beauchamp, Sophonsiba (daughter of Tomey's Turl and Tennie), 101, 120, 122, 180
Beauchamp, Tennie, 58, 70, 71, 78, 83, 85, 88, 101, 107, 120
Beauchamp, Tomey's Turl, II, 118, 169, 177, 178
Beauregard, P. G. T., 76, 77
Bedenberry, Brother, 232
Benbow, Judge, 97, 98, 103, 104, 118, 146, 147
Benbow, Belle Mitchell, 127, 141, 169, 181, 185, 189, 192, 193, 194, 196, 197, 220, 222, 223
Benbow, Cassius Q., 105
Benbow, Horace, 120, 126, 144, 156, 163, 169, 185, 189, 190, 192, 193, 194, 195, 196, 197, 220, 221, 222, 223, 225
Benbow, "Little Belle" Mitchell, 170, 192, 218
Benbow, Narcissa (Sartoris), 127, 179, 180, 181, 182, 184, 188, 189, 191, 192, 193, 195, 197, 208, 220, 221, 222, 227
Benbow, Percy, 147
Benbow, Will, 119, 160, 163, 192
Berry, Louis, 40
Biglin, Luther, 236, 264, 273
Bilbo, Governor, 241, 242
Binford, DeWitt, 219
Binford, Lucius, 140, 181, 210
Bird, Tom Tom, 65, 107, 128, 160, 169, 175, 177, 178, 198
Birdsong, 209, 212, 231, 235, 258, 260
Bishop, Ephriam (sheriff), 271, 273
Bland, Mrs., 168
Bland, Gerald, 126, 168, 180, 187
Bolivar, Uncle Dick, 162
Bon, Charles, 11, 48, 61, 70, 71, 72, 73, 74, 75, 77, 78, 80, 93, 94, 95, 96, 102, 103, 104, 108, 149, 165, 166
Bon, Charles Etienne, 70, 103, 104, 105, 107, 108, 112, 113, 115, 117, 118, 119, 133, 165, 208
Bond, Jim, 115, 118, 136, 144, 165, 166, 167

Bookwright, Calvin, 150
Bookwright, Herman, 181, 184
Bookwright, Odum, 138, 160, 161, 162
Boone, Daniel, 32
Boyd, 146
Boyd, Mrs., 146, 208, 209, 227
Boyd, Amy, 210, 227
Boyd, Howard, 146, 200, 208, 209, 210, 226, 227, 228
Bragg, Braxton, 83, 84, 86, 87, 88
Breckbridge, Gavin, 74, 79, 80, 83
Brown, John, 72
Brown, Johnny Mack, 264
Brownlee, Percival ("Spintrius"), 49, 68, 69, 82, 98, 121
Buchanan, James, 68, 69
Buck, 193
Buffaloe, Mr., 142, 143, 144, 147
Buford (Yankee general), 84
Bunch, Byron, 130, 204, 209, 212, 226, 231, 232, 233, 234
Bundren, Addie, 108, 125, 131, 135, 137, 148, 190, 226, 228, 229, 230
Bundren, Anse, 107, 131, 135, 137, 148, 190, 226, 228, 229, 230
Bundren, Cash, 132, 228, 229, 230
Bundren, Darl, 136, 137, 183, 190, 228, 229, 230
Bundren, Dewey Dell, 174, 228, 229, 230, 234
Bundren, Jewel, 148, 149, 198, 228, 229, 230
Bundren, Vardaman, 189, 228, 229, 230
Burch, Lucas ("Joe Brown"), 226, 230, 231, 232, 233, 234
Burden, Beck, 63
Burden, Calvin, I, 9, 11, 42, 47, 55, 61, 62, 78, 88, 99, 105, 106, 120
Burden, Calvin, II, 9, 11, 66, 98, 105, 106, 120, 163
Burden, Evangeline, 55, 65
Burden, Joanna, 55, 66, 120, 121, 126, 163, 212, 216, 217, 226, 227, 230, 231, 232, 233, 234
Burden, Juana, 97, 118, 120
Burden, Nathaniel, 55, 61, 66, 82, 88, 97, 98, 99, 106, 119, 120, 126
Burden, Sarah, 62
Burgess, 171
Burgoyne, John, 31
Burnside, Ambrose, 81, 82, 83
Butler, Benjamin, 80, 90

Callicoat, David, 36, 37, 38
Carruthers, Miss, 170
Cayley, Miss, 250, 262
Charlie, 154
Christian, Uncle Willy, 101, 125, 175, 203, 205, 225, 227, 230, 235, 236, 237, 238
Christmas, Joe, 24, 66, 104, 127, 128, 130, 132, 133, 135, 136, 143, 146, 163, 169, 171, 173, 174, 176, 177, 183, 208, 212, 216, 217, 226, 227, 230, 231, 232, 233, 234
Cinthy, 69
Clay, Henry, 61
Clayborne, Governor, 41
Cleveland, Grover, 119, 122, 127
Clytemnestra ("Clytie"), 54, 64, 74, 76, 95, 97, 102, 103, 104, 107, 108, 118, 119, 136, 144, 157, 163, 165, 166
Coldfield, Goddhue, 48, 53, 56, 58, 62, 63, 69, 77, 82, 88, 90
Coldfield, Rosa, 41, 42, 62, 63, 64, 65, 67, 69, 73, 76, 77, 82, 90, 95, 97, 98, 118, 120, 147, 165, 166, 167
Columbus, Christopher, 63
Compson, General, 13, 44, 48, 51, 55, 56, 58, 60, 80, 90, 92, 97, 98, 104, 107, 110, 111, 112, 113, 114, 115, 117, 118, 120, 123, 138, 150, 255, 265
Compson, Mrs. (General Compson's wife), 24, 59, 77, 82, 83, 93, 108
Compson, Benjamin, 60, 130, 131, 134, 138, 139, 141, 142, 149, 150, 154, 163, 164, 165, 166, 167, 168, 171, 173, 178, 215, 216, 230, 237, 239, 240
Compson, Candace ("Caddy"), 12, 126, 134, 137, 139, 141, 149, 150, 154, 156, 157, 163, 164, 165, 166, 167, 168, 171, 173, 196, 198, 208, 214, 257, 265
Compson, Caroline Bascomb, 124, 131, 139, 142, 150, 156, 164, 167, 171, 172, 173, 215, 216, 236, 237
Compson, Charles Stuart, 31, 32, 33
Compson, Jason, Jr., 128, 131, 134, 139, 144, 149, 156, 164, 167, 171, 173, 176, 214, 215, 216, 225, 226, 236, 237, 239, 240, 244, 265, 266, 269, 277
Compson, Jason Lycurgus, 31, 42, 43,

45, 47, 50, 53, 60
Compson, Jason Richmond, 100, 116, 124, 131, 138, 139, 141, 142, 156, 157, 164, 165, 167, 168, 171, 173, 176
Compson, Quentin, 13, 97, 102, 126, 133, 134, 135, 137, 139, 144, 146, 149, 150, 154, 155, 156, 157, 163, 164, 165, 166, 167, 168, 170, 172, 173, 176, 180, 210, 265
Compson, Quentin, II (governor), 34, 45, 60
Compson, Miss Quentin, 166, 171, 172, 173, 178, 213, 214, 215, 216, 217, 237
Compson, Quentin Maclachan, 27, 28, 31, 32
Confrey, Mame, 173, 176
Confrey, Max, 173, 176
Coolidge, Calvin, 202
Cooper, Minnie, 10, 125, 185, 200, 217, 224
Cornwallis, Charles, 32
Crawfishford, 40, 41, 43
Crawford, Dr., 117
Crenshaw, Jack, 203
Custer, George Armstrong, 87, 94, 109

Dad, 272
Damuddy (Bascomb), 131, 133, 134, 139
Dandridge, Maggie, 149
Davis, Jefferson, 74, 75, 78, 94, 119
Deacon, 102, 156, 168
de Montigny, Paul, 218, 225
De Soto, Hernando, 27
DeSpain, Major (also de Spain), 76, 88, 98, 101, 102, 104, 107, 110, 111, 114, 118, 119, 123, 129, 130, 133, 274
DeSpain, "Young" Major, 189, 235, 236, 263, 264
DeSpain, Lula, 129
DeSpain, Manfred, 10, 133, 141, 142, 147, 163, 164, 169, 175, 176, 178, 195, 197, 199, 201, 207, 209, 211, 274
de Vitry, Soeur-Blonde, 30, 36, 39
Devries, Colonel, 177, 236, 257, 264, 266, 267, 268, 269, 270
Dick, Col. Nathaniel G., 87, 91
Dodge, Granby, 179, 224, 225

[301]

[302]

[307]